# Proceedings of the Royal Geographical Society of London

by Royal Geographical Society (Great Britain)

Address:
HardPress
8345 NW 66TH ST #2561
MIAMI FL 33166-2626
USA
Email: info@hardpress.net

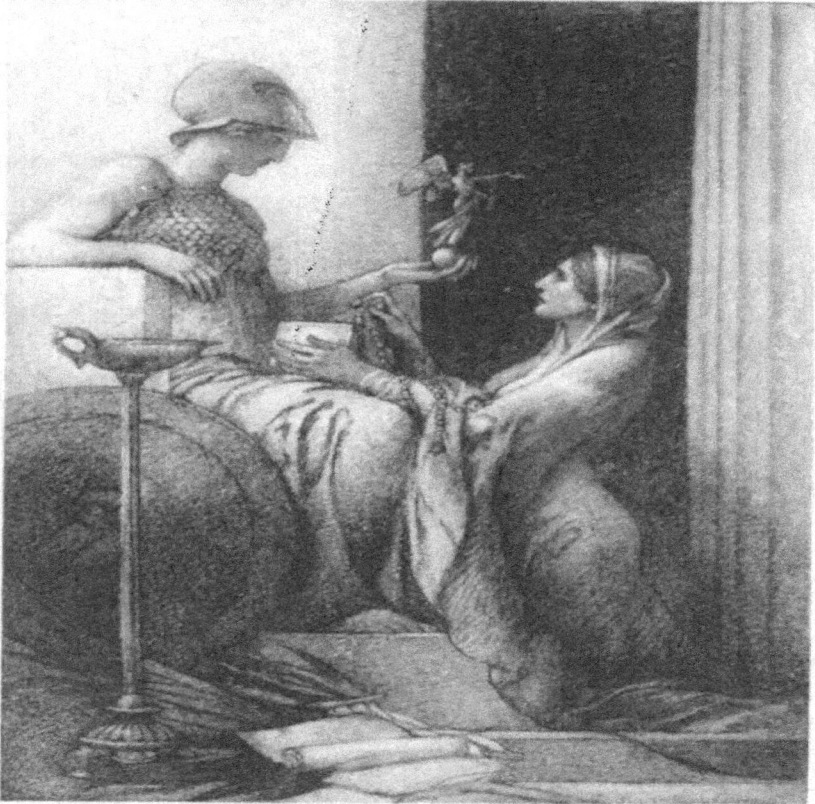

LELAND · STANFORD · JVNIOR · VNIVERSITY

# PROCEEDINGS

OF THE

# ROYAL GEOGRAPHICAL SOCIETY

## OF LONDON.

## Vol. VI.

### SESSION 1861-62.

#### Nos. I. to V.

### EDITED BY F. GALTON AND W. SPOTTISWOODE,
HONORARY SECRETARIES.

*Authors are alone responsible for the contents of their respective statements.*

LONDON:
15, WHITEHALL PLACE.
1862.

LONDON: PRINTED BY WILLIAM CLOWES AND SONS, STAMFORD STREET,
AND CHARING CROSS.

# CONTENTS OF VOL. VI.

*Authors are alone responsible for the contents of their respective statements.*

## No. I.

### ADDITIONAL NOTICES.

## No. II.

## No. III.

## No. IV.

## No. V.

### ADDITIONAL NOTICES.

# PROCEEDINGS

## OF

# THE ROYAL GEOGRAPHICAL SOCIETY OF LONDON.

## SESSION 1861–62.

*First Meeting, Monday, November 11th, 1861.*

SIR RODERICK I. MURCHISON, VICE-PRESIDENT, in the Chair.

PRESENTATIONS. — *Lieutenant-Colonel George P. Evelyn ; Alexander Grant ; and A. Adam Reilly, Esqrs., were presented upon their Election.*

ELECTIONS.—*The Rev. R. Wheeler Bush, M.A. ; the Hon. A. Gough Calthorpe ; Sir John Kirkland ; the Earl of Longford ; Lieutenant-Colonel George H. Money ; Lord George Quin ; the Hon. Thomas J. Hovel Thurlow ; and James Begbie ; John Cheetham, Jun. ; J. Sparrow Crowley, C.E. ; J. Lewis Franklin ; Joseph Goolden ; George Hopcraft ; J. Anderson Rose ; John Thrupp, and Andrew Walls, Esqrs., were elected Fellows.*

ACCESSIONS.—The Accessions to the Library and Map-rooms since the former meeting were numerous. Among the more important were the following :—United States Reports of Explorations and Surveys ; Geology of Arkansas ; Hind's ' Canadian Red River Expedition ;' Krapf's ' Eastern Africa ;' Hutchinson's ' Wanderings among the Ethiopians ;' Tyndall's ' Glaciers of the Alps ;' Jackson's ' What to Observe,' re-edited by Dr. Shaw ; Forbes' ' Norway and its Glaciers ;' Marryat's ' Jutland and the Danish Isles ;' Burton's ' City of the Saints ;' Cleghorn's ' Forests and Gardens of South India ;' Bosworth's King Alfred's ' Description of Europe,' &c. ; the Transactions of various Home and Foreign Scientific Societies ; Russian Maps of the Government of Tver ; Imray's Charts of the China Sea ; Philip's Family and Popular Atlas of Physical Geography ; Stanford's Seat of War in America ; Mouat's Map of the Andaman Isles ; Vce. Bandeira's Map of the Zambesi ; Ethnological Map of Finland ; continuation of Dufour's Map of Switzerland, Carnbee's Atlas, Ordnance Maps and Admiralty Charts, &c. &c. ; and several valuable instruments presented by Walter Ewer, Esq., F.R.G.S.

The Papers read were—

1. *Expedition up the Yang-tse-kiang.*  By Lieutenant-Colonel SAREL, 17th Lancers, F.R.G.S.

THE party composing this expedition left Shanghae on February 11, 1861, with the intention of proceeding up the Yang-tse-kiang, crossing the province of Se-chuen to Lassa, and thence reaching India over the chain of the Himalayas.  However, the first part of their intended journey was alone accomplished, as a state of rebellion and war in the far-west made it utterly impossible to procure boats, land-transport, or even attendants, further than Ping-shan, a small town situated a few miles beyond Su-chow, which itself is in N. lat. 28° 46', N. long. 105° 7'.

The expedition consisted of Lieut.-Colonel Sarel, 17th Lancers; Captain Blakiston, R.A.; Dr. Barton; and the Rev. S. Schreschewsky, of the American mission.  The official report of the journey by Lieut.-Colonel Sarel is printed as a Supplement to the ' Calcutta Gazette ' of September 11, 1861 ; an elaborate chart of the river has been prepared by Captain Blakiston from his surveys; and collections of minerals, plants, and insects, have been despatched to England.

They started in company with the naval expedition under Sir Hope Grant, who steamed as far as Yo-chow.  Here they were left on their own resources, and proceeded up stream in native boats.

The general features of the river above Shanghae are, that it is about 1000 yards wide, flowing through a flat country, with a depth of from 4 to 17 fathoms in main channel, and perfectly navigable as far as I-chang, N. lat. 30° 41', E. long. 111° 3'.  Here the river issues through a contracted channel in a mountainous country, and the boats of the lower Yang-tse do not ascend further. For 78 geographical miles, between I-chang and Quai-chow, the river is narrowed even to 150 yards, and is of great depth and swiftness ; here and there rushing into rapids.  Boats of 120 feet in length, are tracked up this part of its course with severe exertion, but float down with scant pilotage and without danger in mid-stream.  After Quai-chow the river again becomes navigable, but less freely than in its lower course, for its stream is narrower and swifter, and its channel more obstructed with rocks ; however there are rarely less than 8 fathoms in mid-channel.  It receives the Ho-chow river, an important navigable tributary, at Chung-king, and two smaller ones further west, and ceases to be navigable for large vessels at Su-chow, though boats may ascend it further.

The river has an immense rise and fall, the difference between its extreme levels being 27 feet at Han-kow, where its breadth is fully a mile, and 50 feet in the neighbourhood of I-chang, where it is only a quarter of a mile broad.    In the latter place it begins to rise about the beginning of April, continues rising till June, maintains its height till the end of September, and is at its lowest in December.    The time of easiest navigation would be before the river has risen so high as to inundate its banks, and make its main-channel difficult to find.

The political state of the country became exceedingly unsettled from Quai-chow upwards.    The English treaty was nowhere posted, and at one town it had not even been seen.    The Prefect of Quai-chow called it the treaty of Prince Kung.    At Su-chow the rebels were described as overrunning the neighbourhood, while headless bodies, with their hands tied behind their backs, floating at all hours down the stream, verified the Chinese statements.    At Ping-shan, the furthest point reached by the expedition, there was an actual siege and night attack.

The rebels were not the Tai-pings, nor in any way connected with them.    They were called "Tu-feh," or local robbers; there were also plundered peasantry, who took to robbing others for their own subsistence.    The rebels were resisted by the inhabitants of the villages, who banded themselves together, and numerous troops had been despatched and were seen on their way against them.

As to the products of the country;—in addition to other crops, the poppy was largely cultivated above Quai-chow: for many miles it was the universal crop, and its quantity was such as might well interfere with a foreign market.    There are numerous gold-washings, apparently very unproductive, for none but the commonest people were seen employed upon them.    Coal is found in many places, but not of very good quality; it is small and dull-looking. The best coal, and also the most abundant district, is just above Su-chow, where it is quarried high up on the cliffs, and sent down to the river in baskets, sliding on stout bamboo ropes, one full basket pulling up an empty one.    This coal could be boated down to Han-kow in twenty days, and to I-chang in ten.

Native Christians numbered from 2000 to 3000 at Chung-king, out of a population of 200,000, according to the account of the French missionaries who are established there.    Besides the Christians, there are 500 Mussulman families.

The places which hold out the greatest inducement to Europeans to form trading stations, are I-chang and Chung-king.    Steamers could reach I-chang with perfect ease, but thence the rapids and eddies form an obstruction that would require some knowledge of the river, and boats built for the purpose, to surmount in safety.

No serious difficulty was experienced by the expedition on their way except at Chung-king, where the prefect was exceedingly disobliging, and the soldiers threatened to murder them. A bold bearing and show of resistance overcame all this, and the prefect's manner changed to great civility.

The CHAIRMAN said, that about two months ago he received the following letter from Sir H. Robinson, the Governor of Hong-Kong, forwarding the substance of a letter just received from one of the French missionary establishments in the interior of China :—

" You will no doubt be glad to hear the latest accounts of Major Sarel and his party, who are trying to make their way to Calcutta (*via* Lassa) overland from Hankow : I therefore send you the substance of a letter just received here from Monseigneur Desflèches, Vicar-Apostolic of Eastern Sechuen, dated from Chung-king, 15th May last.

" ' The English caravan (travelling party) arrived at Chung-king the 28th April. Monseigneur Desflèches was absent in the country. M. Vincot received them. On Tuesday (30th April) Monseigneur Desflèches returned, and invited them to dinner. The city was in such commotion, and its people, who had never seen Europeans in their costume before, were so threatening, that Dr. Barton and the other gentleman remained on board to guard their property, with the four sepoys ; and Major Sarel and Captain Blakiston accepted the Bishop's invitation. These gentlemen also saw the mandarins of the place, who at first refused, but afterwards granted them chairs (des palanquins). They carried on their boat the flag of an ambassador, being so directed by the authorities at Hankow. They left for Chingtu, the capital of the province, on the 4th or 5th May, expecting to reach the Himalayas about September or October. They were to travel by water to the capital, the land route swarming with rebels, and Monseigneur Desflèches had doubts of their making their way. M. Vincot gives a deplorable account of the state of Sechuen, and calculates the number of the rebels in those parts at over 300,000. The Government troops, he says, are as great ruffians as the rebels, and invariably finish the work of plunder that the latter have begun.

" ' Monseigneur de Narula died in his flight before the rebels on the 6th May, aged 75 years, 42 of which were spent in China.'

" These, I think, are the only points which would interest you in Monseigneur Desflèches' letter.

" By the latest accounts from the Yangtse the navigation of that river has been rendered very difficult in consequence of the rapid rise ; the river having risen 36 feet at Hankow and 21 at Nanking. This, however, does not appear anything more than must be looked for every summer."

These, continued the Chairman, were merely illustrations of the difficulties with which our travellers had to contend, and showed the reasons why they were compelled to abandon their adventurous expedition. They, however, had accomplished much, and the geographical and other information which they had obtained was very valuable. He knew the meeting would agree with him, when he said that the gentleman who had communicated the paper was entitled to their best thanks.

————

2. *The Caucasus.*   By Captain DUNCAN CAMERON, F.R.G.S., late H.B.M.
Vice-Consul at Redout Kaleh, and now Consul at Abyssinia.

IN this paper, after a recapitulation of the mythical marvels of the
Caucasus, such as the Golden Fleece, the Amazons, and Prometheus,
to which some still existing legends bear distant affinity, the author
treated upon its more recent history, the geographical features of the
country, and the peculiarities of its tribes.

The tribes are exceedingly numerous, diverse, and hardly admitting of classification.   For example : the Cossacks, who occupy the
northern face of the Caucasus, date some centuries back, when large
bodies of that restless race moved down from their own plains to
those of the Dnieper and Don, and thence to the Terek, where,
carrying off the daughters of the inhabitants in a Sabine marriage,
they formed a mixed race, which has been continually recruited
from the Don or Ukraine.   Disposed in regiments along the military lines, they vie with the original inhabitants, whose customs
they have in great measure adopted, in their bold bearing, showy
accoutrements, and daring deeds of partisan warfare ; and they
furnish an imposing complement to the regular army of the Caucasus.   Beyond these are Tartars, originally settled by the sea of
Azof, whose history shows four migrations in two centuries.

In selecting one of the numerous races touched upon by Captain
Cameron, as characteristic of the more truly aboriginal inhabitants,
we may take the Tcherkess.   Their constitution is strictly feudal.
Society is divided into several classes of nobles, the principal of
whom are of Arab descent, intermediate classes of freemen, and into
serfs.   As in Europe during the middle ages, every freeman is
expected to be under the protection of a seigneur.   The young
Tcherkess is not educated at home, but is entrusted to a neighbour,
under whom he is perfected in gentle bearing, eloquence, and mar-
tial exercises.   Each great noble is attended by a sort of squire of
the inferior nobility, whose duty is to fight by his side.   The
Tcherkess thus form a regular and numerous Moslem chivalry.
They are turbulent, but brave, and lovers of liberty ; they have
popular assemblies, where the interests of the community are freely
discussed both by the princes and the better class of elder peasants ;
for a great respect is shown to age.   The Tcherkess country is still
a seat of the slave-trade, for which it has been noted since the days
of Herodotus, and its influence has sunk so deeply into the institutions of the people, that the chief privilege of a seigneur over the
peasants of the lower class, is the right of disposing of their issue.
Neither the Tcherkess nor many others of the Caucasian tribes

were devoted to Schamyl; on the contrary, they looked on his levelling system of government with suspicion and dislike. "It was a
rule of priests," they said, "and they were princes." It was only
among the democratic tribes that Schamyl had great power.

The paper concludes with a short account of the exports and
imports of the Caucasus. Among the curiosities of the latter is
found the well known "poudre de Perse" for killing insects, which
has vastly increased in demand. In imports, the cotton goods of
Switzerland rival those of England. Petroleum is an abundant
natural production, but it is not brought into the market to such an
extent as its importance appears to demand. The total average
export of the Caucasus is 192,777*l.*, and import 662,684*l.* This,
however, gives an incomplete idea of the movement of its commerce,
for the Caucasus is a world in itself, and there is a large exchange
of products between different provinces, towns, and villages, each
of which has frequently its own speciality.

The CHAIRMAN said, his friend Captain Cameron had made an attempt to do
that which he (the Chairman) ventured to tell him it was impossible to accomplish, namely, to combine in one short paper the mythology, history, geography,
and ethnology of a vast and very diversified country. The paper, however, contained much of a valuable and interesting character, and he begged to thank
Captain Cameron for his contributions. The Chairman then called upon Sir
Henry Rawlinson and Mr. Danby Seymour, who were acquainted with the
region, to address the Society.

SIR HENRY RAWLINSON, K.C.B., said, that during the last two years, in his
journey to and from Persia, he had had the opportunity of passing and repassing
the Trans-Caucasian provinces. Their geographical features could be described
in a few words. There was, in the first place, a rich alluvial plain on the shores
of the Black Sea—the ancient Colchis, watered by the Phasis and its tributaries, and covered for the most part with dense forest and luxuriant vegetation.
At the distance of 40 or 50 miles from the sea, a chain of hills run down from
the Caucasus towards Ararat, and from the summit of these hills the plateau
sloped gradually down for 500 or 600 miles to the Caspian. This plateau was
generally of a stern and barren character, but the valley of the Cyrus river was
well cultivated throughout, and there was a certain belt of forest running
through the country in a north-west and south-east direction, of extraordinary
beauty. The southern slopes again, of the great range of Caucasus, broken into
innumerable valleys, and studded with villages and vineyards, presented a
landscape of surprising loveliness. The range of hills running south from the
Caucasus to Akhaltzik, beyond Kotais, were especially remarkable for their
beauty : he had never indeed seen or heard of mountain scenery elsewhere of a
more magnificent or picturesque character. Ethnologists found many subjects of interest in that country, but it was especially a school in which they
might learn caution, for there were many languages spoken in it which they
were wholly unable to affiliate. The descent of the greater part of the Caucasian
tribes was a subject of the utmost difficulty, into which he could not now
enter; but he might mention a fact he had observed in reference to one of
them, the Imeretians, as indicating their ancestry—it was the peculiarly thick
and rough character of their hair. He believed it testified to their African
descent, as asserted by Herodotus, and showed that two or three thousand
years had not sufficed to comb straight the woolly hair of the negro. This

appearance of their hair was quite unmistakeable when attention had been directed to it; it struck the gentlemen who were travelling with him quite as forcibly as himself. The hair, however, was the only negro characteristic about them; their features were in no way negro. As to Mingrelia, he considered it to be the finest country in the world, both in the physical features of the land and in the remarkable beauty of its inhabitants. It was a paradise of beauty; neither a plain woman nor a plain man were ever to be seen in it. He recommended those who wished for a pleasant trip to go to the Black Sea and take a run in the Caucasus. They might depend on it they would enjoy the excursion far more than a season spent among the German baths.

After some remarks by Mr. DANBY SEYMOUR, M.P.,

The CHAIRMAN, before adjourning the meeting, wished to announce with respect to China that another expedition was contemplated, and he read the following letter he had received from Mr. Baring, dated Aug. 3, 1861:—

" With respect to your letter of the 17th of November last, submitting for favourable consideration a proposal from Captain E. Smyth, of the Bengal army, to conduct an exploring expedition into Chinese Tartary, I am directed by Sir Charles Wood to inform you that the Government of India have sanctioned—subject to the reply which may be received to a letter addressed by them to Mr. Bruce, Her Majesty's plenipotentiary in China—the proposed expedition, under the conduct of Captain Smyth; and that they have placed under him Lieutenant Jackson of the Bengal Engineers, Dr. J. L. Stewart, an accomplished botanist, and Mr. Joseph Medlicote of the Geological Survey.

" The Asiatic Society of Bengal has been requested to furnish any information, and to offer any suggestions that may be serviceable to the expedition; and I am directed by Sir Charles Wood to add, that any suggestions which the Royal Geographical Society may have to offer, will be forwarded to the Government of India, to be communicated to Captain Smyth, in the event of the reply from Mr. Bruce being satisfactory,* and the exploring party not having started at the time of their receipt."

In addition to that letter he had received one from Mr. Medlicote, the geologist of the expedition, entering more fully into their proposed route, and stating that, while they awaited an answer from Mr. Bruce, they should be very glad of suggestions or other information from people of science in this country.

The CHAIRMAN then drew attention to recent maps of Russia, which were lying on the table, and concluded by stating that the Grand Duke Constantine, who was also the President of the Imperial Geographical Society of St. Petersburg, and was now in England, had given him authority to state that no part of the geography of Russia which was known to H. I. Highness should remain unknown to the geographers of England. He also mentioned that Lütke, the aide-de-camp of the Grand Duke and son of Admiral Lütke, was present.

The meeting was then adjourned to November 25th.

---

*Second Meeting, November 25th, 1861.*

## The EARL DE GREY AND RIPON in the Chair.

PRESENTATIONS.—*The Rev. S. F. Creswell; Sir John Kirkland; Major Alexander Strange; Jonathan S. Crowley, C.E.; and John Thrupp, Esqrs., were presented upon their election.*

ELECTIONS.—*Capt. Frederick Campbell, R.N.; the Earl Cawdor; Capt.*

---

* Intelligence has reached the Society that Mr. Bruce's answer is unfavourable. —ED.

*H. Christian*, R.N.; *Sir Charles Clifford*; *Major-Gen. A. F. Cunynghame*, C.B.; *Capt. Charles Dick*; *the Earl of Donoughmore*; *Rev. William Ellis*; *Capt. Robert J. Hendry*; *Commr. A. Hiley Hoskins*, R.N.; *Sir James J. Randall Mackenzie, Bart.*; *Capt. Rochfort Maguire*, R.N.; *Lord Rollo*; *Don M. F. Paz Soldan*; *Lord Talbot de Malahide*; *Viscount Templeton*; *William C. Baldwin*; *James Bishop*; *Henry Blanshard*; *Julius Brenchley*; *William Burges*; *Herbert Davies*, M.D.; *E. Brown Fitton*; *Julian Goldsmid*; *F. Gover*; *Daniel Grant*; *D. Clewin Griffith*; *John Heugh*; *Deane J. Hoare*; *John Hollingsworth*; *John Holms*; *William Johnson*, R.N.; *J. Pryce Jones*; *Edward Lane*; *John W. Maclure*; *Richard Mann*; *William S. F. Mayers*; *Joseph Milligan*; *Frederick J. Mouat*, M.D.; *Robert Owen*; *George H. Pinckard*; *David Reid*; *James Searight*; *William J. Sharpe*; *Jervoise Smith*; *R. J. Spiers*; *Markham Spofforth*; *Joseph W. Tayler*; *William Ursher*; *Edward H. Walker*; *J. William Walker*; *J. Harrison Watson*; *Charles J. Wingfield, and James A. Youl, Esqrs., were elected Fellows.*

The Papers read were —

1. *Exploration of Central Australia.* By J. MacDouall Stuart, F.R.G.S., and Gold Medallist.

Mr. Stuart left Chambers' Creek on the 1st of January, 1861, with eleven men and forty-nine horses. The first part of his journey was tedious and difficult, owing to the dryness of the country, of which he complains severely. He says, at the Finke's Springs on March 3rd, "I am now in daily expectation of the equinoctial rains, and then I hope to be enabled to push on without further loss of time. The last month has been dreadful slow work; but it has proved the country passable at any season." The first shower fell on March 16th, at the Hugh Springs, and on the 20th his party began to be embarrassed by heavy rains and the consequent bogginess of the ground. He passed Mount Centre on the 6th of April, and reached Attack Creek (the place where he was attacked and repulsed by the natives in his previous journey) on the 25th of April : thenceforward his exploration of new country fairly commenced.

On the 29th of April he arrived at a fine grassy creek with abundance of water, which he called Tomkinson Creek. It formed a station, whence he subsequently made three attempts, in different directions, to reach the northern coast, and where, on the present occasion, he left two of his tired horses to recruit, until the time of his homeward journey.

Four days of travel onwards, brought him to the commencement of large open plains, stretching out of sight to the north, and bounded on the east by a ridge of hills, running also to the northward.   The former of these he called Sturt's Plains, after his old leader in Australian exploration, and the latter Ashburton Range, after the President of the Royal Geographical Society.   It was at this point of his journey where all his difficulties commenced.

The plains were fissured and water-worn by long previous inundations, but now matted over with thick grass, which concealed the crevices and made them exceedingly dangerous to the horses to cross.   There was not the slightest appearance of surface-water. He afterwards mentions his belief that Sturt's Plains are a continuation of some he had met with beyond Mount Centre, and that they might continue to the banks of the Victoria River, the features of the country being nearly the same.

He therefore travelled to Ashburton Range and ascended it, in order to gain a view of the country before him.   To the north lay an extensive open plain, with scarcely a tree on it, and no distant hills were visible, where water might be expected, except some slightly rising ground in the north-west : to which, on the second day after his return to camp, he made his way.

He reached it after a difficult and toilsome journey.   The horses were constantly falling into the fissures before mentioned, which were concealed by grass, at great risk of serious accident.   On arriving he found it to be the bank of a former fresh-water lake, now wholly dried : numbers of old shells lay about it, worn to the thinness of paper by the combined action of the sun and atmosphere.   There was not the slightest indication of water in its neighbourhood, nor anything visible in the distance to hold out hope, excepting one hill-top, too far away in the west for him to attempt; so he was compelled to turn back to the watering-place he had last left.   He thence started afresh in a westerly direction, straight towards the hill-top he had observed from the bank of the dried-up lake.   He reached it, and found it to consist of red, waterless sand-hills, 200 feet high, and thickly covered with scrub.   The view from their top was exceedingly discouraging.   He could see for fully twenty-five miles a-head, and there was no appearance of a change, while entire want of water compelled him to return without delay.

For the third time he started on an altered course, now making directly for the north, over stony and sandy rises, very thick with scrub and trees, and discovered water on May 14th in what he called Lawson Creek, in lat. 17° 15'; whence he had hopes of outflanking the range of sand-hills reached on his previous journey, and of thus reaching the Victoria by a more northern parallel.   He was, however, disappointed in his end, for, on travelling to the west, he came amongst stony rises, covered with scrub so dense that it was impossible to penetrate it. It was the thickest scrub he had ever had to contend against; the horses would not face it, and he was in danger of losing them, for, even at two or three yards' distance, they were wholly screened from sight. His hands and face were lacerated, his clothes and saddle-bags torn to pieces. If the party had gone further they would have lost everything off the horses.

These scrub-covered ridges on the one hand, and the fissured waterless plains on the other, placed a bar to further progress to the north-west; that is to say, in the direction of the Victoria River. They were, as Mr. Stuart says, as complete an impediment as if an inland sea or a wall had been in his way.

Returning to Lawson's Creek, he now made a fourth attempt, but in this case to the north-east, in the direction of Carpentaria. However, he was repulsed by a continuation of the waterless Sturt's Plains, to the aridity of which was superadded the further difficulty of belts of nearly impassable forest.

A fifth attempt to the westward of north, on May 24th, was, in the first instance, much more promising. At a distance of only 14 miles from Lawson's Creek he fell upon a splendid creek of water, in lat. 17° 30', and long. 133° 41'. He saw a large flock of pelicans, and there were mussels and periwinkles in the water, of which the natives must consume a large quantity, judging from the shells on the banks. He called it Newcastle Water, and says it is certainly the gem of Sturt's Plains.

The lagoon proved to be above 9 miles long, 150 yards wide, and 17 feet deep in the middle. It ended towards the north-east in a chain of ponds. Here he was attacked by natives, whom he repelled. He examined the neighbourhood of this water, and on the 30th of May reached even to within 100 miles of Mr. Gregory's last station on the Camfield, but was turned back as before, by the fearfully dense scrub and the want of water.

Again he started from Newcastle Water on the 10th of June, and came on a still thicker scrub than on the former occasion. There was not the least appearance of rising ground, or a change in the country; nothing but the same dreary, dismal forest throughout, which, he says, may in all probability continue to Mr. Gregory's last camp on the Camfield.

He would have dug wells had his party been large enough, when divided into sections, to resist native attacks, and had he possessed means of conveying water to those who would be engaged in sinking the wells. He had not the least doubt but that water could be obtained at a moderate depth, and believed that three or four wells would suffice to carry a party through to the sources of the Camfield.

Lastly, his rations being reduced to four pounds of flour and one pound of dried meat per man per week, he made a push from Newcastle Water, across Sturt's Plains, eastwards towards Carpentaria, but was again driven back by want of water. The ground was dark and dusty, and had wholly swallowed the rain that had fallen upon it.

Mr. Stuart then fell back several stages to Tomkinson Creek, and expended his last efforts in two vain expeditions—one towards the Victoria, where he met with no scrub of serious thickness, but was repulsed by want of water; the second towards Carpentaria, over plains like Sturt's Plains, and equally impracticable for want of water; and the third towards the Victoria River. Finally, on July 12th, he returned towards Adelaide, with exhausted horses and a bare sufficiency of food.

---

2. *Letters from the Governor of West Australia and the Bishop of Perth, accompanying the Journal of an Expedition undertaken by the Brothers* DEMPSTER, *Messrs.* CLARKSON *and* HARPER.

His Excellency's letter is as follows :—

" I ENCLOSE the journal of a small affair undertaken by some young gentlemen who have been my companions in kangaroo-hunting. From a local point of view their discovery is highly interesting, inasmuch as it was believed to be impossible to penetrate far to the northward and eastward of the settled districts of 'Northam,' by reason of dense thickets, which turned Mr. Roe back many years ago. This expedition is, I hope, the forerunner of other and more important discoveries in the same direction; and care will be in future taken to send some scientific observers with the party, which I regret was not the case in the late instance.

" You will observe that the information relative to white men having perished in this locality ten or twelve years ago, is very loose and unreliable. I have questioned the explorers, who can add nothing to what they have stated in their journal, namely, native *hearsay*. The alleged fact of their having horses proves that they could not have been shipwrecked sailors, and I think it highly improbable that any of Leichhardt's party could have reached such a point.

" I begin to look for some tidings of Mr. Frank Gregory's expedition with some anxiety, but without any apprehension, having full confidence in his ability and prudence.

"As our means and prosperity are rapidly on the increase, our settlers will doubtless, ere long, look for more available sheep-land in the unknown waste around us."

THE BISHOP OF PERTH wrote in praise of the members of the Expedition. He corroborated their account of intense cold by his own experience in this unusual season.

### Journal of the Expedition.

Messrs. C. E. Dempster, A. Dempster, B. Clarkson, C. Harper, and a native servant, left Northam on July 3, 1861, and travelled in a pretty straight course to the E.N.E. Every one of the party had two horses, and carried his own provisions of eighty pounds of flour, twenty-two pounds of pork, sixteen pounds of sugar, and three pounds of tea.

Each day's work is described in their printed account, which occupies five columns of a West Australian Journal, the "Independent," of September 13th. The country they passed through, has the rapid alternations usual in Australian scenery, of scrub, grass, and lagoon; but the scrub was never so dense as seriously to embarrass them. The grass was sufficient for their wants, though not over-abundant, and they camped by water on nearly every occasion. The only serious discomfort they endured was owing to persistent hard frost.

Their furthest point was a hill, the most considerable they had seen, which they called Mount Kennedy. They reached it on July 24th, and they place it, by dead reckoning, in s. lat. 30° 28', and E. long. 121° 16'. Here they turned back, because the country was not inviting enough to tempt them further. There were numerous native fires in sight, and the onward route appears to have been as practicable as that which they had already passed over.

The only remarkable feature on their route to Mount Kennedy was an extensive chain of lakes, passing out of sight to the east when viewed from a neighbouring hill. By the side of this hill was a spring, apparently of petroleum. It was situated at about two-thirds of the way between Northam and Mount Kennedy. Their return journey was made by a different route, and they reached home, without loss, on August 23rd. They had been guided by a native, and heard a story from him, which was afterwards corroborated by other natives, that long ago three white men with horses, had reached a large salt water far to the east, and, after travelling about its shores, had turned back and perished.

----

3. *Official Report of the Settlement of Port Denison.*  By
Mr. ELPHINSTONE DALRYMPLE.

MR. DALRYMPLE gives a most satisfactory account of the successful
establishment of the new settlement at Port Denison, in Queensland,
Australia.  He arrived there safely on the 10th of April, in command of the overland expedition, and found the party sent by sea,
already encamped in tents along the shore.  A flagstaff was then
hoisted; the township survey was commenced, and progressed
rapidly; fences and buildings quickly rose; order was kept by the native mounted police and others; and Mr. Dalrymple writes, on the
24th of April, " It is now most deeply gratifying to me to see the
British flag flying over the spot which we found a wilderness; to see
a small, but happy and orderly, population of men, women, and
children, quietly settled, where a few days ago the wild aboriginal
held undisputed sway; cattle and horses feeding over the rich
virgin pastures, and the sounds of industry and civilization, mark-
ing the advance of another great wave of Anglo-Australian energy,
from south to north."  The route traversed by the expedition lay
over a fine pastoral, hilly, and well-watered territory; and to the
path left by the 140 horses and 121 cattle that composed it, is now
added an excellently-marked "tree-line" of 130 miles from Port
Denison to Fort Cooper.

Sir George Bowen, in forwarding this despatch, reports to the
Duke of Newcastle that applications have already been made, chiefly
by settlers from Victoria and New South Wales, for licences to
occupy nearly the whole of the recently proclaimed pastoral district
of Kennedy.  This, alone, embraces a territory exceeding the area
of England and Wales, and reaches within 300 miles of the Gulf of
Carpentaria.  He further adds, that it will probably be shortly his
duty to open another extensive territory, lying to the west of
Queensland.

After some remarks by COUNT STRZELECKI,

COLONEL GAWLER said it was quite refreshing to hear such a combination
of facts accumulating in reference to long-despaired-of Australia.  He would
not occupy the time of the meeting by entering into collateral circumstances,
but would proceed at once to those which had arisen since he personally
visited Australia, when it became the object of his very ardent hopes—the
opening of a line of communication from the south-east provinces to the
north-west coast, by the way of the head of Spencer's Gulf.  He thought that
all who glanced at the map, and looked at the direction of the line of communication, and the wealthy countries beyond it, would see the great importance of
the opening of that line, and, thanks to that fine fellow, that persevering fellow,
Mr. Stuart, it might now really be considered as opened.  It was to be remembered that the part of the country which proved an obstacle to Mr. Stuart's
success in reaching the Victoria River was not more than 90 miles in width.

It was a dense forest, it was true; but while a dense forest was an obstacle to Australian travellers, it was no obstacle to backwoodsmen or the splitters of Australia.   Half a dozen of those men would soon clear away masses of the 90 miles of the dense forest, supposing it continued the whole of the way, which was not likely.   He believed they would cut a road at the rate of 3 or 4 miles a day, and, with a few well-diggers with them, they would be enabled to procure an abundance of water.   Mr. Stuart estimated that three or four wells would be sufficient to make the way open to the Victoria.   The difficulties of the southern part of the route were thought nothing of, and had been overcome with ease, so that they might fairly consider that the whole of the important line from the head of Spencer's Gulf to the north-western coast was open.   They had, too, the satisfaction of considering that it was opening out a well grassed country.   Of course, there were tracts of desert, where there were difficulties to be encountered—some there had been in England itself, such as the moorland between London and the South coast; but, altogether, the accounts were very extraordinary as to the beauty of the soil, the density of the grass, and the abundance of water.   There could not be a more convincing evidence of the traversable nature of the country than the success which had already attended the efforts recently made to explore it.   Mr. Stuart, starting at 18° 30′, reached 28° 30′ in 50 days, a distance of 10 degrees in 50 days, which would average about 15 miles a day for his tired and worn out horses, and men who had long been reduced to four pounds of flour and one pound of dried meat a week.   He attached peculiar importance to the exploration of a route that should connect Spencer's Gulf with the north-west of Australia, inasmuch as it lay directly in the line towards our Asiatic possessions, and abutted on excellent harbours.   The speaker then recommended the careful perusal of Mr. Stuart's Journal, and expressed a hope that now that such progress had been made in exploring Australia, the British Government would step in and assist those who went to the country, by granting them titles and leases of the land which had been discovered, and give the white men as well as the black men some protection.   He concluded by drawing attention to the activity which had been displayed by the Duke of Newcastle in forwarding the medal awarded to Mr. Stuart.   It met him on his recent return to Adelaide, and not only stimulated him, but also the Government and the settlers, so that they were fitting him out with all activity, to enable him to proceed again to the north, to break through the last barrier which existed.

Mr. Baker said that Mr. Stuart had discovered a new country, which was superior to anything which he had passed through before, and had established the fact that the country was well supplied with water in every direction; in fact, he stated that the country could be travelled over at any time, and in any place, without the want of water or of feed for his horses.   Mr. Stuart was going to start again, and he had such confidence in the country, that he was about to take 500 horses to the Gulf of Carpentaria, having found the country so well watered, and the grass in such abundance, as to be capable of sustaining them.   He hoped, if any new colony should be established there after the arrival of Mr. Stuart, that the British Government would give him, as a reward for his services to the country, a large tract of the land, so that it might be handed down to future generations, to show that he, and those who had co-operated with him, were the discoverers of the country for the purposes of the Anglo-Saxon race.   He also expressed a hope that the people who might be discovered inhabiting the land would not be forgotten, and that some successful missionary effort would be made to secure them from the calamities which would otherwise come upon them.

Mr. Crawfurd said that Mr. Stuart's accounts of his discoveries were beyond all praise.   He did not know how the Society was to reward him.

Mr. Stuart had received their medal, and, if there were precedent for it, he thought he should have it again.   Mr. Stuart was a bold, enterprising man, full of sound judgment and great discretion, otherwise he could not have so succeeded.   Australia was a very valuable country.   The fact that it produced five or six millions sterling worth of wool showed its importance, but the production of wool would have its limits—beyond a certain degree from the equator the sheep could not thrive.   Australia was excellent for the production of wool, and for gold, but the gold was diminishing, and, he must say, he agreed with those who preferred New Zealand to Australia for the purpose of colonisation.

The CHAIRMAN then congratulated the Meeting on the interesting nature of the papers read, and the discussions upon them.   He pointed out the great progress which had already taken place in Australia, and trusted that their acquaintance with its vast territory would be followed by its occupation by a large population, the extension of civilization, and advance of the arts of peace.

The Meeting was then adjourned to Dec. 9th.

---

*Third Meeting, Monday, December 9th, 1861.*

### LORD ASHBURTON, PRESIDENT, in the Chair.

PRESENTATIONS.—*The Rev. Charles J. Armistead ; Lieut. Langham Rokeby,* R.N. ; *Don Ramon de Silva Ferro ; E. Brown Fitton ; Edward Lane ; J. Harrison Watson ; and James A. Youl, Esqrs., were presented upon their election.*

ELECTIONS.—*Lord Claude Hamilton ; Captain G. Towers Hilliard ; Sir Christopher Rawlinson ; the Rev. Edward J. Shepherd ; Douglas Henty ; Thomas Hood Hood ; Edward Lawrence ; Robert Low ; William Macpherson ; Henry Martin ; David Ricardo ; and C. Douglas Shepherd, Surg.* R.N., *Esqrs., were elected Fellows.*

EXHIBITIONS. — Logarithmic tables belonging to Mungo Park, accompanied by MS. calculations lately procured on the Niger, and presented by the Foreign Office.   Several photographs of ' Boobies,'—the original inhabitants of Fernando Po,—taken by two Spanish officers, and forwarded by Captain Bedingfeld, R.N., F.R.G.S., were also exhibited.

The PRESIDENT called attention to the remarkable care with which Mungo Park's astronomical tables had been preserved by the Africans into whose hands they had fallen.   The scraps of calculations and manuscript had been compared with a volume of Mungo Park's MSS. in the possession of Mr. Murray, the publisher, and the handwriting had been identified.

The Papers read were—

1. *The British Settlements in Western Africa.*   By Colonel LUKE SMYTH
   O'CONNOR, C.B., F.R.G.S., late Governor of the Gambia.

THIS was a short and slight sketch of the rise and progress of the Gambia, Sierra Leone, and Cape Coast settlements, accompanied by many anecdotes illustrative of African character.  As to the Gambia, which was a noble river, navigable to vessels of 300 tons for a distance of 300 miles from its mouth, little more was known of it beyond the falls of Baraconda than what travellers had told us two-and-a-half centuries ago.  Neither did the author consider this to be wondered at, for the nature of the country, its climate, and especially the jealousy and suspicion of the natives, presented almost insuperable barriers to the advance of the white man. "Aye, aye, Sir," said an old chief, " thankee, thankee ; your words are sweet and your presents good, but, God be praised, we do not want to learn the white man's knowledge.  The cities, the people, the fields, flocks, herds, rivers, forests, are *now* all ours, but once let you get your hand into our nation and you will take the dust from under our feet."

Speaking of the unscrupulous desire to make money, so common to Africans, he said, a negro trader asked his master why he left his own good land and risked his life in Africa?  The white man replied, " To make money."  " Good," said the black trader ; " you are a wise man ; but suppose you die, then whom do you make money for ? "  " For my child," answered the white man.  " Ah ! " exclaimed the African, " why not sell your child and make money of him ? "

The PRESIDENT said he had listened to the paper with great interest, but at the same time with much pain ; for, while they all knew how large a part of the anarchy and misery just alluded to was caused by the misdeeds of our ancestors, it was not so obvious from Col. O'Connor's paper that our settlements on the W. African coast had much tended to mitigate the wrongs we had inflicted.  These settlements had been in our power for many years ; we had lost able men, good servants of the public, in maintaining them ; we now wanted to learn what good had arisen from them.  It was a question on which he sought information from travellers then in the room.  He, the President, had served on a Committee of the House of Lords some years since, when the then Governor of Sierra Leone was under examination.  He had asked him, " What is the condition of the Africans that are taken and set free in your colony ? " and was answered, " They are orderly, well conducted people ; they do all the work of the colony : we could not get on without them."  Again, he (the President) asked, " You have schools, and very good schools : what is the state of the children turned out of those schools ? "  The Governor replied, " Those children do not work ; they are vagabonds, and without the immigration of the liberated Africans we could not get on at all."  He, the President, did not take upon himself to say this was a just statement of the case ; he hoped it was not, and therefore sought testimony to the contrary.

Referring to Dr. Livingstone's endeavour to civilise Africans by first obtaining an influence over them before beginning to preach the truths of religion, the President quoted the advice given by Loyola's successor on the course to be pursued in converting back to Catholicism the then Protestant city of Bologna.  He said, " We will send missionaries to Bologna, but they shall not say one word about religion.  They shall begin first by attending the hospitals, by attending the sick, by attaining influence over them, and establishing their repute as good men.  Then let them begin to preach their religion, and they will be listened to."

Finally, the President called upon Mr. Freeman, the lately appointed Governor of the new British settlement of Lagos, to address the meeting.

MR. FREEMAN said that hitherto he had never visited Western Africa, but that he had resided for some years in Northern Africa, and there in Tunis and Tripoli, and especially in Ghadames, had seen a great deal of the commerce of Central Africa. He could not but be aware of the great importance of Lagos, in offering a new opening to that commerce. Until lately by far the greater part of it had been carried across the Sahara, a distance of five or six months' journey; too long to be remunerative, unless combined with a trade in slaves. But the slave-trade being now abolished in Northern Africa, the traffic across the Sahara was rapidly diminishing, and the commerce of the Soudan was consequently seeking a new outlet in some part of the western coast. Lagos was eminently suited to be that outlet, owing to its neighbourhood to the mouths of the Niger, and means of overland access to the confluence of the Benué and Chadda. Thence Kano, the chief emporium of Central Africa, might be reached in a fortnight, and both Sokoto and Timbuctu were accessible. He thoroughly agreed with the President on the importance of gaining an influence over the Africans before attempting to convert them, and he believed that by opening a trade from Lagos we should obtain that influence.

---

2. *Recent African Explorations :—Proceedings of (a)* SPEKE, (b) PETHERICK, (c) LEJEAN, (d) PENEY, *and* (e) LIVINGSTONE.

(a) *Extracts from a Letter by* Captain SPEKE *to* Lieut.-Col. RIGBY, *H.B.M.'s Consul at Zanzibar, dated Khoko in Western Ugogo, 12th December,* 1860.

" WE are now scarcely knowing what to do. Before us is the desert of M'Gunda M'Kali, and beyond that again the country of Tura—all famished, and without a grain of food to sell us; yet these are not a quarter of the difficulties we have to contend against. Our Kirangozi and nearly all the porters have run away, and our Mozigos are lying on the ground. The rains too are very severe, worse even than an Indian monsoon. Our losses in the rough amount to nine mules, twenty-five slaves of the Sultan, and eighty Wanyamwesis, so you may imagine our dilemma. But we are not out of spirits. Grant is a very dear friend, and being a good sportsman we get through our days wonderfully. At this place alone I have killed two rhinoceroses and three buffaloes, and Grant, a little further back, killed a giraffe. In addition to these, we have killed numbers and many varieties of antelopes, zebras, pigs, and hyenas.

" We often think of you and the great service you have rendered to the expedition by giving us Baraka and the others of your crew; they are the life of the camp. As to Baraka, he is the 'father' of his race, and a general of great distinction among the serviles. I do not know what we should have done without him. Bombay, with all his honesty and kind fellow-feeling, has not half the power of command that Baraka has. Would that I had listened to Bombay when at Zanzibar, and had engaged double the number of his 'free men,' for they do all the work, and do it as an enlightened and disciplined people—so very different from the Sultan's slaves, in whom there is no trust whatever. Many of the Sultan's men I liberated from slavery, and gave them muskets as an earnest of good faith, at the same time telling them they should eventually receive the same amount of wages as all the other 'free men;' but they have deserted me, carrying off their weapons, and so reducing my number of guns.

"Travelling here is much like marching up the grand trunk road in Bengal; the only things we want are a few laws to prevent desertion, and all would be easy. We are moving to-day with ten days' rations, but only in half-marches, sending the men back from each camp, to bring up the remainder of the loads. It is a tiresome business. At Tura I shall leave many things behind, and push on to Kazeh, to hire more men to fetch them up."

### (b) Petherick.

Mr. Petherick's last communication is dated Korosko, August 9th, 1861. He was then engaged in sending his effects across the Nubian desert, by the overland route to Khartum, and was in daily expectation of the arrival of his new boat from Cairo, together with two members of his party who had not yet joined him.

### (c) Lejean.

One if not both of the expeditions that had preceded Mr. Petherick to explore the White Nile, have come to a premature termination. M. Lejean penetrated no further than the Barri country, whence he returned, wearied with the people and suffering from ill-health ; and Dr. Peney, after adding materially to our knowledge of the neighbourhood of Gondakoro, has unhappily died.

### (d) Peney.

The last two letters that were written by Dr. Peney are now just published in the 'Nouvelles Annales des Voyages.' They were addressed to M. Jomard. The first of them is dated Gondakoro, February 20th, 1861. He states that he had returned from a journey due West to the district of Mourou, in the province of Niam-barra. He was eight days in reaching it, but only thirty-one hours of actual travel. He therefore places Mourou on the same parallel of latitude as Gondakoro, and one degree of longitude more to the westward.

There he arrived at the river Itiéy, running to the N.W. It was described to him as continuing the same course through the province of Niam-barra, then through the tribe of the Allah, next bounding the Niam-Niam-Maharaka, then penetrating the Djour country, and finally reaching the Bahr el Ghazal, of which it was one of the principal affluents.

Upwards from Mourou, at a distance of 20 leagues s.e., the river passed through Monda; but of the country above Monda no satisfactory information could be obtained.

Dr. Peney's last letter is dated May 20th, 1861, and is written after his return from a preparatory journey, partly in boats and partly on foot, up and beyond the cataracts of Makedo. His boats had received damage at the commencement of his voyage, and he lost so many ropes and spars as to render them useless for the moment; but he found small lateral arms of the main river, up which he felt assured he could navigate them on a future journey. The natives reported that beyond the limit of his journey, the river spread out into a broad sheet of water, of great depth, but sluggish current. Animated by this account, he was preparing for a second boat expedition southwards in the month of July, as soon as the rising Nile should have made the navigation more practicable, when his plans were cut short by death. His furthest limit was close upon that of Galuffi, and he places it on the same meridian as Gondakoro, and one degree to the south of it. M. Debono was associated with him at the time of his death, but we have no knowledge at present of Debono's movements.

Mr. Galton said that Dr. Peney, in his first journey, seemed to have fallen upon the southernmost portion of Mr. Petherick's route, at a distance of only 60 miles from Gondakoro. Although Mr. Petherick's name does not appear in Dr. Peney's account, which might have been written in entire ignorance of what Mr. Petherick had published, there could be little doubt that the district explored by the two travellers was the same, the tribes' names Mourou and Monda, Niam Niam, and Djour, in addition to the account of the river, being common to both narratives. If this were the case it would involve an enormous amount of rectification of Mr. Petherick's positions, both in actual distance travelled and in the direction of his course from the Bahr el Ghazal. Neither of these corrections surpass the bounds of possibility: for Mr. Petherick's reckoning of 19 miles' journey per diem, in a straight line, is double what other travellers under similar circumstances are found to accomplish; and as to the direction of his route, not only do the rough compass-bearings, on which alone he depended, admit of that large error, but there is the following additional reason to believe in its existence; namely, that the rough map by the brothers Poncet, compiled from various cross routes of traders, places the Djour and Niam Niam countries closely in the position assigned to them by Dr. Peney, and far more eastwards than in the map of Mr. Petherick. Now that the latter traveller has returned to the Soudan, well provided with astronomical instruments and instructed in their use, we may hope for a corresponding degree of accuracy in the geographical data that his future explorations may afford to us.

(e) LIVINGSTONE.

The last news of Dr. Livingstone is dated April 9th, 1861. Extracts of the letter are given as follows, the Doctor having himself written it in the third person :—

"On the 9th of April last, Dr. Livingstone's expedition arrived at Pomony Bay in the island of Johanna, from the river Rovuma.* They had ascended the river only 30 miles, when, halting to wood their ship, a mark made on a tree showed that the water was falling at the rate of 6 or 7 inches a day. They had found some parts carrying no more than 5 or 6 feet of water, and, as they drew nearly 5 feet, they had to return, lest they should be left fixtures till the flood of next year. The cause of this unsuccessful termination is to be attributed to various delays suffered by the *Pioneer* in the voyage out, making her at last quite two months behind the time for a successful trip up the river. After coaling, they left for the Zambesi, intending to go up the Shiré, and then make a road past Murchison Cataract on that river to Lake Nyassa. The distance is only 35 miles, and it is hoped that they will carry a boat up above the cataracts, and by that means explore the lake.

"It is also in contemplation to settle the point whether the Rovuma comes out of Nyassa, as asserted by all the people they met, before going in the *Pioneer* again to that river. The Oxford and Cambridge Mission accompany the expedition up the Shiré, and it is proposed to place these gentlemen on the plateau of 4000 feet above the sea, on which stands Mount Zomba. There they are likely to enjoy good health while pursuing their enterprise. They have had a good deal of fever, but no mortality. The healthy season begins in May.

"The Rovuma will probably turn out to be the best entrance into Eastern Africa. It must, however, be navigated with a vessel of light draught, and with the same skill as is required in the above-bridge London passenger-boats. On the question whether it actually derives its waters from Nyassa, the Doctor thinks that it cannot come out of the Nyassa he discovered, but from some other lake. The reasons he adduces are : the Nyassa is already known to give off one large river, the Shiré. This river never rises nor falls more than 3 feet, nor is its water ever discoloured. The Rovuma rises and falls 6 or more feet, becomes very muddy, and no instance is known of one lake giving off two large rivers. The probability, therefore, is, that if the Rovuma does come out of a Nyassa or Nyanza (lake, or piece of water), it is some other than that dis-

---

* See also *The Rovuma River* (p. 36) in "Additional Notices."

covered by the expedition.   It is well known that lakes having no outlets become brackish in the course of ages.   This is the case with Shirwa, but Nyassa and Tanganyika are sweet.   The former owes its sweetness to the Shiré flowing out of it.   Does Tanganyika owe its sweetness to the Rovuma?"

MR. RAVENSTEIN said he was inclined to believe that the lake generally referred to as Nyassa or Nyanja was not identical with the Nyassa of Livingstone, but that on proceeding for about 70 miles to the north of the debouchure of the Shiré, having the Maravi on the left, we should enter a very narrow channel with a strong current, which, gradually widening, led, in a north-westerly direction, into the upper lake—the great Nyanja.   At Zandenge (say in 13° 15′ s. lat., 35° 10′ e. long.) the width of this channel was very inconsiderable, for people on opposite banks could hail each other. To explain his views with more precision, he would state the assumed latitudes and longitudes of the places he was about to name.   Thus, at Mjenga (13° 5′ s. lat.) it was at most two miles; under 12° 55′ s. lat., 34° 5′ e. long., there was a mountainous island, inserted on the Missionary map, and mentioned by Candido and Dr. Barth's Arab merchant.   Three days' journey to the north of this island was the ferry (Gnombo) Nussewa (12° 35′ s. lat., 34° 30′ e. long.), where, according to Dr. Roscher, the opposite shore could be seen only on a clear day.   Boats crossed the lake here in a day and a half, probably in a south-west direction.   Still further north the opposite shore was not discernible at all, and nothing reliable was known regarding the termination of the lake in that direction.   It had been suggested that Gnombo and Mjenga were situated somewhere near the debouchure of the Shiré, but the great distance from Kilwa, and the shape of the southern extremity of Livingstone's Nyassa, were unfavourable to such a supposition.

There existed apparently great discrepancies in the various itineraries leading to the lake from Kilwa, but all bore internal evidence of leading to neighbouring localities on the same lake: they crossed the river Rovuma about midway, climbed the Njesa mountains before reaching the lake, and in two instances led through Lukelingo (Keringo), the capital of Hiao.   The time occupied on the journey was 60 days according to Mr. Cooley; 56 days according to Baron von Decken; 30 days according to the missionaries.   Dr. Roscher had actually made the journey in about 50 days, and one of his caravans in 25 days.   Great differences in the length of a day's journey were by no means rare in Africa; and Gamitto, on going from Tetté to Lucenda, had made only 2¾ miles' actual progress a day, but 7½ miles on his return.   In the present instance Baron von Decken's journey into the interior, to within 9 days of the Rovuma river, enabled us to estimate the distance from Kilwa to Gnombo, and approximately to fix its position.   The latter was controlled by the route of a Senhor Candido, who had travelled from Tetté in a N.N.W. direction, through the country of the Maravi, had come upon the lake in the country of the Shiva, after 45 days, and crossed it (probably in the direction of Gnombo) in 36 hours.   According to the position assumed, Candido must have travelled at the rate of 5 miles a day.   Another itinerary led to the lake from Mozambique.

The following facts spoke in favour of the northern Nyanja being connected through a narrow channel with a lake further south.   Both Gamitto and Dr. Roscher spoke of a strong current which flowed in that direction.   Candido was positively assured on the upper Nyanja that the Shiré flowed from it; and the Rev. J. Erhardt told us that the Wamuera, dwelling on the western shore of the lake, three days to the south of Mjenga, came to that ferry to be put across.   There was no conclusive evidence of the Rovuma river coming from this lake. Where the routes from Kilwa crossed that river it flowed north and south. It might, however, owe its origin to a lake, which Dr. Krapf placed at 10 days' journey west of Kilwa.

The third Paper read was—

3. *Despatch from Dr. Baikie, Commander of the Niger Expedition, to Earl Russell, dated Lukoja, September 10th, 1861.* Communicated by the FOREIGN OFFICE.

"MY LORD,—The *Sunbeam* arrived on the afternoon of the 31st of August, and by her I received letters and despatches, being the first since 2nd March, 1860. Among them was your Lordship's despatch of June, 1860, recalling the expedition; but, after great consideration, I have ventured to defer my return to England until I can again communicate with your Lordship, and this I have done for the following reasons :—

"1st. Your Lordship has not yet been informed of the present state of affairs here, nor of what has been done here during the past year.

"2nd. My supplies being limited, and my horses having all died, I was prevented from making any lengthened journey; but as I could not be idle, I tried to take advantage of a seemingly favourable state of affairs, and accordingly made a settlement at this spot.

"3rd. The King of Núpe, the most powerful next to the Sultan of Sokoto, being desirous of seeing a market for European produce here, entered into relations with us, and undertook to open various roads for the passage of caravans, traders, and canoes to this place, which promise he has faithfully performed; I on my part, on the strength of the general tenor of my instructions, and faith in Mr. Laird's intentions, giving him to understand that it was the desire of H.M.'s Government to have a trading station here.

"4th. During our late distressed state, the King of Núpe behaved most kindly and liberally towards us, and, besides frequent presents, lent us cowries for our current expenses, so that I am now in his debt 70l. or thereabouts; and during the very limited stay of the steamer here, eleven days and a-half, it was totally impossible to communicate with and pay the king, and it would have been a most ungracious and impolitic act, after his extreme kindness, to have left the place in his debt, and one which I feel assured your Lordship would not have approved of.

"5th. Because, having secured a position here, and the place promising so well, I hardly feel justified in giving it up without first communicating with your Lordship.

"Both the Rev. Mr. Crowther and Captain Walker, agent for the late Mr. Laird's executors, have expressed themselves most favourably impressed with the condition of the place, with its value as a central position and place for trade, and with the importance of keeping it up; and Mr. Crowther will send his views at length to England. I have reduced my staff as much as possible. Mr. Dalton is going to England; I have sent one servant to Sierra Leone, one to Lagos, and another is only prevented from also going by his being at Bida, and the leaving of the steamer before he can possibly reach it; and I am remaining with only two young men and my native followers. I have started a regular market here, and have established the recognition of Sunday as a non-trading day, and the exclusion of slaves from our market. Already traders come to us from Kabbi, Kano, and other parts of Hausa, and we hope, ere long, to see regular caravans with ivory and other produce. I have arranged with the Rev. Mr. Crowther again to try to open a road to Lagos by Ibádan, and at the end of this month I shall send off a messenger by this route to meet Mr. Crowther at Abbeokuta, and to return with other people.

"The step I am taking is, I can assure your Lordship, not lightly adopted. After a prolonged absence from England, to stay another season here without any Europeans, with only a faint prospect of speedy communication, and after all my experience of hunger and difficulty last year, is by no means an inviting prospect. But what I look to are the securing for England a commanding position in Central Africa, and the necessity for making a commencement. I have consulted with the Rev. Mr. Crowther, and that gentleman agrees with me in the expediency of what I am about to do, and in consequence of my determination he has left one of his followers with his family in charge of his mission station at the town of Gbébe on the opposite shore. But I would respectfully request that, should your Lordship see fit to recall me, another may be appointed in my place who should have Consular authority, and whom I might personally introduce as my successor, and who would alike represent England here, and at the same time protect the many people who have trusted the white men, and who have gathered round me."

The meeting was then adjourned to January 13th, 1862.

## ADDITIONAL NOTICES.

### (Printed by order of Council.)

1. *Extract of a Letter on Queensland and New Zealand, from* THOMAS HOOD HOOD, F.R.G.S., Member of the Legislative Council of Queensland, *to* LORD ASHBURTON, President R.G.S.

I HAVE been travelling a good deal lately over the Australian and New Zealand Colonies, and have just returned from a trip with Sir Charles Nicholson to Port Denison, a new settlement we have established in latitude 20°, which will be the shipping port of a large district of tropical Queensland. We are using our best efforts to introduce coolies from India for the purpose of growing cotton, for which there can be no doubt that this colony is well adapted, so far as soil and climate are concerned.

I saw that at a recent meeting of the Royal Geographical Society a gentleman stated that it was very doubtful whether Queensland would produce good wool on account of the latitude. This is a great misapprehension : the value of that article exported last season from the colony was considerable, and in quality it is finer than that grown in the southern colonies. It is now proved that some of the finest pastoral districts lie to the north of the tropic of Capricorn, and before many years elapse it seems highly probable that from some harbour in the Gulf of Carpentaria will be shipped the produce of flocks depastured on Leichhardt's Plains of Promise. We hope shortly to know more of the geography and capabilities of these regions on the return of the various exploring expeditions now out, or about to start, more especially from the two fitted out by the colony of Victoria (with some assistance from Queensland), for the purpose of searching for Mr. Burke and his companions. It is very doubtful whether the ostensible object of the expeditions will be accomplished ; several of the camels taken by the missing explorers have returned to the out stations of South Australia ; and if his party have not perished, they are sure to reach some of the settlements belonging to Queensland before relief can be afforded them. The Colonial war steamer *Victoria* and a transport left Moreton Bay two days ago, with Mr. Landsborough, and a party of 6 men, with 25 horses, to be landed at the Albert River on the north coast, whence they will travel along the eastern borders of the desert country of the interior ; another party, consisting of *Aboriginal* police, under the leadership of a very experienced bushman, Mr. Walker, starts from the settlement of Rockhampton on the FitzRoy River, and makes a course to meet Mr. Landsborough. Should it be found that a large extent of good country exists inland from the gulf, to the west of Gregory's and Leichhardt's tracks, stock will be driven out at once, and the foundation laid of a new colony ; which, from its proximity to the populous countries of Asia, would possess great advantages, and rapidly progress, more especially if commenced as an Imperial one.

I may mention, knowing the interest you take in those matters, that I passed over lately in New Zealand extensive tracts of country in the southern portions of the Middle Island, which are likely to prove highly auriferous, from the geological indications. It is to be regretted should these gold-fields be developed and prove attractive at present ; for the small population in the colony will be diverted from more legitimate occupations, and the healthy tone which pervades the settlers of these provinces, and promised to make New Zealand the England of the southern hemisphere, will be changed to the feverish, discontented one which characterizes the population of a gold country.

It may be interesting to you to know that I discovered at the Antipodes the remains of what I deem to be a species of fossil lizard closely resembling the Plesiosaurus of the Lias. I have sent the fossils to Professor Owen. There is said to be a possibility that the British Museum may still be adorned by a Dinornis : the footsteps of a gigantic bird, it is stated, were seen by a surveyor's party ; they were 14 inches long, and 11 inches wide on the spread, and they had been impressed during the night over the tracks of the men made on the previous day. All the wingless birds existing in New Zealand are nocturnal in their habits, and the general impression from Maori tradition is, that the Moa was a gigantic Apteryx. The district is exceedingly rocky, and full of caves, in some of which it is just possible that a surviving individual may find its hiding places. Exertions are being made (the last steamer's mail brings us intelligence) to ascertain the truth of the report, and if correct, thoroughly to search the wild and unsettled districts where it is said to be. Certainly this will be a most interesting event to naturalists should the search prove successful. I must say I feel somewhat sanguine on the subject, as once, when in that part of the Middle Island, I heard of a very circumstantial account given by a man, who stated that he had seen a great bird go down into a rocky glen one morning at daybreak, but the story was not credited. The surveyor who now makes the statement is understood to be a man of character.

---

2. *Report on the Natural Products and Capabilities of the Shiré and Lower Zambesi Valleys.* By John Kirk, Botanist to the Livingstone Expedition. Dated Senna, Dec. 28th, 1860.

I beg to offer the following Report concerning the capabilities of the regions explored by the expedition under your command for the growth of such articles as are in demand in Europe :—

The countries examined have been those bordering the Zambesi from the east coast to Sesheke, a Makololo town, situated in the centre of the African continent ; likewise the valley of a tributary river, the Shiré, from Lake Nyassa to its confluence with the Zambesi near Moramballa Hill. The highlands of the Batoka and Manganja countries have also been visited. The area thus included extends over 11° of longitude and 5° of latitude ; the greatest height above the sea level being 8000 feet.

The Zambesi forms a large Delta, commencing 60 miles from its mouth ; the coast for about 8 miles inland is muddy, wooded with mangrove, avicennia, and other trees peculiar to such places within the tropics ; the remainder of the Delta consists of rich flat alluvial lands, intersected by many branches of the river. This great tract is covered almost exclusively with gigantic grasses, which keep down all other forms of vegetation, only borassus palms, with a few figs, acacias, or lignum vitæ trees, being able to resist the fires which sweep over these plains during the dry season. The people at present inhabiting the Delta are for the most part fugitives ; the slave trade and war have combined to desolate this rich country, which once produced corn, vege- tables, and fruits in abundance. Near the coast cotton of an inch staple is found growing wild, having sprung up from seed accidentally scattered ; this equals in value much of the Egyptian. Climate and soil are admirably suited, seeing that the plant succeeds so well without cultivation, surrounded by weeds. In the more inland districts it could not raise its head above the dense luxuriance of the other vegetation. The labour required to cultivate cotton here is very small, and the Delta might be made a vast cotton field by encouraging the natives to industry. Many parts of these lands are also suited for the growth of the sugar cane; a little is now raised near the coast, and succeeds well; and it might be raised in most parts even without irrigation. Besides sorghum, pennisetum, maize, setaria, eleusine, and various other sorts of native corn, the Delta also yields wheat during the cold season. Rice of good quality is also cultivated. Tropical fruits succeed well, and near the coast mangos, pine-apples, guavas, cashews, lemons, oranges, and cocoa-nuts are still found where Portuguese settlements had existed in former times.

The climate of the Delta is mild, presenting neither the excessive heat nor cold of the interior; the atmosphere is much moister, and heavy dews are frequent; the prevalence of a sea breeze renders the parts near the coast more healthy than those within the mangroves. The malaria, although an obstacle to the settlement of Europeans, is by no means so intense as that of the west coast; and we have not found a case which resisted treatment, while a cure is commonly effected on the third day. To those passing through or remaining for a short time, there seems to be no danger. But in order that this might become an extensive source of cotton, the permanent residence of Europeans is not necessary; if it were raised by the natives and purchased from them by agents, a steady supply might be depended on; but time would be needed, even under a wise government, to bring the Delta back to a flourishing state.

The valley of the Zambesi, from the Delta to where the river enters the Batoka Hills, presents a very uniform vegetation; that of the valleys and adjacent plains differing from that of the hills, which frequently cross the river. In its course it is joined by the Loangwa and Kafué from the north, and several smaller streams from the south. The forests which clothe this region abound in valuable woods. Lignum vitæ and ebony are both common, so much so that in the region between Tetté and Shupanga we have frequently consumed a ton per day of these alone—the only difficulty experienced being to obtain them of sufficiently small size to enter the badly constructed furnace. There are also many timber trees suitable for machinery and ship-building. A species of Pterocarpus (the "Malompe"), from its lightness and strength, is well adapted for making oars, and is used by the people of the interior for their paddles. The forests, inland from Shupanga, contain the "gunda," from single trees of which, canoes capable of carrying 3 tons are hollowed out.

The hilly regions, especially those between Senna and Tetté, contain the buaze, but it is found in the hills of Mburuma and of the Batoka also. This is the best fibre in the country, being durable when exposed to wet; it is invariably used for fishing-nets, and exists so abundantly that no attempt has been made to cultivate it. The seed also yields a large amount of a drying oil. Between the river bank and the hills there are many wide plains of the richest soil, which in ordinary seasons yield abundant crops, but are liable to suffer from droughts by which the corn crops are cut off, but do not affect the cotton to such an amount. In the damp valleys sugar-cane and wheat are raised, but irrigation would be required to render these crops general. The district to the north of Tetté is the only part in which sugar is manufactured: this is performed in a very rude manner by the natives.

Cotton seems to be the crop best suited for these parts; it is grown in small quantities everywhere; it is a perennial shrub, and springs up the following season even after being burned down; the quality varies very much. That of Kebrabassa is good, also that found beyond the Kafué, but in the intermediate space that chiefly cultivated is of the Kaja or native sort. And the plantations are very small: this is to be accounted for by their distance from the coast, and the very unsettled state of the population, who have been impoverished by successive bands of the Matebele. Above Kebrabassa there are hundreds of miles of the best cotton lands, but until these rapids shall have been shown to be navigable at flood, there exists a considerable land carriage which could not be undertaken unless these parts were in the hands of an active and powerful government.

The valley of the Zambesi, beyond the Victoria Falls, is so far removed from the navigable part leading to the east coast, that its vegetable produce is of comparatively little importance in a commercial point of view; it is also very unhealthy; otherwise it is a very rich country, inhabited by the finest races we have met, both for physical and mental development; they seem free of the suspicion with which a foreigner is regarded in other parts, and are anxious to obtain European articles, of which they see the advantage. In the north, beyond the part reached by us, the sugar-cane is said to be grown, while near Sesheke the cotton-plant attains a size not observed elsewhere; a single plant sometimes covering a space of 12 feet diameter, and forming a stem 8 inches thick. A plantation of such bushes would require only to be kept clean to continue for a lifetime. This had been a season of unusual drought, but there had been a heavy crop of cotton, which was allowed to rot on the ground.

The Batoka highlands, to which attention has been drawn as the first discovered in these latitudes possessing a healthy climate, are situated to the north of the Zambesi, between it and the Kafué. The valley of the Zambesi is there 1000 feet above the sea; the southern slopes are steep, and come down near to the river; the highlands themselves form a vast undulating plain, varying from 3000 to 4000 feet high; they are covered with grass suitable for cattle, and open forests abounding in game; in most parts they are well watered by streams which might be made to irrigate the surrounding parts. The climate is cool and healthy, and during the cold season there are frosts at night. Near the Victoria Falls various native fruit trees have been culti-vated by the natives; a thing almost unknown in other parts of Southern Africa. Cotton is said to be grown in the north, and the parts visited by us, which had been deserted by the inhabitants, seemed in every respect well suited for it. If these regions were more accessible, their value could not be over-estimated, as a European settlement would exercise a most beneficial influ-ence over the interior, and prevent those desolating wars which have stayed the advancement of the people. The whole of this country is free of the Tsetse fly, which is so common in the Zambesi valley; thus cattle and horses might be kept, and an industrious population would soon congregate around any one who could secure to them peace. The obstacles which stand in the way are the difficulties of communication with the coast.

Turning to the valley of the river Shiré, which joins the Zambesi, 80 miles from the coast, near the Hill of Moramballa, we meet a fertile region in immediate communication with the coast, forming the pathway to another still richer, possessing highlands superior in point of position to those of the Batoka, thickly peopled by an industrious race, already extensively engaged in the growth of cotton. The people are of one race and language, but governed by many chiefs, each supreme in his own district. These regions possess the advantages of easy access, and of not having had intercourse with the Portuguese settlements. Previous to our visit Europeans had never been seen by the people, and we were invariably well treated, unless when coming in contact with slave-trading parties from the coast. The first hundred miles of this valley takes a northerly course, the river being deep and navigable the whole way; beyond this, a mountainous region, involving a transport of 35 miles, intervenes between the lower and upper valley, in which the Shiré is again navigable to Lake Nyassa, in latitude s. 14° 30′.

The trade of the interior, on its way to the different coast towns, passes to the south of the lake, crossing the river Shiré. The chiefs in these parts, possessed of neither ivory nor copper, must sell their people if they would purchase foreign goods, and excuses are easily found for such a course. By the present path of trade they are so far removed from the coast that cotton could not repay the carriage, but, by the establishment of commerce on the Shiré, the production of cotton and sugar would open to them a more profitable means of employing labour, and direct the people to industry and the growth of such things as are required in Europe, being advantageous to both parties.

The Lower Shiré valley is 100 miles in length and 20 miles average width, with hills on either side; it is raised only a few feet above the river level, which is much more constant throughout the year than that of the Zambesi. The soil is of the richest description, producing a luxuriant vegetation much like that of the Delta, but possessing more trees, including lignum vitæ and ebony. Near the river the motsakiri tree, whose seed yields oil, is abundant, and there are large spaces occupied by the borassus palm. In the southern part rice is grown extensively, and the crops do not suffer from want of rain. In the northern, bananas, sugar-cane, cassava, and sweet potatoes are cultivated; while every village has large plantations of cotton; the quality being superior to that seen elsewhere. The natives grow it for the manufacture of cloths, a most tedious process when performed without machinery; the picking and spinning are done by hand, and all engage in it from the chief to the poor people. They have never had an opportunity of selling cotton, but seemed delighted with the idea, and would readily enter into its growth on a large scale if they knew that it would be purchased in exchange for cloth and beads. The whole valley is admirably suited for the growth of cotton, while some parts possessing a large amount of salt, which appears on the surface during the dry months, may yield the Sea Island variety, so much esteemed from the great length of its fibre. The only experiment made with this variety of cotton was at Tetté, where it grew from seed brought by the expedition, and continues still, although in a very unfavourable situation. This yielded 1¼ inch staple. The other varieties of seed brought were inferior to what is now in the country.

The Upper Shiré valley is continuous with the southern end of Lake Nyassa, and about 1000 feet above the sea level. The range of hills separating it from Lake Shirwa is distant from 5 to 10 miles. The extent of plain on the west seemed to be much greater. Although not free from fever, this is a much more healthy situation than the Lower Shiré valley; the soil is equally rich, and suitable for sugar-cane and cotton; the latter is a universal accompaniment of every village, some fields being an acre in extent. From its proximity to the highlands this is a promising tract, as it possesses the river leading south to the Zambesi and north to Lake Nyassa.

The highlands of the Manganja country are placed between the river Shiré and Lake Shirwa; they are part of that elevated ridge which extends far along the eastern side of the African continent; their altitude varies from 3000 to 4000 feet, but there are single mountains in the range much exceeding that, the highest being "Zomba," which reaches 8000 feet. The western slopes to the Shiré are steeper than those on the east, which go down to Lake Shirwa, nearly 2000 feet above the sea level. These undulating highlands are watered by many streams which continue flowing the whole year. The climate is cool and pleasant, and in our experience quite free of malaria; those who had suffered when in the valley, feeling a sudden change on ascending the hills.

The cotton of these elevated regions is an annual, from 3 to 4 feet high; it is gathered in August and September, at which season there is no danger of the crop being injured through rain. Sugar-cane is grown in many parts, and would succeed well almost any where, from the abundance of moisture in the soil, and the facilities offered for irrigation by the many perennial streams. European vegetables and fruits, also wheat, could be raised during the cold season. Magnetic iron ore is abundant near the schist rocks which compose the mountain chain, with the exception of the higher peaks; from it the natives manufacture implements of agriculture and war.

Of all the regions explored, the Manganja highlands are the best suited for a settlement conducted by Europeans : possessing a good soil and climate, they command both Upper and Lower Shiré valleys, and lead through Lake Nyassa to the countries far north and west, which now supply most of the ivory, copper, and slaves taken to the coast between Quillimane and Rovuma. It is of easy access from the south, through the Zambesi and Shiré, and possibly another path may be found to it from the north. A vessel of 4 feet might pass at once up the river Shiré at all seasons, as the Zambesi below the confluence is free of the many sand banks which encumber it further up, and render its navigation difficult during the latter months of the dry season.

The flora of the highlands differs entirely from that of the valleys, but bears a resemblance to that of the Batoka country. The grass is in general short compared with that of the plains ; there is an abundance of fine trees, and several sorts of fruits. Many orders of plants, scarcely known below, are here abundant, such as Ranunculaceæ, Proteaceæ, Balsamineæ, Melastomaceæ, Geraniaceæ, Rosaceæ, Piperaceæ, Iridaceæ, &c., while the many ferns show a humid climate compared with the Zambesi valley, where that order of plants is almost absent.

The tsetse fly is unknown among the hills, and very rare in the Upper Shiré valley on the eastern side. In the lower valley, however, it is the natural accompaniment of the large herds of elephants which inhabit the grass plains and marshes.

The expedition has thus shown unlimited tracts of land adapted for cotton, and others suited for sugar-cane; the best for both being near the coast, and enjoying a healthy climate, thickly peopled by a race already engaged in the growth of cotton, all that is required being to develop further a branch of industry now existing, in doing which the slave-trade would be broken and the victims of it turned to industry at home. The only obstruction now standing in the way is the restriction to the free navigation of the Zambesi, which, while closed to others, is not in use by the Portuguese, who have only employed it occasionally for the shipment of slaves, but never for trade. A large supply of lignum vitæ, ebony, buaze fibre, and Indian rubber has also been pointed out, while the abundance of wild indigo seems to indicate a country adapted for its production.

*Special Notice of a few of the more important Vegetable Productions.*

COTTON.—There are two species of the cotton plant cultivated in the countries explored : one of these, known as *Tonje Kaja*, has been in existence for a very long time, and may be indigenous ; no trace of its introduction can be found ; it is found everywhere, but is being replaced by a better sort named *Tonje Manga*, which signifies foreign cotton, and is of modern introduction, having come from the various towns on the east coast. A variety of the Tonje Manga is met with in the interior of the continent, but not found much further east on the Zambesi than the confluence of the Kafué. This may have been introduced from the west coast.

The Tonje Kaja is, according to situation, either perennial or annual ; on the Manganja Hills it is an annual from 2 to 4 feet high, sown in March and gathered in August. In the valleys it forms a shrub, remaining several years in the soil. It is readily known from the other sort by leaf and seed. The cotton is of very short staple, seldom exceeding half an inch ; it very much resembles wool, and adheres strongly to the seed, from which it cannot be entirely removed : this renders it much more troublesome to pick, and an iron roller is employed to facilitate the separation.

The plant is much less prolific than the other, and the only good quality possessed by it is superior strength, on which account some still prefer it. It is the most universally distributed, being seen everywhere from the coast to the valley above the Victoria Falls and along the course of the Shiré. In the region shut off from the coast by Lake Shirwa, it becomes the only sort grown; but the foreign kind is advancing from both north and south, and fast displacing it.

Tonje Manga, the sort of recent introduction, is, like the other, annual or perennial; it is superior in every respect, and attains a much greater size. The staple varies from half an inch to an inch and a quarter, has great lustre, and separates from the seed, which has a clean black coat. What is now produced on the Zambesi and Shiré equals much of the Egyptian, and might be improved by the judicious selection of seed. But there is no necessity for the introduction of new seed, what is now grown on the Shiré being of good quality and very prolific. The variety of Tonje Manga found in the central African valley above the Victoria Falls and as far down as the confluence of the Kafué, differs in the cohesion of the seeds of each cell which form a mass, from the exterior of which the cotton separates easily. The plant attains a great size, and continues seemingly for an indefinite time. Among the ruins of the old town of Sesheke a single plant was measured with a woody stem 8 inches diameter, and covering a space of 12 feet. This year it had yielded an abundant crop of cotton ¾ of an inch in fibre.

Having found cotton throughout the whole extent of country explored, we know what quality may certainly be obtained, while much more may be expected from careful cultivation. The only cotton seed brought by us, superior to that already in the country, was the Sea Island variety: this yielded excellent cotton 1½ inch long when grown under the most disadvantageous circumstances, and the plant still continues at Tetté, although uncared for. Nowhere have we seen cotton which would not be worth exportation, but the best is that of the Manganja country, where the people have given it much attention; thence it might also be exported with least expense, while Europeans, settled in the neighbouring highlands, could direct and superintend the natives of the valleys.

The Delta is excellent cotton ground, but unfit for Europeans, and the present population is very thin and unsettled. Beyond Kebrabassa the Zambesi valley both below and above the Victoria Falls, with the Batoka highlands, might produce a vast supply, and the Batoka hills present a healthy station for residents; but the difficulties at present connected with the rapids of Kebrabassa render this an inferior position in which to commence such an undertaking, which is to be regretted, as the people of the interior seem more disposed to industry than those of the coast.

The specimens of cotton contained in the collection sent to the Royal Gardens at Kew exhibit fully the different qualities found on the Lower Zambesi and on the Shiré. Since then, others have been added from the interior, showing that the cotton grown there is but little inferior.

SUGAR-CANE.—The want of moisture and occurrence of droughts in certain seasons limit the amount of soil adapted for the growth of the sugar-cane. Nevertheless, the greater part of the Delta, the Shiré Valley, the Manganja Hills, with spots near the Zambesi, where joined by tributary streams, are capable of producing it abundantly. In each of these parts we have found it in cultivation, but in small amount. Near the Portuguese settlement of Tetté alone is sugar manufactured, but the process is so rude that it always possesses a bad flavour. The Manganja Hills and tablelands are certainly the regions best suited for its growth, being conducted by Europeans. There the many perennial springs, sources of streams, irrigating the whole country, prevent the failure of crops, and would supply sources of water-power. The only drawback to the Lower Shiré Valley and the Delta is the prevalence of fever; in other respects it is perhaps the best situation for the cane.

The Portuguese have paid as little attention to sugar as they have to cotton : that made at Tetté is not much used by the Europeans.

OILS.—The groundnut succeeds well, and is universally cultivated by the natives; from it oil is expressed, which they use with food, but it has not been made an article of commerce; and the machinery used even at Tetté is of the rudest description.

The Sesamum is also grown from the coast to the Batoka country. Different species of Cucurbitaceous plants yield a pure oil from their seeds, which is employed in cookery.

The Motsakiri tree, of the order Meliaceæ, grows abundantly near the river banks both of the Zambesi and Shiré in all parts ; from its wide distribution this might be obtained in considerable quantity; it separates under exposure to cold into a solid and fluid portion.

Other oils are obtained from the seeds of the Sterculia, and the "Boma" nut (grown extensively at the Victoria Falls) yields a large amount of a pure oil. This is the produce of a large tree which had neither leaf nor flower at the time of our visit to the interior.

INDIAN RUBBER.—Caoutchouc is obtained near Shupanga, from a climbing shrub of the order Apocynaceæ, sub order Carisseæ, the fruit of which is eatable. The stem, sometimes six inches diameter, is covered with a rough bark ; the plant exists abundantly in the forests of Shiringoma, and produces, with little trouble, a large amount of the substance; a little is collected by the natives for domestic uses, but it has not been made an article of export. The process employed is very simple : the outer rough bark being removed, a few punctures are made in the inner, and the milky juice, as it issues, is applied to the skin; by successive applications a ball is soon formed, to the surface of which new layers are added. The many uses to which this substance is now applied, render every additional source of importance.

COFFEE.—This was introduced at an early period, but has become nearly extinct ; at Senna and Tetté there still exist a few plants.

The country near the Portuguese settlements is too dry for coffee to succeed well, but in the Manganja country it would thrive, and probably become naturalized if once introduced into the forests on the hill slopes.

WOODS AND TIMBER.—The *Lignum Vitæ* of this country, produced by a tree of the order Combretaceæ, exactly resembles in all its physical properties that now in use ; the woody layers presenting the same decussation of the fibres. It may be obtained in unlimited amount from the regions between Shupanga and Tetté ; it exists abundantly on the Shiré, and on the Zambesi as far as the Batoka Hills. The trunk is most commonly 18 inches diameter, but met with as much as 4 feet, forming one of the largest of the forest trees. The trees attaining great dimensions are, however, frequently unsound.

*Ebony* is the produce of a small tree of the Leguminosæ, abundant throughout the Zambesi and Shiré Valleys. The trees, when they exceed 6 inches diameter in the black heart wood, are frequently rotten in the heart. Ebony of moderate dimensions may be had in abundance ; the places where it is most common are near Senna, Shupanga, and Zumbo.

The "Mopane," which forms extensive forests, to the exclusion of other trees, yields a wood named here "Iron wood:" it may be had in long pieces of 8 inches diameter ; it is extremely hard and durable, but difficult to work : being proof against the white ant, it is useful for house-building.

The "Malompe," a Pterocarpus yielding a gum similar to kino, produces the wood used up country for the long paddles of the canoes : from its elasticity and lightness it is well adapted for machinery, and for oars seems to be superior to anything now in use. It is most abundant on the hills, but exists at Shupanga. In making paddles the natives split it up with wedges to secure an even grain.

DYE STUFFS.—*Indigo* is a native of the country, found wild near the

Zambesi from the Delta to the Batoka country. The plant is often very luxuriant, reaching 6 feet high in the Shiré valley near Lake Nyassa; at Tetté, on the stony ground near the town, it does not exceed 1 to 2 feet. Judging from small experiments made at Shupanga, where it is particularly abundant, the indigo produced from this species seems to be of good quality.

It is singular that the art of dyeing by means of it should be quite unknown among the natives, nor is it practised among the Portuguese.

*Orchilla weed* may be gathered from the bark of trees in the Delta near the coast, being frequent near the Luabo mouth.

*Fustic.*—A climbing shrub, a species of Maclurea with eatable fruit, exists in the Zambesi valley both above and below Kebrabassa. It seldom, however, attains a sufficient size to form much of the heart wood which contains the colouring matter. If this should be found in sufficient quantity, it would be of value, as the colour is permanent and good.

CEREALS.—There are many cereals now in use among the people : of these, Sorghum, Pennisetum, Eleusine, Setaria, maize, rice, and wheat are the principal ; of these the last three are of most importance to Europeans. The Delta and Lower Shiré valley are the best rice grounds, while wheat requires a constant supply of moisture during the cold season. Thus, without irrigation (which has not been practised since the time of the Jesuits) it can only be grown in the damp hollows, which are under water part of the year ; in such places it is raised in the Delta and near Tetté; but the Manganja highlands are the best suited for it, being cool and more abundantly watered than any other part.

---

3. *On the Batoka Country.* By Mr. CHARLES LIVINGSTONE. Dated " Kongoni mouth of the Zambesi, Jan. 14, 1861."

*Read* April 22, 1861.

THE country of the Batoka, in Central Africa, lies between the 25th and 29th degrees of east longitude and the 16th and 18th of south latitude. It has the river Kafué on the north, the Zambesi on the east and south, and extends west till it touches the low fever-plains of the river Majeela, near Sesheke.

A mountain range running N.E. and S.W. rises abruptly about 15 miles north of the Zambesi, and spreads north and west in a vast undulating table-land, 3000 to 5000 feet above the level of the sea, with extensive grassy plains, through which wind several perennial streams, as the Kalomo, Likone, Ungnesi, &c.

Between this elevated land and the Zambesi, as far west as Thabacheu, the Tetté sandstone is the prevailing rock, while limestone, beds of shale, and seams of coal crop out from the banks of some of the small streams which flow into the Zambesi. North and west of this, granite resembling the Aberdeen variety abounds, and especially so on the Kalomo; while near the Victoria Falls of Mosioatunya, basalt, of apparently recent origin, is the common rock. These broad, elevated lands have a fine healthy climate, well adapted to the European constitution. Fever is unknown. In winter the thermometer sinks during the night as low as 30° Fahr., when thin ice is formed, and during the day the temperature rises to about 68°.

But a few years since these extensive, healthy highlands were well peopled by the Batoka; numerous herds of cattle furnished abundance of milk, and the rich soil largely repaid the labour of the husbandman. Now enormous herds of buffaloes, elephants, antelopes, zebras, &c., fatten on the excellent pasture which formerly supported multitudes of cattle, and not a human being is to be seen. We travelled from Monday morning till late in the Saturday afternoon (from Thabacheu to within 20 miles of Mosioatunya) without meeting a single person, though constantly passing the ruined sites of Batoka villages. These people were driven out of this, the choicest portion of their noble country, by the invasion of Sebituané. Many were killed, and the survivors, except those around the Falls, plundered of their cattle, fled to the banks of the Zambesi and to the rugged hills of Mataba. Scarcely, however, had the conquerors settled down to enjoy their ill-gotten riches when they themselves were attacked by small-pox; and, as soon as its ravages had ceased, the fighting Matibélé compelled them to abandon the country, and seek refuge amidst the fever-swamps of Linyanti.

The Batoka have a mild and pleasant expression of countenance, and are easily distinguished from the other Africans by the singular fashion of wearing no upper front teeth, all persons of both sexes having them knocked out in early life. They seem never to have been a fighting race, but to have lived at peace among themselves, and on good terms with their neighbours. While passing through their country we observed one day a large cairn. Our guide favoured us with the following account of it:—"Once on a time the ancients were going to fight another tribe; they halted here and sat down. After a long consultation they came to the unanimous conclusion that, instead of proceeding to fight and kill their neighbours, and perchance getting themselves killed, it would be more like men to raise this heap of stones as their earnest protest against what the other tribe had done, which they accordingly did, and then returned quietly home again."

But, although the Batoka appear never to have had much stomach for fighting with men, they are remarkably brave hunters of buffaloes and elephants. They rush fearlessly close up to these formidable animals, and kill them with their heavy spears. The Banyai, who have long levied black-mail from all Portuguese traders, were amazed at the daring bravery of the Batoka in coming at once to close quarters with the elephant and despatching him. They had never seen the like before. Does it require one kind of bravery to fight with men, and another and different sort to fight with the fiercest animals? It seems that men may have the one kind in an eminent degree, and yet be without the other.

The Batoka having lived at peace for ages, had evidently attained to a degree of civilization very much in advance of any other tribe we have yet discovered. They *planted* and *cultivated fruit-trees*. Nowhere else has this been the case, not even among the tribes which have been in contact with the Portuguese for two hundred years, and have seen and tasted mangoes, oranges, &c. &c. The natives round Senna and Tetté will on no account plant the stone of a mango. They are firm believers in a superstition that "if any one plants a mango, he will die soon afterwards."

In and around the Batoka villages some of the most valuable timber-trees have been allowed to stand, but every worthless tree has been cut down and rooted out, and the best of the various fruit-trees of the country have been carefully planted and preserved, and also a few trees from whose seeds they extracted oil. We saw fruit-trees which had been planted in regular rows, the trunks being about 3 feet in diameter, and also grand old Motsakiri fruit-trees still bearing abundantly, which had certainly seen a hundred summers.

Two of the ancient Batoka once travelled as far as the river Loangwa. There they saw the massan-tree in fruit, carried some all the way back to the Great Falls, and planted them. Two of the trees are still standing, the only ones of the kind in all that region.

They made a near approach to the custom of even the most refined nations in having permanent graveyards, either on the sides of sacred hills, or under the shady fig-trees near the villages. They reverenced the tombs of their ancestors, and erected monuments of the costliest ivory at the head of the grave, and often even entirely enclosed it with the choicest ivory. Other tribes on the Zambesi throw the body into the river, to be devoured by alligators;

or, sewing it in a mat, place it on the branches of the baobab, or cast it in some gloomy, solitary spot overgrown with thorns and noxious weeds, to be devoured by the foul hyena. But the Batoka reverently buried their dead, and regarded the ground as sacred to their memories. Near the confluence of the Kafué, the chief, accompanied by some of his head men, came to our sleeping-place with a present; their foreheads were marked with white flour, and there was an unusual seriousness in their demeanour.

We were informed that shortly before our arrival they had been accused of witchcraft. Conscious of innocence they accepted the terrible ordeal, or offered to drink the poisoned muavi. For this purpose they made a journey to the sacred hill where reposed the bodies of their ancestors, and, after a solemn appeal to the unseen spirits of their fathers to judge of the innocence of these their children, drank the muavi, vomited, and were therefore declared to be "Not guilty." They believed in the immortality of the soul, and that the souls of their ancestors knew what they were doing, and were pleased or not accordingly. The owners of a large canoe refused to sell it because it belonged to the spirits of their fathers, who helped them in killing the hippopotamus.

Some of the Batoka chiefs must have had a good deal of enterprise. The lands of one in the western part of the country lay on the Zambesi, which protected him on the south; on the east and north was an impassable reedy marsh, filled with water all the year round, leaving only his west border unprotected and open to invasion. He conceived the bold project of digging a broad and deep canal, nearly a mile in length, from the west end of the reedy river to the Zambesi, and actually carried it into execution; thus forming a large island, on which his cattle grazed in safety, and his corn ripened from year to year secure from all marauders.

Another chief, who died a number of years ago, believed that he had discovered a remedy for tsetse bitten cattle. His son showed us the plant, which was new to our botanist, and likewise told us how the medicine was prepared. The bark of the root is dried, and—what will be specially palatable to our homœopathist friends—a dozen tsetse are caught, dried, and ground with the bark to a fine powder. The mixture is administered internally, and the cattle are also smoked, by burning the rest of the plant under them. The treatment is continued some weeks, as often as symptoms of the poison show themselves. This, he frankly said, will not cure all the bitten cattle, for cattle, and men too, die in spite of medicine; but should a herd by accident stray into a tsetse district and get bitten, by this medicine of Kampakampa, his father, some of them could be saved, while without it all would be sure to die.

A remarkably prominent feature in the Batoka character is their enlarged hospitality. No stranger is ever allowed to suffer hunger. They invariably sent to our sleeping-places large presents of the finest white meal, with fat capons "to give it a relish," and great pots of beer to comfort our hearts, with pumpkins, beans, and tobacco; so that, as they said, we "should not sleep hungry nor thirsty."

In travelling from the Kafué to Sinamanes, we often passed several villages in the course of a day's march. In the evening, deputations arrived from those villages at which we could not sleep, with liberal presents of food. It evidently pained them to have strangers pass without partaking of their hospitality. Repeatedly were we hailed from huts, asked to wait a moment and drink a little beer, which they brought with alacrity.

When we halted for the night, it was no uncommon thing for these people to prepare our camp. Entirely of their own accord, some with their hoes quickly smoothed the ground for our beds; others brought bundles of grass and spread it carefully over the spot; some with their small axes speedily made a brush-fence round to shield us from the wind; and if, as occasionally happened, the water was a little distant, others hastened and brought a pot or two of water to cook our food with, and also firewood. They are an industrious people, and very fond of agriculture. For hours at a time have we marched through unbroken corn-fields of nearly a mile in width. They erect numerous granaries for the reception of the grain, which give their villages the appearance of being unusually large ; and when the water of the Zambesi has subsided they place the grain, tied up in bundles of grass, well plastered over with clay, on low sand islands, as a protection against the attacks of marauding mice and men.

Owing to the ravages of the weevil, the native corn can hardly be preserved until the following crop comes in. However largely they may cultivate, and abundant the harvest, it must all be consumed the same year in which it is grown. This may account for their making so much of it into beer. The beer they brew is not the sour and intoxicating kind found among other tribes, but sweet, and highly nutritious, with only a slight degree of acidity to render it a pleasant drink. We never saw a single case of intoxication among them, though all drank great quantities of beer. They were all plump, and in good condition.

Both men and boys were eager to work for very small pay. Our men could hire any number of them to carry their burdens for a few beads a-day or a bit of cloth. The miserly and extra-dirty cook had an old pair of trowsers some of us had given him, and which he had long worn himself : with one of the decayed legs of his trowsers he hired a man to carry his heavy load a whole day ; a second man carried it the next day for the other leg ; and what remained of the old trowsers, minus the buttons, procured the labour of another man for the third day.

They have their wandering minstrels. One of these, apparently a genuine poet, attached himself to our company for several days, and, whenever we halted, sang our praise to the villagers, in harmonious numbers of 4 and 5 feet respectively. Another, though less gifted son of song, belonged to the Batoka of our own party. Every evening, while the others were talking or sleeping, he played on his sansah and rehearsed his songs. In composing extempore he was never at a loss : if the words refused to come, he halted not, but eked out the measure with a h—m, h—m, h—m. We did not observe many musical instruments among them : perhaps since their exile from the finest portion of their country, like the Jewish captives by the rivers of Babylon, they have hung their harps upon the willows.

A peculiar order of men is established among them, the order of the Endah Pézés (Go-Nakeds). The badge of this order, as the name suggests, consists in the entire absence of the slightest shred of clothing. They are in the state in which Adam is reported to have been before his invention of the fig-leaf apparel. We began to see members of this order about two days above the junction of the Kafué ; two or three might be seen in a village. The numbers steadily increased, until in a short time every man and boy wore the badge of the Endah Pézés. The chief of one of the first villages, a noble, generous fellow, was one, as were likewise two or three of his men. In the afternoon he visited us in the full dress of his order, viz., a tobacco-pipe, nothing else whatever, the stem about 2 feet long, wound round with polished iron. He gave us a liberal present. Early next morning he came, accompanied by his wife and daughter, with two large pots of beer, in order that we might refresh ourselves before starting. Both the women, as comely and modest-looking as we have seen in Africa, were well clothed and adorned.

The women, in fact, are all well clothed, and have many ornaments. Some wear tin ear-rings all round the ear, no fewer than nine often in each ear. There was nothing to indicate that they had the slightest idea of there being anything peculiar in the no-dress-at-all style of their order. They rub their bodies with red ochre. Some plait a fillet two inches wide, of the inner bark of trees, shave the wool off the lower part of the head to an inch above the ears, tie this fillet on, having rubbed it and the wool which is left with the red ochre mixed in oil. It gives them the appearance of having on a neat forage-cap. This, with some strings of beads, a little polished iron wire round the arms, the never-failing pipe, and a small pair of iron tongs to lift up a coal to light it with, constitute all the clothing the most dandyfied Endah Pézé ever wears.

They raise immense quantities of tobacco on the banks of the Zambesi in the winter months, and are, perhaps, the most inveterate smokers in the world. The pipe is seldom out of their hands. They are as polite smokers as any ever found in a railway carriage. When they came with a present, although it was their own country, before lighting their pipes they asked if we had any objections to their smoking beside us, which of course, contrary to railway travellers, we never had. They have invented a novel mode of smoking, which may interest those who are fond of the weed at home. They take a whiff, puff out the grosser smoke, then by a sudden inhalation before all is out contrive to catch, as they say, and swallow the pure spirit of the tobacco, its real essence, which common smokers lose entirely. Their tobacco is said to be very strong; it is certainly very cheap; a few strings of beads will purchase as much as will last any reasonable smoker half a year. Their government, whatever it may have been formerly, is now that of separate and independent chiefs. The language is a dialect of that which is spoken by the natives on the Zambesi below them, and particularly marked by the characteristic use of the letter $r$, to the apparently total exclusion of the letter $l$. They have not been visited by any regular trader for many a day until shortly after we passed. A party of trading slaves, belonging to the two half-caste Portuguese who last year, with 400 slaves armed with the old Sepoy flint muskets, so treacherously assassinated the chief and 20 of his men near Zumba, and then took possession of all his lands on the Zambesi and Loangwa, followed in our spoor, and bought large quantities of ivory and a number of young slave-girls for a few beads. They also purchased 10 large new canoes for 6 strings of coarse white or red beads a-piece, or 2 fathoms of American calico. As traders are now sure to go to them with beads and cloth, the order of the Endah Pézés will in a short time be numbered among the things that were; for it is to be regretted that these traders belong to a nation whose subjects buy and sell slaves, and are the guilty agents for carrying on the slave-trade in all this part of Eastern Africa.

———

4. *The River Rovuma.* Extract from " Pilotage remarks " of D. J. MAY, R.N., in charge of the *Pioneer*, Dr. Livingstone's Expedition.

THE river Rovuma is about 12 miles north-westward of Cape Delgado, in lat. 10° 28' s., long. 40° 30' E.; the entrance is 1 mile in breadth, situated on the south side of a bay 6 miles in length and 3 in breadth, formed by Rovuma Point on the south, and the island of Nizambary on the north.

In rounding Rovuma Point, the entrance of the river is not easily made out until it bears s.w. (there being many other smaller openings to the north and south of it), on which bearing a vessel may anchor in 5 or 7 fathoms. During the time the *Pioneer* was here she anchored for a fortnight off the entrance, when the ebb-tide made out of the river the whole time, overcoming the flood-tide, which in springs rises to 18 feet, and in neaps to 5 feet.

The navigable entrance to the river is only ¼ of a mile, owing to projecting sand-banks on both sides; and, although there is no bar, it is dangerous for boats to attempt the entrance between half-flood and half-ebb, on account of the over-falls caused by the sudden change in the depth from 3 to 17 fathoms.

About 2 miles inside the entrance commence a series of sand-banks, which obstruct the channel, rendering the navigation very intricate, by a narrow passage which runs from one side of the river abruptly to the other, with a depth of only 5 or 6 feet in many places.

At the beginning of March, 1861, the river Rovuma was at its maximum height of the season. It subsided, and then rose again towards the close of the month to nearly its original height, and it was between these periods that our examination was made. We reached 30 miles up the river, and, as the water began to fall rapidly, it was thought best to return to the entrance to clear the shoal patches, over which we barely carried 5 feet. At the point of our turning there appeared no more difficulty to our further progress, but the falling tide would not permit it.

The navigation of the river is not only intricate, but it has a down-current of 3 knots per hour, and near the mouth a pulling boat could not stem it. Wood for steaming purposes is easily procurable, especially near the sea. The inhabitants were few: they were shy and timid, and could only give us a scanty supply of provisions. The water of the river on our first using it affected every one on board, but it ceased doing so when we became accustomed to it. Comparing the Rovuma with the Niger, as to their qualities as rivers, and comparing also the people and productions about them, the Rovuma is most markedly inferior; but it may yet be shown that we have much more to learn about it.

I do not think it very unhealthy, although, on our return to the mouth, nearly every person on board the *Pioneer* became ill. I attribute the sickness to exposure and to the hard work we had just experienced, and to our being anchored off a foul mud-creek, close to a mangrove forest, for convenience of wooding.

A comparison of the rivers Shiré and Rovuma will incline to the conclusion that they do not proceed from the same source. The Shiré is deep, clear, and subject to little variation of rise or fall; the Rovuma is shallow, muddy, and, according to Krapf, was but a small stream when he passed its mouth.

# PROCEEDINGS

OF

# THE ROYAL GEOGRAPHICAL SOCIETY OF LONDON.

## SESSION 1861–62.

*Fourth Meeting, Monday, January 13th, 1862.*

SIR RODERICK I. MURCHISON, VICE-PRESIDENT, in the Chair.

PRESENTATIONS.—*Lord Rollo ; Deane J. Hoare ; John Holmes ; and W. Johnson, R.N., Esqrs., were presented upon their Election.*

ELECTIONS. — *Commr. Richard Charles Mayne, R.N. ; Rev. Jordan Palmer, M.A. ; Sir Joshua Rowe, C.B. ; Colonel H. Dalrymple White, C.B. ; George F. Banks, Surg., R.N. ; Alfred Barton ; Latimer Clark ; James Goddard, Jun. ; James M'Cosh, M.D. ; Thomas Martin ; Henry Nourse ; George D. Ramsay ; Augustus Thorne ; and William F. Webb, Esqrs., were elected Fellows.*

ACCESSIONS.—Among the Accessions to the Library and Map-rooms since the former meeting were—Ravenstein's 'Russians on the Amur ;' Abstracts of the Principal Lines of Spirit Levelling in Scotland, by the Ordnance Survey ; Haast's 'Report on the Nelson Province of New Zealand ;' Sykes' 'Notes on Progress of Trade of England with China ;' Davidson's 'Directory for Pacific Coast of the United States ;' 'Description de l'Afrique,' by Dapper ; Mouat's 'Rough Notes of a Trip to Reunion, the Mauritius, and Ceylon ;' Transactions of various Scientific Societies at home and abroad ; complete suit of a Japanese Warrior, from Consul Pemberton Hodgson, &c. &c.

EXHIBITIONS.—Several Photographs taken in the Andaman Islands, and various bows and arrows, nets and drinking-vessels, used by the Aborigines of these islands, were exhibited.

The CHAIRMAN, in opening the meeting, said it was his duty to announce that the Council of the Society had forwarded to the Secretary of State for presentation to Her Majesty, the following Address of Condolence on the death of the late Prince Consort, which had been duly acknowledged by H.M. Secretary of State for the Home Department :—

" MAY IT PLEASE YOUR MAJESTY,

" WE, the President and Council of the Royal Geographical Society, respectfully tender the expression of our heartfelt condolence to your Majesty on the mournful occasion of the decease of your illustrious Consort.

" Profoundly grieved as the heart of the nation has been by this sad calamity, we, uniting with the multitude of His Royal Highness's admirers, urgently desire to testify our deep sense of the irreparable loss which science and art have sustained by the death of our gifted and enlightened Vice-Patron.

" As men enabled from the nature of our pursuits to take a wide retrospect of the many good deeds of His Royal Highness, we specially advert to the well-known and gratefully acknowledged facts that your Majesty's lamented Consort largely promoted and diffused scientific knowledge both by precept and example ; and, to the great advantage of your people, successfully applied such knowledge to the improvement of the various industries of Britain and her Colonies.

" Representing a scientific Society of which your Majesty is the gracious Patron, we repeat the expression of our profound sympathy, and earnestly pray that, with the aid of Divine Providence, your Majesty may be enabled so to sustain your heavy bereavement as long to continue to be a blessing to your faithful and loyal people.

" *January 4th*, 1862."


The Chairman, in continuation, greatly regretted that their President was prevented by illness from attending the meeting and taking the chair, as it was Lord Ashburton's especial wish to address the Society upon this mournful subject. His Lordship would, however, take the opportunity of doing so on a future occasion, and would doubtless expatiate fully thereon at the ensuing anniversary.

ANNOUNCEMENTS.—The Chairman announced to the meeting two very important geographical facts, which would probably be the subjects of future papers read before the Society. 1st. A letter from Sir Henry Barkly, Governor of Victoria, stating that Messrs. Burke and Wills had crossed the Australian Continent to the Gulf of Carpentaria, and returned to Cooper's Creek, where they had miserably perished from starvation (see pp. 53 and 68). 2ndly. That a letter had been received from Mr. Thornton, who accompanied Baron von der Decken, stating that they had returned to Mombas, after reaching and partly ascending Kilimanjaro; whose top was covered with snow, and whose height was trigonometrically measured to be about 20,000 feet (see p. 47).

The Papers read were—

1. *Brief Narrative of an Expedition to the Andaman Islands, in 1857.* By F. J. MOUAT, M.D., of the Bengal Army, F.R.G.S., &c.

A COMMISSION was appointed by the Governor-General of India, in 1857, to examine the Andaman Islands, with a view of selecting a suitable spot for a penal settlement. The mutineers of the great Indian Rebellion were to be sent there, and the islands were ultimately to form a station for the reception of all felons who were sentenced to transportation from India. Dr. Mouat was appointed the chief of the commission; his associates were Dr. George Playfair, to whom the medical and scientific duties were assigned, and Lieut. Heathcote, who undertook the hydrography.

Very little recent intelligence was procurable about these islands, though part of their coasts had been carefully surveyed by Lieut. Blair, in 1789, and a penal settlement had actually been established upon them at the same date, but abandoned, in 1795, on account of its unhealthiness. Col. Colebrook, afterwards Surveyor-General of India, had visited the Andamans, and published a short vocabulary of the language of the natives. Others also had published short accounts in the beginning of this century; but of late years no information whatever had been obtained about the Andamans, except through the narratives of shipwrecked persons, who invariably represented the aborigines as exceedingly savage and hostile. Dr. Helps endeavoured to explore the islands in 1840, but he was murdered shortly after his arrival. The Andamaners were usually reputed cannibals.

Dr. Mouat's commission was accompanied by a large escort, including a useful body of Burmese convicts sent to aid them in pioneering. They sailed to their destination in a steamer of light draught, and ultimately proceeded in making a thorough examination of the coasts of the Andamans, except where the abundance of coral reefs made safe navigation and useful harbours an impossibility. The natives were found to be exceedingly numerous and hostile, and their stealthy habits made it necessary for the exploring party to proceed with exceeding vigilance; especially as the island was covered by a dense vegetation, which seriously embarrassed the movements of the travellers, and hid the advances of the natives. The entire islands, up to the very hill tops, which reached 2000 feet in altitude, were clothed by a forest-growth of such remarkable thickness that no eminence could be climbed without cutting a pathway. No spots were found sufficiently open to admit of safe encampment, and, in consequence, the party were obliged to return every night to their ships, and to content themselves with a limited range of exploration from the coast.

Several good harbours were found. Port Cornwallis, the site of the old settlement, is a magnificent one: it is land-locked and picturesque; but a bank of mud, uncovered at low-water, was there to account for its unhealthiness.

The botanical features of the Andaman Islands somewhat resemble those of Sumatra: fine timber-trees were found in the forest. As regards animals, the only mammal seen was a small black hog of a peculiar species. Rats and monkeys were said to exist. A harmless green snake was the only discovered reptile. Scorpions and centipedes were found in abundance. Birds were neither numerous nor varied in species.

Numerous efforts were made to communicate in a friendly way with the natives, but all failed utterly. The Sepoys who have latterly escaped from the penal settlement into the bush—for the station has been established since Dr. Mouat's visit—have been equally unsuccessful: they have usually been murdered, and those who returned can hardly account for their good fortune in being permitted to do so. One intelligent Hindoo informant, who lived upwards of a year among the natives, brought back a full and very interesting account of their social habits. He agrees with others in his description of their habitual hatred and ferocity to strangers, but adds that, to one another, they were kindly disposed. He wholly repudiates the charge of cannibalism brought against them. In the many huts Dr. Mouat examined, which had just before been quitted by their inhabitants, he could find no traces whatever of such a practice. Yet they have customs which seem sufficient to have suggested this charge; they prize the bones of their deceased relatives, and, as they are remarkably migratory, they always carry the bones with them. The dead are buried in a sitting posture; and, months afterwards, the bones are exhumed, wept over, and divided amongst the relatives. The chief mourner wears the skull, hung from his neck, upon his back, and carries it for more than a year.

A native was captured during an attack upon Dr. Mouat's expedition, and was brought by him to Calcutta. Though exceedingly ferocious at the time of his capture, it was remarkable how completely and quickly his ferocity left him. He became attached to the sailors, and they to him. He showed himself remarkably docile and imitative, and adopted dress and civilised habits with readiness and constancy.

Dr. Mouat considers the whole of the Andaman group to be inhabited by one single race of men. They are diminutive, but perfectly shaped ; they bear no discoverable resemblance to any other race of men. He estimates their number, partly from facts adduced by the Indian Sepoys above mentioned, and corroborated by what he saw, as perhaps attaining to 15,000.

---

2. *On the Trade between the Eastern Archipelago and New Guinea and its Islands.*  By A. RUSSELL WALLACE, F.R.G.S.

THE portion of New Guinea with which trade is regularly maintained from the Eastern Archipelago, includes Geelvink Bay and the north-western part of the island, on both coasts, as far as the 137th degree of longitude. It also includes the adjacent islands of Jobie, Waigaiou, &c., and the more distant ones of Ké and Aru. The entrepot, whence the trade is directly carried on, is a small island, called Kilwaru, scarcely 50 yards across, between Ceram Laut and Keffing, which has a good anchorage on both sides of it.

The only articles of commercial value procured from the interior of New Guinea, are Mussoi bark—which gives an aromatic oil used in Java to rub over the skin—and wild nutmegs. From the coasts and islands come bêche-de-mer, mother-of-pearl, and tortoiseshell, in abundance. There are also pearls, birds of paradise, sago, raw and in cakes, and rice in the husk. Few of these articles go to Europe. The Chinese are the only consumers of bêche-de-mer ; the Philippine Islands take the tortoiseshells, and even the pearls and birds of paradise mostly go to China. The goods with which they are all bought, are bar-iron, calico, cheap German knives, &c., and the trade is mainly carried on in native prahus.

Of all this New Guinea district the Aru Islands are the most important. There is a great competition of trade in them ; and calicos and handkerchiefs may be obtained even cheaper there than in the towns where they are actually produced. Fifteen large prahus, carrying a cargo worth 15,000*l*., and about one hundred small ones, were seen at the Aru Islands at one time, in 1857, when the author visited them. The Ké islanders are the boat-builders of the far East. The Goram group are inhabited by traders.

The staff of life in these islands is sago. A good sized sago-palm will give 1800 cakes of three to the lb., of which five are the ordinary quantity consumed by a man in a day. Hence a single tree may be considered equal to the support of a man throughout the year. The labour to prepare the food is as follows:—Two men, working moderately, will finish a tree in five days, and two women will bake the whole in about five days more; so we may estimate that, with ten days' labour, a man may produce food for a whole year. This is, if he possesses trees of his own; for all the sago-palms are become private property, and cost about 9*s*. each. Again, the cost of labour being 4*d*. a-day, and the cost of the tree 9*s*., the expense of one year's food for a man is only 12*s*.

PROFESSOR OWEN said the uniform accounts that had reached him of the diminutive stature and low animal life of the natives of the Andaman Islands, had made him peculiarly desirous to acquire the means of comparing their physical characters with those of other forms of the human race. It was therefore with great pleasure that he received for the purpose of examination, he believed, the first skeleton of a male Andamaner which had ever reached Europe. It was through the thoughtfulness for the needs of science manifested by Dr. Mouat, that the specimen was secured which had been submitted to him by that gentleman, and which he had liberally presented to the British Museum. Professor Owen said that the specimen closely accorded with the attribute of the diminutive stature of the Andamaners. The bones were those of a man to all appearance in the prime of life, who evidently did not exceed four feet ten inches in height. As to the character of the bones, he might say he never saw any in texture or in the development of their processes or ridges, or in any of those characteristics which indicated the complete mastery of the frame by a healthy individual—so strongly marked as in those of the little man whose skeleton he had received from Dr. Mouat. His first attention was directed to the ankle, the feet, and that most characteristic member the great toe; and he found all that related to the power of maintaining an upright posture was as well and as perfectly marked in the small skeleton as in one of the highest specimens of the human race. The next point to be considered was the character of the cranium; because the first questions which had been mooted by ethnologists with regard to those little, low-placed savages, as the Andamaners were called, were,—Whence did they come?—with what other race of the human species were they allied? There had been a conjecture that they might possibly have been derived from the negroes imported for slave labour by the Portuguese—that they might have got stranded on the island owing to the wreck of some vessel while bringing them from Africa. Another opinion, founded upon the mere analogy of their dark colour, was that they might be an offshoot of the Papuans that inhabited New Guinea and Australasia. And, thirdly, it had been conjectured that the Andaman Islands might have been peopled by immigrants from the Burmese coast of the continent of Asia. He found, however, that the skull of the skeleton he had examined decidedly showed that it was not the cranium of the black West-African negro, or of the dark Papuan. In comparing the skull with the Papuans, he found it had not the same lowness and flatness of the brow, nor the frontal ridge overhanging the sunken origin of the nasals, nor the prominence of the cheek bones, nor the degree of prognathism of the jaws, nor the thickness of the cranium, nor the large proportional size of the molars ; there was nothing, in fact, in its family character which resembled the skull of the Papuan.   Still more decided were the evidences that the Andamaner was no member of the race of the typical negroes : least of all those western negroes from whom the Portuguese and the other slave-importers had derived their slaves.   Neither did the cranium, as a whole, exhibit marks of close or special affinity to the Malay or the Mongolian.   There was nothing osteological to lead him to infer that the Andamaners had been derived from the Burmese or from any people now inhabiting the continent of Asia.   The skull of the present Mincopie was well shaped, neither too long nor too short : its walls were not thicker than those of Europeans.   The capacity of the cranium was certainly small, the skull being proportioned to the stature, and the forehead was neither high nor broad ; but the bones of the face were developed in a medium degree, with the exception of a slight projection of the upper jaw, such as he-had seen developed in some of the lower Europeans, and which might be connected in some degree with protracted suckling of the infant by the mothers, and by the habitual use of the incisors in feeding, which was common to uncivilized people.   These were the chief facts he had derived from the study of the skeleton of the Andamaner.   They, of course, suggested certain ideas to his mind.   The first was this :—Why should ethnologists, when they came to study the natives of an insulated group of people like the Andamaners, deem it necessary to determine to what contemporaneous people they were allied, on the assumption that they had been derived from some existing and neighbouring land ?   Geological science had established the fact of continuous and progressive, though extremely slow, mutations of land and sea ; and had taught them that the continents of modern geography were only the last phases of those mutations.   How long the human species had existed, and how far they had been contemporaneous with such mutations, were the preliminary questions which presented themselves in grappling with the problem suggested by a peculiar insular race like the Mincopies.   Certain it was, that geologists had conceived that the islands on the south of the present great continent of Asia might be remnants of some antecedent very distinct group of land ; and naturalists—and he would more especially mention Sir J. Emerson Tennent, who had paid so great attention to the fauna of Ceylon—had brought to their knowledge a host of facts confirmatory of the idea that Ceylon was not a dismemberment of India, but part of a distinct and antecedent continent.   In confirmation of that idea, they had the result of the geological researches of Cautley, Faulkner and others in India, which seemed to show that the Himalayas had risen, lifting up the fossiliferous beds on their present slopes, within comparatively recent geographical time ; proving that India had been the site of one of the latest of those great systems of upheaving forces that resulted in the formation of new continents. Was it not, then, possible that the Andamaners might have come from *nowhere*—that was to say, from no actual contiguous and separate land, but might be the representatives of an old race belonging to a former continent that had almost disappeared ?   He would add, that the Adamaners were true men, showing no special affinity to any lower form of the animal kingdom.   They were active, bold, plucky little fellows ; and they had as much wit as their notions of daily and annual happiness required.   Their islands yielded a sufficiency of food in the form of quadrupeds, such as an indigenous species of wild hog, of fishes, of shell-fish, and various indigenous fruits : their arts had progressed in the degree requisite to enable them to obtain that food.

As climbers, as swimmers, as runners, as leapers, they appeared to exhibit how admirably the human frame was adapted for mastery over the earth, in whatever limit and kind of sphere the bimanous species might become placed.

MR. CRAWFURD agreed entirely with Professor Owen with respect to the physical and intellectual appearance of the Andamans. They were small, compact, and well put together; and, for the purposes of savage life, he did not think they were deficient. Upon the whole, the Andamans were an ingenious people, as far as their means extended. He thought they were a great deal superior to the people of Australia: for the Australians were unable to make a boat; they were ignorant of navigation, and they had never invented the bow and arrow.

The meeting was then adjourned to Monday, Jan. 27th.

***

*Fifth Meeting, Monday, January 27th, 1862.*

CAPTAIN R. COLLINSON, R.N., VICE-PRESIDENT, in the Chair.

PRESENTATIONS.—*Rev. Jordan Palmer, M.A.; Sir Christopher Rawlinson; Sir Joshua Rowe; Douglas Henty; Henry Martin; and Thomas Martin, Esqrs., were presented upon their election.*

ELECTIONS.—*Lieut.-Commander W. Digby Mackworth Dolben, R.N.; Captain Horace Mantagu; Lieut.-Colonel A. Park; the Earl of Pomfret; Major Charles S. Showers; Edwin Adams; James Hiscutt Crossman; Alfred Head; J. Binny Key; Clement Davidson Leggatt; George Lumsden; Colin J. Mackenzie; Robert Russell Notman; John Samuel Phené; Robert Prislo Roupell, Q.C.; Henry Ayshford Sanford; Franklin Travers; John Wardlaw; and John Watney, Junr., Esqrs., were elected Fellows.*

ACCESSIONS.—Among the accessions to the Library and Map-Rooms since the former Meeting were—Waugh's 'Report on the Survey of India, 1858-59;' Casalis's 'Basutos;' Murray's 'Pitcairn;' Thomson's Plan of the Province of Otago; Sketch-map of the Ogun River, by Captains Bedingfield and Burton; Admiralty Plan of Shanghai; Ordnance Maps; Admiralty Charts, &c. &c.

EXHIBITIONS.—A photograph of the Tuapeka Gold-Fields in New Zealand; Danish Plan of the River Volta; and Maury's Map of the United States, were exhibited at the Meeting.

ANNOUNCEMENTS.—McDouall Stuart. The CHAIRMAN desired the following extracts to be read from a letter addressed by Messrs. Chambers and Fincke to Lord Ashburton, dated October 26th, 1861:—

" We again take the liberty to address you, to give particulars of our progress in fitting out the present party, under the command of Mr. Stuart, to complete the crossing of our continent from south to north. On the 22nd instant, Mr. Keckwick (second in command)

and Mr. Woodforde started for Chambers's Creek with four of our horses. And on their arrival they will at once commence preparing the food necessary for the party; and we expect that by the time this is done the whole party will be there assembled, and at once make their final start for the Newcastle water.

Yesterday five men, with thirty horses, took their departure, who will travel by easy stages to the north till they are joined by Mr. Stuart and Mr. Waterhouse (the naturalist). The entire strength of the party will be eleven men, with seventy horses. They are fitted out most liberally with every necessary. They carry with them water-bottles that will hold 70 gallons, and by this means Mr. Stuart will be able to form depôts ahead; and we now entertain no doubt of his making his way through the last 80 miles which he has yet to accomplish.

The Papers read were—

1. *Expedition to Kilimanjaro* (*in company with the Baron von der Decken*). By R. THORNTON, F.R.G.S., late Geologist to the Zambesi Expedition.

THE letter from which the following extracts are made contains the only information that has yet reached the Society on the successful issue of their journey. The extracts contain all that is purely geographical in the letter, but there are in addition minute notes on the geology of the district visited.

" Our route lay from Mombas to the south-west over the Shimba, thence north-west to the Kadiaro, then south-west to the Pare, then north to the Lake Yipe, thence through Dafeta to Kilema, where we made one attempt to ascend the Kilimanjaro, but had to turn back at about 8000 feet. We then went round by the foot of the mountain to Madjami; thence we returned by Dafeta, Lake Yipe, Pare, and the north foot of Usambara, to Wanga on the coast, which we reached on the 101st day from Mombas. We have made a tolerable map of our journey, the country through which we passed being very favourable for triangulation; though, from not being allowed to ascend the mountains of Pare and Usambara, and the want of two or three stations which circumstances prevented our taking, the map is not nearly so complete as I could wish it to be. The triangulation is checked by several latitudes and a lunar distance at Kilema. I have not yet plotted out the whole of the map, but I hope to complete and send it shortly.

" Our journey, on the whole, has been tolerably successful. We did not succeed in reaching the top of Kilimanjaro; but I have its altitude from six different stations, connected by tolerable triangles, at

distances varying from 15 to 50 miles.    From these I believe the
height of the Kilimanjaro to be about 20,000 feet.    Its shape varies
much, as seen from different points of view; but, from all places
we have seen it, its base rises very gradually from a great plane.
The outline of the top, as seen from Madjami, is a great dome (but
this face is nearly flat): as seen from the east, it is conical, with
the apex cut off, forming a little plane, sloping a little to the north.
The southern slope of this cone is much steeper than the northern.
Several miles to the north-east of the top a great conical peak rises
to about 17,000 feet; and about 50 miles to the west of Kilimanjaro a great conical mountain, named Meru, rises from the great
plain of the Massai to perhaps 18,000 feet.

"As seen from the east, the snow forms only a thick cap to the
Kilimanjaro, with a broad tongue creeping down the south slope;
and, when the sun is high, several long streaks of snow are seen
lying in small ravines descending from the cap.    As seen from
Madjami, the snow partially covers the south-west face of the dome
(about a quarter the height of the mountain), but several large bare
patches of rock show out above the snow.    The snow here seems to
lie at its steepest possible angle, so that fresh snow falling on this
side must at once slip down to the foot of the face of the dome.    In
one evening, at Madjami, we saw three such slips of snow in about
an hour's time.    On the eastern peak a few patches of snow are
seen when the sun is high.

"All parts of the mountain we saw are composed of lava of subariel origin.    From not reaching the top, and having seen only the
south-east, south, and south-west parts of the mountain, I cannot
speak with certainty of its structure; but I think that the Kilimanjaro is the north-eastern part of an old subariel volcano, the
south-western and larger part having sunk down several thousand
feet, and been partially broken up by faults.    The great fault
separating these two parts lies about north-west and south-east, and
forms a very steep, long, flat south-west face to the mountain; and
a high, very rugged mountain mass, lying a few miles to the north
of Madjami, may be the relics of the top of the original mountain.

"We have not reached the axis of structure of Eastern Africa;
but very far to the south-west from Kilema are seen, on a clear day,
three very high rugged mountains (as high as the Meru mountain),
with conical tops, which, if not volcanic—and I think their sides
are too steep and shapes too irregular for ordinary volcanoes—may
be composed of the axial granite.

The Lake Ype is shallow, and rapidly filling up.    You will see
its size and position best when I send you our map.    On its north side

it receives the River Loomi (of Rebmann), and at its west end sends out a river which, after joining the Jagga river, flows south through the plain lying between the Ugono and Anuisha ranges to the river of Pangani.   Between the Kilimanjaro and Anusha ranges is a small watershed, which sends the rivers of Western Madjami to the west.

" Mr. Rebmann's map and description, as given in the first volume of the ' Missionary Intelligencer,' give a very fair idea of the country, and, considering he had no instruments, his map is very accurate."

2. *Ascent of the Ogun, or Abbeokuta River.*   By Captain RICHARD BURTON, F.R.G.S., H. M. Consul at Fernando Po, with Captain BEDINGFIELD, R.N., F.R.G.S., and Dr. EALES, R.N.

CAPTAIN BURTON's characteristic letter will be found printed at length at p. 64.   It is therefore unnecessary to do more here than shortly allude to it.   He visited Abbeokuta; and his remarks show that, while impressed with the cotton-producing powers of the soil, he takes a less favourable view than is usual, of the civilized progress to which the inhabitants have actually attained.   He points out that the new colony of Lagos is deficient in a sanatorium, which should be sought in the mountainous country of the Cameroons.   A minute survey of the River Ogun, by himself and Captain Bedingfield, accompanies the letter.

3. *Journal of the Proceedings of H. M. S. 'Bloodhound' up the River Volta, West Coast of Africa, under* Commander DOLBEN, R.N., F.R.G.S.

THE author, conveying his Excellency the Governor of Cape Coast Castle, steamed to the mouth of the Volta, a river near Lagos, with a view of ascending it,—a feat that had never before been accomplished by white men.   A rapid survey of the bar proved it was not that impassable barrier it had always been reputed, and that its features had become exceedingly different from those described in the sailing directory.   An expedition of four well-armed boats, manned by thirty-nine men, then proceeded to enter the river. They crossed the bar without difficulty on October 28th, 1861, in 11 feet water.   The *Bloodhound* herself could have been taken across it.

Partly sailing and partly rowing, the expedition ascended the river for 120 miles without difficulty or molestation, when their voyage was brought to an abrupt close by rapids.   Though impracticable to ship's boats, the rapids are not absolutely impassable, for the small strong native canoes can be forced through them to

Pong, a town which is situated at their head, 5 miles above the furthest point reached by the expedition. Above Pong the Volta is again navigable. Its stream was considerable. Immediately below the rapids it had a depth of 10 feet right across from bank to bank and a width of three-quarters of a mile. The natives were a fine race of men. The climate appeared healthy; for none of the party suffered during the five days they were in the river, notwithstanding exposure and severe work. The principal products were cotton, palm-oil, Indian-corn, and cassava. The water of the river was palatable, and fish abundant.

The CHAIRMAN said the first paper which had been read had reference to one of those important geographical problems which they must all rejoice to learn had been solved. It was not indeed that elaborate account, accompanied by a map, which they hoped to have communicated to them by the authority of the leader of the expedition, the Baron von der Decken, but it was a private letter from his associate, the geologist Mr. Thornton. The letter was nevertheless so ably written, and treated of such exceedingly interesting topics, that it was felt best to submit it to the Society without further delay. There was not now any doubt in the world that Kilimanjaro was really and truly a snow-capped mountain, and that its height, if not 20,000 feet, was something very nigh to it. He regretted that Sir R. Murchison was unable to be present, for he would have done justice to the important geological facts communicated by Mr. Thornton. He (the Chairman) felt no doubt that the information now received on the physical structure of the district of Kilimanjaro would materially influence our speculations on the position of the eastern affluents of the White Nile.

MAJOR-GEN. SIR HENRY RAWLINSON, K.C.B., said it was most satisfactory to have the problem of Kilimanjaro at last solved. They must remember that for a long period it had been a question of doubt amongst geographers whether the mountain really existed at all, and, if it did, whether it was of the height it was stated to be. For a long time it was supposed that the white top that was seen was simply quartz or dolomite which glittered in the sun, and was mistaken for snow. However the evidence now received fully verified the statement of Mr. Rebmann; for to him belonged—and he (Sir Henry Rawlinson) hoped would be attributed, without any sort of jealousy on the part of England—the honours of that discovery. The note he had in his hand was from Lieut.-Col. Pelly, who had succeeded Col. Rigby as the agent of the British Government at Zanzibar. He was a gentleman of considerable geographical experience (having recently performed a very interesting journey from Teheran through Afghanistan to India), and was anxious to further as far as he could, both officially and privately, the exploration of central Africa. Sir H. Rawlinson then proceeded to read the following communication:—

"MY DEAR SIR HENRY,                    Zanzibar, 23 Nov., 1861.
    "I arrived here on the 16th ult., having coasted along the African shore from the Mozambique to Zanzibar, touching at Iboo, and the other ports en route.
    "Since arrival here I have been in the *Ariel* up to the equator, touching at Mombas and Lamoo. The country is finer, and the climate better than I had expected to find them.
    "Baron von der Decken, just returned from the mountain of Kilimanjaro, dined with me last evening. He is much pleased with his African excursion. Kilimanjaro has perpetual snow on it, though close to the line; and he estimates its height by triangulation at 20,000 feet.

"I am becoming much interested in the line of the Ozi River, and I cannot help fancying that explorations taken along it to the ranges on its N.W. would be the most worth of all, and might also discover the real sources of the Nile."

COL. SYKES said they really owed the solution of the problem to which reference had been made, to Baron von der Decken, who, out of his own means and his love of research, had undertaken to travel in Africa. The Baron's original object was not the discovery of which they now heard, but an expedition in another part of Eastern Africa, whence he was driven back under circumstances of considerable personal danger ; but, nothing daunted, he renewed his explorations, and this time in the direction of Kilimanjaro. The existence of that mountain had been pooh-poohed in England, where it was looked upon as a myth. It was said by some that the supposed snow was quartz, and by others that it was a thing *in nubibus* ; but they now found that the snow-capped mountain was a real fact. He was very glad that the problem had been solved by one who undertook the research from his own resources ; the more so as he had taken a personal interest in the discoveries of Krapf and Rebmann, the German missionaries, and had brought them to the notice of the Society, in his paper upon Zanzibar. He congratulated the Baron heartily upon his success, and desired to render unmitigated homage to the zeal of a foreigner.

MR. GALTON would add a few words supplementary to the remarks of Col. Sykes. The Baron von der Decken visited England for a few days previous to sailing to Africa ; but it was at a time of the year when there were no evening meetings of the Society, and consequently few of its members had the opportunity of making his acquaintance. Baron von der Decken was a Hanoverian gentleman of rank, who had been an ardent Algerian sportsman-traveller ; but having scientific tastes, and becoming desirous of a wider field of travel, selected the east coast of Africa as the place of his future explorations. The Baron had hoped that Dr. Röscher, who was then exploring those districts, would have associated himself with him ; but learnt, on his arrival at Zanzibar, that Röscher had been murdered near the Nyassa. Baron von der Decken then followed his steps, to secure his papers, but was ultimately driven back by the hostility of the natives. Subsequently, on his return to Zanzibar, he fell in with Mr. Thornton, who had originally been attached as geologist to Dr. Livingstone's expedition, but had latterly thrown up his appointment, and he induced Mr. Thornton to accompany him. He (Mr. Galton) was glad to believe that as this was not the first expedition of Baron von der Decken, so it would not be his last ; for Dr. Barth, with whom the Baron was in regular communication, had been asked to write to England to procure a portable boat, by which an exploration might be carried on of the lakes mentioned in Mr. Thornton's paper.

It was not to be thought that Kilimanjaro was the sole object of interest in that portion of Africa. Even as a mountain Kilimanjaro was by no means, of necessity, the most important, although it was the one of which most had been heard. Mr. Thornton mentioned no less than five other mountains that he had seen, ranging between 17,000 and 18,000 feet, and his views did not extend to either Kenia or Doengo Engai.

In reference to the letter read by Sir H. Rawlinson on the Ozi River, he might say that when he himself was exploring Africa eleven years ago, he had an English sailor-boy in his service, who had been one of the crew of a small trading schooner which had ascended the Ozi for twenty-five days. The boy had been greatly impressed by the size of the river, and, making allowance for the inaccurate and exaggerated recollections of non-educated persons who did not test their estimates of size by measurement, or at least by considerate examination, he had carried away a strong belief in the importance of that river.

The CHAIRMAN then invited discussion on the second and third papers.

After a few remarks by MR. TAYLOR, Consul at Abbeokuta,

COMMANDER STRICKLAND, R.N., described the natives of Abbeokuta, whom he had seen at Sierra Leone, on their own coast, and in the Brazils, stating that they exhibited extraordinary aptitude for trade. They were, in fact, called the Jews of Africa. Many of them had been taken as slaves, and when they were landed at Sierra Leone they were given a mere subsistence for six months, and then were left to shift for themselves; but after a few years spent in cultivating the soil and selling the produce, many of these Abbeokutans improved their position, and at last they so prospered as to have small shops and to rank among the chief people engaged in the retail trade of the colony. Not a few of them had gone so far as to establish commercial relations with England, importing English goods for sale to the Mahommedan traders who came from the interior. He believed that Abbeokuta afforded an excellent field for promoting civilization amongst the Africans. In the Brazils they formed a separate community of free blacks.

In reply to questions from MR. CRAWFURD,

CONSUL TAYLOR said he could not state that he had any great hopes that they could at this moment procure a large supply of cotton from Africa; but he believed the natives of Africa had every capacity and facility for providing an increased supply. In the case of palm-oil there had been a very large addition to the quantity exported, and he did not see why the produce of cotton should not also be increased.

COMMANDER STRICKLAND, R.N., thought now they had taken possession of Lagos, they should proclaim peace. If they wanted cotton they must stop all war. If they declared in Lagos their intention to punish those who made war, he believed they would secure peace, and would soon have abundant cotton from that country. He earnestly urged the duty of the white nations to give peace to these black races whom they had taught to sell each other into bondage, and whose original state of civilization they had been the cause of destroying. He quoted, from the journals of early voyagers, descriptions of the flourishing state of this part of Africa before the slave hunts for foreign exportation were got up through the white man's influence.

The meeting was then adjourned to Monday, February 10th.

---

*Sixth Meeting, February 10th, 1862.*

SIR RODERICK I. MURCHISON, VICE-PRESIDENT, in the Chair.

ELECTIONS.—*Dr. F. L. G. Gunn; Dr. S. Day Goss, M.D.; Capt. Edward Whitby; Charles Buxton, M.P.; Thomas Brookes; James Hall; Robert Hanbury, M.P.; John Jerdein; James Levick; William Marshall; Robert Deane Parker; and Arthur Roberts, Esqrs., were elected Fellows.*

ACCESSIONS.—The following were among the accessions to the Library and Map-rooms since the former meeting:—'Bombay Magnetical and Meteorological Observations for 1859;' Waugh's 'Instructions for Topographical Surveying;' Colton's Map of the United States; Transactions of the Pesth Academy of Sciences, &c.

EXHIBITIONS.—Geological Specimens from Charles Harper's and the Dempsters' Exploring Expedition to the East of York, West Australia; and some "Nardoo" seeds, taken from the patch on which Burke died, at Cooper's Creek; as also a specimen of the Nardoo plant, were exhibited.

The Papers read were—

1. *Despatch from His Excellency* Sir Henry Barclay, *Governor of Victoria, on the Expedition which, under the late* Mr. R. O'Hara Burke *and* Mr. W. J. Wills, *with* Messrs. Grey *and* King, *succeeded in crossing the Australian Continent from Melbourne to the Gulf of Carpentaria.*\*

[Communicated by His Grace the Duke of Newcastle.]

---

2. *Journals of the Expedition, with the Astronomical Observations of* Mr. W. J. Wills.

[Communicated by Governor Barkly to Sir Roderick I. Murchison.]

The sad intelligence reached Melbourne on the 2nd of November, that Messrs. Burke and Wills, the leaders of the Victoria Camel Expedition, had perished of starvation at Cooper's Creek, after having successfully accomplished the object of their mission by opening a road across the continent to the Gulf of Carpentaria.

On arriving at Cooper's Creek, they found the small depôt they had left there had been abandoned the same morning, and that the large relief party they expected from the Darling had never arrived. One of the two men who travelled with them, alone survives: the journal and route-map have been saved. The geographical results of the expedition are as follows :—

The distance from Menindee on the Darling to Torowato Swamp, lat. 30° 2', long. 142° 36', was about 200 miles, and the road lay through a fine grazing country. There was no difficulty about water, as creeks or water-holes, many of them important ones, were found at distances never exceeding 20 miles.

From Torowato to Wright's Creek (lat. 28° 48', long. 142° 53') the road was good; thence to Cooper's Creek it was stony, but not impracticable. The feed on Cooper's Creek was satisfactory; but the flies, mosquitos, and rats which abounded there, made it a very disagreeable residence. Wills has no doubt but that Wright's Creek was the lower part of the Warrego River. Burke considered that the road from the Darling to Cooper's Creek ought to be established more to the westward than the line he followed.

Four excursions were made without success from the easterly part of Cooper's Creek, to discover a practicable route due northward, according to instructions. On one occasion Mr. Wills travelled

---

\* The principal part of this despatch is printed in p. 68.

90 miles without finding water. The whole country had a deplorably arid appearance.

Mr. Burke's account of the journey from Cooper's Creek to Carpentaria, which he buried in a bottle on his return, is : " We have discovered a practicable route to Carpentaria, the principal portion of which lies in the 140th meridian of east longitude. Between this and the Stony Desert there is some good country. From thence to the tropic the country is dry and stony. Between the tropic and Carpentaria a considerable portion is rangy (i. e. hilly), but it is well watered and richly grassed." Mr. Wills' more detailed report fully bears out this description.

The longitudes of four points in the route have been worked out carefully at the William's Town Observatory, from Mr. Wills' records of lunar distances and eclipses of Jupiter's satellites. These careful reductions are based on Greenwich observations, and modify Wills' approximate determinations, which were, of course, calculated from the 'Nautical Almanack' data. They are as follows :—

| Latitude. | | | Longitude. |
|---|---|---|---|
| 17° 54' | .. | .. | No observation. |
| 18° 12' | .. | .. | 140° 59' |
| 18° 16' | .. | .. | 141° 28' |
| 18° 22' | .. | .. | 141° 15' |
| 19° 14' | .. | .. | 140° 55' |

By correcting Mr. Wills' route-map according to these more accurate results, we have probably an exact knowledge of the path taken by the expedition. His latitudes are numerous.

---

The third Paper read was—

3. *Proceedings of the Exploring Party, under* Mr. F. T. Gregory, *in North West Australia.*

Mr. F. Gregory sailed to Nickol Bay, on the north-west coast of Australia, and commenced his explorations on June 11th, a considerably later period than he had desired. He travelled till October 21st, passing over more than 2000 miles in consecutive expeditions from the coast, following the courses of different rivers, but on no one occasion penetrating very far into the interior. His results are the discovery of numerous periodical rivers and a vast amount of grazing country within the tropics, of which not less than 2 or 3 million acres lay within the limits of his route. The physical features of the land present a succession of terraces rising inland for nearly 200 miles, more or less broken by volcanic hills near the coast.  The highest elevation seen was nearly 4000 feet. The maximum October temperature in Nickol Bay during October was 92°, and the minimum 70°: the heat was not inconveniently felt during the journey.  Mr. F. Gregory's map has not yet been completed and forwarded; but the report that has been received, bears evidence to a careful survey of the country examined by him.

:

------

The fourth Paper read was—

4. *Letter from* Capt. Cadell *to* Sir Roderick I. Murchison, *on the Country to the East and North of the Grey and Stanley Ranges.*

" I do myself the honour of herewith forwarding a rough tracing of some new ' features ' which are found to exist to the eastward and north-eastward of the Grey and Stanley ranges.

" The most noticeable feature in the tracing is the Booro Pooro or Gonnewarra, which, from its magnitude, we imagine to be identical with the Neville of Sir Thomas Mitchell.  In August last its breadth, twenty miles from Mount Vision, was about 30 yards, with a depth of about 11 feet.  It eventually appears to expend itself on the plains.  It will now be seen that this region is much better watered than the respected Sturt was led to expect from the natives; and in a few years, when stock shall have trodden down and formed the topsoil, which at present acts but as a sponge to absorb the rains as they fall, it will really be a fairly watered country and decidedly favourable for pastoral purposes.  And I should not be surprised to see nature cutting fresh watercourses, notwithstanding that those at present existing are deep and well defined.

" ' Country ' has been taken up largely both on the Paroo and Warrego.  The Grey and Stanley ranges are under tender, and runs have been applied for on and in the neighbourhood of the Gonnewarra.  The tracing was made from information I received when on the Darling the other day; and I account for the longitudes not agreeing with those of Wills, as that observer in his maps was very considerably to the eastward of Sturt's positions.  When out at the back of the Anna branch a short time ago with my friend Mr. Haverfield, we found that the "backwaters" of the Darling had at some time and during great floods extended nearly if not over the South Australian boundary line (141st meridian).  Lake Cawndilla overflowing fills Lake Tondour, which in its turn sends its waters down through a depressed line of flooded country to a lake (or lakes) of vast extent, which have not been filled for many years.

" I may add that all our western flowing rivers seem to carry down uniformly larger volumes of water than they did in former years."

MR. LAUCHLAN MACKINNON having been called upon by the President, said that it was many years ago—as far back, indeed, as 1839—that he was engaged in an expedition into the interior of Australia that might, in a manner, be considered an exploring one, though its main object was of a commercial character.   At the time of which he spoke there was nothing so exciting to youthful enterprise in that country as the overland journey from Sydney to the then newly formed colony of South Australia, of which Adelaide was the capital.   At that time South Australia had an immense extent of unoccupied pasture-lands of the finest quality ready for the reception of flocks and herds.   The first sheep, cattle, and horses had to be imported by sea from England, Tasmania, and New South Wales.   The obvious disadvantages of this expensive and tedious mode of stocking the lands of the new colony stimulated the enterprise of Bonny, Hawdon, Eyre, and others, and the result was that a practicable route for stock was discovered, along the Morumbidgee and Murray Rivers, from New South Wales to South Australia.   He himself was the leader of one of the earliest parties who traversed that route.   The party started from Sydney in the middle of 1839, and arrived in safety at Adelaide in about three months.   At that time a great portion of the country was quite unknown.   He met large tribes of natives, but he succeeded in passing through them without much difficulty.   He, however, found one thing to be necessary in order to carry out the work he had undertaken to a successful issue, and that was, not to separate himself from his commissariat; and he believed that if, in Messrs. Burke and Wills' expedition, the same principle had been adhered to, they would not now have had to mourn over the loss of those gallant men.   There was no problem in social science so extraordinary as that which was in process of development in Australia.   It was but seventy-four years since the first settlers arrived in Sydney and formed a colony that had since become the parent of other magnificent colonies.   On the shores of Port Jackson, where seventy-five years ago the native savages were the only occupants, stood the fine city of Sydney, with an Anglo-Saxon population numbering some 60,000 or 70,000.   As late as 1836 the colony of Victoria was a mere run for kangaroos and savages, but now it was the habitation of civilised men.   He believed that there were results in that colony which were quite unparalleled in the history of colonisation.   It was in the year 1837 that the first land was sold in Victoria.   When he arrived in Melbourne, in 1840, its population numbered about 150, while that of the whole district of Port Phillip, as it was then called, did not exceed 3000.   Melbourne itself was then but a hamlet in the midst of a forest, yet the energy and enterprise of its inhabitants had rendered it, within the short period that had intervened, one of the finest and most prosperous cities in the world.   When he left Melbourne in 1857, just seventeen years after he had first arrived there, its population had risen to 95,000, while that of the whole colony had increased to nearly 600,000.   The city itself had become one of extreme beauty from the substantial and tastefully ornamented character of its buildings.   The streets were wide and handsome, macadamized in the centres, and paved at the sides with flagging taken out at great cost from the north of Scotland.   The entire city was lighted with gas.   Works, constructed on the best principles known to modern science, at a cost of 800,000l., supplied the town most abundantly with water.   The rapid increase of material prosperity in Victoria was so remarkable that he could not refrain from giving them a few more statistical facts, which would speak for themselves. When he went to Victoria in 1840, its whole public revenue, from all sources, was about 10,000*l.* a year ; the value of its exports was about 70,000*l.* a year : when he left in 1857, its public revenue was 3,330,000*l.* a year, and its exports had reached to nearly 15,000,000*l.* sterling. The greater part of this amount was made up of gold, the produce of the rich mines which abounded in Victoria. But, independently of the gold, the resources of Australia in agriculture and in her flocks and herds had been such as to render these colonies highly prosperous and affluent before the advent of the golden era. As regarded the government of the colonies, there were matters which had not been satisfactory. It was yet to be seen how far democratic institutions were consistent with constitutional government. He trusted that problem would be worked out satisfactorily. As regarded the unfortunate expedition of Burke and Wills, every one must deplore the melancholy fate of the gallant and persevering men. He was glad to see that the countrymen of Wills, in the town of Totness, Devonshire, were about to pay a mark of respect to his memory, by raising a monument; and he hoped that every one who felt an interest in the progress of discovery in Australia would seek an opportunity of adding their mite towards raising a monument to so worthy a man. He considered that before Burke and Wills left Cooper's Creek, they ought to have established a large depôt at that place, to ensure sufficient food upon which they might fall back ; but, instead of that, their enthusiasm led them to go ahead of their party, imagining that those they were leaving in charge would be able to reach Cooper's Creek in time, but the sub-leaders were not equal to the task, and hence the melancholy result of that successful, yet disastrous, expedition.

Captain Bagot said, they once had the impression that Australia, generally speaking, was a desert—that it was a country presenting but few spots which might be turned to account. This idea which was entertained in England was not surprising, because he could bear witness to the fact that it was held by those living in Australia itself, until the people there became better acquainted with the country. His friend, Mr. Mackinnon, had stated elsewhere that, when taking cattle across the portion of country over which he had travelled, they had to traverse a salt-bush desert. The cattle which were with him even declared it to be a desert, for they would not touch the bush, and many were lost because they had nothing to feed upon. He thought it was two years after Mr. Mackinnon traversed the country that his son went into it. He was travelling until his provision-wallet was exhausted; he was tired and hungry, and had nothing to depend upon but his rifle for subsistence, and he was looking for something which he might deprive of life to preserve his own life ; he saw a bullock, shot it, and found it exceedingly fat. After he had feasted upon the animal he had the good sense to examine its stomach, for the purpose of seeing on what food it had become so fat. He opened the stomach, and found nothing but salt-bush in it. His son returned to Adelaide immediately, arranged with the Government for a large tract of land, and he now had on it 7000 or 8000 as fine beasts as could be seen, and they had been all fed upon the salt-bush. His friend, Mr. Eyre, had passed into that country, to the north of Spencer's Gulf, and, on his return, declared that he believed it to be a land which was perfectly useless : yet upon that very country there were now something like 2,000,000 of sheep. It was believed that even the plains of Adelaide were useless brickfields, but upon those plains enough breadstuffs were now raised, not only to feed the population of South Australia, but also to supply a large proportion of the gold-diggers in Victoria. South Australia has for many years exported as much breadstuffs each year as would supply her own con-

sumption for two years.   He thought these few facts would serve to show
that, whatever may have been the opinions formed on a first cursory glance
at it, the land of Australia, as far as it is known, is not a desert; while the
recent explorations of Burke and Wills and of Stuart remove the preconceived
opinion of the desert condition of the vast interior of that mighty continent.

After some remarks by MR. MARSH, M.P.,

MR. SAUNDERS expressed his belief that the coast of Carpentaria, owing to
its peculiar local advantages, would attain to a more flourishing position than
any other part of Australia; and he urged the necessity of establishing there
a new settlement as a means of creating a very beneficial influence upon commercial operations, especially throughout the adjacent archipelago.

MR. HENRY AYSHFORD SANFORD, on being called on by the Chairman, spoke
in reference to the resources of Western Australia, and to the causes of its present
inferiority to the other colonies on that continent.   He said that the colony
was established in 1829, when the Government officials received large tracts of
the best land then known in the colony, a great part of which, from want of
capital and labour, are still lying untenanted.   Again, the land was divided
amongst the original colonists in proportion to the cost of the articles—whatever
might have been their usefulness—brought by each from home; and in 1830
upwards of 2000 persons, with property amounting to the value of 100,000*l*.,
arrived in the colony; but, from the impossibility of apportioning the different
tracts of land to the various applicants (there being then but a Surveyor-
General and an Assistant-Surveyor in the colony) and from want of labour,
the country was not able to be cultivated to any great extent; and at one time
the colonists were reduced to nearly a state of starvation.   From that time the
colony underwent various vicissitudes till 1850, when the introduction of
convicts (then rejected by the other Australian colonies) supplied to a certain
extent the defects of the want of labour; and the employment of these, under
the moral force system (which has been attended with the greatest success),
first raised the prospects of the colony.   To show the success of the system,
in 1859, 21 convictions at the sessions were as follows :—11 free-men, and but
3 conditional-pardon men and 7 ticket-of-leave men, out of a population of
about 15,000 souls.   A further advance has been made by the new Land
Regulations; and he, Mr. Sanford, could state, from his own knowledge, that
where, in 1857, scarcely 400 acres were under cultivation, a district not less
than 12 miles long by from 2 to 3 miles wide was, in 1861, one succession of
corn-fields.

He added that the southern part of the colony produced in large quantities
the jarrah wood, most excellent for buildings, railway purposes, &c. &c., being
capable of resisting the attacks of the white ant, as also so much esteemed for
ships, piles, and all water purposes (resisting the attacks of the *Teredo navalis*),
that at this moment it is being imported to England for the purpose of being
used in the royal navy yards.   Copper and lead ore were found in great abundance, with an extraordinarily rich percentage of ore, within an easy distance
of good and safe ports.   Coal has also been discovered, and there exists but
little doubt that there are extensive coal-fields also within a short distance of
the sea.   He referred them to the Exhibition of this year, where they would
have the opportunity of seeing and testing the accuracy of his statements as to
the great natural advantages of the country.   He thought that a great part of
the meeting were doubtless well aware that to the exploring energy, perse-
verance, and skill of the Messrs. Gregory the colonists were in a great measure
indebted for their knowledge of the agricultural and mineral resources of their
adopted country; and the report that had been read that evening of Mr. Frank
Gregory's last successful explorations in the north-west opened new and extensive fields to the settlers for the extension of their flocks and herds, and very
possibly for the cultivation of the cotton-plant.

Messrs. Dempsters, Clarkson, and Harper had also discovered, 300 miles east of York, large tracts of land, with plenty of water, and well adapted for pastoral purposes ; but the principal interest attached to their trip was the intelligence they had obtained of what might prove a clue to the fate of the Leichardt expedition, and he had been informed it was the intention of the Colonial Government to prosecute further inquiries in the ensuing wet season.  He believed the colony only required *labour*, and he trusted that Government would persevere in sending out convicts, and, if so, he believed sufficient capital would speedily be introduced to work the mineral and other resources of the country ; and Western Australia would yet rank among one of the most prosperous colonies of that wonderful continent.

The meeting was then adjourned to the 24th of February.

# ADDITIONAL NOTICES.

(Printed by order of Council.)

1. *Abstract of Capt. Duncan Cameron's Paper on the Ethnology of the Caucasus.*  By W. SPOTTISWOODE, Esq.

THE establishment of Cossacks in the Caucasus dates some centuries back, when large bodies of them moved down from their own plains to the Dnieper and the Don, and thence to the Terek, where they formed a mixed race, which, however, has been continually recruited from the Don or the Ukraine. These were systematically augmented by Peter the Great and his successors. Catharine the Great, in particular, transferred thither the turbulent Zaporogue Cossacks.  Continually recruited by desperadoes from the surrounding states, they rendered themselves at one time seriously formidable, frequently carrying devastation into Russia and Poland, Turkey and the Crimean Khanships.  In 1775 their government was suppressed by Catharine II.  They were subsequently allowed to serve against Turkey, and, as a reward for their exploits, they were granted in 1789 the territory which they now occupy on the Black Sea.

The Cossacks of the Caucasian line still retain some vestiges of the self-government which distinguished their rude, free communities.  They have no nobles, and acknowledge no difference between families, except distinction gained in the field or military rank.  Disposed in regiments along the different military lines, they furnish an imposing complement to the regular army of the Caucasus.  Their artillery, with that of the Don Cossacks, is reckoned the best in Russia.  Some of their early settlements have become the nuclei of important towns.  Thus Kizliar, established in 1715, numbers 9305 inhabitants ; Mozdok, established in 1777, 10,970 ; Stavropol, established the same year, 14,368.

Beyond the Cossacks are the Nogai Tatars, a widely different race, whose history, however, is no less characteristic.  At the beginning of the seventeenth century they passed from the Sea of Azov to the north-east of the Caspian, between Tobolsk and the Jaik.  Pressed by the Kalmuks, they afterwards submitted to Russian sway, pitching their tents for a time near Astrakhan.

At the beginning of the last century we find them crossing the Dnieper, and placing themselves under Turkey, but returning in 1770 to their old camping-grounds in Russian territory.

The Nogais are divided into the Trans-Kuban and the Kumyk hordes. The Trans-Kuban Nogais occupy the left and part of the right banks of the Kuban, from the post-station, Batalpashinsk, to the mouth of the Laba, as well as the tract at the foot of Beshtau, near Piatigorsk. The Kumyk Nogais live between the Sulak and Terek rivers ; some of them are nomadic, others cultivate rice, madder, and the vine, and are rich in flocks and herds. Besides these there are the Karatchai Tatars, the Urustpievs at the sources of the Baksan, and the Malka. The total Tatar population here is 45,000.

Passing to the mountaineers, the Tcherkess, Abkhasian, Suanetian, Ossetian, and Immerian, and after them the Tchetchen and Lesghian groups, claim our attention. A great diversity of race and language not only separates these people from one another, but renders their classification difficult.

The Tcherkess were called Zukoi by Greek geographers, and placed by them in the Crimea and Western Caucasus. In the time of George Interiano, who wrote in the year 1702, the Tcherkess country included the whole of the eastern shore of the Palus Mœotis, from the Don to the Cimmerian Bosphorus, whence however they were expelled by the Muscovites and Tatars.

The Tcherkess call themselves Adigh. They at present occupy the northern face of the Caucasus and the Kuban to the fortress of Anapa, and thence southwards, along the eastern shore of the Black Sea, from the mouth of the Kuban to the river Bsyb or Kobosh. They are divided into communities, of which the principal are the Natochuadj, Schapsukhs, Ubykhs, Temirgois, and Kabardians. The constitution of the Tcherkess is strictly feudal. Their country is still a seat of the slave-trade, and its influence has sunk so deeply into their institutions that the chief privilege of the seigneurs over the peasants is the right of selling their issue. Among the higher orders, however, the custom of disposing of their female relatives to strangers takes something of the form of a family alliance. The Sultans formerly availed themselves largely of this usage to strengthen their influence among the Tcherkess. Thus the Abadsekhs always call the reigning Sultan their cousin, on account of their numerous contributions to Imperial harims.

The main body of the Tcherkess group is still opposed to Russian domination, which has, however, sufficiently established itself in Kabarda and along the coast. Their total population is fixed at 290,540.

To the south of the Tcherkess are the Abkhasians, a people resembling them in many of their usages, but different in personal appearance, and far more wild and lawless. Their tongue is harsh and barbarous in the extreme. It is told that a Sultan once sent a certain learned Effendi to the Caucasus to collect information regarding languages. He brought back vocabularies of many ; but on being asked about Abkhasian, produced a bag of pebbles which he rattled. " That," he said, " is the Abkhasian."

They are divided into the Abkhasians proper, subjects of the reigning Prince of Abkhasia, under Russian protection, the Ssadds, Besselbeis, and other smaller communities, all distinguished by their passion for rapine, murder and blood-revenge. The total population of the Abkhasian group is 144,346.

Next come the Suaneti, the " gens Suanarum " of Pliny and Procopius ; a wild, unruly people, but whose country, strewn with remnants of Greek architecture, attests an order and civilization long since passed away. These occupy the mountain territory between Mingrelia and Abkhasia, on the south-west, and Kabarda on the north-east. Their language is said to be cognate with the Persian.* The Suaneti have long been hermetically sealed to external influence

---

* It is a branch of the Georgian.—W. S.

by the wild character of their country; and it was by a Prince of their race that the last Governor-General of Imeritia, was openly assassinated at Kutais, in 1857. A road is, however, being pierced by the Russians through their territory, which is said to be rich in metals. Their population is about 11,000.

The Ossetes, bordering on these, occupy part of the mountain territory, between Kutais, Tiflis and Vladikavkas. They constitute one of the most interesting people in the Caucasus. Their language has been pronounced by Klaproth to be Indo-Germanic. Their manners bear a striking resemblance to those of the Germanic race, and the furniture of their houses struck Haxthausen as singularly resembling that of the peasants in Westphalia. They are believed to be a fragment of the Alani of the middle ages, who, according to Moses of Choreni, and others, were originally located near the Caucasus, and are classed by Procopius among the Gothic tribes; and, supposing this to be true, they thus become directly linked with our European history. They call themselves Tagiran, and the Alani also called themselves Iran.

The Ossetes are a handsome race; gifted with great eloquence and ability; proud, true to their word, and hospitable, but great robbers, as their proverb, " Whatever is found on the high road is God's gift," sufficiently testifies. Their form of society is aristocratic, but based on family clanships. Their religion consists of a mixture of Heathenism, Christianity, and Islam. The prophet Elijah plays a great part in their religious observances; and they offer pagan sacrifices at certain caves which he is said to have inhabited, as well as on old altars the relics of their former faith, which seems to have extended throughout the Caucasus. If an Ossete is injured by another he slays a cat, a dog, or an ass, on the grave of the wrongdoer's ancestors, believing that, unless he is satisfied, their souls will be degraded to occupy the animal slain.

Beyond these are the Khevsur, a Christian people, an offshoot of the old Georgian race, inhabiting the mountain tract about the sources of the Argun, and they have long formed a barrier to the fanatic Mussulman tribes of Daghestan and Upper Georgia.

The Christianity of the Khevsur is of a loose kind, and tinged with paganism. But his faith in the sign of the cross is unbounded; he crosses himself at sight of a church, crosses himself when he sneezes, crosses himself when he lights a lucifer in a strong wind, and wears the cross as a badge on his coat of mail. The population of the Khevsurs, with that of their kindred tribes of Pschaves and Tuschetes, amounts to 11,546.

Lastly, we arrive at the Tchetchians and Lesghians, two separate people, speaking different languages, inhabiting Daghestan and the adjacent mountain country towards Vladikavkas. They differ from the Tcherkess in eschewing aristocratic government; every man among them being free, equal, and noble. Until Shamil's time they were broken up into small democratic communities, keeping themselves so jealously apart that their language has been split into innumerable dialects. Blood-revenge is common, and the males of a family are often exterminated by this desperate substitute for regular law.

Of the races to the south of the Caucasus, namely, the Georgians and Armenians, little need be said. Among the former society is based on a feudality as complicated as that of any European state in the middle ages; kings, nobles, and clergy, forming a regular hierarchy, not unlike that of the old Germanic empire. Society in Georgia is still divided into nobles and serfs. The existence, indeed, of serfdom is one of the greatest drawbacks to the development of the resources of the country. The Georgians were at one time masters of a large, wealthy, and powerful kingdom, but the invasion of Tamerlane overthrew this, and it never recovered the shock. Its remnants, gathered together for a brief period, were again formally divided by Alexander II., in

1442. From that period the Georgian race sank into an anarchy, only broken at the close of last century by the establishment of Russian domination.

[The following population-table of the Caucasus is taken from Russian sources :—

| Tribe. | | | | | | | No. of Souls. |
|---|---|---|---|---|---|---|---|
| Abkhasians | .. | .. | .. | .. | .. | .. | 144,552 |
| Svaneth | .. | .. | .. | .. | .. | .. | 1,639 |
| Adigh | .. | .. | .. | .. | .. | .. | 290,549 |
| Ubykh | .. | .. | .. | .. | .. | .. | 25,000 |
| Turkish tribes | .. | .. | .. | .. | .. | .. | 44,989 |
| Ossetes | .. | .. | .. | .. | .. | .. | 27,339 |
| Tchetchians | .. | .. | .. | .. | .. | .. | 117,080 |
| Tumenes | .. | .. | .. | .. | .. | .. | 4,719 |
| Pshavs | .. | .. | .. | .. | .. | .. | 4,232 |
| Khevsurs | .. | .. | .. | .. | .. | .. | 2,505 |
| Lesghians and Daghestans | | | .. | .. | .. | .. | 397,761 |
| | | | | | | | 1,060,365 |

The languages of the Caucasus have been but little investigated ; but it has been ascertained that, with one exception, they belong to what is called the Turanian, *i. e.* neither to the Semitic nor to the Indo-Germanic family. The exception is the Ossete (Tren or Tronen), a distinctly Indo-Germanic language, a full grammar and vocabulary of which was published by Sjögren at St. Petersburg in 1844. An excellent sketch of a classification of the Caucasian languages is to be found in Prof. Max Müller's ' Languages of the Seat of War,' 1855.—W. SPOTTISWOODE.]

---

2. *Memorandum—Earthquake of Erzerum, June,* 1859. By ROBERT A. O. DALYELL, Esq., F.R.G.S., H.B.M. Consul at Erzerum.

THE first shock took place on the 1st June, about 8 A.M.: it was very sensibly felt, but did very little damage.*

On the 2nd June, about 10·30 A.M., another shock occurred, lasting about 8 seconds ; and was followed about 11·30 A.M. by another, but of shorter duration.

The vibrations were horizontal ; but, during the more violent shocks, a slight vertical motion is stated by some persons to have been perceptible. The direction of the shock appears to have been nearly from south-west to north-east.

On the 4th June a severe shock was felt at Tabreez, in Persia, which, however, did no damage to the town.

Schamaki, a town in the Caucasus, near the Caspian, has suffered very severely by a shock which occurred there within a day or two after the shock here ; but the Russian Consul informs me that his letters make no mention of the shock as having been felt in other parts of the Caucasus.

I have been unable to obtain accurate information as to how far the shock of the 2nd instant was felt at intermediate points towards the north and north-east, but it does not appear to have been felt at any great distance to the southward. The shocks of the 1st and 2nd were felt in various villages in the plain of Erzerum ; but, so far as I can ascertain, were not perceptible in the district of Tortoum. On the days of the shocks mentioned, the weather

---

* Erzerum is situated in latitude 39° 55' 20", and longitude 41° 18' 31". Height above the sea 6114 feet ; geological formations resembling those of the Caucasus ; mountains apparently metalliferous ; population about 35,000.

was sultry and lowering; but not, however, it is said, very much different from that usually prevailing at this season.

At a village, called Souk Tchermik,* in the neighbourhood, a mineral spring, the water of which is usually of a blue colour, became darkened in colour, and retained such colour for two days.

The sense of disquietude mentioned by Humboldt, as affecting the lower animals during similar phenomenon, was very remarkable in the barking, on the occasion even of slight shocks, of the numerous dogs with which the town abounds.

For considerably more than a month, after the 2nd June, slight shocks continued to occur about once in the twenty-four hours: one or two were rather severe, but did not occasion any damage.

Slight shocks appear to be of frequent occurrence at Erzerum: they are not confined to a particular period of the year, but seem to be most frequent in spring.

The following is the official return of casualties furnished to the Pacha:—Killed, four hundred and sixty Mussulmans; eleven Gregorian Armenian Christians; one Catholic Armenian Christian; two Greek Christians.

The Turkish quarters of the town were those which suffered most severely. Four thousand five hundred houses were quite destroyed, or very seriously damaged; twelve mosques suffered more or less; nine minarets were quite destroyed; seven Turkish schools were completely destroyed; five baths, many of the fountains, and eight hundred and fifty shops were rendered useless. The khans, in which merchandize is deposited, being usually vaulted, have suffered very little.

The loss of life is probably not overstated: it would have been much greater had not the 2nd June been a great festival (the Ascension). Few, comparatively, of the population, either Mussulmans or Christians, were in the bazaars, and many of the latter were absent from their houses.

The very solidly built walls of the fortress, the palace of the Pacha, the Austrian, British, Persian, and Russian Consulates, all among the most solidly constructed buildings of the town, have sustained much damage.

The pyramidal top of the Lalé Pacha minaret was, by one shock, moved a considerable distance on the column, of which it forms the summit; and, by another shock, was brought back to its original position.

The Central Government has afforded some assistance to the poorer inhabitants in rebuilding, and a commissioner has arrived from Constantinople.

At about an hour's distance from Erzerum to the south, there is a point in the mountains surrounding the plain, which would appear to be the crater of an extinct volcano; † and a mountain of the range, forming the plain of Erzerum to the south, is easily recognizable by its form as an ancient crater. ‡

There are traditions in the country of a great earthquake which occurred about one hundred years ago, and by which, though the damage at Erzerum was not great, the villages in the plain of Passim, about twelve miles from Erzerum to the east, suffered severely.

It is said in the country that the lake of Tortoum § was, up to that date, much smaller than it is at present, and was then deepened by the falling of a mountain, which altered the course of the Tortoum Chai.

---

* At many points in the plain of Erzerum there are hot mineral springs. Souk Tchermik is a cold spring, but its temperature is somewhat warmer in winter than in summer.

† See Hamilton's ' Researches in Asia Minor,' vol. 1, p. 178.

‡ It is described in Wagner's ' Reise nach Persian,' Leipsig, 1852, ch. vii.

§ For description of lake of Tortoum, see Kurzon's ' Armenia,' p. 155; and for description of remarkable geological formations, valley of Tortoum, see Hamilton's ' Researches in Asia Minor,' vol. 1, ch. xiii.

The appearance of the locality seems to me to confirm this tradition; and, although my want of geological knowledge does not enable me to form any accurate opinion, I should consider that the whole country to the north-east of the lake of Tortoum bears evident traces of volcanic disturbances. The walls of two churches, the one at Ishkirt, the other at Vank (near the lake of Tortoum), are cracked in the manner I should be inclined to attribute to the action of an earthquake; and I would mention a remarkable rift known in the country by the name of the Dunya Buzurgu (Greatness of the World): this rift splits the mountain from top to bottom, and is about fifteen feet broad at the entrance. It took me from twenty minutes to half an hour to ride through it. The strata on the opposite sides correspond; and, though a small stream flows through it, I should think, from its depth, the chasm can hardly have been formed by the action of water.

After careful inquiry on the spot I was unable to ascertain that shocks have, within memory, been felt in the valley of Tortoum, or on the districts to the north-east; and I am inclined to believe that the slight shocks which I have above mentioned as a frequent occurrence are (except as they may form part of a wider system) confined to the town and plain of Erzerum; and I am disposed to think are scarcely felt in that part of the plain which lies to the north of the branch of the Euphrates, which divides it into two portions.

I have, however, ascertained that within the last two years shocks, but apparently slighter in character than those experienced in this neighbourhood, have been felt at many points in the area, which would be bounded by lines drawn between Erzerum, Tiflis, Van, and Bayazid; but I am unable to collect sufficient information to connect the dates or directions of such shocks with the dates or directions of those experienced here.

In conclusion, I may state that many buildings of solid construction have, for instance, at Van and its neighbourhood (about 200 years ago), at Bayazid, about sixty or seventy (?) years since, been destroyed, or have severely suffered by earthquakes; although the shocks experienced of late appear, in this part of Turkey, to have been most severe in this immediate vicinity.*

---

3. *Letter from* Capt. RICHARD BURTON, F.R.G.S., H.M. Consul to Fernando Po, *to* Dr. NORTON SHAW.

ENCLOSED is a compass-sketch of the Ogun or Abeokuta river, which has not yet been regularly surveyed.

Captain Bedingfield, Dr. Eales of the *Prometheus*, and I left Lagos on the 29th October, in the first and second gigs, manned by Krumen.

Our line was across the large lagoon called in maps the Cradoo Waters: the word should be written Koradu, and the name is derived from a well-known market-town opposite Lagos. After two hours' rowing we entered the Agboi Creek, a short cut running nearly northwards. You will find it roughly laid down in Lieut. Glover's map, whereas the Ogun river sweeps round to the east.

On our return we came out by the mouth of the Ogun, which was nearly choked with grass. These rivers have no influents in their lower courses, and the soppy, muddy nature of their deltas, combined with want of waterfall, makes them shrink in volume as they near the sea.

After three hours' paddling up the fetid Agbai, and encountering a sharp tornado on the way, we entered the main river, a goodly stream, about 100

---

* Monsieur Abich, a distinguished Russian Seisologist, has published an account of the earthquake at Erzerum, of June 1859, and the earthquake at Schamake of the same period.

yards broad, belted on both sides with an immense growth of forest and little affected by the tide.    After sunset we neared the village Igáon, which, in the dry season, is the terminus of the boat traffic : a path leads from it to Abeokuta, the main road being on the other side, viz. the west of the Ogun river.

The next day took us to a miserable mass of huts on the left bank, Mabban—a fine specimen of maritime Africa—all mud, miasma, and mosquitos.

Our third night was spent at Takpana, a large hamlet surrounded by well-cultivated fields ; maize, manioc, and sweet potatoes.    The aspect of the country had improved ; the walls of dense vegetation upon the banks had yielded to the Guinea-grass, and the stream had become shallow, and showed sandbanks and boulders.    My companion compared it to the upper part of the Zambezi river.

At 11 A.M., on the 1st November, we landed at Agbarneya, the southern " port " of Abeokuta, distant about 8 miles from Ake, our destination.

The river is navigable for boats as far as Aro, some 6 miles higher up ; above that point a ridge of rocks crosses the bed and forms an impassable rapid.    Small canoes can thread it for a short distance in the upper waters ; but the general style of ferry is a large calabash, which the traveller takes to his bosom.    At Agbarneya we were met by Messrs. Wilcoxon and Roper, of the Church Missionary Society, who obligingly escorted us up to the town of Ake, from which the alake or chief derives his title, and we found quarters in the hospitable home of Dr. Harrison.

Our stay at Abeokuta lasted a week, from the 1st to the 8th November.    It was consumed in " palaver " touching the war with Ibadan, kidnapping, slaving, and human sacrifice.    A revolting case of sacrifice had just occurred, and hardly had we returned to Lagos than we were informed of another.    The Egbas, or people of Abeokuta, are one of the weak semi-monarchical African tribes ; " every man," as their proverb says, " is king in his own house." The chiefs are influential and refractory as the sheïks of a Bedouin tribe ; and the alake, though aspiring to regal title, has not half the power nor a quarter of the state of the pettiest Indian rajah.    Abeokuta has been so often described that I shall say little about it.    The population has apparently been underestimated by travellers and limited to 100,000 ; I should prefer 150,000.    The extreme circumference of the walls is about 27 miles.    Most of the interior, however, is granite knob and field ; and in point of uncleanness it beats anything I ever saw.    The frontispiece to ' Sunrise within the Tropics ' should be called " what Abeokuta ought to be."    Like the little book itself, it is all couleur de rose—Africa, with an Italian tint.

There is no mistake, however, about cotton-growing in these regions.    It can be carried out all over Yoruba ; a kingdom once extending from the Volta river to the Niger, and including Benin and Dahomy : but, to give it due extension, wars must cease and treaties must be made with the several chiefs. I would here correct a mistake, universally made by those who have written upon the subject. The land is not, as stated by Mr. Campbell and others, common property, nor will the people allow strangers to take it.    Litigation upon the subject is quite as general as in England ; and if, as Sir Culling Eardley proposes, free negroes and mulattos were sent here from America, there would follow the agrarian wars and troubles of New Zealand.    Even in the towns a stranger cannot obtain building-ground, except it be granted with the understanding that it is not alienated in perpetuity, but shall revert, when no longer in use, to the original proprietor.

If you want a colony in West Africa, send it to me, near the Cameroons. At some future time I will (D. V.) enter fully into the subject.    Suffice it to say for the present that Lagos requires a sanatorium—the nearest now being Teneriffe and Ascension ; and the Oil rivers want a key, after losing Fernando Po.    At Abeokuta the cotton is grown in the farms.    I was shown the green seed or upland (short staple ), and the black seed or long staple.    There is, moreover, a very valuable kind, called "akashe," soft as silk. Eight seeds are sold for a penny. Before the war, the export was doubling every year; since then it has declined. The Cotton Association of Manchester exported 20,000 bales in 1839-60, and received only 3447. With the return of peace it will revive. The wars are conducted in the usual African style. Seventeen thousand men meet, blaze away with "long Danes" from the hip all the day, retire and advance, as if by mutual consent, and separate with the loss of half-a-dozen killed and wounded: and this stuff they call fighting! It is serious only to the allies, who, being weaker than those who assist them, are sold off by way of commissariat. The Egbas of Abeokuta are nominally fighting to defend their friends the Ijáyes against a common foe, the Ibadans. It is generally asserted that the unhappy Ijáyes have at this time lost 20,000 of their number by famine and the slave-market. The real *casus belli* lies deep; the Abeokutans are determined to monopolize transit-dues by keeping the northern people from the coast. Every African tribe knows that it cannot prosper without seaboard, and then the war began.

We were informed that the King of Dahomy was busy sacrificing before beginning his annual slave-hunt. It is the practice of this amiable monarch, as of his predecessors, to muster his forces, arm, drill, train them, and march them round the capital till the spirit moves him to rush in a particular direction and drive and harry the land.

Concerning Dahomy, however, I must warn you that there is a vast amount of fabling, which originates with certain slave-dealers, who think to alarm strangers by spreading abroad all manner of horrible tales. To this category belongs the report that his Majesty sadly wants to catch an English officer, to be used as a stirrup when mounting his charger. The Amazons may be reduced from 6000 to 2000. Messrs. Duncan and Forbes were, I believe, imposed upon by seeing the warlike dames marching out of one gate and in to another. A similar story is told concerning commissariat bullocks in the good old times of India. I have no doubt that the Amazons, like the tender begums of Oude and Hyderabad, are mighty contemptible troops; and I should like to have a chance of seeing them tackled by an equal number of stout English charwomen, armed with the British broomstick. After taking leave of the alake, we left Abeokuta on the 8th November, and on the 9th I found myself once more under the comfortable roof of my excellent friend the Acting Governor of Lagos, Mr. McCoskry. The trip has led me to doubt that sunrise has yet taken place within the tropics, though not to question that it can take place.

On the 21st ult. I left Lagos in H. M. S. *Bloodhound*, Lieut.-Commander Mackworth Dolben, which Captain Bedingfield kindly detached for the purpose of visiting the Oil rivers. We entered the Nun river on the 24th November, passed through the Akassa Creek, whose waters saw for the first time a man-of-war; visited Brass and Fish towns, and we are now proposing to sound the bar of St. Nicholas river.

You will probably hear from me by the next mail, unless I happen to be on the top of Cameron's Mountain.

---

4. *A Missionary Journey up the Cavalha River, and the Report of a large River flowing near the Source of the former.* By the Rev. C. C. HOFFMAN.

### Communicated by Mr. JOHN MARSHALL of Cape Palmas, West Africa.

AT your request I furnish you, with pleasure, with a few particulars of a missionary tour I made to the interior last July. On the 9th of July we left Cavalla, the station of Bishop Payne, and reached the Cavalha river after a walk of an hour and a half. That afternoon we ascended the river about 5 miles to Burbo. On the 10th we made 25 or 30 miles, and on the 11th about the same number, when we reached our landing-place, Kekre in Webbo, say 70 miles from the mouth of the river. The river varied in depth from 2½ to 4½ fathoms. Numerous towns, belonging to eight or ten tribes, whose territory extends on both sides of the river, are on its banks. In three of the tribes we have mission-stations, in charge of native catechists. The language is similar and understood by each other. We were always kindly received. Krekre is only a short distance from the rapids, which extend a mile or two below the falls. The river is divided by islands, making three falls, the highest about twelve feet. Above this, for a couple of days' journey, the river is obstructed by rapids, and there are in all five falls, beyond which the river runs for a long distance in a north-easterly direction. The land becomes hilly; hills are seen in all directions. For ourselves, we left the river at Krekre, and proceeded to our mission-station at Bohlem, 3 miles from the river, where we passed the night. Bohlem is finely situated on a hill surrounded by hills. The weather was cool and pleasant. On Friday, the 12th July, the thermometer stood at 63° at 6 A.M. We had a good fire in the stove to make ourselves comfortable. Saturday, we started at 6 A.M., in a north-easterly direction. Walking was laborious over hills covered with a fine growth of timber, the roots of which impeded our progress. We passed many streams; the ground was rich, and the rice was standing in the farms 5 feet high. At night we reached the Diebo tribe, having travelled about 25 miles during the day. By this people, who occupy four towns, we were kindly received; very few of them had ever seen the face of a white man. We rested on Sunday the 14th, except to visit two towns for preaching. The Greybo language had here to be translated into that which the people spoke; it was similar to the Greybo, but not sufficiently alike for the people to hear well. We learned from our guide that there were twelve tribes beyond us, under the jurisdiction of one man who lived two days' journey from us.

We were obliged to return to Cape Palmas, being unable to proceed further; we met with no hindrances from the natives. One important fact, however, I learned from one of the natives with whom I conversed about the country towards the interior. It was this: that near the source of the Cavalha river another river flows from the hills, by which the natives receive English goods, cloths, salt, guns, &c., from vessels at its mouth. This river they call *Niga*. The natives in the interior make cotton cloths, some of which I saw. I have very little doubt but that one of the sources of the Niger will be found a few weeks' travel east of Cape Palmas, and that this is the river to which the native referred. Our journey home was speedily made, taking but one day on the river.

---

5. *Excursion from Queensland towards the Interior of Australia.* By E. B. Cornish, Esq.

### Communicated by F. Walker, Esq.

The following is the extract from the letter of my correspondent in Queensland, Australia, which I promised to send. It appears to me valuable, as showing how near the enterprise of the squatters in Queensland has approached to the line of march of Burke, Wills, and Grey, in their recent and fatal passage to the Gulf of Carpentaria.

" You are aware that I was going, when I last wrote, to look at some country William Landsborough had discovered to the westward. On the 24th June five of us started from Broadsound. As I was in haste, and as Landsborough did not wish more fuss than was necessary to be made (the district in which it is situated not being yet proclaimed), we parted on Peek Downs,—Landsborough and Kemmis made for Fort Cooper: Buchanan (who jointly with Landsborough discovered the country), I, and a black fellow started for the westward.

Never was there a party better equipped for a short exploring trip. We had 16 picked horses, 5 of them carrying packs. Our provisions consisted of 40 lbs. of prime dried beef, cured with sugar, 120 lbs. of flour, and tea and sugar in abundance. On the 1st July we camped on Phillip's Creek, near the Mount of that name, crossed the range at Shepherd's Awl, and steered by compass west by south; crossed the Belyando on the fourth day, and when 20 miles west of it saw Mount *Narrien,* which bore from us east by south, and we estimated its distance to be about 45 miles. About 20 miles further on we crossed the watershed of a large river (not laid down in the maps), which we supposed to be the Cape of Leichardt. From that river to the river which we named the Landsborough (*quære* the Thomson of Mitchell)—or rather to the good country which commences about 30 miles from it, a distance of 130 to 160 miles —we crossed no creeks of any consequence, and the chief part of the country produced nothing but desert-grass. We were generally lucky, however, in getting nice spots to camp on, and we kept our horses in good condition. I must say, with regard to this good country, that, notwithstanding the distance was 100 miles further from the Belyando than it was thought to be, it was quite up to what had been said of it. In fact, I never saw it equalled in Australia, take its position and distance from a shipping port out of consideration. The river runs south-west, has in places a great number of channels, and is evidently subject to very high floods. The position of this country at its centre we found to be E. long. 143° 40', S. lat. 22° 30'. On our return we travelled 50 miles on one of the main branches or tributaries of the river, the country of which was well watered and at places very fine; but after leaving this creek we did not cross a watercourse of any description for 90 miles, and the country was almost entirely covered with desert-grass until we approached the Cape. We were lucky, however, in getting water at times in puddles, and, although our horses were pulled down, we ourselves did not suffer. We reached Fort Cooper on our return in 35 days from our starting at Broadsound.

---

6. *Extracts from a Despatch from* Governor Sir H. Barkly *to the* Duke of Newcastle, *on* Burke's *Expedition.*

The mystery in which the fate of the Victorian Exploring Expedition was shrouded, when I lately alluded to it, was soon afterwards dispelled on the arrival of Mr. Brahe from the relief party under Mr. Howitt, with intelligence that King, the sole survivor, had been found living among the natives on Cooper's Creek: his companions Burke, Wills, and Grey, having perished from exhaustion on returning from the Gulf of Carpentaria, which it now appears they reached in safety in the month of February last.

How thoroughly indeed the gallant band accomplished their perilous mission will be seen from the journals and charts of their leaders, which are fortunately preserved to us, and serve incontestably to prove that, without detracting from the credit due to McDouall Stuart, whose route was unknown to them and far distant from that they followed, to Burke and Wills exclusively belongs the honour of first crossing the Australian continent from sea to sea.

The details of their discoveries and of their sufferings will be best learned from the simple and touching narrative which poor Wills left behind him, coupled with the statement of King, which has been taken down by Mr. Howitt. But I will continue, for your Grace's information, the brief sketch of the history of the expedition begun in my despatch of the 20th July, No. 64.

I then mentioned that Mr. Burke had quitted the depôt on Cooper's Creek on the 16th December last, with half his party, leaving the other half there under Mr. Brahe, whom he promoted to the rank of petty officer on the occasion, but with the expectation that the command would almost immediately be assumed by Mr. Wright, whom he had directed to join him as soon as possible with the stores left behind at the Darling. I described also how Mr. Brahe, after waiting beyond the time Mr. Burke had anticipated being absent, and hearing nothing either of his or Wright's party, abandoned the depôt on the afternoon of the 21st April, first burying such provisions as he could spare, after retaining enough to carry him to the Darling.

It now appears that on the evening of that very day, by a strange fatality which seems thenceforth to have prevailed to the end, Burke, Wills, and King (Grey having died four days before), reached the depôt in far too weak and exhausted a state to follow the retreating party with the slightest hope of overtaking them, though that night they slept only 14 miles off.

They found the food that had been left for them, and, after remaining some days to recruit, resolved, most unfortunately, instead of returning the way they had come, to try and reach the out-settlements of South Australia, not above 150 miles distant. Had they taken the route to Menindie, they would have almost immediately met Mr. Wright's advancing party. Depositing a letter, therefore, to this effect in a bottle, which they replaced in the "cache," but again, by fatal mischance, neglecting to alter the inscription which Mr. Brahe had left on an adjacent tree, or to leave any outward sign of their visit, they started on a south-west course. But misfortune pursued their steps; one of the two camels which survived got bogged inextricably, and the other became so weak that they thought it best to kill it for food: and, after wandering on till their limbs would carry them no further, they decided to return, at a point where, though they knew it not, scarce 50 miles remained to be accomplished, and just as Mount Hopeless would have appeared above the horizon had they continued their route for even another day.

Meanwhile Brahe, as described in my previous despatch, revisited the depôt in company with Wright, whom he had met some days after leaving it; but, perceiving no change, they, as a climax to this sad chapter of accidents, resumed their final journey to the Darling without opening the cache or discovering the letter which Burke had substituted for theirs in the bottle.

Thus left to perish in the wilderness, the hapless explorers determined, as a last resource, to seek succour from the aborigines, whom they had at first viewed with suspicion. This was freely and generously afforded so far as it was in their power to give it; but the season was now mid-winter, the clothes of the unfortunates were in rags, and the scanty diet of fish and "nardoo" (the spores of a species of marsilea, which the natives make into bread) was too innutritious to restore frames weakened by previous over-exertion and want of nourishment, and with minds depressed by disappointment and despair, both Burke and Wills gradually sank under their privations, dying about the end of June, whilst we in Melbourne were still ignorant of the abandonment of the depôt, as well as of the obstacles which so long delayed Mr. Wright's arrival at it.

So fell two as gallant spirits as ever sacrificed life for the extension of science or the cause of mankind! Both were in their prime; both resigned comfort and competency to embark in an enterprize by which they hoped to render their names glorious; both died without a murmur, evincing their loyalty and devotion to their country to the last.

How far the sufferings of these devoted men arose from preventible causes, and in what degree any person or persons are to blame for the disastrous termination of a scheme apparently so carefully devised, and which up to a certain point was eminently successful, are questions still to be determined, and regarding which I express no opinion, because a commission has been appointed by this Government to investigate the whole matter.

The liveliest sympathy was manifested by the entire community on receipt of the glorious though disastrous news ; both Houses of Parliament passing resolutions expressive of profound regret at the death of the explorers and of an earnest desire that every mark of respect should be shown to their memory. And it has since been settled, in pursuance of these resolutions, that Mr. Howitt shall be commissioned to send down their remains for a public funeral, and that a monument shall be erected to record an achievement of which Victoria may well feel proud.

Apart, indeed, from the interest which must ever attach to the melancholy fate of these brave men, the results obtained by the expedition are of the very highest importance, both to geographical science and to the progress of civilisation in Australia. The limits of the Stony Desert are proved to extend very little farther north than the point to which Sturt penetrated so many years ago, whilst the country beyond is even more adapted for settlement than that which McDouall Stuart has discovered to the westward of it. According to the summary which poor Burke himself deposited on his return to the depôt, " there is a practicable route to Carpentaria, chiefly along the 140th meridian of east longitude. There is some good country between Cooper's Creek and the Stony Desert, thence to the tropic all is dry and barren ; but between the Desert and the Gulf a considerable portion, though rangy (i. e. hilly) is well watered and richly grassed."

It has been remarked, too, by the transcriber of Wills's field-book, that " the expedition, except when actually crossing the Desert, never passed a day in which they did not traverse the banks of, or cross, a creek or other watercourse."

Such, in fact, is the impression made on the squatters by the accounts received, that the occupation of " Burke's Land " with stock is already seriously contemplated ; and there seems little reason to doubt that in the course of a few years the journey from Melbourne to Carpentaria will be performed with comparative facility by passing from station to station. To show the rapidity with which this sort of settlement proceeds in Australia, I may mention that much of the country between the Darling and Cooper's Creek, which the several parties from Victoria have traversed, is already taken up, so that not only sheep but cattle are now depastured within 25 miles of Mount Bulloo, not far from which Burke's expedition struck the creek in question, stretching thence easterly along the Queensland boundary in an almost unbroken chain. To the westward also the country towards the South Australian settlements is likely to be occupied ere long.

I hope to be able to enclose a tracing of the entire route of the Burke and Wills expedition ; but the Surveyor-General has, of course, experienced some difficulty in connecting the various rough charts and checking the calculations as to longitude, &c. A fuller description of some parts of the country may also be obtainable when King can be further examined ; and there can be little doubt that our knowledge of the portion bordering on the Gulf of Carpentaria will be much extended by the labours of the surveyors on board Her Majesty's corvette or colonial steamer *Victoria*, as well as by the party likewise despatched for the relief of Burke overland from Queensland.

It seems, indeed, not improbable that one or other of these parties, on discovering the record left by the explorers at the mouth of the Flinders River (not the " Albert," as they conjectured), and supposing them never to have got back to their depôt on Cooper's Creek, may pursue their tracks to the southward until themselves in danger ; and it has been deemed advisable, in order to guard against any casualty of this sort, as well as for the purpose of connecting Burke's tropical discoveries with the depôt by the best practicable route, to instruct Mr. Howitt to establish his headquarters for the summer there, making short excursions in every direction around, which, without exposing his men to serious risk, will be better for them than idleness or inactivity.

Some time may thus elapse before the full value and extent of these discoveries can be ascertained; but meanwhile it may be asserted, without fear of contradiction, that to the liberality and enterprise of one of her youngest colonial offshoots, backed by the heroic self-devotion of Burke and Wills, Great Britain owes the acquisition of millions of available acres, destined at no distant day to swell her imports and afford fresh markets for her manufactures.

---

### 7. On the Gold-Fields of Tuapeka, in New Zealand.
### By J. THOMPSON, Esq.

HEREWITH I have the pleasure of sending a photograph of the gully or valley in which so much gold has been found in this province. The gully is called "Gabriel's," after J. Gabriel Read, the discoverer. It is situated 35 miles west from Dunedin, and 30 north from the mouth of Clutha River, Otago Province. When I was there, a month ago, 6000 people were employed in digging. The photograph will require a lens to analyze the picture; as the naked eye will not discover all the figures represented. I also enclose a small map of the province, lithographed in my office, which will show you the Tuapeka gold-field. I have marked in yellow other spots where gold has been found, but which are not yet worked. I would have sent information to the Society before, but was desirous of seeing the rush over before spreading the news. Much misery is entailed by these blindfold rushes that take place in Australia. The advance of the gold-field will now, however, rest on its own merits, as the excitement has cooled down. The escort brings gold down to Dunedin once a fortnight, and on the last two occasions brought down 12,000 and 16,000 ounces respectively; the digging population being about 6000 to 8000. What I am desirous of laying before the Society is a sketch of the formations of the province, from which its eminent members will be able to anticipate the results of the discovery to this small but interesting colony of Scotchmen.

I may premise that Mr. Ligur, now Surveyor-General of Victoria, was the first to discover gold in this province; since which time it has been detected by various parties, myself included: but no field of enticing richness was found out till Gabriel Read published his discovery. I visited the field when it was first worked, and afterwards when it was in full operation.

The province, which I have traversed in all directions, has great sameness of formation, the mountains consisting of schists and clay-slates. Granites, amygdaloids, and porphyries are found at the Bluff and in the mountains due north from that harbour; I have seen them nowhere else. The seaboards and river-valleys consist of sedimentary formations; such as sand-beds, conglomerates of quartz, pebbles, limestones, coal (rather lignite), and clay-beds. Here and there very frequently basalt, trap, and metamorphic rocks protrude. often in hexagonal prisms. The quartz conglomerates are very abundant, and consist of rounded quartz, cemented by an iron cement; in places taking the appearance of burnt earth. The limestones appear very modern (geologically speaking); I have found recent shells, vertebræ of the *Moa*, bones of small birds, beak included, in this formation. The prevailing formation, however, is schistose, and is almost universally traversed by small veins of quartz, or else nodules of quartz; and the débris of this formation is found in the river-beds, consisting of rounded quartz or flakes of schist. The quartz veins are generally ferruginous. Quartz reefs have not yet been found to my knowledge, though I have seen blocks of pure quartz 20 feet cube in size. However, quartz pebbles are very abundant everywhere, especially on the sea-coast between the Bluff Harbour and the Watuara. Inland of this, hills actually covered with quartz pebbles are found.

The gold has been found in the gravel and shales of the valleys, 2 to 15 feet from the surface; but much dry digging is going on over the adjacent hills, which pays fair wages, that is, 10s. to 20s. per diem. The largest nugget that I have seen weighed 2 oz. 2 dwts. The gold is generally small and scaly. In the deep sinkings now going on (20 to 30 feet), quartz boulders are said to be arrived at, but I have not seen them. This summer will give the field a fair trial, as fully 20,000 diggers will be at work in all directions.

In this map you will observe that the interior lakes have been delineated : this summer they are to be actually surveyed. The scenery about them is very rugged and grand. I explored the northern lakes during 1858, along the base of the Southern Alps. Mount Cook, 13,000 feet in height, is a glorious giant. It would be difficult to ascend, being conical, and covered with snow in Midsummer down to 6000 feet elevation. The upper valley of the Waitaki, which I traversed *alone* to near the base of Mount Cook, was wild and sterile in the extreme. The waters of the Pukaki Lake are as white as milk. Mount Aspiring and Mount Stokes are also splendid features. The country which I then surveyed was unoccupied ; now every portion is taken up for pastoral purposes.

It will be noticed that a new province has been detached from Otago, and named Smithland. If Mr. Tucket were to come back he would be convinced that they can grow wheat without covering the shocks with tarpaulins. The old whalers told him this to prevent a settlement being formed near them, and led to his very unfavourable report in the Society's Journal.

More satisfactory information will, I hope, soon be given by Dr. Hector, a geologist engaged by the Otago Government to explore its resources.

# PROCEEDINGS

OF

# THE ROYAL GEOGRAPHICAL SOCIETY OF LONDON.

SESSION 1861-62.

*Seventh Meeting, Monday, February 24th, 1862.*

LORD ASHBURTON, PRESIDENT, in the Chair.

PRESENTATIONS.—*Rev. Robert Wheeler Bush ; Lord George Quin ; Major Charles S. Showers ; Capt. Edward Whitby ; George F. Chambers ; Samuel Day Goss, M.D. ; and Edward Lawrence, Esqrs., were presented upon their election.*

ELECTIONS.—*Lieutenant-Colonel R. Stuart Baynes ; Sir William Holmes ; Lieutenant-General W. T. Knollys ; Sir Charles Edward Trevelyan, K.C.B. ; Lieutenant Arthur Wing, R.N. ; A. Grooss Duff, M.D. ; Harry Emanuel ; James Alexander Guthrie ; Henry Wilkes Trotman ; Spencer St. John, H.M. Consul-General, Haiti ; Henry Bridgeman Simpson ; and Harrington Tuke, M.D., Esqrs., were elected Fellows.*

ACCESSIONS.—Among the Accessions to the Library and Map-rooms since the former meeting were—M'Cosh's ' Advice to Officers in India ;' Kennedy's ' Ethnological and Linguistic Essays ;' General Atlas by Visscher ; American Atlas, by Jeffreys ; Admiralty Charts, &c., &c., &c.

EXHIBITIONS. — Several Photographs of Mendoza, after the late earthquake, were exhibited by Mr. Hinchliff ; and diagrams illustrating Commander Bedford Pim's proposed Transit-Route across Central America were also laid on the table.

The Noble PRESIDENT wished, before the Papers were read, to refer to the deep regret he had felt at his inability, owing to indisposition, to attend the meetings of the Society during the present year, and more especially the first of those meetings. When he had taken leave of them at the close of the past year, he had expressed a hope that when they next reassembled they should do so in peace. At that time the only dark cloud that apparently loomed in their horizon lay upon America, but by the time the Society met again a deep and irreparable loss had befallen them. He believed there was not one of those then assembled who did not feel that the greatest patron of science had been lost to the country by the death of his Royal Highness the Prince Consort, and it was the duty of their President to give utterance to feelings which they all entertained. However, the time for doing so had now passed by, and he could only once more express his regret that he was unable to be present on that occasion.

The Papers read were—

1. *Report on the Brazilian Province of the Paraná.* By the Hon. H. P. VEREKER, H.B.M. Consul at Rio Grande do Sul.

THE Brazilian province of the Paraná is thinly peopled, and has been much neglected. It lies between the Atlantic and the province of Uruguay, and between the S. latitudes 22° and 28°. Its surface rises gradually, in well-wooded and well-watered districts, from the seaboard to the heights of the Serra do Mar and the hills of St. Paul. Thence to the westward lies a large diversified plain, containing the capital, Curityba, and other towns, the furthest of which is Guarapuava, at the extreme limits of civilization. Beyond are immense unexplored forests, reaching to the confines of the province on the Paraná and Uruguay. They are intersected by numerous rivers, which are, for the most part, little known, but will doubtless afford routes for future commerce. As yet there are no ports upon any of them. The only considerable harbour on the Atlantic is Paranagua, which has never been regularly surveyed. It is an immense sheet of water, apparently deep and navigable throughout.

A description is given in the paper of nine small colonies that are established in different parts of the country. One of the most interesting and the most fertile is that of South Theresa, founded in 1847 by the late Dr. Faivre, a Frenchman, and consisting in 1850 of 180 Brazilians and 20 French. In addition to these are many small settlements of Germans and others, and their number is on the increase.

---

2. *A Sketch of Nicaragua.* By GERALD RAOUL PERRY, Esq., H.B.M. Vice-Consul for that State.

NICARAGUA, one of the five sovereign states of Central America, is about half the area of Great Britain, but contains a population of only a quarter of a million, of whom nearly a half reside in towns. The country is mostly a dead level, covered with perennial forest, growing on a soil of apparently extreme fertility. Its climate has two marked seasons—the wet and the dry—of which the former is called the winter, on account of its chilliness, though the sun is at that time vertical. The whole territory is eminently volcanic, such hills as there are being either active or extinct volcanoes. The chief exports of Nicaragua are hides (about 50,000 annually) and various woods. One-half of its population are pure Indians, and the rest, excepting very few pure Spaniards, are of intermixed races.

Nearly the whole are Roman Catholics and speak Spanish. They are exceedingly illiterate; even the Chief Justice doubted whether or no London was a town in England. Nicaragua has been chiefly famous for its civil wars. Its Government—as those in the four neighbouring Central American republics—consists of a President, elected for four years, and a Senate, and a House of Representatives.

---

3. *Proposed Transit-Route across Central America, from a new Harbour in Nicaragua.* By COMMANDER BEDFORD PIM, R.N., F.R.G.S.

THE author was stationed in H.M.S. *Gorgon*, on the Atlantic seaboard of America, from 1859 to 1861, having surveyed the Pacific coasts of the same isthmus on a previous occasion. He argues from the history, the politics, and the geography of Central America, that no line of transit can promise greater advantages than one through Nicaragua. Hitherto, Greytown has been the only known harbour on its Atlantic coast. Greytown was the terminus of the Nicaraguan river and lake route, which formerly competed with the Panama transit; but at the present moment, as established by the author's survey, there are only 11 feet of water above its bar, and the entire harbour is rapidly silting up, so that in a few years it will be transformed into an enclosed lagoon, like that of Blewfields.

This difficulty of access to Nicaragua is cleared away by Commander Pim's discovery of an excellent bay immediately to the south of Monkey Point, previously unknown as a harbour, and even unnamed. He calls it "Gorgon Bay," and proposes it as the terminus of a railway, to abut on Lake Nicaragua, at San Miguelito, whence passengers would cross the lake by steamers (two of which, belonging to the old abandoned enterprise, are now lying there in good order), and would finally pass through a shallow canal, to be dug either to San Juan del Sur, or to Salinas Bay, across the neck of land, 12 miles broad, which separates the Lake Nicaragua from the Pacific.

As a commencement to this undertaking, Commander Pim has bought the entire shore of Gorgon Bay, and some small islands opposite, from the King of Mosquito, whom he describes as an intelligent Indian, of ancient descent, well-educated at Jamaica, and speaking English as his own language.

Commander Pim travelled by canoe up the river San Juan and across the lake of Nicaragua to Managua, to communicate with Sir C. Wyke, the British Plenipotentiary, and, both going and returning, he visited San Miguelito. He was unable to make more than a cursory survey of its harbour, owing to a fear of exciting suspicion among the natives, but he satisfied himself of its fitness for the lake terminus of his proposed route. A survey of the country between San Miguelito and Gorgon Bay, of which no description is given in this paper, might be made during the next dry season, and the necessary concession from the Nicaraguan Government for constructing a railroad could be obtained on the same occasion.

Commander Pim insists on the necessity of a route being established across Central America, which should be free from the predominant influence of the United States, and considers that a railway would be as advantageous to commerce as a canal.

The old Nicaraguan water-line, after conveying thousands across the isthmus, was abandoned, owing to political troubles, and consequent insecurity of life and property, during the sojourn of the filibuster Walker in the country, and also, as reported, to an arrangement with the Panama line, by which competition was to be withdrawn. The present state of Greytown Harbour has made it impossible to restore the old line of traffic at any future time, without enormous cost (see p. 112).

SIR R. I. MURCHISON said, that though he had no observations to offer with reference to the subject of the paper, he thought he ought not to sit on his Lordship's left hand without stating that he himself occupied the chair at the time when the news reached England that Commander Pim had, by his journey across the ice, been the means of enabling Sir Robert M'Clure to return to England. They should also recollect that it was Commander Pim who offered to traverse Siberia ; indeed he (Sir R. Murchison) himself was the individual who went to Earl Russell with a view of inducing his Lordship to support Commander Pim in that proposed expedition in search of Sir John Franklin. To the honour of Earl Russell it should be borne in mind that his Lordship, then First Lord of the Treasury, advanced 500*l*. in aid of the project, which failed on account of the difficulty pointed out by the Russian Government in supplying the wants of any expedition in those scantily peopled regions. Then Commander Pim distinguished himself in the Russian war, when he submitted a plan and volunteered his services for an attack upon Kronstadt ; and, lastly, he was engaged and severely wounded in China, where he was ultimately promoted to the rank of Commander. He was delighted to find that Commander Pim had exhibited the same zeal in dealing with the-subject of Central America that he had displayed on many previous occasions.

ADMIRAL SIR EDWARD BELCHER, after relating his experience of Nicaragua in 1837-9, observed that no reliable data had been given by Commander Pim in regard to the scheme propounded by him. His visits to the northern villages on Lake Managua, as well as that to Gorgon Bay, afforded nothing to guide the engineer ; while the mountains seen from the towns of Matiares and Managua, which cannot be seen from any part of the northern side of the lake to which his visit was confined, running apparently across his proposed line of railroad, had yet to be examined. In addition to these, the difficulties which well-tried men had found far from imaginary in the arduous prosecution of the Atrato and Honduras schemes, independently of fever and possibly volcanic difficulties, might destroy many valuable lives before even a road could be cleared. They had heard of the difficulties at Panama in finding men to work in that comparatively healthy climate ; and when they came to those regions where Nelson and Collingwood thought " no Christians should be sent," he feared the chances were much against success. It had been his (Sir E. Belcher's) lot to work very much in equatorial climates, but the fact which had made the strongest impression on his mind was the clearing of a site for a fort at Pasangan, on the island of Basilan, in a beautiful climate, near the equator, in the Eastern Archipelago. The forest was well cleared by fire, and the fort was built, yet malaria seized the troops, and the supply of water, which was originally abundant, suddenly failed. He was disposed to support every new and feasible improvement either in roads or railways, and most heartily did he wish success to all such projectors. But the loss of life, loss of capital, inadequate return for the outlay, and, lastly, the instability of any guarantees in those Central American countries, rendered him very suspicious as to the propriety of investment in such a scheme as that of Commander Pim's. First, there was the railroad—that line has to be made healthy; next the Lake crossing, with very doubtful security for landing; then a canal to the sea, to what could not be properly termed a *port*, for in 1838 no vessel could embark cargo there—this canal would have to be locked down to the sea from at least 80 feet above it; lastly, they came to a point not discussed by Commander Pim—the lake at times was deficient in water. Indeed, the Nicaragua route has failed from this cause. Will the State consent to drain it by a canal?

He felt some surprise that no effort had yet been made to cut a railway from Vera Cruz to the queen of ports, Acapulco, and to continue the packet-service thence to San Francisco and British Columbia. So soon as the troubles of Mexico ceased, and she began to make use of her former sources of wealth, might we not expect this idea to be realized? Money she has in abundance: cotton she may produce, and send eastward to compete with the Americans. Messrs. Barron and Forbes at Tepic introduced the Lowell girls from Boston, constructed mills, and produced cloths quite equal to British and paid 15 per cent. the first year! Looking to the millions of coined specie which are annually transported to San Blas, to be shipped to Panama or round Cape Horn, with her other immense resources, Mexico has the means, when treasure paid as it now does 15 per cent., to remunerate any undertaking of this nature.

Panama must still engross the trade of Valparaiso and of the ports nearest to it. But what has it done, even with its beautiful harbour, to develop the trading resources of the Pacific since 1337?

MR. GERSTENBERG said, that Commander Pim was in error in stating that all idea of gaining the Atlantic and Pacific Oceans by a canal had been abandoned. It is true the French had given up the scheme of the Nicaraguan Canal, owing to the insuperable difficulties presented by the rapids and the very high elevations. Humboldt's favourite plan of the Atrato route had also been abandoned, chiefly on account of the long and difficult river navigation it involved. But another route, also recommended by Humboldt, and repeatedly explored by various travellers, namely, that from Caledonia Bay to the Gulf of San Miguel, has been taken up afresh by some French gentlemen. Two expeditions had already been sent out, headed by the engineers Messrs. Bourdiol and De Champeville, and the geologist Mr. De Puydt. The second expedition was accompanied by the Abbé Amodru, who was well received by the Indians, a number of whom brought to him their children for baptism. The accounts of a practicable passage were so encouraging that a third expedition was in course of preparation, which, like the previous ones, was to enjoy the benefit of the protection of a French vessel of war. A gentleman actively interested in that grand enterprise had informed him that the leaders of this third expedition were to visit London on their way to the Gulf of San Miguel; and they would be most happy to submit to the Royal Geographical Society the results of their former explorations, and their plans for the future.

He was not himself disinclined to entertain favourably the Nicaraguan railway scheme of Commander Pim, if satisfactory information should be given him to show that it would be a good commercial speculation.    Commander Pim had not given him the requisite information on that point.    It would be a question whether the railway scheme would pay ; but before he said more upon that point he, as a commercial man, would tell Commander Pim that he was not correct in stating that the idea of a canal must be abandoned in favour of a railway because at present they required only quickness in conveying the traffic, and not cheapness.    The quickness in the conveying traffic was at present effected by the Panama line : they could travel nearly as quickly by that route as by the Nicaraguan line.    But the chief consideration at present was the cutting off of the immense sea voyage.    There were hundreds of thousands of tons of goods shipped from England to China and other parts of the world, and cutting off the sea voyage was the great desideratum.    At present no goods could be sent except those of considerable value, as the charges were so excessive that they would considerably exceed the value of the goods themselves.    Even articles of tolerable value, such as tobacco, which had occasionally been sent from Western America, had produced loss, in consequence of the cost of sending them by the Panama Railway.    It was now stated that if another line were to be made the cost would be reduced ; but they must not forget that the line of Panama was only 47 miles.    The Nicaraguan line would be considerably longer ; there would be great ascents, and the cost would be large.    It was doubtful, therefore, whether capitalists would undertake Commander Pim's scheme as a commercial speculation ; for they must not forget that, notwithstanding its high charge, the Panama line had only produced 15 per cent., which was not so high a percentage as was obtained from some of the French undertakings.    He was, however, of opinion that if capital could be found for the Nicaraguan line, it was likely to give such a stimulus as would tend to the development of the resources of the country, and that ultimately the greatly increased value of the land, and worth of its productions, would amply repay any expenditure which might have been incurred.    He quite thought that it was desirable that a transit route should be independent of any political influence—that it should be secured as a free transit for all the world.    Now it had been stated that the Panama Railway was the property of the Americans, but that was not correct ; British subjects had a direct interest in the railway.    The American Government paid a certain sum to the Granada Government, and the Granada Government owed money to England ; and they had apportioned part of that which they received from America in liquidation of the debt.    The Granada Government had not yet paid what they had undertaken to pay ; but it was said that their neglect was due to the supineness of England in this respect.    The Foreign Office had sent an expedition to Mexico, not to collect debts, but for something very similar ; and he thought that if it should suit the English Government, as on a recent occasion, not to show the white feather in matters relating to America, it might then be found very convenient, at some future occasion, to recollect that British bondholders had a lien upon the Panama Railway which entitled them to the protection of their Government.

COMMANDER PIM, in reply, said that there was little to add to that which he had already brought before the Society.    He was earnestly desirous that his country should reap the great commercial and political advantages which must result from the possession of an independent highway across Central America.    The proposed line would be about 130 miles in length ; the Panama Railway was stated to pay 12 per cent., he thought it paid more ; however, be that as it may, the promoters of his proposed line would have a valuable precedent to guide and cheer them.    He had not stated that the Nicaraguan Canal scheme was abandoned, he merely said it could not succeed, because the Atlantic Harbour had silted up so much that the cost of deepening it must be enormous.    Without a good harbour at each end, he thought every one would admit that no transit project was practicable.    As regards Greytown, seven years ago there were 24 feet on the bar, but now there were only 11 feet. As to Gorgon Bay, there was no impediment whatever to its navigation by day or night. He was astonished at the remarks which had fallen from Sir Edward Belcher. Some of the obstacles and dangers enumerated by him existed, in a great measure, only in that officer's imagination; and he, Commander Pim, was happy to inform the Society that he had himself overcome them without difficulty. He hoped to see vessels of the *Great Eastern* class, on either side of his proposed route, connecting England with Australia, New Zealand, Japan, and British Columbia. Such a project, he thought, would be befitting a nation like Great Britain; which ought clearly to possess a sure and rapid means of access to her distant colonies and possessions, independent of any political disturbance.

The meeting was then adjourned to March 10th.

---

*Eighth Meeting, Monday, March 10th,* 1862.

## LORD ASHBURTON, President, in the Chair.

ELECTIONS.—*Lieut. James Murray Grant; H. B. H. Birchill; Frederick Elliot Blackstone; John F. Laurie; William Leslie, M.P.; John Thomas Quin; James Rae; Joseph Rigby; Russell Morland Skinner; Henry Arthur Dillon Surridge; and William Wells, Esqrs., were elected Fellows.*

ACCESSIONS.—Among the Accessions to the Library and Maprooms since the former Meeting were—Rosser's 'Notes on the South Atlantic;' Map of Peru, showing the deposit of Nitrate of Soda; Sheets 6, 12, and 14 of Philip's Imperial Atlas, &c., &c.

EXHIBITIONS.—Maps, Plans, and Views, illustrating the Paper by M. Mouhot, were exhibited at the Meeting.

The PRESIDENT announced that a letter had been received from Mr. Consul Petherick, alluding to a serious affray in which he and his large party had been engaged, and referring for further particulars to a communication previously sent to Sir R. Murchison, which has not yet reached its destination. Mr. Petherick enclosed a copy of the following letter, which he had sent to Captain Speke :—

" Khartoum, 15th Nov., 1861.

" MY DEAR SPEKE,—I pray God this may be delivered safely to you by my agent, Abd el Majid, who with a strong party, consisting of some seventy men, well armed and equipped, will proceed in search of you the moment he arrives at Gondokoro.

" We—that is to say, my wife and self, accompanied by a medical man and photographer—after a tedious journey up the Nile and a vexatious delay of six weeks at Korosko, owing to a deficiency of camels necessary for crossing the desert of Aboo Hamad, arrived here a month ago.

" Had it not been for a serious illness from which I am now recovering, we should have left at the same time as Abd el Majid to attempt a meeting.

" The latter also has been detained by the unheard of rise of the Nile this season, and the consequent backwardness of the north winds and cool season.

" Abd el Majid's instructions are to proceed to meet you from Gondokoro viâ my establishment at Niambara, on the west bank of the Nile, some four to five days' journey in the interior, where he will reinforce himself with some thirty men, in addition to the forty he proceeds with from here; and, unless he meets you in the neighbourhood of Gondokoro, he is to continue due south in the direction of the Lake Nyanza, which, as he proceeds, he is to inquire for, until my wife and self come up with him.

"Should Abd el Majid effect a happy meeting with you, prior to my arrival, he is to place himself and men at your disposal, return and conduct you to the boats, and make them over to you for your disposal.

"The bearer has in charge some provisions, quinine—which latter I trust you will not require—and clothing for your immediate requirements; and hoping that all may go well, with my best wishes to Grant and yourself,

"Believe me, my dear Speke,

"Yours ever sincerely,

"JOHN PETHERICK.

"P.S. Papers and magazines for your amusement are sent with the bearer; but the letters and Proceedings of the Royal Geographical Society, according to you their gold medal, I prefer for greater safety conveying to you myself.

"God bless you both.

"J. P."

The PRESIDENT said the first paper that would be read would give an account, by a French gentleman, of Cambodia. Cambodia was not like Borneo or any other wild district, of whose past history we knew little, and which had comparatively little interest for us in the future: it was at the present moment the scene of a struggle between the French and the natives, and there was a prospect of a French empire being ultimately established in that country. Cambodia has been the scene of a remarkable civilisation. We have the relation of a Chinese envoy to Cambodia, at the end of the thirteenth century, who gives an account of the wonders of the capital, of which the ruins still exist;—great ruins of a city with five double gates, displaying not only masses of masonry with large carvings, but many monuments of interest. When the Portuguese arrived in that country, Cambodia was still a seat of empire. Unfortunately, towards the end of the last century, a disputed succession took place. Siam on the one hand, and the Annamites, who are the opponents of the French on the other, divided the country between them; and the whole land has been made desolate, the population has decreased, and in every way it has fallen below its former state of prosperity. In 1860 the French made demonstrations against Cambodia. In 1861 they took its capital Saigon; and there was every prospect of their extending their conquests and establishing themselves permanently in the land.

---

The Papers read were—

1. *Travels in Cambodia.* By M. MOUHOT.

M. MOUHOT traversed Cambodia from east to west, and also ascended the Mékon River to the frontier of Laos. He returned to the coast by crossing the waterparting between it and the basin of the Menam River, and descending to Bankok.

The Mékon is a vast melancholy-looking river, three miles broad, covered with islands, and flowing with the rapidity of a torrent: its shores are covered with aquatic birds, but its waters are almost deserted by canoes. A plain, covered with coarse herbage, separates it from the forest by which Cambodia is overspread, and which can rarely be traversed except by cutting a way. That forest is exceedingly unhealthy. M. Mouhot reached Brelum, a village in lat. 11° 58', long. 107° 12', inhabited by a secluded race of wild people, whose customs are minutely described, differing in features from the Cambodians and Laos tribes, and forming one of a series of similar groups widely distributed in the less accessible parts of Cochin-China, Cambodia, and Burmah. They are believed by M. Mouhot to be aborigines of the land. Two Catholic missionaries were resident at Brelum.

Subsequently the author visited the large Buddhist ruins of Ongior, of which he has brought back numerous sketches. He speaks of the mineral wealth of Cambodia; its iron, gold, lead, and copper. In the islands of Phu-Quoc or Koh-Tron, belonging to Cochin-China, and near to Kom-pot, there are rich mines of coal, similar to our cannel coal, from which ornaments are made. Several extinct volcanoes exist in Petchaburi, of heights not exceeding 2000 feet above the sea-level, and there are two active ones in an island called Ko-mun, lat. 12° 30', long. 101° 50', in the Gulf of Siam.

DR. HODGKIN stated that besides the two letters, portions of which had been read, and the drawings and charts, M. Mouhot had likewise sent an elaborate description of the ruins which he found at Ongior and in its vicinity. The plans on the table would give some idea of the magnitude of these ruins. A great part of the manuscript which accompanied them described their structure and workmanship. They were constructed chiefly of granite, and many of the stones were not only of very large size, but were elaborately carved. The workmanship of some of them was described as exquisite, and the designs were not so deficient in artistic taste as one might suppose. Many of them represented imaginary animals, such as serpents with many heads; others represented beasts of burden, horses, elephants, and bullocks. These temples were situated in a district which was now completely embedded in a forest very difficult of access, and were so much in ruins that trees were growing upon the roofs, and many of the galleries were in a state of great decay. The base and a large portion of the elevation were constructed of a ferruginous rock; but for the upper part blocks of granite were used, so exquisitely cut as to require no mortar to fill the interstices, and carved with relievos relating to mythological subjects, indicative of Bhuddism. M. Mouhot had copied some of the inscriptions, which, from their antiquity, the natives who accompanied him were unable to read. The characters so nearly resembled the Siamese, that Dr. H. had no doubt that a skilful archæologist would have very little difficulty in deciphering them. He believed that the remains in question would be found equal in value to those which had been recently explored in Central America; and he felt convinced that when the descriptions were published, M. Mouhot would be thought deserving of great respect.

MR. CRAWFURD said it was about forty years since he visited the country, but his recollection of it continued vivid to this day. Most people knew very little about Cambodia; its very name was only familiar to us in that of its product, gamboge, which word was nothing else than a corruption of Cambodia. It was one of five or six States lying between India and China, whose inhabitants had lived under a second or third rate civilisation, at all times—never equal, whether physically, morally, or intellectually, to the Chinese or even to the Hindoos. At the present time Cambodia was a poor little State, having been encroached upon by the Siamese to the north, and by the people of Annam, the inhabitants of Tonquin, and of Cochin-China to the south. M. Mouhot had given us an account of a country that no European had ever visited before. With respect to that gentleman's belief that certain wild tribes, whom he described, had descended from Thibet, he, Mr. Crawfurd, rather thought that his ethnology was at fault. For his part he believed these wild people to be no other than natives of the country, mere mountaineers, who had escaped from the bondage and hence from the civilisation of the plains. Such people existed in Hindostan, in Siam, in the Burmese empire, in Cochin-China, and in China itself: in fact, they were of no distinct origin, but simply the natives of the country in a rude, savage, uncivilised state.

With respect to the French, he did not know on what grounds they had gone to Cambodia. They had obtained possession of one spot which was eminently fitted for a settlement. The finest river in all India, so far as European shipping was concerned, was the river at Saigon, which he had himself ascended about fourteen miles, and found it navigable even for an old "seventy-four." He believed it was the intention of the French to attempt the conquest of the whole of Cochin-China. If they effected it and occupied it, they would find it a monstrous difficulty. It would prove another Algeria, with the additional disadvantage of being 15,000 miles off instead of 500, and within the torrid instead of the temperate zone. The climate was very hot; the country was covered with forests; the malaria and the heat rendered it unsuitable for the European constitution. If they made an advance upon the Cochin-Chinese capital, they would find the enterprise one of great difficulty. From Saigon to the northern confines of Cochin-China the distance is 1500 miles, and the capital itself could not be less than seven or eight hundred miles from Saigon, situated on a small river navigable only for large boats, with a narrow mouth and two considerable fortresses, one on each side, at its mouth. When they arrived they would find one of the largest and most regular fortifications in the East. He believed it was the most regular after Fort William in Bengal, and a great deal larger than Fort William. It was constructed by the French, and now they will have considerable difficulty in conquering their own work. The French had a perfect right to be in Cochin-China, and being there would not only do us no harm but even good, however questionable the benefit to themselves; for their presence amounted to the substitution of a friendly and civilized government for a rude and inhospitable one.

The drawings on the table were exceedingly curious and interesting. They were admirably done, and they exhibited representations of some remarkable monuments, evidently of Bhuddist origin. They reminded him very much, though inferior in quality and beauty, of the monuments of the island of Java.

He never heard of volcanoes when he was in Cambodia; but he had no doubt that M. Mouhot's information was correct, though it appeared he did not describe them from his own personal experience.

He would add a word upon the alphabets which were upon the table. The Cambodians had invented a written phonetic character, which they used at the present time; therefore there could be no difficulty in understanding a Cambodian manuscript. But there were several of those now exhibited which were of more or less antiquity. One of them seemed to be the alphabet which was used by the Cambodians in their religious rites. The figure of Bhudda showed that the Cambodians were worshippers of Bhudda.

2. *Route from Toangoo to the Shan States.*    By EDWARD O'REILY, Esq.

THE Commissioners of Pegu gave instructions to open a road of 70 miles, from Toangoo, in Burmah, to the fertile Shan states on the other side of the Poung Loung ranges, immediately adjacent to the eastward of them.    Mr. O'Reily was despatched on this mission. His party consisted of a few Burmese, and four elephants; and he travelled in short stages of two, three, or four miles, with occasional long halts, while the natives pioneered a road in front of him. The way lay across five ridges, of which the highest rose 7425 feet above the sea-level, and over a large amount of elevated and rugged land, inhabited by Karens, the aborigines of these regions; they are generally wild, though many of them are Christianized by Baptist missionaries.    The journey was successfully accomplished, and the road is now open.

Mr. CRAWFURD said he had letters from Colonel Phayre, the Lieutenant-Governor of Pegu, stating that these Karens were coming over to us in great numbers, and that upon one occasion he had gone out for the express purpose of receiving into British territory five thousand of them.    A great number of them were converted to Christianity, and he was happy to think that the good work was commenced by a personal friend of his own, the late Rev. Dr. Judson, an American Baptist minister, who accompanied him when he went on a mission to the Burmese capital thirty-five years ago. Colonel Phayre was about to send descriptions of the numerous tribes that inhabited the territory under his administration, accompanied by correct photographs.

---

3. *On the N.W. Coast of Borneo.*    By SPENCER ST. JOHN, F.R.G.S., late Consul-General for Borneo.

THE north-west provinces of Borneo contain the harbour of Sapangar, the best of any in the island, and also the mountain of Kina Balu, the highest of any in the Archipelago.    It is 13,700 feet above the sea-level, according to Sir E. Belcher's trigonometrical measurement, which recent ascents corroborate, though the barometers of those who made them, were broken before the actual top was reached.    There are no navigable rivers in the north-west of Borneo, neither are there roads leading over the hills, though it would be easy to make them.    The tribes who live in the interior are therefore beyond the present reach of commerce; so much so that those who reside on the Lake of Kina Balu are never visited by people from the coast.    The aborigines are essentially agriculturists, and raise rice, sweet potatoes, yams, maize, sugar-cane, tobacco, and cotton; but their mode of cultivation is confined to merely scratching the ground.    The tenure of land on the plains is

as well established as in much more civilized countries.   The manufactures of the people are trifling.   They consist of salt, made from
the ashes of a palm, and cloth, woven from native cotton.   The
natives have earned a good character for honesty.

MR. CRAWFURD said his friend Mr. St. John had been fifteen years in Borneo,
and no Englishman knew so much of it as he did, unless it were Sir James
Brooke.   It would be interesting to mention the striking influences produced
by the difference in the geological formation of the islands in the east.   Here
was Borneo, a country of primary formation, peopled by a hundred different
tribes, the majority of whom were savage like the Dyaks.   The only people
of the island who had attained any amount of civilisation were strangers to
the country, Malays and Chinese.   From one to two millions would be the
utmost population of this monster island, which was about eight times the size
of Ireland.   Compare it for a moment with a country of volcanic formation, the
island of Java.   Java contained, not one million, but twelve millions of people
in comfortable circumstances—a result greatly due to its geological formation,
which was nearly throughout volcanic, with many high mountains furnishing
perennial supplies of water.   There were two small islands a little further to
the east, which, together, were about one-eightieth part of the size of
Borneo ; and yet their population was almost as great, amounting to upwards
of a million.   We ought, therefore, to be careful in judging of the value
of a country by the mere size of it.   Yet he must say that Borneo possessed
a value which the other more fertile islands had not: it promised to be
a country productive in minerals.   He believed there were some 100,000
Chinese working the gold-mines of Borneo, just as they were working the
gold-mines of California and Australia.   It contained a great deal of mineral
wealth, gold and antimony—nearly all the antimony that was consumed in
this country in the manufacture of printers' type came from Borneo—and it
might be that it contained other metals besides.

The PRESIDENT regretted that the late hour of the evening rendered it necessary to bring the discussion to a close.

The meeting was then adjourned to March 24.

---

*Ninth Meeting, Monday, March 24th, 1862.*

### LORD ASHBURTON, PRESIDENT, in the Chair.

PRESENTATIONS.—*Lieutenant-General W. T. Knollys ; Herbert Davies,*
M.D. ; *John Thomas Quin ; Arthur Roberts ; and Russell Morland Skinner,*
*Esqrs., were presented upon their election.*

ELECTIONS.—*Lord Ebury ; Rear-Admiral Charles Eden,* C.B. ; *Mr.*
*Alderman Thomas Quested Finnis ; Lieutenant-Colonel W. W. H. Greathed,*
C.B. ; *Lieutenant Edmund Hope Verney,* R.N. ; *Colonel C. P. Beauchamp*
*Walker,* C.B. ; *John Bowie ; William Caward ; Archibald Hamilton ; F. J.*
*Sargood ; John Todd ; Francis Fox Tuckett ; and Edward Bean Underhill,*
*Esqrs., were elected Fellows.*

ACCESSIONS.—Among the accessions to the Library and Map-rooms
since the former Meeting were—'King's Campaigning in Kaffir-
land ;' 'Mercantile Navy List,' 1862 ; General Fraser's Map of

Ceylon, by Mr. Arrowsmith; Dolben's Map of the River Volta; Admiralty and Ordnance Maps, &c., &c.

EXHIBITIONS. — Several Views on the Yang-tse-kiang, by Dr. Barton; and numerous Chinese Sketches by Lieutenant Oliver, R.A., were exhibited.

The Papers read were—

1. *Notes on the Country to the West of Canton.* By LIEUTENANT OLIVER, R.A.

LIEUTENANT OLIVER joined a party who ascended the Canton River for 93 miles. His description of the journey is contained in a collection of private family letters, illustrated with numerous pen-and-ink etchings. Several of his larger drawings in outline were also exhibited to the Society. His short voyage is chiefly interesting in showing the respect with which foreigners are now treated in China, as compared with the comparatively recent insolence of the Canton mob. His furthest point was Shin-king, a town in whose immediate neighbourhood lie the Ten-foo mountains, famous in Chinese literature for their beauty. The travellers visited them, and were delighted with the varied foliage of the woods that clothed them, and with the ornate character of their general scenery.

They visited a Buddhist monastery and a large stalactite cave, and had interviews with different officials, and finally returned to Canton, after eight days' absence on a very agreeable expedition.

---

2. *On the Exploring Expedition to the Western Borders of China, and the Upper Waters of the Yang-tse-kiang.* By DR. A. BARTON, F.R.G.S.

AN account of this journey, written from China by Lieut.-Colonel Sarel, was read before the Society on November 11th, and will be found reported in abstract, at p. 2 of the present volume of the Proceedings. Since then, Dr. Barton and Captain Blakiston, members of the same joint expedition, have returned to England; and a second paper, by Dr. Barton, was submitted to the Society, accompanied by his own sketches, and by Captain Blakiston's elaborate survey of nine hundred miles of the river. It relates to a country that cannot be described as previously unknown, because the Jesuits had mapped it in the olden times before the persecution, and Catholic missionaries have continued to penetrate the country in native disguise; but nothing approaching to a scientific or even a satisfactory description of the upper waters of the Yang-tse-kiang existed previously to the present time.

Dr. Barton describes the deplorable condition of the towns of the lower portions of the river since the invasion of the rebels. Ching-kiang-foo formerly contained 600,000 inhabitants, and was one of the most flourishing cities; it is now mostly a heap of ruins, and contains but 2000 imperial soldiers. At Nankin there was even greater distress and misery, nine-tenths of that great city has become a mass of jungle and ruins. At Woo-hoo he walked through two miles of brick-bats, three feet deep, the remains of a once populous suburb; and people were seen on all sides starving, and others recently dead from want. The scenes he witnessed were too horrible to describe. After passing An-king, the highest point in possession of the rebels, the contrast was marked and cheering, the country on both banks was green, with young wheat; populous villages skirted the water's edge; the people were well fed, fat, and healthy; the old women were working at the loom, buffalo and oxen were at the plough, the labourer was everywhere seen in the fields; and farms and hamlets, surrounded with stacks of corn, dotted the undulating country. At the picturesque city of Yo-chow, situated on the great Sung-ting lake, the party, which thus far had availed themselves of the kind permission of Admiral Sir James Hope to accompany his naval expedition, were left on their own resources. They found the upper Yang-tse, where it entered the lake, to be considerably narrower than the river below; and they began their slow and ardous journey of from 12 to 20 miles per day, by means of sailing, tracking, poling from the bank, and sculling, according to circumstances, and making fast to the muddy walls of the shore at night. The natives were invariably civil and ready to barter; it was only from the soldiers that any trouble was experienced, though the whole population crowded and jostled to see the strangers. The river passes through a level country, with a tortuous course, between high mud walls, which are flooded during the inundations; and on either side of it rose embankments of great age and strength, maintained in good order by the Government, to confine inundations. They are about 100 yards in width at the base, and 30 at the top; the deposits, from successive floods, have raised the land on the river side to near their summits, while on the other side they rise 40 feet above the plain. The embankments cease above Kin-chow, where the country becomes undulating, and distant hills are seen against the western horizon: these are reached at Ichang, where the river issues from a deep and narrow gorge after a series of violent rapids. Here the boats of the lower river have to be changed for smaller ones, fitted to be dragged up the rapids; whose difficulties lie, not in hidden rocks

or shoal water, but simply in the violence of the contracted stream.
As the party entered the gorge, the contrast was great to what they
had witnessed during the past two months.   They had hitherto
ascended a wide and quiet stream passing through an open
country, and now it suddenly narrowed from 1000 to 250 yards,
and rushed impetuously through a gloomy narrow gorge between
perpendicular banks of 500 feet in height, with narrow chasms
on either hand, and cascades pouring down them.   The scenery
varied at every turn; sometimes the gorge was filled with mist,
and the water was like a boiling cauldron.   Lama hermits occupied
caverns high up, which were reached from the water by a chain
or a rope.   Occasionally there was a small hamlet with terraces of
cultivation, and temples were perched on the rocks, which were
worn in the strangest forms.   The tracking of the vessel up the
rapids is a most toilsome business, but managed with great dex-
terity, and accidents rarely happen.   The entire length of obstructed
navigation, during which the river passes through other gorges like
those of Ichang, is 78 geographical miles; then Quai-chow is reached,
and the country opens out, and the river becomes more easily navigable.   Here the poppy begins to be cultivated largely, and for
two hundred miles in succession the river-banks produced little else
than that drug and tobacco.   Dr. Barton never witnessed any bad
effects from its moderate use: it is extensively smoked by men,
women, and children.

Above Wan, and before arriving at a village called Ku-lin,
three Chinese visited the boat with great respect, saying they
were Christians and belonged to a large Christian community,
and rejoiced in the coming of holy men from the Western
Ocean; and that they hoped henceforth their religion would cease
to be persecuted, now Christian Englishmen travelled without
disguise.   On reaching the village, the banks were lined with the
people, and every hospitality was shown to the travellers.   The
church was a miserable building, containing the usual Romish
decorations: they were told there was formerly a larger church,
which the mandarins had pulled down.   Dr. Barton pays a high
tribute to the zeal and self-sacrifice of the Romish missionaries.

Chung-king was next reached, and is described as a vast city,
divided in two parts by the river, and built on sand-cliffs in a most
important position.   Here were many Christians, and Monseigneur
Desflèches, the Vicar-Apostolic of Eastern Sechuen resided in the
place.   They were indebted to his good offices in being warned
of an intended attack from the soldiers of the place, which they
were thus able to avoid by a little management.   At Su-chow,

where large quantities of coal are obtained, the immediate neighbourhood of a vast rebellion was reached. Numbers of headless bodies continually floated past them down the stream. It had been the original intention of the party to leave the river long previously and to travel by land, but it was represented as an impossibility that they should do so, owing to the disturbed state of the country. They therefore adhered to the river, hoping ultimately to be able to force a way. Their hopes were finally disappointed at Ping-shan, where the rebels had moved down to the river-banks, and whilst the explorers were anchored off the town, it was actually attacked by the insurgents. After running considerable risk, and further progress being impossible, as no natives would accompany them farther, they were obliged to return, and they accomplished their downward voyage in safety. Their dates in ascending the river were as follows: they left Wu-chow on March 16; reached Ichang on April 1; and Ping-shan on May 25th.

The PRESIDENT thought it would facilitate the discussion if he touched upon the points where more information was required. In the first place, as to whence the Taeping insurrection had arisen, and how it was that anarchy was extending so widely throughout the oldest existing Government in the world —whether it proceeded from national decay or from the weakness of the hands of Government; lastly, they would like to hear more about the Jesuit settlements in China. As geographers, they were particularly indebted to the Jesuits. All that they knew of Chinese history and of the interior of the country came from them. It was wonderful how much they had accomplished. He believed if the Jesuits and Jansenists had not quarrelled at Rome, China might have been almost, if not altogether, Christianised.

MR. CONSUL PARKES, on being called upon by the President, said it was a very great pleasure to him to find himself again in the rooms of the Geographical Society; and if it was in his power to contribute to their information for a few minutes, that would be an additional gratification. He was exceedingly glad to be in the position of a second to his friend Dr. Barton on this occasion, because he had the privilege of being a companion of his for part of the way in that voyage which he had described. It was with no ordinary feelings of emotion that he saw the little junk with the four men on board who undertook that voyage part company from the expedition under Admiral Hope at Hankow. He was sure they received a very hearty cheer from all those who saw them thus go forth; and he was exceedingly happy to meet his friend Dr. Barton in that place, and to welcome him back from the very interesting voyage he had made. He (Mr. Parkes) thought himself, whatever his opinion might be worth, that this exploration was one of the most interesting that had been heard of for some time. As Dr. Barton summed it up, they had navigated a river for 1800 miles, 900 miles of which were perfectly new, never having been traversed by any European before, unless by some Jesuit in disguise. In our quarter of the world a journey of 900 or 1800 miles is no great difficulty: but in China it is a very great novelty to have accomplished, especially on new ground; because our relations with China have hitherto been such that we were forbidden by our treaties to penetrate the interior of that country. Many Englishmen, especially those who had lived there some time and who were interested in the country by a knowledge of the language and other circumstances, have often wished for the opportunity of exploring this inner land; but they were not allowed to do so. The treaties forbade them to go more than 30 miles from the ports on the coast: they had five ports on the coast, and they were limited to 30 or 40 miles from those ports. That was the greatest distance to which an Englishman could legally attain. Therefore whenever a man did penetrate 100 miles or so into the interior, it was thought he had achieved a very great thing. Now those rules are changed, and here at once they saw their friends going 1800 miles on a stretch—starting on the extreme east on the one side, and not stopping till they got almost to the extreme west of the empire on the other side.

The object of that exploration, he believed, was to try to reach India. He did not know whether any of the gentlemen themselves felt any disappointment at not reaching India, but he thought they had achieved a greater service to commerce and to science by keeping to the river as far as Ping-shan instead of deviating to India: for they had been the means of making known to us nearly the whole length of the Yang-tse-Kiang as far as it could be made practically available. Through their exertions we have now a practical and intimate knowledge of the whole of that great river, so far as, either on account of the natural obstacles or on account of political difficulties, it is at present navigable. The importance of the Yang-tse-Kiang will be in the course of a few years far better known to Englishmen than it is now. It will be one of the greatest arteries of English commerce with China; and, although some of the names upon its banks were strange to us now, they might in a very few years become as familiar as the names of places in Europe. A change has come over the times, and now the Englishman and the foreigner can travel throughout the length and breadth of China without let or hindrance, except such as may arise from the disordered state of the country, and which it was hoped might in the end be mended.

As regards the Taepings, he must say Dr. Barton had not exaggerated the condition of the country when his party first commenced the ascent of the river. He described the states of Chin-Kiang, Nankin, and Woo-hoo, three cities which only ten years ago had enormous populations. These cities are now little more than ruinous heaps, and the same desolation extends also to the great provinces of which they are the chief *entrepôts*. The rebellion rose in 1849 in the out-of-the-way province of Kwangse. Kwangse is a wild and mountainous province, one of the rudest in the empire. There the rebellion, or disorder, or brigandage, or whatever they might choose to call it, festered and rankled for three or four years, until, having acquired a sufficient number of supporters to enable greater enterprises to be undertaken, the insurgents descended on the Hoo-nan plains, and were carried along by the Seang river to the Tung-ting lake and the Yang-tse-Kiang. Favoured by the broad and rapid current of that great river, they met with little to impede their progress until they arrived at Nankin, which, on account of old associations as the former capital of China, and being still at that time the next place in political importance to Pekin itself, they seized and fixed upon as their head-quarters. Although on their way to Nankin, or at various times since its capture, they overran the seven central provinces of China, they at present remain in only three of these, viz., Ngan-hwuy, Keangsoo, and Chehkeang, not occupying, however, the whole of the three, but probably about half of each, or say an area of 66,000 square miles; the population of which, before they were overrun, numbered, according to the usually received census, 49,000,000 souls. It would be very difficult to form an estimate of the population of those provinces now; but in Ngan-hwuy, which was formerly said to support 34,000,000, the rebels, according to their own statement, were now unable to obtain supplies sufficient for their own subsistence.

Dr. Barton said the rebels held 180 miles of the river. They did so at the time the expedition passed up, but now they are reduced to about 60 or

70 miles. Indeed it cannot be said that they hold the waters of the Yang-tse-Kiang at all. They do not possess any navy or flotilla, so that they cannot impede the navigation of the river by foreign vessels. As an earnest of what the commerce of that great river will eventually be, he might tell them that from the 1st of April to the 10th of December last year, during the eight months that the river had been open, 152 foreign vessels passed up from Shanghae to Hankow, some of them performing two trips; besides 170 junks in foreign employ. And the estimate for the trade which is expected to be done on that river alone in 1862 is 10,000,000*l*. They might hope great good would result to China from such a traffic. Anybody travelling over the districts now laid desolate would see that a warm stream of commerce poured through that main artery of the empire is just what is wanted to revive them, and that nothing would be more likely to check the rebellion than giving employment to starving multitudes.

The question may arise, " How is it that such hordes of rebels are heard of ?" It is not difficult to account for, when they considered the population of those provinces that have just been mentioned. In China, in most of the provinces—certainly in all those on the coast and on the main rivers—the population presses very severely upon production. There is a very dense population and the means taken by the Government to meet the wants of that population are notoriously insufficient. There is no Poor-law in China ; there is nothing that is worthy of the name of police. Now, if they imagined England—where they considered themselves pretty well-behaved—without a Poor-law and without police, they could easily understand that the Chartists, and men of that ilk, would stand a much better chance than they did now. It was not difficult, therefore, when any bold fellow or unscrupulous man had gathered around him some few hundreds, not to say a few thousands, of companions, to run the gauntlet through the finest provinces of the empire, and hold his own for a long time against the Government or any power they could bring to bear against him. On the other hand, while these rebels do nothing but destroy and plunder wherever they go, the Imperialists, or Government, do very little indeed to protect their own people. They have been accustomed to rule their country very much by moral suasion. They are fond of a paper executive : not only in the sense of having an army on paper, but by the issuing of pompous proclamations on large sheets of paper, daubed over with red ink, and commanding the people to " Respect this," " Tremble," " Honour," and " Obey," and all that sort of thing, which, so long as there is no trouble given, does very well. But the moment the Government receives a shock, these people cease to " tremble," " honour," and " obey," and begin to do that which is right in their own eyes. It was very discreditable to the Government that these rebels should have been able to hold their position so long in what the Chinese themselves call the very heart of the empire—to have pounced upon it in the first instance, and to have gained the footing they have. Unfortunately China, for the last few years, has been ruled by a petty clique of inert and inefficient mandarins ; the consequence is that at Pekin there has been a paralyzed state of affairs, which has spread through the provinces. Again, there was another thing to be remembered, and that is the absence of any national feeling among the Chinese, such as we understand by the term. A Chinaman in one province will care very little about what is going on in another province. There may be anarchy or rebellion elsewhere, and he will not stir a foot or trouble his head about it. And not only so with the common people, but with the authorities also. The authorities at Pekin when they hear of trouble in any provincial Government are too much accustomed to say, " That is the business of the particular Vice-Roy ; he must look to it. If he does not settle affairs, we will punish him. He has got into trouble, and must get out of it as well as he can." The consequence is that insurrections are very common in many parts of China. Dr. Barton has mentioned several that came under his own observation. He (Mr. Parkes) recollected a memorial to the Emperor nine years ago, naming eight or ten rebellions that were then going on in different parts of the country. In fact it was difficult to find out a province in which some disturbance or other was not heard of. It should be remarked, however, at the same time, that, notwithstanding this terrible prevalence of disorder, there is not a single province in the whole eighteen in which the functions of the Imperial Government are entirely suspended : so he could not quite agree with the conclusion of Dr. Barton, that there was no Imperial rule in China. There was Imperial rule all over China, but it was weak and imperfect, according to our notions. All this was intelligible when they considered what China was. It was ruled by a stationary despotism which had long put a stop to all progress, and for probably as much as 1200 years the political condition of the country had not advanced. No doubt its isolation from the rest of the world has had a great deal to do with that result ; and had it not been invaded at various times by the Tartar race,—and thus for a time obtained from those wild tribes a certain amount of vigour, although of a rude kind,—in all probability the Empire of China would have been broken up before now, and would no longer be the great whole it still is. There is no doubt that China at the present day is in a very similar condition to that which marked the end of the previous dynasty. The previous dynasty was a Chinese dynasty,—the Ming dynasty. Misrule, or weak government, had caused at that time the same or a greater spread of disorder than that which we now see. Some six or eight rebel armies were in the field, fighting against the Government or among themselves. At last one of their armies got up to Pekin, and the usual result followed—torpor was succeeded by despair, the Emperor killed himself, and his generals called to their aid the Manchoo Tartars, who quickly responded to the invitation, but when they had reconquered the country kept it for themselves. And so, at the present time, the Chinese are quite ripe for invasion. No doubt, a band of strong invaders would be able to establish themselves in the country, just as easily as the Manchoo Tartars did 219 years ago. But he did not see at present where that invasion was to come from, and he trusted we might never see it. China in the mean time has become differently situated with respect to other nations ; it has now entered into relations with the West. Two centuries ago it knew nothing of the Western people : a few Jesuits were settled in the country, but it had no political or commercial relations with Europe. It is to be hoped that the Chinese will now be disposed to learn something from the Western nations, notwithstanding their conceit and prejudice against foreigners. The vigour they want in their administration might be obtained by the aid of those foreigners, whom they have hitherto been accustomed to despise, and who are placed by the late treaty in a favourable position for giving information of the kind the Chinese require.

Many have found difficulty in understanding how it was the English have often had differences with China. One reason was that they have never, until lately, been able to get to the head-quarters of the Government of China. If they sustained a grievance or anything went wrong, they could seldom obtain redress, because the local authorities knew perfectly well that as complaints could not reach the supreme Government at Pekin, they might be neglected with impunity. The consequence was, that foreigners had to adopt the law of reprisals, and reprisals lead to serious collisions.

One thing in Dr. Barton's paper will have struck their attention. When travelling on the upper Yang-tse, he saw fields upon fields, miles in extent, of poppy-cultivation. Many have hitherto thought that England was poisoning China with opium, that China got all its opium from India, and that opium was the cause of one of the collisions referred to just now. This statement of Dr. Barton will, however, show that the Chinese knew perfectly well what opium was before the English took it to them, and that they have long grown opium themselves. At Hankow, one of the ports recently opened, native opium is so cheap that it will not pay to import foreign opium.  In fact, the English importation of opium into China is what the importation of French brandy is into England.  The Indian opium is of a superior quality to the Chinese opium, and is preferred by the Chinese, much in the same way that Englishmen prefer Cognac to brandy of home manufacture.  These facts served to dispel one popular fallacy, which was that the first time we went to war it was in order to make the Chinese smoke opium.  They smoked opium long before we had any commerce with China ; and, although it suited Commissioner Lin to represent the English in very black colours at the time, as being importers of opium, it is doubtful whether the Government acted in good faith in taking no steps to prevent the cultivation of opium in their own country.  It mattered little whether foreigners imported at that time 25,000 or 30,000 chests, when the Chinese had in the very heart of their own country hundreds of miles under poppy-cultivation.  Besides, we know the quantity of opium we import ; and that that quantity forms the supply of only about three millions of smokers,—a very small proportion, indeed, out of the whole population.  It might not, therefore, be too much to say, that for one Chinaman who smokes foreign opium, eight or nine will smoke opium of their own manufacture.

The Yang-tse-Kiang is a most important river.  A river which can be navigated to Hankow, 640 miles, by vessels drawing 20 feet of water, and having never less than 3½ fathoms as far as Ichang, 360 miles further on, is no mean river.  There is probably no other river in the world possessing such facilities for commerce.  Our doubts as to the difficulties of the navigation have been dispelled, because those vessels which run now between Shanghai and Hankow, do so with little difficulty, and do not experience that necessity for numerous pilots that was at one time feared would be required.  There is no doubt about it, that if vessels suited to river-navigation are sent out,—not heavy sea-going vessels, but vessels specially built for the purpose,—the river will admit of easy navigation.

As to whether the present Government gives some hope of a stronger rule, and of more security to life and property ; it may be said they do so, as far as good words go.  At the same time it is scarcely fair to judge of them, because their opportunity of improvement has been so limited.  They came into power on the 8th of last November only.  China is a slow-going country, and we must not expect to hear much of them for a few months to come.  But if good words, an earnest wish to listen and to be informed of the true state of affairs, and an inquiring mind, are some proofs of a will to work out reforms, then Prince Kung in his communications with our minister, Mr. Bruce, has shown that disposition.  One remarkable instance which denotes a change of feeling as bearing upon our affairs may be alluded to.  It is that when Prince Kung came into power the other day—by seizing upon his opponents, the other party in power, and putting them completely out of the way in the manner he did—one of the first charges brought against them for high treason to their own country was their treacherous behaviour on a certain occasion in 1861, when they seized foreign officers, and thus degraded China in the eyes of the whole world.  It is very extraordinary to hear such language from the lips of a Chinese minister, or to find mandarins willing to admit that China can be degraded in the eyes of the world, or to feel any scruples of conscience upon an act of that kind.

Dr. Barton has told a very touching incident that occurred to him, when, upon arriving at a distant part of his journey, he met with some native Christians who received and welcomed him as a brother Christian.  An occurrence of that kind, taking place in a remote quarter of the world, would speak most directly to our best and innermost feelings.  Too much cannot be said in favour of these Jesuit missionaries, who thus with their lives in their hands have continued to go to the innermost parts of that country, and maintain their churches in the way they have done.  At the same time, it should be remembered that the Roman Catholics have long been established in China, and that they had a splendid start there.  They first reached China in the sixteenth century, and actually established themselves at Canton, as early as 1581.  Then they gradually worked their way up to Pekin, where they were received into favour and employed at Court.  Probably in no part of the world did missionaries ever make converts of the same high class, or were they so aided by their converts, as in China.  They held their own and more than their own until the Tartar rebellion, when the country became in the distracted state, or worse than that, in which it is now.  At that time, some of the Romish missionaries sided with the Tartars and some sided with the Chinese.  They were to be found everywhere; there was not a province in which they were not located.  And when the Tartar dynasty established themselves they still continued to be employed, suffering persecutions occasionally; for one can never be certain what the Chinese will do—they are a capricious people, doing one thing one day and the contrary the next.  Still the Jesuits were employed on all sorts of services.  They were ready to undertake anything, from reforming the Imperial calendar to casting cannon, with that ready adaptiveness for which Jesuit priests are distinguished.  But in an unhappy moment they went a point too far; they split upon that rock, of which we have seen instances elsewhere, not stopping nicely short of that line where spiritual power ceases and temporal power begins: they undertook to determine what the Chinese should and should not do in respect of some of their political institutions.  To mention one among other instances, one party among them prevailed on the Pope to decree that the Chinese should not worship their ancestors: the severest test probably that they could have imposed, for all the religious feeling that a Chinese can be said to have, appears to centre in the great respect which he has for his ancestors.  Well, the Pope issued a Bull putting a stop to that and other ceremonies.  The Emperor met the Bull with a counter edict, because he thought it infringed upon his own authority, and the consequence was a decree of expulsion.  All the missionaries forfeited their position, and they were ordered to leave the country, and some of them were treated severely.  That occurred in 1723.  They have never recovered their position, and from that time to this they have had to conduct their religious services underhand.  It is astonishing with what fidelity their converts clung to them still; affording them safe concealment in recesses, cottages, and small out-of-the-way places, and how, mainly through the fidelity of these converts, the Church has been kept up to its present numbers of, I believe, 400,000 souls.  I think a late Propaganda return gives, as the Romish strength in China, fifteen bishops, seven or eight coadjutors, eighty foreign missionaries, ninety native priests, and about 400,000 converts; and the funds sent for the support of these men from the Propaganda are about 400,000 francs, or say 16,000l. a year.

That is a short outline of the proceedings of the Romish missionaries.  But we should not depreciate the endeavours that Protestant missionaries have also been making during a much shorter period and under greater disadvantages.  It is true that the Romish missionaries by much self-denial and sacrifice have continued to remain with their flocks in the interior of the country; and fresh recruits, as they are sent out from time to time, are passed on into the interior.  When our first missionaries came out, they were very few in number until the first treaty was made with China.  By that treaty it was rendered penal for any Englishman to travel further into the country than 30 or 40 miles from the ports.  It may be thought that zeal might have carried the missionaries beyond these bounds; but it would have been at the risk of being brought back again and handed over to the consuls for punishment: I believe there must have been many a struggle in the breast of a zealous missionary at that time, between what zeal prompted him to do and what the ordinance required him to abstain from. At the same time, though the missionaries remained at the ports, there had hitherto been work enough and more than enough for such numbers as had always gone out. But now that China has been thrown open to all Englishmen, whether merchant or missionary, it is probable they will penetrate into the interior as far as where they find their Romish brethren already established.

He ought to mention that he had only a day or two ago seen a letter from a gentleman belonging to the missionary body, and a Fellow of this society,—Dr. Lockhart,—from which he would read a short extract. It is interesting, not only as showing what a single missionary can do and is doing, but also as denoting an improvment in our position generally in China. Dr. Lockhart left England last summer and reached Pekin in October. He was allowed by Mr. Bruce to open a hospital there. He is a lay missionary. In respect of the matter of hospitals, Protestant missionaries have certainly done more than the Romish missionaries. At the ports they were in a legal position and could do their work in public and could open hospitals; whereas the Romish missionary, living in disguise in the country, could not open hospitals. The hospitals have certainly succeeded. It is a subject to which Missionary Societies should give their attention, and thus strengthen their labours in China in particular, by as many medical societies as they can afford to support. Practical as the Chinaman is, and this not being the age of miracles, we must work with human means. And there is no more tangible way of appealing to his understanding than by doing some bodily good to him; by showing him in the first instance that we are willing to take care of his body as well as of his soul. Dr. Lockhart writes under date 21st December, 1861, to this effect:—

"This is a fine sphere for work. You would be amused to see the broad street at my door. There is plenty of room, as the Imperial Canal runs along the street, and the road on my side is 40 feet wide. This space is filled with carriages and carts, and patients and their friends; and numerous itinerant cooks set up their kitchens all round, giving the place the look of a fair. And if by chance I go near the door, a cry is raised of "There is the Ta foo, Lo Ta foo" (i.e. the great doctor, the great doctor Lo).

"For five days this week I attended to 600 patients a day, and on one day to 800. To-day I have had 621 in all, 212 being women. Among them there were some most respectable people; one, the son of the President of the Board of Punishments, a very high officer; also a Mongol princess, who is blind, on whom I am going to perform an operation. She is a tall, handsome woman, very pleasing in manner. At first she came in a common cart with two women, all plainly dressed; but now she comes in her own carriage with attendants and out-riders, all in full dress. She is a princess by birth and also by marriage. Many of the women come in full dress, especially the Tartar women, who are a much finer race than the Chinese. Besides the crowd of patients, I have every day quite a levée of officials, their wives and children. I have never before had patients in China of the rank that come to me here. One lady, wife of the officer in charge of the Examination Hall, from whom I have removed a tumour, lives in my outer quadrangle, and will go home in a day or two, when she shall have recovered from the operation."

One feature that is particularly satisfactory is the circumstance of so many people of rank coming to Dr. Lockhart. There has been no want of attendants at the hospitals previously established at the different ports: but they have generally been the halt, the maimed, and the blind; people from hedges, ditches, and bye-ways, who are always very numerous in China. But, hitherto, it has been very seldom that people of the higher classes have so far laid aside their prejudices as to be ready to accept assistance from foreign physicians. We may now see in Pekin what is to be hoped will prove a return to the old state of things, a foreign physician attended by people of the highest as well as the lowest rank—a circumstance which gives promise that missionaries of all classes, not only medical and clerical, but Protestant as well as Romish, may soon be occupying the same position of respect and influence in China that their Jesuit brethren held before they were expelled.

The PRESIDENT introduced Captain Blakiston, another member of the Expedition.

CAPTAIN BLAKISTON, R.A., said, it had been thought by some that the Yang-tse-Kiang was probably navigable above Pingshan, as far as Batang, and that ultimately there might be communication between China and India. He considered that very unlikely indeed. He had heard of falls on the river some 100 li above Pingshan, which was to be expected, as the country is very mountainous. Between Batang and Sudya which is actually on the Brahmapootra, intervenes a distance of over 200 miles; and 200 miles of land transport is a great obstacle to commerce. With regard to the lower portion of the river, it can be navigated with vessels fit to sail round the Cape of Good Hope, as far as Ichang, about a thousand miles from Shanghai. But above that, the river narrows suddenly from half a mile to 250 yards. There it rushes through gorges in the mountains; and in those gorges there are rapids. The Expedition never found any want of water in these rapids, but they found the current exceedingly strong; so strong that no river steamer in China could get 12 miles above Ichang. Not until they employed steamers like those on the Upper Mississippi, with disconnected wheels, one capable of turning one way and the other the contrary way, would they see steamers go far above Ichang. The current of this contracted part of the river is from 5 to 6 knots an hour, and in many places it runs 10 and 12. Steamers might be pulled up with ropes, but there would be considerable labour in that. There would be no difficulty about coal; it would be found as far as Pingshan. It appears to be of much the same formation throughout. There is a sandstone, and every now and then limestone crops out with coal. At present, however, coal can be brought cheaper through the Tung-ting lake. The rivers which run into that lake supply Hankow.

The PRESIDENT desired to ask Captain Blakiston, as he had travelled over part of the route of the French missionary Huc, whether he found the particulars contained in his work correct?

CAPTAIN BLAKISTON replied it had always been supposed that the Abbé Huc's descriptions were imaginary. He found them to be quite the reverse. In every point of which he had an opportunity of judging, he found Huc perfectly correct, except with respect to the amount of populations, and everybody knows how difficult it is to estimate that. If you ask a Chinaman how many people there are in a city he will say, "some myriads." With regard to the geography of the river, he (Captain Blakiston) mapped it for about 900 miles above where they left the Admiral; and the position of the river has come out pretty much as it is placed in the ordinary maps of China, which are based on those which were drawn up by the Jesuit missionaries. He found very slight errors, indeed. With reference to the naval survey between Hankow and Yo-chow, a distance of 140 miles, the survey had been carried on by "dead reckoning." Commander Ward went to Yo-chow without having been able to obtain any astronomical observation. He (Capt. Blakiston) found that in 140 miles of survey by dead reckoning there were only two miles of error, and was glad to record it in proof of the accuracy of which naval surveying is capable in skilful hands.

The meeting was then adjourned to April 14th.

*Tenth Meeting, Monday, April 14th,* 1862.

## LORD ASHBURTON, PRESIDENT, in the Chair.

ELECTIONS.—*Commander E. John Pollard, R.N. ; Colonel C. Palmer Rigby ; Isaac Braithwaite ; Richard Cockerton ; James V. H. Irwin ; John Jones ; Charles P. Pauli ; and James T. White, Esqrs., were elected Fellows.*

ACCESSIONS.—Among the Accessions to the Library and Map-rooms since the former meeting were — Pugh's ' Queensland Almanack,' with Map ; Sheet No. 8 of Dufour's Atlas of Switzerland ; seventeen sheets of the Topographical Map of the Netherlands ; Maps of Savoy and Piedmont ; Canton of Glarus ; Pontine Marshes ; Gulf of Japan, by Malte-Brun ; Ordnance Maps ; Admiralty Charts, &c., &c.

EXHIBITIONS.—Views of the Fiji Islands, and specimens of their natural productions ; Panoramic View of the Kashmir Mountains ; and Ziegler's Geological Map of the World, were exhibited.

The Papers read were :—

1. *The Fiji Islands, their Commercial Resources, &c.*   By Mr. BENSUSAN.

---

2. *Remarks on the late Government Mission to the Fiji Islands.*   By BERTHOLD SEEMANN, Ph. Dr.

DR. SEEMANN was a member of the Commission sent under Colonel Smythe, R.A., to investigate circumstances connected with the proffered cession of the Fiji islands to the British Crown. The islands are now visited by traders from many nations ; and the object of their inhabitants in appealing to England, was to extricate themselves from political embarrassments which were becoming fastened upon them.

The report of the Commission was favourable to the bonâ fide nature of the proposal and also to the value of the islands as fertile, healthy, and convenient stopping places for the traffic to Australia by way of Panama. The question of the acceptance of their sovereignty was under the consideration of the British Government.

The Fiji group owe their origin to a volcanic upraising and to the growth of corals ; the islands are usually hilly, and present an unbroken mass of trees on their southern side, while their northern slopes are grassy and watered by streams descending from the central highlands, whose ridges condense the vapour of the trade-winds.

A great variety of vegetation is found in the islands : its predominant appearance is tropical. The mangrove-swamps are confined to the deltas of the rivers, and the islands are singularly exempt from malignant fever.

Their fertility may be estimated from the fact that, though partially and imperfectly cultivated, they support a population of 200,000, and supply provisions to foreign vessels and yield an immense export of cocoanut-oil, obtained by a wasteful process. Their fertility appears still more remarkable on considering the variety of their vegetable productions useful to man. Sugar, coffee, tamarinds, and tobacco are cultivated with success; so are four oil-yielding and five starch-yielding plants; four different spices; twelve edible roots; eleven potherbs; thirty-six edible fruits; and a vast number of medicinal, fibrous, scent-yielding, and ornamental plants, besides a long list of first-class timber-trees. It was the abundance of sandal-wood that first attracted Europeans to their shores.

They promise an excellent field for the best qualities of cotton; the undulating ground, the neighbourhood of the sea, and the absence of frost being cogent reasons in favour of its growth : the inhabitants are also beginning to work for wages. Experiments in raising cotton have already been tried with remarkable success, both by the author and by others.

Dr. Seemann bears witness to the laudable influence of the Wesleyan missionaries over the islanders, who recently were savage cannibals. He considers the religion which Christianity is beginning to supplant, as well worthy of philosophical study. Their belief is in a Supreme Deity, and in future rewards and punishments. They worship their ancestors. The chiefs are a taller, better developed, and in every respect a more able caste of men than the rest; it follows from this that mere height of stature in a stranger is an important claim upon the consideration of the islanders.

Mr. Bensusan's paper was chiefly an elaborate compilation from recent authorities on the Fiji group. While he acknowledges the extreme fertility of the islands and the skill of the natives in agriculture and rude mechanical arts, he doubts whether labour can be procured for extensive cotton-culture. He says the natives will positively not work; that they have no wants. The spontaneous supply of food far exceeds what they are in need of. They make their own scanty dresses, build their own houses, make their own canoes, their own mats to lie upon, their own pottery utensils for cooking, and are independent of the white man, though they fear him and respect his ingenuity. Printed cottons, hardware, groceries, and other articles, which are wholly unsaleable elsewhere, are shipped to Fiji. Many persons are already engaged in trade, and there is room for more.

After the Papers had been read,

The Rev. GEORGE PRITCHARD (formerly Her Majesty's Consul at Tahiti) said, having occasionally visited the Fiji group during the thirty-three years that he had spent on the islands in the Pacific, he could bear testimony to the truthfulness of the statements made in the papers which had just been read. The beauty of the scenery must be seen to be appreciated. Of the many descriptions by voyagers, he had seen none that in his opinion had done justice to those "gems" of the Pacific Ocean. They were remarkably fertile, and most of them possessed valuable seaports, which ships of any draught could enter without difficulty, and anchor in safety between the coral-reef and the shore.

With reference to the cession of the Fiji islands, he thought it most desirable, both on political and commercial grounds, that the proposition should be favourably entertained by the Government of this country. In a political point of view, it would be good policy on the part of Great Britain to possess themselves of the Fiji group, in order to arrest the extension of French influence in the Pacific, which, with the possession of Tahiti and New Caledonia already in their hands, would be attended with serious inconvenience to us in case of war with that power.

Commercially, the possession of these islands by Great Britain was exceedingly important. In view of the difficulty of obtaining cotton from the United States, it is very desirable that we should have independent sources of supply. If properly cultivated, the Fiji islands were capable of producing an immense quantity of excellent cotton, equal in quality to the best of that grown in the United States; and not only on the Fijian islands, but it could also be largely produced in the other groups of islands, where he had seen it growing luxuriantly, at all times. One remarkable circumstance connected with the growth of cotton in the Pacific was this : in the United States, he was informed, the cotton-seed was planted annually, and bore only one crop; on the South Sea islands the seed, when once planted, would continue to bear perpetually for from ten to fifteen years.

There was another important point connected with this subject, which deserved the consideration of shipowners. At present, ships carrying out cargoes to Australia had the greatest difficulty in obtaining return cargoes, and many of them, he was assured, came back in ballast. He had known ships himself to go 4000 miles in search of a cargo. Now, if cotton were grown on the Fiji islands, vessels returning by way of Cape Horn could easily call at these islands, load with cotton, and bring it home at a moderate freight. The islands possessed admirable harbours, in some of which ships of any burden could enter without difficulty, with plenty of room to beat in and out even in a contrary wind.

Then, the islands produced immense quantities of cocoa-nut oil, arrow-root, béche-de-la-mer, timber suitable for ship-building, and fancy woods for furniture; so that a valuable commerce could be carried on. He was delighted to see in the *Times* the other day an article, stating that during the last year our commerce with the South Sea islands was treble what it was in the preceding year. This showed how commerce was extending, and if our Government would accept the cession of the islands, he believed it would result in opening up a large and valuable commercial intercourse with this country.

The PRESIDENT wished to ask Dr. Seemann a few questions bearing upon the growth of cotton. In the first place, he should like to know what the tenure of land was in the islands, because if the land was altogether occupied by the natives, and we were to take possession of the islands, we should find ourselves very much in the same position that we found ourselves in New Zealand, where quarrels soon broke out. Therefore he would ask whether there were any unoccupied lands which our colonists could take possession of? Secondly, as we were told the natives would not labour, he should like to know whether there was a prospect of obtaining labour from the neighbouring islands, instead of sending for Coolies?

DR. SEEMANN said land in the Figi islands was owned by a class of gentry, who seemed to have a perfect right to dispose of their land with the consent of their chief. A great deal of land had been disposed of by these people at good prices, with which all parties appeared perfectly satisfied. Generally, after a bargain, they went to the British or American Consul and registered the sale. He did not think any disputes had arisen about the selling of the land. With respect to labour, he believed it could be procured without difficulty. The Fijians were agriculturists and cultivated a number of plants, taking great pains with them. Besides, the neighbouring islands would furnish labourers. It was found that the Polynesians would work better when removed from their native to other islands. The Fijian islands contained a great many Polynesians. There was a cocoa-nut establishment, employing sixty men or more, all active fellows. They were well paid, and were cheerful and contented. He did not think there would be any difficulty at all about the labour; in fact, he had gone into that question in his official report.

The PRESIDENT: Would you state what facilities there are for the cultivation of cotton?

DR. SEEMANN stated that cotton grew very rapidly indeed. There were six different kinds of cotton already naturalised in the islands, which had been brought there by traders. The cotton grew wild, and produced a very good crop. He had himself established a plantation which, after the first three months, began to yield. It was New Orleans cotton, quite equal to the best American cotton. It was certainly true, as the Rev. G. Pritchard stated, that the seed, when once planted, would produce crops for several years. The plant was never killed by frost.

MR. CRAWFURD said he differed very considerably from the two gentlemen who had addressed the meeting. He would first point out what might be called Oriental Negroland. It commenced in New Guinea or Papua, at the Equator exactly,—ran down very nearly to the tropic of Capricorn, and then ran up to the north-east, terminating at these very islands of Fiji. The people were here all negroes; but negroes of distinct races, differing in language, in person, and in intellectual qualities.

The negroes of Papua or New Guinea were a very powerful, stalwart race. Some of them he had seen, bore a considerable resemblance to African negroes, but they were a totally different race from them. The negroes of the Fiji islands were of the same general description, with many minor differences. Between these two principal branches of the negro race there were others of a very inferior class. He believed the Fijians, one and all, were, or had been, cannibals; such at least as had not been converted by those bold, intrepid, conscientious men, the missionaries, who had been doing a world of good among them, and had eradicated the practice in many places. In Captain Erskine's book, written some years ago, there was an account of thirteen captives who were brought in, and before the missionaries or their wives could interfere, ten out of the thirteen were roasted and eaten: the remaining three were spared through the intercession of the wives of the missionaries. He believed also, on the authority of Captain Erskine, that the immolation of parents still continued.

There were some curious differences between these people and the Polynesians, or brown-complexioned race of the islands of the Pacific. The Polynesian, for example, could never pronounce an English or any other European

Every word with them must end with a vowel; indeed, every syllable also : whereas the negroes, on the other hand, could pronounce English perfectly, for they had an abundance of consonants. The Polynesians, who were a fair race, had not above half-a-dozen, or at most eight or nine consonants.

Then there was another distinction which Captain Cook drew, and which was true still. The Polynesians, the fairer race, were all thieves—dexterous thieves ; the negroes were all honest, and Captain Erskine said that, notwithstanding their many vices, referring to cannibalism and the immolation of their parents, they were upon the whole a most energetic race, and he had higher hopes of them than of any other in the whole of the Pacific Ocean.

To come to the cotton question, he could not conceive anything more at fault than the statements of the previous speakers. These islands, if they could all produce cotton, would not yield a week's consumption for this kingdom. There was a very small proportion of the land of that country capable of growing cotton. The mountains were not; nor were the mountain sides ; nor was the sea-shore, as was shown by the vast quantity of cocoa-nuts produced there. Cocoa-nuts grew in the sand; cotton would not grow in the sand. The cocoa-nut grew best close to the sea-shore, and would not thrive at any great distance from it ; and the greater the quantity of cocoa-nut grown on these islands, the less the quantity of cotton that could be grown. The whole area of these islands was said to contain about 20,000 square miles. He could only make it 5500, and that would never suffice for an abundant supply of cotton even if the entire surface were cultivated with that plant. It might produce very fine cotton, equal to Sea Island cotton ; but as to producing 800 lbs. per acre, that is what no cotton ever did. He had paid considerable attention to South Carolina and Georgia cotton, which was what was called Sea Island cotton, as it must be grown near the sea-side ; and the average produce was 150 lbs. per acre, whereas the average of the inland cotton was nearer 300 lbs.

With respect to the cession to this country, he believed Her Majesty's Government had not the slightest intention to take the Fiji islands. He hoped they never would. The islands would be totally useless to us, and a burden ; indeed, we already had too many of this class of colonies.

Sir Edward Belcher said he really hoped with all his heart that the British Government would accept this cession. We required some port in those seas to enable our vessels to refit as well as enable us to watch our enemies in time of war. He was quite sure that the Americans would be too glad to take the islands if we rejected them. They were situated on the line leading to China. Any vessel wishing to make a rapid passage, if she fetched the Fijis, could complete her water and make a clean run outside the Phillippine islands to China.

With respect to cotton, he thought Mr. Crawfurd was greatly in error. He was inclined to take the part of the other two gentlemen. He had visited nearly all the islands in the South Seas, as well as the western intertropical coasts of America, and he found that cotton grew luxuriantly in every part. In the Sandwich islands Captain Charlton, our consul there, persuaded the natives to cultivate a very large portion of ground. The cotton was of the finest quality, and the Americans who had settled there declared it as fine as they had ever seen produced in America. But a change came over the mind of the American missionaries. Whether they were jealous of cotton being grown there or not, they persuaded the natives that it was impious to grow cotton, when the land produced them food enough without. They compelled the natives to root up every tree and destroyed the whole of the cotton in the Sandwich islands. That happened in 1825 or 1826. At Tahiti, about the same time, they found cotton also under cultivation in small patches in gardens : it produced very large pods and very fine staple. He had also travelled through the cotton-growing countries of America, particularly about New Orleans and Texas. He found there, although the temperature sometimes fell as low as 12°, that the staple was as fine as it was in any other part of America. He felt perfectly confident that, better than bringing home a cargo of timber, or coming home in ballast, it would be a very great advantage if our merchant vessels coming home from Australia could pick up a cargo of cotton.

There were many other articles grown in the Fiji, of interest to us, besides cotton. The islands abounded in fruit and in cocoa-nuts. Indeed, the natives planted cocoa-nuts because they had nothing else to plant for export. In seven years every cocoa-nut planted was valued at four shillings sterling; consequently, where they had only the cocoa-nut tree to plant and could allow nature to rear them up, it was not worth their while to cultivate the ground. But if we could make it an object with them to cultivate the land, he had no doubt they would produce good cotton, and, with care, equal to any that we got from America.

The islands also produced fancy woods and fair timber. With respect to timber, there were no good spars produced, after leaving Australia, until you reach the Fijis. None of the timber of the other islands for spars was worth a farthing, being very porous and not possessing the requisite density and elasticity; therefore, should a vessel lose her spars, the timber of the Fiji islands would be found very serviceable.

SIR RODERICK MURCHISON announced that Dr. Seemann was about to publish, at his own expense and risk, an account, not only of the expedition, but describing in detail and with illustrations all the plants of these remarkable islands. There were many varieties of genera and species of plants which had hitherto been wholly unknown to the botanists and naturalists of Europe. He therefore hoped there were many gentlemen present, who, with the noble Lord in the chair and himself, would support the laudable publication of the 'Flora Vitiensis' by Dr. Berthold Seemann.

---

*Eleventh Meeting, Monday, 28th April,* 1862.

MAJOR-GENERAL PORTLOCK, VICE-PRESIDENT, in the Chair.

PRESENTATIONS.—*Isaac Braithwaite and F. J. Sargood, Esqrs., were presented upon their election.*

ELECTIONS.—*Sir Daniel Cooper ; Captain R. J. Henry ; Lieut.-Colonel Sir John Stephen Robinson, Bart. ; the Rev. Thomas Scott ; George Arbuthnot ; Peter Bicker-Caarten ; Charles Brett ; G. Willoughby Hemans,* C.E. *; Henry T. Parker ; Berthold Seemann,* PH. DR. *; Henry Sprigg ; Henry Sterry ; George Tyler, and R. Dobie Wilson, Esqrs., were elected Fellows.*

ACCESSIONS.—Among the accessions to the Library and Map-rooms since the former meeting were—Vol. ii. of Messrs. Schlagintweit's 'India and High Asia,' with Atlas ; Part xiii. of the ' Imperial Dictionary of Universal Biography ;' Admiralty Chart of Shanghai and Environs ; four sheets of Carnbée's Atlas of Netherlands India ; Part ii. of Philip's Imperial Library Atlas, &c. &c.

The Papers read were :—

1. *The Surface Currents in the Bay of Bengal, during the South-west Monsoon.* By Lieutenant J. A. HEATHCOTE, I.N.

THE currents of the Bay of Bengal have not hitherto been accurately determined. Horsburgh gives a short general account, but his conclusions are based on analogy rather than on fact; and Lieutenant Fergusson's charts of the Indian and China seas are drawn on a small scale, and are inaccurate for the Bay of Bengal.

The materials from which the present paper has been compiled were mainly gathered from the log-books of a large number of the old East-India Company's traders, which have been carefully scrutinised by Lieutenant Heathcote. They have a value exceeding any that is obtainable in the present day, now that improved methods of astronomical determination make "dead reckoning" (or the calculation of a vessel's position from the simple data of her course and speed) of minor importance. Currents are estimated by comparing the true position of a ship, whether determined astronomically or by sight of land, with her expected position as calculated by dead reckoning: it is obvious that these comparisons are of value in those cases alone where both elements are given with scrupulous accuracy.

The author's investigations are limited, at present, to the currents of the South-west Monsoon; but that season is the one in which the greatest dangers present themselves, and a trustworthy knowledge of currents is of the most importance.

Copious extracts from the paper are given at p. 114, in "Additional Notices."

MR. CRAWFURD said the paper appeared to him to be a most able and judicious one, and the author deserved their most hearty thanks. The question was of prodigious importance in relation to our commerce in those seas. He believed the exports and imports to Bombay amounted to about ninety millions annually; the commerce of Calcutta was about the same; and the commerce of the Straits of Malacca amounted to from ten to twelve millions. In short, we had close upon two hundred millions sterling of British property passing up and down this gulf.

MR. GEORGE DUNCAN said he felt very ill qualified to address the meeting, but he was not quite prepared to agree with all the statements contained in the paper. He had made six consecutive voyages to Calcutta, and had traversed the Bay of Bengal, and, therefore, he had obtained some experience in the matter. In the south-west monsoon the currents varied very much. In the early part of the south-west monsoon there was a strong current passing up on the west side of the Bay of Bengal; but in the later part of the south-west monsoon there was a strong current setting in the opposite direction. The north-east monsoon, having blown for six months nearly, has blown the water below the level; and therefore during the latter part of the north-east monsoon he had been carried along the coast of Coromandel by a north-easterly current at least 60 or 70 miles a day; and during the first part of the south-westerly winds, he had beat down on the west side, in the month of August, and had been carried 50 miles with a current setting to the south-westward. So that to say that throughout the south-west monsoon a certain definite current prevailed in the Bay of Bengal would be a great mistake. After the rains had fallen in India, and the rivers had been swelled, a great quantity of water was thrown into the upper part of the Bay of Bengal. The surface of the water was pressed upon by the south-west monsoon, and not allowed to find its way readily to the southward again, it therefore formed a current along the shore. Ships leaving the river Hooghly in the latter part of July and the beginning of August regularly made it a point to keep close to the west shore, where they got, not only good smooth water, but a strong current setting southward. It was, therefore, a mistake to suppose that during the south-west monsoon a steady current set in in the direction indicated.

MR. R. SAUNDERS considered Lieut. Heathcote's paper to be framed more on imaginary views than on sound practical data. So well understood were the currents in the Bay of Bengal, that few shipwrecks happen on its shores; and when they had occurred, in his experience since 1829, he never remembered an instance in which fault was traceable to undefined currents.

DR. HODGKIN thought it would interest the meeting to be reminded, that it was the mutual action of large oceanic currents, in the Eastern Seas, that led the late Dr. Young to the explanation of the phenomena due to interferences of the undulations of light. He considered there was some reason to doubt an opinion of the gentlemen who had addressed them, that the large rivers flowing into the head of the Bay of Bengal exercised an important influence on its currents. In illustration of his objection, he would remark that a friend of his had an idea, many years ago, that it would be possible to propel vessels through the sea by forcing a stream of water from their sterns, on the same simple principle that rockets are propelled through the air. His friend tried the experiment; but found the method wholly unsuccessful, in consequence of an immediate diffusion of the expelled current of water through that in which the vessel floated. Now it appeared to him that a diffusion of the same nature would very likely take place, when a river poured its waters into the sea, and that no defined current of any considerable length was likely to be caused by it.

LIEUT. HEATHCOTE, in reply, doubted if his statement had been clearly understood either by Mr. Duncan or Mr. Saunders.

---

3. *Notes of a Visit to the Elburz Mountains and ascent of Demavend.*
By R. G. WATSON, Esq.

ON July 23rd, the party consisting of the Prussian minister at Teheran; Dr. Brugsehes, the secretary to the mission; Dr. Dolmaye, of the Teheran college; and three other gentlemen including the author, with six guides, started on this expedition. They left the neighbourhood of Teheran, and reached Abigarm, the last village on the way to the mountain, on the evening of the 26th, where they met Captain Nicholas and another French officer, who had recently attempted an ascent. M. Nicholas considered he had arrived within 300 or 400 feet of the crater. They encamped on the 24th in the valley of the Lar, where one of the party caught 199 trout after eight hours' fishing. On the 27th they pitched their tents at the termination of the regular path towards Demavend, at a place where herdsmen have piled stones in circles, and where water boiled at 189° when the air was at 60°. The valley through which they had passed was clothed with magnificent scarlet poppies and thistles, and other plants not so familiar to English eyes. A day was lost at the encampment in a vain endeavour to repair an injured barometer, and on the 29th the ascent began. The horses had to be left after an hour, when the first snow was reached; then came two hours of loose stones; then (apparently) one and a half hour of bare rock, too steep for the snow to lie on; and here, within twenty minutes of a cliff of rock, which shut out further view, they found many matches and pieces of paper, and a guide told them that it was the highest point to which M. Nicholas had ascended. On reaching the cliff of rock, the guides wished to make them believe they were close to the summit, and that it was impossible, at that early season of the year, to proceed higher: and they were nearly returning, as M. Nicholas did, under that belief. However, Dr. Dolmaye pushed forward across an incline of snow to the left, where he fell, but checked himself after a few yards of descent with the help of his alpenstock. Five of the party with five guides crossed the incline safely; the remaining gentleman could not proceed further, and was left with a guide. Then came a still steeper snow slope, up which they had to scramble, and for which ropes ought to have been provided, for there was one especially awkward corner which had to be turned, and there was no visible termination, through the mists below, to the steep incline of snow, over which they had to pass. An hour after, another mass of snow was crossed, then the clouds were surmounted and the lovely peak of Demavend stood clearly above in full sunshine, giving to the sulphur, with which it was covered, the appearance of pale gold. They pushed on quickly through the snow and sulphur, and reached the edge of the crater which forms the summit of the mountain. The crater appeared about 40 or 50 feet in diameter; it was thickly covered with snow, and of no great depth. The cold was so great, and the view so entirely obscured with clouds, that they contented themselves with a very short stay, and went to a cave 50 or 60 feet below the summit, where they tried to light a fire in order to take the temperature of boiling water, for they had no barometer. It was then half-past twelve o'clock. They had been seven and a half hours from their starting point, in reaching the summit of the mountain, and had walked for nearly three hours from the spot where M. Nicholas had been told that he was within 400 feet of the crater. The ground outside the little cavern was so hot from volcanic heat, that it was necessary to change seats every few minutes; and it was impossible not to expect that some day the mountain might pour forth its smothered flames.

The cave was filled with fumes of sulphur, and it took the party an hour and a half to make the water boil, though paper, matches, cotton, wood, charcoal, and spirits of wine were used in abundance. [The results are, as might be expected, discordant. The average of six observations was 177°.3 Fahr., and the interval between the extremes was 4°.5, representing more than 2000 feet of altitude; but if the *highest* observed temperature be taken, viz. 179°.8, as probably the only case in which the water was boiling satisfactorily, the results are nearly accordant with the triangulated measurements (see Anniversary Address, 1861, p. 194). The temperature of the external air was 41°, and assuming the sea-level temperature at 74°, and the sea-level barometer at 30·00, we obtain the altitude of 18,865 feet for the summit of Demavend, against the 18,550 of the Russian survey.—F. G.] The party returned with great speed, glissading down the snow, and reached their tents in two hours.

MR. MARSHALL said he was not acquainted immediately with the country of which this paper treated, but he had travelled in the neighbouring country of Daghestan, which formed the most eastern portion of the Caucasian range. At the foot of it lay the eastern part of Georgia, where some of the finest wine in the world was grown. There was no country where the people drank such quantities of it. He never saw such a drunken country in his life. It was quite impossible for any stranger to go there and hold his own among the people, unless he set to and drank hard like everybody else. The ladies assisted at these drinking bouts, though they did not drink themselves. Rising above the plain of Georgia were the Caucasus Mountains. They were well-wooded, ranging at what he would roughly estimate at 10,000 feet in height. Comparing them with Switzerland, which was perhaps the best-known mountainous country to Englishmen, instead of pines they were clothed with birch, beech, and such like forest-trees, which gave to the mountains a much more varied and picturesque appearance than the pines. They differ from the mountains of Switzerland in other respects, and especially in the rarity of glaciers, which was partly due to the formation of the mountains not admitting of hollow slopes for the snow to repose in. The inhabitants of the country were rude and uncivilised and still very savage in their habits. It was only some three or four years since that Schamyl — for this was his country—was taken prisoner. The men were not handsome, and the women were decidedly the reverse. As an instance of the way in which they conduct their quarrels, he stated that it was the custom when a man was murdered to erect over his grave a kind of flagstaff, where it remained until his murder had been avenged by his friends, and in almost every village grave-yard he saw poles of this kind standing. Before he reached the country he was told he should have the greatest difficulty in penetrating it, owing to the jealousy of Russian officials. So far from this being the case, he was bound to acknowledge that he should not have been able to travel in the country but for the escorts and horses provided by the Russians, from whom he experienced the greatest courtesy and civility.

GENERAL MONTEITH said Mount Ararat still held its position as the highest mountain in that part of Asia. It was close upon 19,000 feet high, and had a direct rise of 16,000 feet from the plain in which it stood, presenting a magnificent appearance from the unintercepted view which the spectator had of it. He attempted the ascent when he was there, but failed in consequence of coming upon some glaciers 50 or 60 feet high, and abounding in fissures which it was useless attempting to cross.

THE CHAIRMAN, in closing the sitting, said they must not judge of the value or interest of the paper on Demavend, by the comparative absence of remarks made upon it. It was only very recently that this chain of mountains had come under their special observation. They had records of it many years ago, but the close observation now bestowed upon it was only of recent origin.

*Twelfth Meeting, Monday, May 12th, 1862.*

SIR RODERICK I. MURCHISON, VICE-PRESIDENT, in the Chair.

PRESENTATIONS.—*The Rev. Edwin Prodgers; Capt. E. Wynne Roberts; Charles P. Pauli, and W. Levering Salting, Esqrs., were presented upon their election.*

ELECTIONS.—*Captain Francis John Bolton; Colonel John L. Peyton; Frederick Palgrave Barlee; Thomas Jacomb, Junr.; George Mackenzie, and Richard Pelham Warren, Esqrs., were elected Fellows.*

ACCESSIONS.—Among the accessions to the Library and Map-rooms since the former meeting were—Beardmore's 'Manual of Hydrology;' Stanford's Map of London; Ravenstein's Plan of Frankfurt; continuation of the Maps of the 'Dispatch' Atlas, &c., &c.

EXHIBITIONS.—A model of a stern-wheel Steamboat, adapted for the navigation of the Fraser River, was exhibited at the meeting by Mr. Kelly.

The Papers read were :—

1. *Description of the Ruins of Cassope.*   By Lieutenant-Colonel T. B. COLLINSON, R.E.

CASSOPE occupies the summit of a mountain which overlooks the whole of the Gulf of Arta: the extent of its ruins and its commanding position testify to its having formerly been an important stronghold of the ancient Epirote nation. The crest of the mountain was occupied by the Acropolis; 150 feet below it lies a plateau of 1000 × 200 yards, closely covered with the foundations of ancient buildings, crammed into the only space which the natural features of the mountain made available to the townsmen. Colonel Collinson compares the probable density of its former population with that of the modern Corfu. Corfu, within the walls, is one-third greater in extent, and contains 16,000 inhabitants; hence the population of the ancient Cassope may be estimated at 12,000. The ruins have been visited and minutely described by Colonel Leake and by Mr. Hughes: the intention of the present paper is to add some details, and to correct others. One of the most remarkable of Colonel Collinson's observations is the discovery of an unmistakeable specimen of a regular arch in these ancient buildings. It is the roof of an underground chamber or tomb, described by Colonel Leake, and named by him the " Vasilospito," or King's house. He had observed the roof, but ascribed its structure to horizontal courses of stone, whereas Colonel Collinson finds it to consist of regular voussoirs of three or four to the span. It is possibly the oldest specimen of the true arch extant in Europe. There are other instances among the ruins, of spurious arches; namely, horizontal lintels of stone, whose under sides have been hewed away. One of these is found in the gallery leading to the Vasilospito, and another forms an entrance through the city walls. The walls consist of polygonal stones that average 3 × 2 × 1½ feet in size, and are laid together without mortar. The theatres and other objects were minutely described by Colonel Collinson, who exhibited photographs of the ruins, taken at the time of his visit.

---

2. *Explorations in Vancouver Island.* By Commander RICHARD C. MAYNE, R.N., F.R.G.S.

ALBERNIE is a deep bay on the western coast of Vancouver Island, and lies in about the same latitude as Nanaimo and Namoose, on the eastern shore. No overland communication between them had been attempted previously to Captain Mayne's journey, which was set on foot in order to discover whether any overland route was possible.

Two prominent mountains, called Arrowsmith and Moriarty, stand on either side of the direct line of communication. It was satisfactorily ascertained during the journey that they were connected by a high snow-covered ridge, which made it out of the question to establish a road between them. The actual route followed by Captain Mayne, lay to the north of these mountains, and passed alongside a small lake; then it bent considerably to the south, in order to strike its eastern destination. There are no natural difficulties in this circuitous track, to interfere with the establishment of a road, if exception be made of the shores of the small lake, where further inspection appears advisable. The greater part of the way lies over level country well suited for settlement, and the highest pass need not exceed 700 feet.

---

3. *British Columbia.* By WILLIAM KELLY, Esq., F.R.G.S.

THE object of Mr. Kelly was to invite attention to the disadvantages under which British Columbia labours, owing to the expense and delay of communicating with the mother country. He described its climate and productions as closely corresponding to those of England, and eminently suited to British emigrants, who, however, as a class, were debarred from going there by the long voyage round Cape Horn, or by the shorter, though costly, route across Panama.

He also described its varied mineral products; and gave data, from which he estimated the yield of gold, since its first discovery in 1858, or during the last two and a half years, at 1,200,000*l*. He then showed that the direct line from Canada, mostly through British territory and through the Vermilion Pass, was of such a nature that, by using existing railroads and establishing an overland mail of the same character as those established elsewhere in America, twenty-five days would suffice for communicating between Portland on the Atlantic and New Westminster on the Pacific. The author looked forward to the time when a chain of settlements should connect Canada with the Rocky Mountains; through which emigrants with their cattle and family waggons could travel leisurely and securely, where wants could be recruited and accidents repaired, while a still poorer class of men might work their way, step by step, to their goal.

The CHAIRMAN said the subject of British Columbia had been brought before them on previous occasions by their medallist Palliser, and more particularly by Dr. Hector, who had especially pointed out the desirability of opening a passenger route over the Vermilion Pass. The subject was indeed worthy of the consideration of the Society. With regard to the development of gold, it seemed to him that this country was about to open out to us a complete new California, and that the very same ridge which had been found to be auriferous all through the chain of the Andes—not the Rocky mountains, but a chain considerably to the westward of it—had been found to be auriferous all the way northward, extending through British Columbia, and probably extending to Russian North America. Captain Mayne, in addition to his exploration of Vancouver Island, had also penetrated into the interior of British Columbia; and he would, therefore, call upon him to communicate what he had seen of the wealth and productions of this vast region.

CAPTAIN MAYNE said, as the road from the eastward across the Rocky Mountains had been referred to, he would make a few observations upon that topic. That route was by no means so practicable as people thought, and those companies who talked about driving four-horse spring waggons from the Lake of the Woods to British Columbia, would either starve the people they took or leave them in the Rocky Mountains, for they would certainly never get them over them. Dr. Hector, Palliser, or Blakiston, who had explored the country, would tell them they had the greatest difficulty in getting their horses through the passes. They had to stop and cut through fallen timber, and it took them many days, going about a mile an hour. Although ultimately this road might be made, yet at present we were much too sanguine about it; and emigrants who thought of going by that route would feel most grievously disappointed, that is, if they lived to be disappointed, which he rather doubted. The better-known way by Victoria had been frequently described. The emigrants could either go from New York by steamer to Panama, or by our own steamers from St. Thomas to Panama, then up by the American steamer to San Francisco, and thence on to Victoria. New York was the best point to start from, because they avoided being kept waiting at Panama, a circumstance which frequently occurred, by taking our West India mail-steamer. Having reached Victoria, the first start was to New Westminster by steamer. From New Westminster, to go to Cariboo, they went up the Fraser River and Harrison Lake to Fort Douglas, where they left the steamer. They then traversed a road, which waggons could be driven along with the greatest ease, constructed last year by the Royal Engineers. He had himself walked 30 miles easily in the day, which showed that the road was pretty good. Then they crossed the Lillooet Lake, a distance of 15 miles to Pemberton. Here they came upon another trail for 25 miles up to Anderson Lake, which is 14 miles long. There were two lakes, Anderson and Seton, both of which are 14 miles long, separated from each other by a narrow neck of land of about a mile or a mile and a half. That brought them to Kayouth. This place Kayouth could also be reached by the Fraser River. Instead of going up to Fort Douglas, they could go to Fort Hope by the steamer, and possibly if the stream was not very rapid they could get to Yale. At Yale the rapids commenced, where the river rushed between immense perpendicular rocks so rapidly that no steamer could possibly get through them. Sometimes the current came down at 17 or 18 knots. He timed it at 16 knots, but the water was not then at its highest. From Yale to Lytton he found the trail excessively dangerous. At some parts he went round the face of the rocks on poles hung from the tops of the cliffs with deers' hide, and he hung over the cliff at an altitude of 300 feet perpendicular above the river below, and the only means of proceeding with safety was by pressing close against the face of the rock. That danger had since been avoided by the trail being cut at the back of the rock. They then crossed the river, and the trail was very good for some way farther. But on the whole that was not so easy a route as by Harrison Lake, on which all the work was done by horses and mules. From Kayouth they could either cross the river at once, or cross higher up and then keep the east bank to Fountain and Pavillon. From Pavillon there were two trails. One led up by the Fraser, passable only to foot passengers, to Alexandria, and then up to Fort St. George; and as the Hudson's Bay Company had constant communication with Fort James, Fort George and M'Leod's Fort, no doubt the trail led up to them. The road by which the diggings were reached went east along the Pavillon Lake, till it met the Chapeau and Bonaparte and Bentinck River. It crossed them and went to the northward up the valley of the Bonaparte River, past several small lakes and rivers, to the Quesnelle Lake, and that brought you at once to the Cariboo country. Very rich diggings were worked the year before last on the Quesnelle Lake; but the diggings in Cariboo were found to be so much richer, that all the miners left for Cariboo, and rushed up to Swift River and the little streams in the neighbourhood.

With respect to the richness of the Cariboo diggings, he had no doubt the account of Mr. Fraser, the *Times* correspondent, was perfectly correct. Mr. Nind, the gold commissioner in that country, who was at present in England, told him the other day that he saw three men take up the sluices, which are the trays at the bottom of the troughs in which the gold is washed, after one day's work, and take out 195 ounces of gold—all but five dollars. It would give some idea of the size of the lumps of gold to hear that there was no quicksilver used at Cariboo, the fine gold being allowed to pass away. On one occasion some men realised 9000 dollars of gold as the result of three months' labour. They said they were getting 25 dollars a-day. Other men reported having got 73 ounces in a day, and that food and everything there were comparatively cheap. During the first winter the great difficulty was to get food. Two months before his arrival at Pavillon they were paying 75 cents per lb. for flour. That was before this route by Harrison Lake was opened.

It was a great question now in the colony whether some route would not be found to Cariboo easier than by going up the whole length of the Fraser River, which was very rapid even as far as it was navigable. It was thought by many that some route would be found from one of the inlets which indent the whole coast, which would afford a much shorter and easier way. With this object nearly all the inlets had been examined. The one which was at present engrossing the attention of the colony was the route from Bellhoula or Bell-whoala, at the head of the Bentinck arm. This was the route by which Sir Alexander Mackenzie crossed in 1789. He went up the West Road River, then came down on the Bentinck arm at Bellhoula, to which he gave the name of Rascal's village. Last year Mr. Mackenzie, one of the Hudson's Bay officers, and Mr. Barnston, crossed from Alexandria to Bentinck arm in almost a direct line. They took eleven days to cross, and Mr. Barnston, in a letter to Mr. Nind, stated that the trail for the whole distance from Alexandria to the coast range was on a kind of table-land, which was studded in every direction with immense meadows. He said he thought the journey might be performed easily in ten days. Another route had been tried by Mr. Macdonald, coming down the Stuart River to Fort George, which promised some day to be the route to Cariboo, leaving out the Fraser altogether.

Dr. RAE knew nothing of the country west of the Rocky Mountains; but with regard to the eastern country from Lake Winnipeg and Lake Superior to the Rocky Mountains, he had been over that part only so late as last year. As to the facilities of travelling over it, he could not agree with the author of the paper. Some years hence there might be roads and facilities similar to what Mr. Kelly contemplated; but at the present time they certainly did not exist. He would describe his own experience last year with a hunting party. They took four days from Toronto to St. Paul; from that to Red River occupied nine days. From Red River up west to the south Saskatchewan, travelling very hard, having excellent horses and two horses to each man, it took them from sixteen to eighteen days. They were then eight or ten days from the Rocky Mountains. They travelled at least double the rate that any party going with one horse could travel. Therefore he came to the conclusion that it would at least take ten weeks to reach the Rocky Mountains from England, in the present state of the country. Regarding the game in that country, the young gentlemen of the party were anxious to kill any and all kinds of game. They travelled over several hundred miles before they could kill an animal larger than a badger. They had the ablest hunters in the country, all picked men, the Red River half-breds, and their object was entirely to kill game. Yet that was the result of their hunting. They should have starved had they not carried plenty of provisions with them. Had they been a large party, such as that contemplating to go out there, they could not possibly have got provisions at the Hudson's Bay Company establishments. The buffalo are so peculiar in their migrations, that they travelled for hundreds of miles over one of the finest old buffalo prairies in that part of the world and did not see a single animal. The Indians were starving, could not get anything to eat, and were obliged to eat the skins. They travelled over a better route for game than emigrants would take. Going up to the Red River settlement, which is easily arrived at from Canada in twelve or fifteen days by steamer, the usual time from the settlement to the Rocky Mountains was from forty-five to fifty days with carts. One gentleman came from Edmonton, which was six or eight days from the Rocky Mountains, in nineteen days last year; but he had three relays of horses, with three horses to each man, and he travelled day and night. Therefore he agreed with Captain Mayne that it would be very dangerous indeed for any large body of men to attempt to reach the Fraser River by that route. He thought it would be attended with a sacrifice of life. In Canada last year the idea of opening up this route had excited a good deal of attention, and numerous letters had appeared on the subject. The advantage of going round by Victoria is that they can start at any season of the year. They can go in a vessel nearly the whole way, and they can take baggage and all that they want to the diggings. If they went by the Rocky Mountains and got to the diggings, they would have to obtain the articles that they wanted there, instead of taking them round in a vessel with them and going up the Fraser River. In saying this, he was only speaking of what he would do himself. Whether as a rich man or as a poor man, he would not in the present state of the country recommend a single individual to try the overland route.

After some remarks from the REV. J. GARRETT, urging the immediate value of Columbia as a field for British emigration and the practicability of an overland route to that colony, and on the value of Indian labour,

CAPTAIN MAYNE replied that Mr. Garrett entirely mistook both himself and Dr. Rae in supposing they were of opinion that the route across the Rocky Mountains would never be made. All that they said was that the parties who were advertising to send "four-horse spring waggons" by the Rocky Mountain route would starve the people whom they took. Mr. Garrett, in dealing with the question of emigration, had left out of consideration the expense of living after people reached the colony. It was an exceedingly expensive colony, and it would not do for the Government or for societies to send people, especially women, to British Columbia and drop them there. If they were now sent by sea round Cape Horn, they would land at Victoria in the middle of winter, and it would be impossible for them to get to the diggings till the spring; therefore, they would have to wait four or five months at Victoria doing nothing, and where they could not get a dinner under a dollar. The question of Indian labour was too large a question to be entered into. If anybody wanted to know anything about their character, he could not do better than look to the printed journals of Mr. Duncan, who was by far the most experienced missionary in that country. With respect to the country of the Sasketchewan River, Mr. Hind did not give a flourishing account of it as suitable for a roadway. Captain Palliser says of it in the Blue Book, that "it is too tedious, difficult, and expensive for the generality of settlers." A great deal of it would have to be piled, before anything like a good road could be made. This was another reason why emigrants should not be sent that way at present. Mr. Garrett was mistaken in thinking the Indians would ever work as miners. They got the coal at the pit's mouth and carried it down in little baskets to their canoes, that was all; and he knew the manager he referred to would never think of sending them into the pit to work out the coal, and their doing anything could never be depended on. Mr. Pemberton's evidence respecting the interior, he would receive with great caution, because it was well-known he had never travelled in the interior. He once went to Yale, sixty miles up the river, and he once made a short journey across the island ; but as to the interior of the country, Mr. Pemberton knew it merely from hearsay or the same reports to which they all had access.

The CHAIRMAN, before adjourning the sitting, introduced M. Jules Gérard. the well-known "lion-slayer" of Algeria, and announced that on a future occasion that gentleman would bring under notice a project of his own for the formation of a Society (*Société Africaine*) connected with discoveries in the interior of Africa, and in furtherance of the objects of the Acclimatization Society of Paris.

The meeting was then adjourned to the Anniversary on the 26th of May.

# ADDITIONAL NOTICES.

### (Printed by order of Council.)

1. *Extract from a Paper* by Commander BEDFORD PIM, R.N., *on a New Transit-Route through Central America.*[*]

THE immediate coast-line extending from Cape Gracias à Dios to Navy Bay, Aspinwall, or Colon (by each of which names the Atlantic terminus of the Panama railway is known) is for the most part low and uninteresting, although in some places, even in Mosquito, a spur of the great central chain of mountains reaches quite to the sea-shore, and diversifies the otherwise monotonous aspect by slight, cliffy, projecting headlands. Numerous rivers of more or less volume intersect the country; but they all have a dangerous bar, and therefore none but light-draught vessels can be used for their navigation. From Cape Gracias as far south as Blewfields Lagoon many islands and coral-reefs are distributed at a greater or less distance from the shore, but from the latter place right round to Navy Bay the sea is singularly free from any impediment to navigation. The land is clothed to the water's edge with dense tropical vegetation, which gives to it a very uniform appearance; indeed for miles on either side of Greytown, or, as it is now called, San Juan de Nicaragua, the general aspect is so unvaried that it is often very difficult to distinguish the proper anchorage; and ships, however well navigated, frequently miss the entrance, and, falling to leeward, take days to beat up against the wind and currents.

There are only two harbours between the points I have mentioned; these are the Chiriqui Lagoon and Greytown. The former is very spacious and commodious, comprising within itself many excellent anchorages; but as regards the latter, it will not be much longer worthy the name, as the detritus brought down by the river San Juan is rapidly silting it up. In April, 1860, I made a most careful survey of the port, and, after reducing my work to the same scale as the Admiralty chart constructed some years previously, I placed my own plan in red ink upon it, and the result was most startling. Indeed, I consider the rapid filling up of Greytown Harbour the most curious instance of the kind I have ever heard of. The sand-spit which forms the outer enclosure of the harbour has grown towards the mainland (and therefore narrowed the entrance) more than 100 feet; the deepest water I could obtain between the points was only 11 feet, which is the more remarkable when it is remembered that two years before, the frigate *Eurydice* sailed out of the port without the least inconvenience, taking a depth of at least four fathoms. In short, there is every reason to believe that Greytown Harbour will soon become a Lagoon, like Blewfields, Pearl Rey, and Cape Gracias Lagoon; the latter of which was a harbour, superior to Grey Town, when Lord Nelson was there in the latter part of the last century.

*Gorgon Bay* (the Atlantic Terminus of the New Route).—Leaving Blewfields, we ran down in a few hours to Gorgon Bay, and came to in this well-sheltered anchorage for two or three days. During our stay the master and myself sketched in the outlines of the land, and obtained some soundings, which upon a subsequent visit were verified. The fine bay included between Monkey Point and Little Monkey Point is completely sheltered from the Northers, the only destructive winds on this coast; hurricanes are unknown. This large expanse, which comprises a distance of about 5 miles from point to point, and a depth of about 2 miles, is further increased by two islands off its outer point, the nearest $\frac{3}{4}$ mile, the next $\frac{1}{4}$ mile more dis-

---

* See p. 75.

tant from the mainland, which if joined to the point by a breakwater would make the most capacious and safe anchorage in this part of the world. The contour of the bay is broken into small indentations, from the headlands of which wooden piers might be thrown out for the convenience of loading and unloading small craft. As a site for a settlement the locality appears well suited ; the land is rich, rising about 100 feet above the sea-level, with abundance of good wholesome water, but quite free from swamps or other lurking-places of fever : in fact it is drained by the peculiarity of its formation, and well ventilated by the prevalent N.E. trade-wind.

The undulation caused by the strong trade-wind rolls into the bay between Monkey Point and the islands, and therefore renders it prudent to anchor about 1½ mile off shore in 4½ fathoms, otherwise we could have gone much closer in. If a breakwater were made, ships could come quite close, as the bottom, of soft mud, shelves very gradually towards the beach, and rocks or shoals are unknown. There is stone in abundance, both on Monkey Point and the islands, well adapted for the construction of a breakwater; it could easily be quarried and the work completed in a short time, as the greatest depth of water is 4¾ fathoms.

A lighthouse on the outer island and a red light on the beach would render the roadstead easy of access in any weather or at any hour of the night.

I hope I have made it plain that the bay (which is without a name on our charts, but which I have designated Gorgon Bay) possesses capabilities and resources which eminently qualify it for a healthy and agreeable settlement, a convenient emporium for the trade of the interior, and a suitable terminus for a great transit-route ; indeed the Royal Mail Packet Company have already directed their captains to anchor there instead of at Greytown Roadstead.

*Corn Islands.*—The "Corn Islands" are two in number, called Great and Little ; they are both moderately high and very pretty. A coral-reef nearly surrounds each, and makes it necessary to approach with great care and caution. There is a very fair anchorage on the lee side of either island in about 5 fathoms water.

The great island—which, by the by, simply affords a pleasant walk all round it, and is not, therefore, very great—is peopled by about 200 Creoles and Negroes. Their language is English, and they have a small portion of land under cultivation ; sufficient, however (such is the richness of the soil), not only to supply their own wants but to afford a large amount of stock to vessels calling. Bullocks, pigs, goats, fowls, ducks, turkeys, and a great variety of fruit and vegetables can always be procured. Cotton of the finest sort was at one time exported in considerable quantities ; but since the emancipation of the negroes, which was effected here as summarily as elsewhere, all commercial enterprise has ceased, if a very small trade in cocoa-nuts be excepted.

Little Corn Island is chiefly grazing land, and affords excellent pasturage for herds of cattle, which, however, are not bred on the island but imported from Cape Gracias à Dios. The channel between the Great and Little Island is about 6 miles broad and is deep and safe. About 20 of the Great Corn Islanders generally live on the Little Island to look after the cattle, collect cocoa-nuts, and pick guava, of which great quantities grow wild on the south side, and prove excellent food for pigs. Its scenery is still more pretty than that of the Great Island, and its healthiness is proverbial ; the few cases of sickness which occur may be traced to imprudent exposure to the weather. In short, I was much struck with the Corn Islands. Their proximity to Gorgon Bay, their salubrity and charming scenery, as well as the abundant supply of fresh meat, fruit, and vegetables, which can always be obtained, will make their vicinity to the future railway most valuable to those employed upon the works, whenever change and recreation may be deemed desirable. As a sanatarium, the Corn Islands will be invaluable, and I have already made certain arrangements to ensure their full usefulness.

2.—*Extracts from a Paper on the Surface Currents of the Bay of Bengal during the S.W. Monsoon.* By Lieut. J. A. HEATHCOTE, I.N. (*See* p. 101).

*Ceylon.*—From the s.w. corner of the peninsula of India, the current of the s.w. monsoon runs in a direction varying from s.e. to s.s.e., according to the distance from the land, and at the rate of ½ to 1¼ mile per hour, until, about the latitude of Point de Galle, it is diverted into a more easterly course. On the line between Cape Comorin and Point de Galle, there is a strong set into the Gulf of Manaar, which begins from 30 to 35 miles outside this line and may prove a source of danger. Vessels from Bombay to the eastward should therefore be careful to keep within the limits of the favourable s.e. current. South of Ceylon, within 30 miles of the coast, the current runs strongly to the eastward from ¾ to 2 miles an hour; but farther south, that is, between the parallels of 4° and 5°, its direction is more southerly or about s.s.e. On the east coast of Ceylon a strong current exists to s.s.e. and s., taking more or less the direction of the land, and running at the rate of ½ to 1¼ mile an hour, or as much as 40 miles a day.

The inaccuracy of a deduction of Horsburgh is here apparent. He states the current at this season to be here running in an entirely opposite direction, that is to the northward; for he argues that, as it runs to the southward in the n.e. monsoon, it must run in a contrary direction in the opposite monsoon. Such, however, is not the case. This southerly current is well established; not only are numerous instances of its effects on record, but the result of my own investigations has also been confirmed by the observation of officers very recently employed on the survey of the east coast of Ceylon. This current is felt from 40 to 50 miles off shore, and from its eastern limits a north-easterly set begins.* At the Basses Rocks it is met by that already described as setting eastward off the s. coast of the island; and they both together then take a north-easterly, and afterwards an east-north-easterly direction across the bay; except that in the vicinity of the parallel of 5° n. the set is less northerly, while s. of that parallel it becomes east-south-easterly.

*Coromandel.*—On the coast of Coromandel a north-easterly set prevails within 30 miles of the shore, as far n. as the parallel of 15°; outside these limits it turns to the north-eastward. North of the parallel of 15° it takes the direction of the land as far as Gordeware Point, and thence trends in an easterly and afterwards a north-easterly direction across the bay. From False Point nearly to Vizagapatam we have a strong s.e. current of ¾ to 1½ mile per hour, within 30 miles of the coast; but, farther to the eastward, it gradually succumbs to the influence of the wind and joins the general set, first in a north-easterly and then in an easterly direction across the bay.

*Arakan.*—On approaching the coast of Arakan it becomes more north-easterly, and finally is governed by the form of that land, and runs strongly to the north-north-westward. It thus becomes a very dangerous current for vessels making Akyar during the s.w. monsoon. In such cases it is frequently necessary to heave-to off the port during the night; and if the existence of this current be not known, and proper precaution be not taken to keep to the southward, the vessel may be drifted into dangerous proximity to the reefs to the eastward of the harbour. In some of the works on this subject all mention of this current is omitted, in others it is represented as running in a

---

* I think it very possible that future observations may prove that this current is a return of that which flows with great velocity round the s.e. corner of Ceylon to the n.e., a portion of which may be found to bend to the n.w.; for, under circumstances somewhat analogous, a return current of this description is found off Cape Guardafui in Africa.

contrary direction; it is therefore the more necessary to call attention to it, as either the want of information on the one hand, or the existence of erroneous information on the other, may lead to injury to the greatly increasing trade of Akyah.

*Circulation of Currents and Tidal Wave.*—This north-easterly current along the coast of Arakan may probably have a very intimate connection with the southerly current on the coast of Ganjam. They may both belong to the same system of circulation, the Arakan current finding its way to the westward along the sea face of the Sunderbunds, and becoming the southerly current at False Point, and being again thrown on the coast of Arakan as before described. But, if this be the case, any positive trace of the westerly movement is not to be discerned, or at least is most difficult to recognise in the peculiar rotatory tides which are found to seaward of the Sunderbunds. These tides set, at different periods of each tide, towards every point of the compass. The flood begins at w., at the first quarter it flows w.n.w., at half-flood it is about n., the last quarter being to e.n.e. The ebb begins at e., half-ebb runs about s., and the last quarter ebb w.s.w., thus forming a complete rotation. But although these rotatory tides go far to hide the current itself, its effects while working its way to the westward are observable in the configuration of the sand-banks off the mouths of the Ganges. The current would here exert its greatest force, and these sands are curved to the westward in a remarkable manner, their very form proving that they are under an influence stronger than that which bends the banks off the mouths of the Hooghly into their south-south-easterly position ; the latter being due to the s.w. monsoon itself, while the former is the effect of the current of the same monsoon concentrated, as it were in a funnel, by the shores of Arakan. That the position of the banks off the mouths of the Ganges is *not* caused by the n.e. monsoon admits of but little doubt; for this portion of the sea is peculiarly sheltered from the n.e. winds, and they cannot be supposed to exert a force sufficient to affect the position of these sand-banks, as, were it so, the effects of this force would be apparent in a much greater degree to the westward, and the sands at the entrance to the Hooghly would lie in a south-westerly direction instead of their present south-easterly one.

*S.E. Current.*—A strong current to the south-eastward at the rate of $\frac{3}{4}$ to $1\frac{1}{4}$ mile per hour begins about lat. 18° and long. 90°, and flows down towards Preparis Island, and then turns more easterly into the Gulf of Martaban. There is, no doubt, an accumulation of waters in the n.e. portion of the bay caused by the steady blowing of the s.w. monsoon across the whole breadth of the sea ; and this current seems to be the result of their waters attempting to find an exit. It may be of important advantage to ships from Calcutta bound to ports to the eastward, for it will materially help them in getting to the southward against the wind. From its eastern edge the currents turn off to the north-eastward, until near the coast of Pegu they become governed by the form of the land, and take a course to the north-north-westward, joining those on the coast of Arakan already described.

*Andaman Islands.*—The Andaman Islands, which have lately formed the subject of an interesting paper read before this Society, play an important part in the system of currents of the s.w. monsoon. They present an obstruction to the general set of the waters in the middle of the sea ; and the same phenomena are observable in their vicinity as are to be seen wherever fluids in motion meet with an impediment under similar conditions. The currents rushing to the eastward round the n. and s. extremes of the islands meet at a short distance beyond them, and become confused and irregular, and throw up high ripplings ; while immediately under the shelter of the islands an eddy is found, running to the northward from $\frac{1}{2}$ to 1 mile per hour. That portion of the sea to the westward of the Andaman Islands is wisely avoided during the s.w. monsoon, the reefs lying to windward of the islands presenting dangers to which every prudent mariner would gladly give a wide birth; and I have therefore been unable to find examples of actual experience of the currents to the w. of the Andamans.　But it is more than probable that the north-easterly set extends close up to the islands; the waters becoming, in a certain measure, heaped up on their w. side, and making their way through them and round them wherever they find an opening.　Evidence of this action is particularly observable at the eastern mouth of the narrow strait which separates the South and Middle Andaman.　This strait was closely examined on the occasion of the expedition—of which Dr. Mouat was the head—appointed, towards the close of the Indian mutinies, to select a site for a penal settlement in these islands.　1 may remark, *en passant*, that the manuscript of the original survey of the Great Andaman by Lieutenant Blair, executed at different periods between 1788 and 1796, and drawn on a large scale, was in the hands of the expedition, and was found to be beautifully accurate in all its details.　It was our sure guide in the intricacies of channels of which no other knowledge but that afforded by this chart was to be obtained; and in those few places where it is deficient in the representation of details, we found that they had not been passed over until it had been ascertained that they could be of no practical utility.　The geographical position of these islands has also been determined so far satisfactorily, that though it may not be incapable of a still nearer approach to exact truth, yet it has, 1 believe attained already to a higher degree of accuracy than can be claimed for the positions at present assigned to many places of far higher commercial importance.

*Middle Strait, Great Andaman.*—The strait between the Middle and South Andaman is one of peculiar formation; it is for the most part a narrow deep crevice, between the mountains by which it is bounded on both sides, and which are in no part distant from it much more than 300 yards, while at places the rocks completely overhang it.　The channel is thus narrowed at one or two points to about 80 yards, its general breadth being from 400 to 500 yards.　Its depth varies, but it is mostly deepest where it is narrowest, 25 fathoms being found where the rocks abut immediately upon the channel, and 6 fathoms where they are more distant; a depth of from 12 to 14 fathoms is, however, very generally found throughout the narrow part of the strait, its western portion where it runs N. and S. being both broader and shallower. Its western entrance from the sea has now a depth of from 4 to 6 fathoms, it having been filled up to some extent during the last seventy years, while the interior of the strait has suffered scarcely any perceptible change.　We found no variation in the depth, nor in the contour of the shore; even small islets of less than 50 yards in length appearing in precisely the same state both as to size, elevation, and position, as represented by the first surveyor.　But while the depths before mentioned are found in the strait itself, its eastern mouth is almost closed by a bank of sand and mud, which has but from 6 to 10 feet water on it; and this, I believe, may be looked upon as the effect of the current of the s.w. monsoon, which being driven, as before described, upon the w. coast of the island, finds its way through this narrow strait, and deposits at its exit the sediment which it had taken up or set in motion on its passage.　The area of drainage of this strait, though small, is sufficient to throw into it a considerable quantity of silt and sand; and the very form of this bank indicates that it has come out *from* the strait, and not that it has been thrown *into* the strait by any effort of the winds and currents of the N.E. monsoon; and, moreover, were this latter the case, some corresponding effects would surely be observable at some of the other openings on the same side of the island, such as Port Cornwallis, the entrances N. and S. of Sound Island, and Port Blair, at all which places instead of shoals we find deep water.　The strait between North and Middle Andaman is completely closed; it is now no longer a strait, if it ever was one: and this is not at all certain, for Blair had not the opportunity of surveying it; he probably found it impossible to enter even in a boat, as we did.

In the open sea between the Mergui Archipelago and the Andamans, the influence of the prevailing wind again shows itself in a north-easterly set of ½ mile to 1¼ mile per hour.

A south-easterly and south-south-easterly current sets with considerable force down through the Mergui Archipelago and past the Seyer Islands; and from lat. 10° N. and long. 95° E., a strong current in the same direction sets, at the rate of ¾ to 1¾ mile per hour, into the entrance of the Malacca Strait. This current may probably be found some degrees farther to the eastward; but I have been unable to gather any facts in support of such a theory, though I know of nothing in opposition to it.

*Sumatra.*—On the N. coast of Sumatra the current of the s.w. monsoon follows the form of the land to the westward; but this portion of the sea is sheltered from the influence of the wind. A slight return current to the eastward may be experienced in about lat. 6¼° N.

Between Acheen Head and the Great Nicobar an extraordinary current is found running to the south-westward in the teeth of the monsoon at the rate of ¾ to 1¼ mile per hour; it extends to the parallel of 5° N., and nearly to the 92° meridian, when it turns to the s. and s.E. Where this current meets the ordinary north-easterly set strong ripplings are observed. It may be taken advantage of by ships bound westward from the straits of Malacca, but it is at present but little known.

---

3.—*Extract from a Letter on Queensland from* SIR CHARLES NICHOLSON, Bart., F.R.G.S., *to* Governor SIR G. F. BOWEN.

Communicated by the DUKE OF NEWCASTLE, F.R.G.S.,

August 22, 1861.

" WITH fine weather and a good steamer, the trip from Rockhampton to Port Denison may be rendered both short and agreeable. The coast-line for the whole distance is bold and well-marked, and the hills with which it is backed often present bold and picturesque outlines. After leaving the broad expanse of Keppel Bay, and the secure shelter and anchorage it affords, the course of a vessel is an open sea-way, in which a few rocky and well-marked islets occur. These are sufficiently prominent to prevent any impediment to navigation by night. After reaching the Percy Islands, and from thence on to the entrance of Port Denison, a succession of islands, seemingly countless in number, and varying in size from a single rocky projection to areas of some square miles in extent, are scattered along the whole coast. They are generally clothed with grass and wood, the latter consisting apparently of the 'Araucaria Cookei.' The outlines they present are generally most striking. Occasionally with bold and rocky summits, some of which must be little short of 1000 feet in height, at other times presenting grassy slopes stretching up amongst the deep-wooded sides of hills, it is difficult to imagine anything more beautiful than the *tout ensemble* thus presented to the eye of the traveller whilst gliding through the waters of these Australian Cyclades. Some of them must have permanent water, as a small cascade may be seen in a ravine on one of the most striking of the group, which, if I recollect rightly, is known on the chart as 'Prudhoe Island.' Secure landing may be found in most of these islands, in the numerous little sandy beaches and bays with which their sides are environed.

" On approaching Port Denison the scenery becomes bolder on the coast. Mount Dryander attains an altitude of nearly 3000 feet. Cape Conway is an abrupt rocky promontory, and Gloucester Island, which faces one of the sides of the bay, presents a long serrated ridge of granitic rocks, which at a distance seem destitute of all vegetation, and remind the traveller who has been in the Red Sea, of the mountains of the Sinaitic Peninsula, and of Aden. On rounding Gloucester Island the waters of Port Denison are reached, presenting a broad and nearly circular basin, the largest diameter of which is probably five or six miles. It is nearly land-locked, although exposed somewhat to the south-east. The point forming the north entrance is a peninsula, which at high water forms an island, with an abrupt cliff rising some four or five hundred feet towards the sea, and gradually sloping off towards the west into a bed of mangrove-swamps. The view from this promontory is very imposing. To the east the bold mural precipices of Gloucester Island, to the south the lofty isolated peak of Mount Roma ; and, stretching to the far-west, a succession of hills and undulating plains. The bay of Port Denison is unfortunately shallow, its greatest depth in the centre not exceeding 25 feet. The shores are low and shelving, and some difficulty (in the absence of a jetty or pier) is encountered in landing except at high water. At other times boats are unable to reach the shore, and the only means of landing are, as far as passengers are concerned, the back and shoulders of a sturdy aboriginal black ; or, in the case of goods, a bullock or horse-team, which has to be driven some 200 or 300 feet into the sea.

"The site of the future town (named after Governor Sir George Bowen) appears to be judiciously selected on a small ridge on the northern side of the bay. It is proposed to connect this with the peninsula forming the northern entrance of the bay by means of a causeway.

"The great drawback to the settlement appears to be a deficiency of fresh water. This all-essential article is at present supplied from some native wells. Such a source must evidently be limited and precarious. The River Don, which is within four miles, will, however, it is said, furnish if needed an adequate supply of water to the inhabitants, if the native wells fail.

"The country immediately adjacent to the township, and beyond the mangrove-swamps, consists of a rich, light, sandy soil, apparently well adapted for the growth of cotton, and other tropical vegetable productions. An extensive and fertile tract of country, consisting of open bush, is said to extend for a considerable distance inland, and to be well adapted for grazing purposes. A station has been already formed 40 miles from the township, and the natives have as yet given no serious trouble to the white population.

"From all that I can collect we may, I think, safely infer that the future town of Bowen will acquire considerable importance as the centre of a fertile country, and as an outlet for the pastoral districts of the Kennedy, for the wool and tallow which they will ere long produce. There are, however, I apprehend, some serious drawbacks to its prosperity. These will be chiefly found to consist in the insufficient supply of fresh water, in the shallowness of the basin of the harbour, the low shelving beach, and the difficulty and labour which now attend the landing of goods and passengers. These drawbacks are, however, capable of removal or mitigation.

"I believe that an important step has been taken in the occupation of this part of the coast of North-Eastern Australia. All credit and honour are due to Mr. Dalrymple, by whose zeal and energy this new locality has been opened up, and is now being settled upon what, I trust, will be a prosperous basis.

"Before leaving the settlement I met with several parties of young men, who had just returned from explorations to the north and north-west, in search of pastoral 'runs.' It is impossible not to be struck by the courage, enterprize, and endurance, of these pioneers of civilization in the Australian wilderness. One party, consisting of three Europeans and an aboriginal boy, had been absent in the bush for upwards of five months, during which interval they had never met with any white man and had been frequently menaced by the blacks. For a considerable period prior to their return they had been living upon a diminished ration of flour and bacon, and were in a great degree dependent for subsistence upon fish and native animals. Their journey had extended as far as the basaltic table-land of Leichhardt, towards the sources of the Burdekin. They purpose occupying a large pastoral tract in this region, and were thinking of bringing stock from Melbourne by sea. The point they had fixed upon for stations was nearly abreast of Rockingham Bay.

"One important point connected with the progressive occupation of the north-east coast of Australia is the hastening of the period when steam communication with India and Europe will follow this route. Port Denison is only 600 miles from Cape York, and the latter not more than 1100 miles from Timor, from which a regular line of steam communication exists with the various Dutch East Indian settlements, and thence to Singapore. Some 1600 or 1700 miles is all that is really at present needed in steam communication to connect Queensland with the Old World. Why do we not supply the small link thus wanted to complete the golden chain that so nearly encircles the civilized world?"

# PROCEEDINGS

OF

# THE ROYAL GEOGRAPHICAL SOCIETY
# OF LONDON.

## SESSION 1861—62.

*Thirteenth Meeting* (ANNIVERSARY), 1 P.M., *May 26th*, 1862.

### LORD ASHBURTON, PRESIDENT, in the Chair.

THE Minutes of the previous Meeting having been read and confirmed, and the regulations respecting the Anniversary Meetings having been read, the President appointed John Hogg and James Macqueen, Esqrs., Scrutineers for the Ballot.

Captain the Hon. James R. Drummond, R.N., C.B.; Lieutenant-Colonel Elkington; Captain Edward Donald Malcolm; Captain John Puget; Sir Henry Young; James Anderson; Samuel Bruce; Eugène Claude; John Baily Darvall; Henry Schuback Hood; Henry Lannoy Hunter; Frederick Isaac; Leonard Jaques; George Mitchell; William Parry; Mark Richardson; and William Whitmore, Esqrs., were proposed as Candidates for election at the next Meeting.

The Report of the Council, with the Balance Sheet for 1861, and the Estimate for 1862, was then read and adopted, and the motion,* as recommended by the Council at p. 6 of the Council Report, was carried.

The President then delivered the FOUNDER'S GOLD MEDAL to the Duke of Newcastle, on behalf of the late Richard O'Hara Burke, in remembrance of that gallant explorer, who, with his companion Wills, perished, after having traversed the continent of Australia from south to north—as also a GOLD WATCH on behalf of Mr. John King, the sole survivor of the expedition under Burke, as a recompense for his faithful and meritorious conduct; and the PATRON'S GOLD MEDAL to Captain Thomas Blakiston, of the Royal Artillery, for his survey of the Yang-tze-Kiang from Yo-chow to Ping-shan,

---

* " That the words The ' *two* Secretaries of the Society shall be Honorary Secretaries,' &c., be The ' *three* Secretaries,' &c. ; and that Mr. William Spottiswoode be proposed as the new Honorary Secretary."

extending nine hundred miles beyond the farthest point previously reached by Englishmen.

The Anniversary Address was next read, and a unanimous vote of thanks was passed, with a request that the President would allow it to be printed.

At the conclusion of the Ballot, the Scrutineers reported that the following changes, advised by the Council, had been adopted :— Lord Ashburton, the President, retiring at the expiration of his second year of office, to be succeeded by Sir Roderick I. Murchison ; and the vacancy among the Vice-Presidents, occasioned by the election of Sir Roderick I. Murchison, as President, to be filled by Lord Ashburton ; and the vacancies caused among the Ordinary Councillors occasioned by Mr. William Spottiswoode being made an additional Honorary Secretary, and by the retirement of Earl de Grey and Ripon ; Lieutenant-General C. R. Fox ; W. J. Hamilton ; Austen H. Layard, M.P. ; Major-General Sir Justin Sheil ; and Colonel W. H. Sykes, M.P., to be supplied by the Right Hon. H. U. Addington ; Earl Ducie ; Cyril C. Graham ; Clements R. Markham ; John Rae, M.D. ; E. Osborne Smith ; and John Walker, Esqrs.

Thanks having been voted to the President, Vice-Presidents, Members of Council, and Scrutineers, the President finally directed attention to the usual Anniversary Dinner, and the Meeting adjourned.

# PRESENTATION

# GOLD MEDALS

## To the Representative of the late RICHARD O'HARA BURKE AND TO CAPTAIN BLAKISTON, R.A.

THE PRESIDENT said—The first duty which I have to perform is to present the medals. But before I do so I may, perhaps, be allowed to remind you that these honours are not the gift of a society of private gentlemen, who have assumed to themselves the right of so distinguishing certain merits of their own selection, according to rules fixed by their own good pleasure; these medals are the gift of that supreme authority of this realm which is the source of all public honour and distinction. And just as peerages and knighthoods are given by the Crown, at the instance of the Prime Minister; just as Victoria Crosses are given by the Crown, at the instance of the Commander-in-Chief, so the Crown has selected the President and Council of the Royal Geographical Society to award the honours which it considers to be due to those who have most distinguished themselves by the furtherance of geographical science and discovery.

If you will look back to our records, you will see that this Royal trust has been fulfilled by the President and Council of the Royal Geographical Society with scrupulous fidelity; you will find no trace of political bias, or of personal favour, or of what is more difficult to resist, the influence of popular sympathies. Now it is this distinction, proceeding from the highest power of the realm, and assigned by the most competent and impartial judges, that I am about to present.

I will request Dr. Shaw to read the formal judicial decision, by which the Council of the Royal Geographical Society has awarded the Founder's premium for this year.

Dr. Shaw then read as follows :—" The Founder's Gold Medal has been awarded to the representative of the late Richard O'Hara Burke, in remembrance of that gallant explorer, who, with his com-

M 2

panion Wills, perished after having traversed the continent of
Australia from south to north.   The Council have also awarded to
Mr. John King, the sole survivor of the expedition under Burke, a
gold watch, with a suitable inscription, as a recompense for his
faithful and meritorious conduct."

The President then addressed the Duke of Newcastle, her
Majesty's Secretary of State for the Colonies, as follows :—

"My LORD DUKE,—We rejoice to see you here within our walls,
that we may have the opportunity of testifying to you our thanks
for the cordial and liberal manner in which you have accepted the
co-operation of this Society whenever we could in any way contribute to the public service.   The colonies over which you preside
must see in your presence this day new evidence of the interest
taken by Her Majesty's Government in every event which bears
upon their permanent welfare ; and there have been few events
within the history of our Australian colonies destined to have a
more beneficial influence upon their progress than this passage
from sea to sea by the expedition of the late Mr. Burke.

"I consign this medal to your hands, to be delivered to his
nearest relative.   Oh ! that this posthumous tribute of a nation's
gratitude could in any way assuage the sorrow and mitigate the
bereavement of the many friends and admirers whom he has left to
bewail his loss."

The DUKE OF NEWCASTLE assured the meeting that he attended there
in fulfilment of what he considered a public duty, at once painful and
agreeable—painful because he received at the hands of the President
this token of admiration of one of England's great men, for trans-
mission not to him for whose merits it had been bestowed, and who
was now cold on the shores of that great country on which he had conferred such great benefits, but to those relatives who, like the colony
itself, must look back upon his memory with affectionate admiration.
At the same time it was a pleasurable duty, because it showed that
this Society, as well as the country at large, had not been insensible
to the merits of the individual or the services he had rendered to
science and civilization.   These medals, as it had been correctly
stated by the Chairman, were not conferred at the option of private
individuals, but by the Crown, through the instrumentality of the
President and Fellows of that Society ; but the medals must bear
an additional value when it was recollected that they were not
bestowed upon any arbitrary principles, but by gentlemen eminent
for their knowledge and experience, and who were well calculated
to appreciate the merit they rewarded.   Standing before them as
he did, entrusted by Her Majesty with the seals of the Colonial
Office, he felt bound to express his admiration of the colony of

Victoria in instituting this expedition. That was perhaps the one of the Australian colonies least interested in the result of Mr. Burke's expedition; at the same time it entered upon it with that public spirit which had actuated this country in similar expeditions —a desire to benefit science and to extend civilization throughout Australia, of which the colony of Victoria formed so important a part. But if credit was due to Victoria for this, it was also due to that colony to acknowledge that it set on foot other expeditions when the fate of Mr. Burke was held in the balance, and when it was hoped that expeditions might afford aid, or probably effect his rescue. It would be unnecessary to say much upon the individual merits of Mr. Burke, for most of those present had read that touching despatch of Sir Henry Barkly in which he narrated the circumstances of Mr. Burke's untimely fate. In him they had lost a man as eminent, as gallant, and as great as that intrepid brother who perished on the banks of the Danube. He felt certain that the Society had done well in awarding its medal to so distinguished an explorer. It would not be proper for him to pledge the Colonial Office to anything on such an occasion, but he would say that on all such matters as that the authorities of that office looked to the Royal Geographical Society as a guide and instructor, and, although it might not be always possible to follow what was suggested, it would always be with great deference that they received suggestions, and with great reluctance that they were unable to carry them out. On the part of the friends of Mr. Burke he thanked the Society, and assured them that the medal should be duly transmitted to them.

At the desire of the President, the terms of the award of the Patron's Gold Medal were then read as follows:—"The Patron's Gold Medal has been awarded to Captain Blakiston, of the Royal Artillery, for his survey of the river Yang-tze-Kiang, from Yochow to Ping-shan, extending nine hundred miles beyond the farthest point previously reached by Englishmen."

The PRESIDENT then said,—

" CAPTAIN BLAKISTON,—Having already had the pleasure of being associated with you in private life, I rejoice that it should be from my hands that you receive this honourable distinction, awarded you by the Council of the Royal Geographical Society."

CAPTAIN BLAKISTON, R.A., expressed his gratification at receiving the medal, but regretted that in a private expedition any distinction had to be made. He wished that it could be divided into four portions, so that each of his companions might receive a share; but that not being possible, he should consider that he held it in trust for them.

He tendered his thanks to the President and Council for the award, and to the members present for their flattering reception, and concluded by saying that he should ever remember that the " Upper Yang-tze Expedition" had gained one of the highest honours accessible to geographers.

# ADDRESS

TO THE

# ROYAL GEOGRAPHICAL SOCIETY OF LONDON;

*Delivered at the Anniversary Meeting on the 26th May, 1862,*

BY THE LORD ASHBURTON,

PRESIDENT.

## OBITUARY.

IN the Report which has been read, you have heard of the increasing numbers of this Society—numbers which begin even to exceed the space which we can assign to them. But at the same time there is another review to make—the melancholy review of our losses. There have passed away from amongst us men of European reputations, lamented not only by the friends they loved, but by the public they have served; who have laboured in their day not only for the generation among whom they lived, but for all time and for all humanity. As the narrow circle of kindred within which a man has lived hasten with pious reverence to celebrate solemn obsequies over his tomb, so the wider circle within which he has worked find a pride and glory in recording the worth and recounting the actions of the fellow-labourer they deplore.

I begin our melancholy list by recording the death of our Royal Vice-Patron, the late Prince Consort. His vigilant eye was not confined to the science of geography alone; it extended to every science, every pursuit which could in any way contribute to the welfare of his fellow men. Our grief for the irreparable loss we have ourselves sustained has been still further intensified by our sympathy with that great Lady, our Queen and Governor, in whom we glory, on whom we have concentrated all that we have of respect, admiration, and love.

The Prince alone could, from his universal and accurate knowledge, from his exalted position, carry out to their successful completion, a course of measures by which he hoped to secure for his adopted country an honourable supremacy in every department of science and of art. Such I believe to have been the determinate purpose of our great Patron. He has passed away from amongst us, and where shall we find his like? Where shall we find such power, such knowledge, such earnest zeal, such deliberate wisdom, such patient endurance of opposition?

Where shall we find a constancy inspired by love to us, and elevated by the aspirations of a noble mind for the advancement of mankind? On every public and private occasion he gave to men distinguished in art, science, or literature, that social position to which they were entitled. He exerted himself by every means in his power to enlarge the sphere of education.

He organized and completed the Great Exhibition of 1851. It was then, when we came into direct conflict with other nations, that our manufacturers found that for the higher branches of their respective arts they must have French designers, French painters, and Italian modellers. They became conscious of their inferiority in taste and workmanship; they found the want of such public institutions as had facilitated in foreign countries the cultivation of the artist and the mechanic.

Public opinion thus roused, enabled the Government to carry out the Prince's views, by the establishment of schools of art and science throughout the country.

Already in 1855, enlightened foreigners were struck by the progress which had been made in four short years. Eight more have now elapsed; improvement has been going on in an accelerated ratio. A measure of progress is applied this year, by the Exhibition of 1862, to test the success of the Prince's plans and labours; but the originator of them all is not there, to hear the universal voice of praise and gratitude. His far-seeing eye is closed, his fostering hand is cold. Science has lost her noblest patron, England her surest guide.

Thomas William ATKINSON, the Siberian traveller, was born of humble parents at Cawthorne, a village in the West-Riding of Yorkshire, on the 6th of March, 1799, and the only education he received was at its village-school. At the age of eight years he followed the plough, at ten he began to earn his own livelihood as a bricklayer's labourer and quarryman, and afterwards worked in a stonemason's yard.

In 1819 he was employed as mason in rebuilding St. Mary's (the old) Church at Barnsley, where he distinguished himself by carving some unusually fine work, and showed so much talent that he was strongly recommended to try his fortune in a larger sphere.

In accordance with this advice he went to London, and in 1827 he established himself in Upper Stamford Street, Borough, as an architect. In 1842 he left England for Hamburgh, where he was engaged during 1845 in the reconstruction of the church of St. Nicholas, and where he obtained some patronage from the King of Prussia.

He next visited Egypt and Greece, and in 1846, by the advice of Baron Humboldt, went to Russia. He there formed the project of an artist's journey into Siberia ; and the Emperor of Russia granted him the rare privilege of a *blank* pass throughout his Asiatic dominions. The crowning effort of Mr. Atkinson's life then commenced ; he started on his journey through southern Siberia, the Kirghis Steppes, and parts of Central Asia.

On his return he wrote his Travels, entitled ' Oriental and Western Siberia,' in 1858, and ' The Upper and Lower Amoor,' &c. in 1860.

James BRANT, C.B., was a gentleman well known to many travellers and tourists, from his long official connection with Eastern countries. He was appointed Vice-Consul at Trebizond, in 1830, and Consul at Erzeroum in 1836, where he remained till the close of the Russian war, and then was transferred to the Consulship of Damascus. He retired from the service in 1830, and died suddenly last year at the age of seventy.

Captain Walter Colquhoun GRANT, the author of an able and vivid description of Vancouver's Island, published in Vol. xxvii. of our Journal, died at Saugor, Central India, aged thirty-nine. He was the only son of the late chief of the intelligence department of the army commanded by the Duke of Wellington in the Peninsula. He did good service in the Crimean war, and again in India he assisted in the siege of Lucknow, and succeeded to the command of the regiment of irregular cavalry known as 1st Hodson's Horse. One of Captain Grant's last acts was to prepare and transmit to this Society a map and paper on Sikkim, which, however, have not yet reached their destination.

James Ormiston M'WILLIAM, M.D., F.R.S., was chief medical officer to the disastrous expedition in 1841, under Captain Trotter, R.N., in which his name is familiar to all who are conversant with the history of Niger enterprise. During the return voyage of the afflicted party, when the survivors were mostly fever-stricken, Dr. M'William displayed an energy and devotion which demanded and obtained the most grateful acknowledgment. His experience gained on this fearful occasion has been of marked utility to after travellers, and is recorded in his well-known ' Medical History of the Niger Expedition.'

The Rev. Dr. Joseph WOLFF, whose name is so intimately associated with Eastern travel, was the son of a Rabbi, and was born at Weilersbach, in the year 1795. He was converted to Christianity through his acquaintance with the Count of Stolberg and Bishop Seiler, and was prevailed upon to enter the Monastery of the Redemptorists at Val-Saint, near Tribourg. Being unable to convince himself of the truth of Romanism as taught there, he left Val-Saint and came to London; and after studying the Oriental languages under Dr. Lee of Cambridge, and theology under the late Rev. Charles Simeon, commenced his travels for the purpose of proclaiming the Gospel to the Jews, Mohamedans, and Pagans. He travelled in Mesopotamia, Persia, Teflis, and the Crimea; incessantly preaching at every town and village he came to. From 1831 to 1834, Dr. Wolff proceeded to search for the Ten Tribes. A full account of all these wanderings and of his second journey to Bokhara, in order, if possible, to effect the liberation of Colonel Stoddart and Captain Conolly, as also of his visit to the United States, will be found in his works.

I have now recorded the sad list of those who have, by their labours, contributed to geographical science and discovery. There are others whose cheerful presence we miss, sedulous attendants of our meetings, contributors to our funds. But they came to learn, not to instruct; they came to enjoy the fruits which others, with toil and danger, had sown and reaped.

-----

## ADMIRALTY SURVEYS.

The Coast Surveys in course of execution under the orders of the Admiralty, both at home and abroad, have made the usual progress during the past year. They are conducted by twenty different surveying parties, one-half of whom are employed on the coasts of the United Kingdom; the remainder in the colonies of Australia, Cape of Good Hope, West Indies, Nova Scotia, New-foundland, and Vancouver Island; and on the foreign coasts of Syria, Cyrenaica, in Banka Strait, China, and Japan.

*England.*—The Coast Survey of the British Isles is so nearly complete that the account of its advance from year to year must necessarily be made up of minor topographical details, which would be out of place in a general view of the progress of geography all over the globe, were it not for their important bearing on the safety of navigation, and their being of special interest to the numerous class connected with the vast commercial marine of the country. Beginning then with the south coast: the shores of the Solent, Southampton Water, and Portsmouth harbour have been re-examined by Mr. Scott Taylor, R.N., in order to insert the several changes that have been caused by the progress of the nation and the require-ments of trade during the last sixteen years, when the former survey was made. Questions, too, connected with deep-water docks, and the extension of Portsmouth harbour, have led to a critical examination of the early surveys of this region—and apparently the depth of water on Portsmouth Bar is found to be precisely the same.

In the Channel Islands Mr. Richards, R.N., is continuing his re-examination, and, by patiently struggling against the rapid tides that prevail around that group, has succeeded in discovering many small rocks which might have wrecked a vessel. On the coast of Devon Captain Stokes, R.N., with his staff, has completed the survey of the Yealm river and the soundings in Bigbury Bay; and the chart of Plymouth Sound by Commander Cox, on the scale of 6 inches to a mile, has been published. In the Scilly Isles Captain George Williams has made much progress in the re-examination of that intricate group. In the Bristol Channel Commander Alldridge has continued the survey of the coast of Glamorganshire, and sounded over 180 square miles of ground; while Mr. Calver, R.N., with his staff, on the east coast, has continued the survey of the upper part of the Humber from Hull to Goole, has re-examined the eastern gatway leading into Yarmouth Roads, and the Shingles channel at the mouth of the Thames.

*Scotland.*—In Argyllshire Commander Bedford and his staff have surveyed 14 miles of the open north-west coast of Mull, and 9 miles of Loch Linnhe, with 76 miles of the shores of Loch Awe, besides sounding over an area of 60 miles. Captain Otter and staff have surveyed Loch Lomond, the Sound of Barra in the Hebrides, a portion of the Isles of Harris and Benbecula, and a part of Rum ; while Mr. Jeffery has brought to a close the survey of the coast of Inverness-shire.

*Ireland.*—On the east coast of Ireland Mr. Hoskyn has been engaged on the upper part of Lough Strangford and on the coast of Down, and has sounded over an area of 65 miles.  On the south coast Commander Edye has filled up the off-shore soundings that were wanting in our charts over an area of 1200 square miles ; he has also sounded an area of 800 miles on the north coast.  A general chart of the west coast of Ireland, on the scale of two-tenths of an inch to a mile, with numerous small plans, has been published by the Admiralty during the past year ; as also Dingle and Ventry harbours and Blasket Sound, and the outlying fishing-bank and almost inaccessible islet of Rockall.

*Mediterranean.*—While carefully sounding the bottom and pioneering the way for the electric submarine cable between Malta and Alexandria, Captain Spratt, with his staff, in the *Medina,* has taken advantage of the opportunity afforded to re-examine the north coast of Africa by Cyrenaica, and to correct its outline; also to make plans of the roadsteads of Tripoli, Benghazi, &c.  One of the first uses to which the submarine telegraph was put was to determine the meridian distance between Malta and Alexandria.  This has been successfully accomplished by Captains Spratt and Mansell ; and the result of these measurements gives 16° 6′ 3″ as the difference, or 29° 51′ 42″ as the longitude of the lighthouse at Alexandria ; this determination differs only 14″ from that already obtained by chronometric measurements.  On the coast of Syria Commander Mansell and his staff have completed a second sheet of the coast from Markab to Cape Bianco, and connected with it several important points in the interior, as Ba'albek, Hermon, Jibbel, Sunnín, and others.

The charts connected with the Mediterranean which have been published during the past year are as follows :—Valetta harbour, Malta, on the scale of 11 inches to a mile ; Rhodes Island, on the scale of eight-tenths of an inch, with enlarged plans of the ports ; Scarpanto and Casso islands, on the scale of 1 inch ; the western portion of Crete, on the scale of half an inch, with views and plans of ports, completing the survey of this rich and beautiful island ; Euripo Strait, in Greece, on the scale of 3 inches ; and a general chart of the Delta of the Danube, on half an inch, with the Sulina mouth of that river, showing the increased depth that has been gained over the bar by the recent works which have been carried out by the International Commission.

*Africa.*—On the west coast of Africa the river Volta has been explored as far as the first rapids at about 50 miles from its mouth, the Ogún for 40 miles from Lagos to within 4 miles of Abeokúta, and the St. Nicholas and Brass branches for 25 miles from the sea; and the sketch-map of each has been published at the Admiralty. In the Cape Colony Mr. Francis Skead, R.N., is engaged on the coast near Hout Bay. In the early part of the year he accompanied Mr. May, R.N., in Dr. Livingstone's new steamer to the Zambesi, and made an improved sketch of the five mouths of that river, and more correctly determined their position, while Mr. May proceeded with Dr. Livingstone and Bishop Mackenzie to the river Rovúma, and explored it for 30 miles from its mouth, which was as far as the falling water would allow them to ascend : the sketch of this river, on the scale of 1 inch to a mile, has been published. In the Red Sea a plan of Dissee Island and harbour, and Commander Mansell's re-survey of the Strait of Jubal, with the Ashraffi reef and islet, have been engraved; and it is gratifying to be enabled to add that the intelligent Viceroy of Egypt, His Highness Said Pasha, has caused three lights to be established to facilitate the navigation of that narrow sea—one on Zafarana point, already lighted ; one on the Ashraffi reef, at the southern entrance of the Gulf of Suez, which will be lighted shortly ; and a third on the Dædalus reef, which is to be lighted towards the close of the year.

*Asia.*—The chart of the Persian Gulf, to which I referred last year, by Commander Constable and Lieutenant Stiffe, of Her Majesty's Indian Navy, has been published at the Admiralty in two sheets, on the scale of a quarter of an inch to a mile, with plans of several small ports and various views of headlands : it is accompanied by a memorandum on the former charts of this gulf, with a table of positions; and the Sailing Directions are far advanced in printing. The whole work is highly creditable to the surveying officers of the Indian Navy ; and the chart is one of those selected to be sent as a specimen to the International Exhibition. A plan of Bahrein has also been completed by Lieutenant Whish.

In India a gap in the Malabar coast—Thullknob to Borin pagoda —has recently been filled up by Lieut. Williams, I.N.; and thus the whole of the west coast of the peninsula south of Bombay has been surveyed. Lieut. Taylor, I.N., is engaged in writing the

Sailing Directions from Cape Comorin to the entrance of the Persian Gulf; while Lieut. Ward is making progress with those on the south coast of Arabia from Ras al Had to Bab el Mandeb, including Sokotra and the Gulf of Aden. There still remains some portions of this eastern region which it would be highly desirable to examine; and it is understood that the Secretary of State for India in Council has decided that the work shall be done; and I believe that it may help to advance the cause of geography by giving a brief summary of these gaps, coupled with the expression of the wish of the Geographical Society that an early opportunity may offer for their being filled up. They are as follows :—1. The coast of Malacca from the Sakshan River to Pulo Penang, about 300 miles. 2. Coast of Orissa from Santapilly rocks to Point Palmyras, about the same distance. 3. The coast from Chittagong to Akyab, at the head of the Bay of Bengal. 4. The re-examination of the group of the Andaman Isles. 5. The west coast of India from Bombay northwards to Danú, about 100 miles. 6. Bombay harbour on a large scale, so as to admit of docks and other engineering works being planned upon it. 7. The Batnah coast from Maskat to the entrance of the Persian Gulf, 250 miles. 8. The coast of Africa from Ras Bir to the entrance of the Red Sea, 15 miles. 9. A series of chronometric measurements throughout the Bay of Bengal and to Singapore. 10. A similar series from Bombay westwards to Suez and to the outlying islands in the Indian Ocean.

These two last can only be well done by a vessel specially devoted to the service, carrying a batch of at least thirteen chronometers. There is no work that could be undertaken that would place the hydrography of those seas on a firmer basis than the measurements last named; and I believe that I do but give utterance to the hearty desire of this Society in expressing a wish that, before the accomplished surveyors of the Indian Navy are dispersed abroad, Her Majesty's Secretary of State for India, than whom no one knows better the value of accurate geographical information, may be pleased to set this seal to the labours of Ross, Horsburgh, Moresby, Elwon, Grieve, Haines, Ethersey, and other officers of the Indian Navy, who, during the past half-century, have patiently borne the toil and heat of the day to furnish the mariner with charts by which he may with safety navigate those Eastern seas.

In the Banka and Gaspar Straits, and near Linga, Mr. Stanton, R.N., in H. M. S. *Saracen*, has materially corrected our charts during the past year. It may serve to show our ignorance of the geography of these regions in the middle of the nineteenth century, when I state that the populous town of Palambang, in Sumatra, was found to be 14 miles in error in latitude in all our best maps and charts, being placed that much too far to the south. A chart of Singapore, by Mr. John Richards, R.N., has recently been published by the Admiralty on the scale of 12 inches to a mile; it shows at a glance the docks, coal-wharfs, and other accommodation at that flourishing entrepôt of the trade of the East.

*China and Japan.*—One hundred and twenty miles of the upper -part of the Yang-tze-Kiang above Hankow has been explored as far as Yo-chow-foo, at the entrance of the Tung-ting Lake, as far as 500 miles above Nanking, during the past year. In addition to this service, Captain Ward in the *Actæon*, and Lieut. Bullock in the *Dove*, have been employed on the southern coast of Japan. In the mean time some of the results of their labours of former years have recently been published by the Admiralty—as Port Adams in the Gulf of Pechili; the Liau river up to Niu-chwang, one of the trading ports under the treaty; Chifu or Yentai harbour; Talien-whan Bay, Wei-hai-wei and Lungmun harbours; Hai-yun Island, containing Thornton Haven, Pechili Strait, and a general chart of the Gulfs of Pechili and Liau-tung. The *Actæon* has just arrived in England, after five years' absence in the China Seas, during which very material additions have been made by her officers and crew to our knowledge of the coast, rivers, and outlying islands of China and Japan.

*Australia.*—Allusion was made in the Address from the Chair of last year to the wise liberality of the Australian colonies in sharing with the Admiralty the expenses of an organised system of coast surveys. Parties, under the command, respectively, of Commanders Sidney, Cox, Hutchison, Lieut. Brooker, and Mr. J. Jeffreys of the Royal Navy, are now established in New South Wales, Victoria, South Australia, Tasmania, and Queensland; detailed plans of places locally important have been received, and the steady progress of an efficient examination of the extensive lines of seaboard of the several provinces may now be confidently anticipated.

To keep pace with the rapid extension of colonization on the shores of the intertropical part of the east coast, a series of charts to connect with the detailed surveys of the late Captains Owen, Stanley, and Blackwood (which extended from Torres Strait to $18\frac{1}{2}°$ south), are in the course of construction, compiled from the detached and partial examinations of our naval surveyors from the time of Cook to the present date, to be eventually connected, it is to be hoped, by the rising generation.

Charts of the Coral Sea, embracing on a small scale all these coast features, and giving the recent surveys of Captain Denham, R.N., have been published, and prove a great boon to the navigator. The labours of this officer in the Australian seas, extending over nine years' service, deserve more than a passing notice; but, limited necessarily in this Address in time and space, a summary of the more salient statistical features can alone be given. 200 sheets, as I am informed, of charts, plans, and drawings, are completed and in progress; 163 positions catalogued; the variation of the compass tested afloat 2410 times, and 191 times on shore; 41 islands and 42 ocean reefs and sunken shoals surveyed; 700 miles of edge of soundings contoured; and 23 fabulous dangers erased from the charts.

The most favourable accounts have been received of the security of the passage through Torres Strait by the great north-east channel; and the testimony appears to be overwhelming in its favour compared with those by Raine islet and the numerous treacherous openings through the barrier reefs near the 12th parallel of south latitude. The merchant-ship *Castilian*, drawing 20 feet, has recently made two voyages through the north-east channel in sixteen hours. We cannot here forbear paying a passing tribute to the valued labours of the late Captain Francis Blackwood, R.N., who so successfully and clearly defined this remarkable and valuable channel.

A general chart of Australia in two sheets, with the adjacent islands and seas between its northern coast and the equator, has also been completed during the past year. The authorities and materials for this chart have been most extensive: in addition to the well-known names of Flinders, King, Wickham, Stokes, Stanley, Blackwood, Yule, and Denham, the recently-published Dutch charts of the Arafura, Banda, and Java seas have been consulted, and the northern coast of New Guinea, the shores of New Ireland and New Britain, as resulting from various French surveys extending over half a century, connected by the more recent chronometric measurements of Sir E. Belcher—the whole chart being thus reduced to the common meridian of Fort Macquarie, Sydney, New South Wales.

*Vancouver Island.*—Crossing the Pacific Ocean to the thriving colony of British Columbia, we find that Captain George Richards, in H. M. S. *Hecate*, with his staff of assistants, has surveyed 700 miles, much of it open sea-coast or the exposed entrances of the great sounds on the west side of Vancouver Island; during which time the party thoroughly sounded over an area of 400 square miles in Barclay and Clayoquot or Clakkot sounds, and more generally over 1400 miles off the entrance to Fuca Strait. In the course of the past year plans have been published at the Admiralty of Esquimalt and Victoria harbours, on the large scale of 10 inches to the mile; of Haro Strait and Middle Channel, on the scale of 1 inch; and Sailing Directions generally for the straits, harbours, and rivers of this district.

*Newfoundland.*—The re-examination of the south coast of Newfoundland, under Captain Orlebar and his assistants, has made good progress during the past season, in the course of which 200 miles of sea and harbour coast-line have been mapped in six large sheets, generally on the scale of 3 inches to a mile. At the same time, plans of Placentia harbour, Port Basque, and St. Pierre Island, on the same scale, have been published, as well as Pope and Tangier harbours in Nova Scotia—the latter place becoming of importance on account of the immediate vicinity of the gold-diggings which have been discovered.

*Bay of Fundy.*—The tedious survey of this bay of fogs and rapid tides is at length complete, and Captain Shortland and his staff have moved on to the south-eastern part of the coast of Nova-Scotia. In the course of the past season they have mapped 27 miles of open coast and 154 miles of harbour and river shore-line, sounding over an area of 260 square miles. On this eastern coast of America the unhappy civil war, and the uncertain state of political affairs, has led to the publication of forty-two sheets of the several charts and plans taken from the admirable United States Coast Survey, with the Sailing Directions that accompany them.

*West Indies.*—The survey of the group of the Grenadines has been completed by Mr. Parsons, R.N., and his assistants, and they are now moving on to the island of Sta. Lucia and the port of Castries. In the course of the year they have mapped 45 miles of coast-line, and sounded over an area of 310 square miles. The chart of Grenada, on the scale of 1 inch, and the plan of St. George's harbour, on the scale of 20 inches, have been published. Also, in Texas, plans of the entrances of Rio Grande and Brazos river, with the San Luis, Aransas, and Sabine passes.

*Variation of the Compass.*—Resulting from the investigations that have been in progress for some time past (which have been alluded to in former Addresses) by Mr. Frederick J. Evans, R.N., F.R.S., Superintendent of the Compass Department of the Admiralty, and Mr. Archibald Smith, F.R.S., whose gratuitous labours in this cause are beyond all praise, a Manual embracing ample practical and theoretical rules for ascertaining and applying the deviation of the compass in ships is on the eve of publication. This Manual has appended to it charts of the lines of equal variation, dip, and horizontal force, by the examination of which the seaman may become familiar with the distribution of these elements, so important as a correlative branch of science to that of navigation under the great impending changes in naval architecture. It is a gratifying feature that these researches should have preceded the sudden demand for a new order of iron war-ships. In connexion with this subject, Mr. Burdwood, R.N., of the Hydrographic Office, has computed and published Tables of the sun's true bearing or azimuth for the parallels of 49° and 50° N., which will enable the mariner at once to determine the amount of variation and local deviation combined by a simple compass-bearing of the sun either in the morning or the evening—thus affording a constant check to the ever-changing deviation in an iron ship, according to whether she heels to starboard or port, which in many cases is an unsuspected source of danger.

Besides the surveys above enumerated as in progress in different parts of the world, the labours of the Hydrographic Office during the past year have consisted in the publication, under the immediate superintendence of Captain George A. Bedford, R.N., Assistant Hydrographer, of about ninety new and corrected charts and plans, some of which I have already mentioned. There have also been published the usual Tide Tables for two thousand places on the face of the globe, Light and Hydrographic Notices acquainting the mariner at once with the slighest change or discovery of rock or shoal that can affect the safety of navigation. Mr. Michael Walker, too, has taken advantage of the leisure afforded by his retirement from office, and has examined and corrected about five hundred of the Maritime Positions, chiefly in the Eastern seas, recently published in the 7th edition of Raper's 'Practice of Navigation.'

## ORDNANCE SURVEY.*

The publication of 'The Trigonometrical Survey of the United Kingdom' is now completed, and is comprised in seven quarto volumes, viz. :—

I. The Principal Triangulation, with the Figure, Dimensions, and Mean Specific Gravity of the Earth derived therefrom, 2 vols.

II. Levelling, taken in Ireland, 1 vol.

III. Levelling, taken in England and Wales, 2 vols.

IV. Levelling, taken in Scotland, 2 vols.

Thus this great work, which was commenced in 1783, under General Roy, R.E., is at length finished.

In last year's estimates the sum of 1000*l.* was taken to enable the director of the survey to extend the triangulation of England through France to the frontiers of Belgium, so as to form a connection between the triangulations of England and Belgium. This operation has been completed. The stations selected to form the connexion across the Channel were St. Peter's Church, between Margate and Ramsgate; Coldham, on the high ground north of Folkestone; and Fairlight, a few miles north of Hastings. From these three stations observations were taken to the church at Gravelines, to Mont Couple, near Wissant, and Mont Lambert, near Boulogne.

From these three last-named stations a station raised 74 feet above the level of the ground at Harlettes, between Boulogne and St. Omer, was observed, and then the churches at Cassel and Dunkirk, and then the station at Mont Kemmel, near Ypres, in Belgium. The triangle, Dunkirk, Cassel, and Mont Kemmel, is common to the triangulations of France and Belgium, and is now also made part of the extended triangulation of this country, and the lengths of its sides will therefore be independently determined by the geometricians of the three countries from the measured bases in the three countries, and a comparison of the results will be highly interesting; but the French officers who were ordered to observe at the same stations that ours observed at, not having been able last year to take the observations across the Channel, the comparison cannot yet be made. They have now, however, returned to this country to recommence their work, and it is to be hoped they will be able to finish it this summer.

During last year the Belgian geometricians were engaged in con-

* Colonel Sir Henry James, R.E., Superintendent of the Ordnance Survey.

necting their triangulation with that of Prussia, and the Prussians
in connecting theirs with that of Russia; and thus we shall shortly
have a connected triangulation, extending from the west of Ireland
to the Oural mountains, and the means of computing the length of
an arc of parallel of about 75° in length.

The electric telegraph now furnishes the means by which the
difference of longitude between distant places can be determined
with greater precision than they could formerly be by the trans-
mission of chronometers from one station to another.

The Astronomer Royal will therefore this year re-determine the
difference of longitude between Valentia, in the s.w. of Ireland,
and the observatory at Greenwich, by means of the electric telegraph; and as it will be necessary for the director of the survey to
connect the station selected by the Astronomer Royal at Valentia
with the triangulation of the kingdom, a joint expedition is now
about to proceed to Valentia for this double purpose, and to complete the quota of work assigned to us for the measurement of this
great arc of parallel.

The engraving of the complete map of Ireland in outline, on the
scale of one inch to a mile, was finished last year, and the hill
features are now being engraved. There are 205 sheets in this
map.

The progress of the Cadastral Survey in the north of England and
Scotland has been greatly retarded in consequence of the very
numerous and extensive surveys which have been made by the
Ordnance in the south of England for purposes connected with the
defences of the kingdom.

But as all these have been made on the scales adopted for the
National Survey, and the plans have been drawn as so many
sheets of a complete survey of the counties to which the places
belong, they will form a part of the Cadastral Survey of England
and Wales, should such a measure be decided on; and as the committee of the House of Commons, of which Lord Bury was chairman, which was appointed last year to report upon "the expediency
of extending the Cadastral Survey to those portions of the United
Kingdom which have been surveyed upon the scale of one inch to a
mile only," have reported in favour of it, the cost of the surveys
made for the defences will go to diminish the cost of the Cadastral
Survey.

In the north of England, Yorkshire and Lancashire have been
published on the 6-inch scale; Westmoreland and Durham on the
25-inch scale; and the survey is in progress in Northumberland

and Cumberland. A large portion of each of these counties has already been published, and they will be finished this year. The last sheets of the 1-inch map of England and Wales are in the hands of the engravers; we may, therefore, expect that this map, which was begun in 1784, will now be soon finished. In Scotland all the southern counties have been published either on the 25-inch or 6-inch scales; and the counties of Forfar, Perth, Stirling, and Dumbarton are in course of publication; and the survey is proceeding in Perthshire, Kincardineshire, and Buteshire. The 1-inch map of Scotland is also in course of publication.

The plans of the eight northern counties of Ireland have been revised and made perfect in every detail, like the plans of the southern counties. This perfect revision was rendered necessary to enable the Government valuators to mark upon the plans every property and tenement; and this has now been done throughout the whole of Ireland. The Ordnance plans are now invariably used for the transfer of land under the Landed Estates Court, the cost of preparing the plans for the court being charged to the carriage of the sale of the property; and the same arrangement will doubtless be introduced here as soon as some progress is made in the Cadastral Survey.

Sir Henry James has this year published six sheets of the Marginal Lines for the sheets of a map of the whole world, on the scale of 2 inches to a mile; the object in view being to have a map constructed on the largest scale required for geographical purposes, the sheets of which can be put together to form a connected map of any part of the world, however large or however small; and to avoid the confusion arising when we attempt to put together maps of different countries, as they are now constructed on different scales and on different projections.

This is a great undertaking, and one which will require the cooperation of a great number of people and some years to accomplish; but the advantages to be derived from having such a grand map of the world are obvious; and it is right that the topographical department of such a country as ours should undertake to make it.

In a discussion upon the relative merits of several projections for large portions of the earth's surface which has been published in the last number of the 'Philosophical Magazine,' it has been demonstrated, that, assuming the errors which all projections of a spherical surface on a plane must necessarily have, viz., distortion in form and distortion in area, are equally objectionable, the distance of the point of projection adopted by Sir Henry James in his geometrical projection of two-thirds of the sphere, will, for the projection of a hemisphere, give the least possible distortion of form and area, and that the misrepresentation will be a minimum. If we draw a circle and two diameters in it at right angles to each other, one may be taken to represent the plane of projection for the concave hemisphere above it, and the point of sight or projection is at the distance of half the radius in the prolongation of the other beyond its circle. It is now demonstrated that this is the best possible projection for a hemisphere, and it should therefore be adopted by all geographers.

## METEOROLOGY.*

In Meteorology some degree of increased interest has been caused by various discussions and publications, besides an organised system of forecasting weather and giving cautionary notice of expected storms.

In treating so complicated and extensive a subject as that of our atmosphere and its movements, it is extremely difficult to combine mathematical exactness with the results of experience obtained by practical ocular observation and much reflection ; but to some extent this has been effected recently, the Board of Trade having arranged telegraphic and frequent communication between widely-separated stations and a central office in London ; by which a means of *feeling*—indeed one may say *mentally seeing*—successive simultaneous states of the atmosphere over the greater extent of our islands is established ; and an insight into its dynamical laws has been thus obtained, to which each passing month has added elucidation and value.

Possibly at this time, when extensions of our arrangements to the Continent are contemplated in France, in Hanover, and in Prussia (although *here* there are still persons who doubt, if they do not entirely disbelieve their utility), it may be desirable to circulate an explicit description of the basis, and the nature, of those forecasts and occasional warnings, which have been proved during the past year.

The first cautionary or storm-warning signals were made in February, 1861 ; since which time similar warnings have been given, as occasions needed.

In August, 1861, the first published "forecasts" of weather were tried ; and after another half-year had elapsed for gaining experience

---

* Admiral FitzRoy, Director of the Meteorological Department, Board of Trade.

by varied tentative arrangements, the present system was established.
Twenty reports are now received each morning (except Sundays),
and ten each afternoon, besides five from the Continent.    Double
forecasts (two days in advance) are published, with the full tables
(on which they chiefly depend), and are sent to six daily papers, to
one weekly, to Lloyds', to the Admiralty, and to the Horse Guards,
besides the Board of Trade.

These forecasts add almost nothing to the pecuniary expense of
the system, while their usefulness practically is said to be more
and more recognised.* Warnings of storms arise out of them, and
(scarcely enough considered) the satisfaction of knowing that no
very bad weather is imminent may be very great to a person about
to cross the sea.    Thus their negative evidence may be actually
little less valuable than the positive.

Prophecies or predictions they are not: the term forecast is strictly
applicable to such an *opinion* as is the result of a scientific combination and calculation, liable to be occasionally, though rarely, marred
by an unexpected "downrush"† of southerly wind, or by a rapid
electrical action not yet sufficiently indicated to our extremely
limited sight and feeling.   We shall know more and more by degrees.
At present it is satisfactory to know that the measures practised
daily in these proceedings do not depend solely on one individual:
they are the results of facts exactly recorded, and deductions from
their consideration, for which rules have been given.   An assistant
is able to share their responsibility now, and others are advancing
in the subject of dynamical meteorology.

In order to enable the reader to judge of the basis on which rules
for forecasting probable weather are founded, some degree of explanation may here be offered—as the method is new in its combinations, although depending on old or well-known principles.

Air-currents sometimes flow side by side, though in opposite directions, as "parallel streams," for hundreds or even thousands of miles.
Sometimes they are more or less superposed: occasionally, indeed
frequently, crossing at various angles; sometimes combining, and by
the composition of their forces and qualities causing those varieties of
weather that are experienced as the wind veers more toward or from
the equator or the nearest pole; and sometimes so antagonistic in

---

* At a recent meeting of the Shareholders of the Great Western Docks at
Stonehouse, Plymouth, it was stated officially that "the deficiency (in revenue) is
to be attributed chiefly to the absence of vessels requiring the use of the graving-
docks for the purpose of repairing the damages occasioned by storms and casualties at sea."
† Herschel.

their angular collision as to cause those large circular eddies or rotatory storms, called cyclones, which are really like the greater storms in all parts of the world, although they do not quite assimilate to local whirlwinds, dust-storms, and other commotions of atmosphere, which seem to be more electrical in their characteristics, if not in their origin.

Whenever a polar current prevails at any place, or is *approaching*, the air becomes heavier, and the barometer high, or rising. When the opposite (equatorial or tropical) prevails or approaches, the mercury is low or falls, because the air is, or is becoming, specifically lighter, and these changes take place slowly. Whenever, from any causes—electrical, chemical, or simply mechanical—either current, or any combination of currents, ceases to press onwards without being opposed, a gradual lightening of the atmosphere, through a greater or less area of hundreds or perhaps thousands of miles occurs, not suddenly, but very gradually, and the barometer falls : there is less tension.

To restore equilibrium, the nearest *disposable* body of air (so to speak), or most moveable, advances first; but an impulse at the same time may be given to other and greater masses that—though later in arriving—may be stronger, last longer, and cause greater pressure, mechanically as well as by combination. Air, like water, mingles slowly, either from above or laterally.

Taking, with Dové, north-east and south-west (true) as the " wind-poles," all intermediate directions are found to be more or less assimilated to the characteristics of those extremes, as they are nearer one or other ; while all the variations of pressure or tension, many of those caused by temperature, and all varieties of winds, may be clearly and directly traced to the operations of two constant principal currents—equatorial or tropical, and polar—our north-east and south-west.

It has been proved that storms—indeed all the greater circulations of atmosphere in the zone between the tropics and polar regions—have an eastward motion bodily, while circulating around a centrical area. Within the tropics it is otherwise, or westward,—till they *recurve*, moving first toward the *nearer* pole, direct, and then eastward, with more or less direction toward the same pole.

Clear distinction should be made between those ever alternate and often conflicting main currents—tropical or polar, and the local effects of their union or antagonism, namely, mixed winds—whether westerly or easterly, with occasional eddies, or cyclones, on a larger or on a smaller scale.

The lower current does not ordinarily extend far upward (only some few thousand yards), and highlands, mountains, especially *ranges* of mountains, alter and impede its progress, so that a variety of eddy winds, or streams of wind, with local and apparently anomalous effects, are frequently caused.

Heat, electrical action, or cold; condensation of vapour into hail, snow, rain, or fog; or its other changes, namely, evaporation, rarefaction, and expansion—absorbing heat, and therefore causing *cold* —immediately cause currents of air, in a degree proportional to such influence; inducing horizontal motion and dynamical force.

The polar current always *advances* from the polar quarter while *laterally* moving eastward (like a ship making lee-way), being pressed towards the east by the tropical flow which advances from the south-westward, usually above and at an angle with the polar stream or current of air, often mixing with it, but at times *separately* penetrating downward, then sweeping and warming the earth's surface, uncombined with the polar current even while feeling its approaching influence, and thus, as it were, forcing passages between streams of chilling polar air that at the same time are moving in opposite and nearly parallel directions.

At times, after a continuance of tropical air-current, or during its general prevalence, a polar flow or separate stream of air (electric, cold, dry, and of greater pressure or tension than the prevailing body of air then next the earth) passes above, chilling and otherwise influencing the lower air through which, at some places, it penetrates completely.

These movements of air-currents are shown by clouds crossing the heavenly bodies, by the visible characteristics of those clouds, and by simultaneous observations of temperature, tension, force of wind, and its true direction, at many places.

It is very interesting as well as practically useful to mark how these inroads or mixtures of air-currents occur, and to note their beginnings or endings at a few places considerably separated; such, for instance, as Copenhagen and Lisbon, Galway and Heligoland, Jersey and Aberdeen, Queenstown (or Valentia) and Berwick or Yarmouth, with intermediate places. But this special feature may be better referred to after a few other considerations have been submitted as preliminary.

Dynamical force, pressure of air in motion, is generated by disturbed equilibrium, whether electrically by heat or cold, mechanically by aqueous expansion into gas, by contraction into rain, snow, or ice, or by previously induced action of air-currents among themselves, with their inertia.

Hence it follows that no great disturbance of equable temperature, tension, dryness, or moisture, can occur without a proportionate dynamical force, tending to cause currents of air, or wind, however resisted, deflected, or otherwise affected by similar and simultaneous actions, more or less in opposition or in combination.

Sometimes their opposition is so equal, and equilibrium is so complete, that a calm is the result, no sensible movement horizontally along the earth's surface being perceptible.

Frequently combination occurs, and dynamical effects are produced in proportion. These are particularly evident in the meetings of tropical and polar winds (by the west), by their subsequent continuance in strength as mixed winds, and by the concurrence or combination of cyclones.

Successive, or rather consecutive, gyrations, circuits, or cyclones, often affect one another, acting as temporary mutual checks, until a combination and joint action occurs; their union causing then much greater effects, as may be seen even in water-currents as well as in the atmosphere itself.

Between the tropics and the polar regions, or in temperate zones, the main currents are incessantly active, while more or less antagonistic, from the causes above mentioned; besides which, wherever considerable changes of temperature, development of electricity, heavy rain, or these in combination, cause temporary disturbance of atmospheric equilibrium (or a much altered tension of air), those grand agents of nature, the two great currents, speedily move by the *least resisting lines* to restore equilibrium, or fill the comparative void. One current arrives, probably, or acts, sooner than the other; but invariably collision occurs of some kind or degree, usually occasioning a circuit, a cyclonic (or ellipsonic) gyration, however little noticed when gentle or moderate in force.

As there must be resistance to moving air (or a conflict of currents) to cause gyration, and as there are no such causes on a large scale near the equator, there are no storms (except local squalls) in very low latitudes.

It is at some distance, from about 5° to 20°, from the equator that hurricanes are occasionally felt in their violence. They originate in or near those hot and densely-clouded spaces, sometimes spoken of as the " *cloud-ring*," where aggregated aqueous vapour is at times condensed into heavy rain (partly with vivid electrical action), and a comparative vacuum is suddenly caused, towards which air rushes from all sides. That which arrives from a higher latitude has a westwardly, that from a lower an eastwardly, tendency, due to the earth's rotation and to the change of latitude, whence a chief cause of the cyclone's invariable rotation in one direction, as above explained.

The hurricane, or cyclone, is impelled to the west in low latitudes, because the tendency of both currents there is to the westward along the surface, although one—the tropical—is much less so, and becomes actually easterly near the tropic, after which its equatorial centrifugal force is more and more evident, while the westwardly tendency of the polar current diminishes; and, therefore, at that latitude hurricane cyclones cease to move westward (recurve), go then easterly, and on toward the polar quarter.

Great and important changes of weather and wind are preceded as well as accompanied, by notable alterations in the state of the atmosphere.

Such changes, being indicated at some places sooner than at others around the British islands, give frequent premonitions; and therefore great differences of pressure (or tension) shown by barometer, of temperature, of dryness or moisture, and direction of wind, should be considered as *signs of changes likely to occur soon.*

It will be observed, on any continued comparison of weather reports, that during the stronger winds a far greater degree of uniformity and regularity is shown than during the prevalence of moderate or light breezes; and this should be remembered in forecasting weather.

When neither of the greater and more extensive atmospheric currents is sweeping across the British islands (currents of which the causes are remote, and on a large scale), the nature or character of our winds approaches, and is rather like that of land and sea breezes in low latitudes, especially in summer.

Either the cooler sea-wind is drawn in over land heated by the summer sun, or cold air from frosty heights, snow-covered land, or chilly valleys, moves towards the sea, which is so uniform in temperature for many weeks together, changing so slowly and but little, in comparison with land, during the year. These light variables may at such times be numerous, simultaneously, around the compass on the various coasts of the British islands.

Frequently it has been asked, " In this country, how much rise or fall of the glasses may foretell remarkable change or a dangerous storm?" To which can now be replied, "Great changes or storms are usually shown by falls of barometer exceeding half an inch, and by differences of temperature exceeding about fifteen degrees. Nearly a tenth of an inch an hour is a fall presaging a storm or very heavy rain. The more rapidly such changes occur, the more risk there is of dangerous atmospheric commotion."

As all barometric instruments often, if not usually, show what may be expected, a day or even days in advance, rather than the weather of the present or next few hours; and as wind, or its direction, affects them much more than rain or snow, due allowance should always be made for days as well as for hours to come.

The general effect of storms is felt unequally in these islands, and less inland than on our coasts. Wind is diminished or checked by its passage over land. The mountain ranges of Wales or Scotland, rising two to four thousand feet above the ocean level, have great power to alter the direction and probably the velocity of wind, independently of alterations caused by changes of temperature at elevations.

Extensive changes, showing differences of pressure above or below the normal or mean level, amounting to nearly an inch, or thereabouts, are certain to be followed by a marked commotion of the elements in the course of a few days. If the fall has been sudden, or the rise very rapid, swift but brief will be the resulting elementary movement; if slow or gradual, time will elapse before the change, and the altered state of weather will take place more gradually, but last longer.

Notice may thus be obtained and given a few hours, or a day, or even some days, before any important change in the weather actually occurs.

Having such knowledge, it obviously follows that telegraphic warning may be sent in any direction reached by the wires; and that occasionally, on the occurrence of very ominous signs—barometric and other, including always those of the heavens—such cautions may be given before storms as will tend to diminish the risks and loss of life so frequent on our exposed and tempestuous shores. Barometers show the alterations in tension—or, so to speak, the pulsations, on a large scale—of atmosphere; and diagrams express to practised observers what the "indicator-card" of a steam-cylinder shows to a skilful engineer.

Our own islands have very peculiar facilities for meteorological communication by telegraph between outlying stations on the sea-coast and a central place, all being at nearly the same level, and nearly all comparatively uninfluenced by mountain ranges.

And now the results are, that, having daily knowledge of the weather (including ordinary facts of a meteorological nature) at the extreme limits and centre of our British islands, we are warned of any great change taking place ; the greater atmospherical changes being measured by days rather than by hours. Only local changes, however violent they may be occasionally (and dangerous in proportion to their suddenness and violence), only those changes are unfelt at a distance, and do not influence great breadths—such as hundreds of miles area of atmosphere—horizontally.

Some special, and to many persons entirely new, considerations should here be mentioned, as they are now practically valuable in connection with forecasting weather.

When opposing currents of air meet, their masses must continue in motion a certain time, either rotating, or ascending, or going onward horizontally in combination.

Masses of air, either of polar or tropical origin, so to speak, returning (when driven back by stronger opposition), at first, and for a certain time, retain the characteristics of their peculiar and very different natures.

In our latitudes there is a continuous alternation of air-currents, each specifically different, and denoting approach by marked characteristics ; and we have proved, by successive series of simultaneous statical observations over a wide range—embracing Scotland, Ireland, all England, and adjacent islands—that, while these alternating or circuitously-moving currents are thus incessantly passing, the whole body of atmosphere, filling our temperate zone, is moving gradually *towards the east*, at an average rate of about 5 geographical miles an hour (from 2 to 8 miles).

During strong westerly winds this eastward motion is greatly increased, and in easterly gales it is proportionately diminished, as measured by its passage along a horizontal surface of earth or ocean.

Knowing these circumstances, and having accurate statical observations of these various currents at selected outlying stations, showing pressure (or tension), temperature, and relative dryness, with the direction and estimated horizontal force of wind at *each place simultaneously*, the dynamical consequences are already measurable approximately on geometrical principles ; and, judging by the past, there appears to be reasonable ground for expectation that meteorological dynamics will be soon subjected to mathematical

analysis and accurate formulas.    The facts now weighed and measured mentally—in what may be correctly called forecasting weather
—are the direction and force of air-currents or wind, reported tele-
graphically to the central station in London from many distant
stations, their respective tension and temperature, moisture or
dryness, and their changes since former recent observations.
These show whether any or either movement or change is on the
increase or decrease; whether a polar current is moving laterally
off, passing from our stations towards Europe, or approaching us
from the Atlantic; whether moving direct towards the south-westward with great velocity, or with slow progress.    If moving fast
in the direction of its length, it will approach England more from
the east—its speed direct being 20 to 50 or 80 miles an hour;
while its constant lateral or easterly tendency (like a ship's leeway
in a current), being only 5 miles an hour, is then insensible to us
(though clearly deducible from other facts ascertained), and is that
much in alteration of actual direction, as well as of what would
otherwise be the velocity of that polar current.

With the opposite principal current—the equatorial or south-
westerly, more briefly and correctly, tropical—similar but opposite
results occur.    The direct motion from a south-westerly quarter is
accelerated sensibly to our perception by part of the eastward constant (about 5 miles hourly), and therefore a body of air approaches
us sooner (other things being equal) from the westward than it
does from the eastward.

To seamen accustomed to navigate in ships making leeway while
in currents setting variously over the ground, such movements,
complicated as they may appear, are familiar.    There are the
ship's headway, leeway, and drift to be considered, in combination
with the motion or current-rate of the buoyant water, and that perhaps an upper current, differing from one beneath, while each is
passing across the bottom or bed of the sea beneath all.

But the motes circling in a beam of light across a draught of
dusty air may perhaps show what is meant by such combined and
varying motions of fluid, elastic, and mobile air, as are here mentioned.

One important consideration is the disposal or progress of bodies of
air united, or mixed, or contiguous to each other, after their meeting
—either directly opposed or at an angle—on the earth's (or ocean's)
surface.    They do not vanish.    They cannot go directly upwards,

against gravitation; westward they cannot (generally) go when there is collision or meeting, because the momentum, elasticity, and extent of the tropical "antitrade," * or south-wester, usually overpowers any direct polar current, or rises over it and more or less affects the subordinate one below by the friction of its eastward pressure. Downward there is no exit; eastwardly (towards the east) the accumulating air must go, and this tendency continued causes the varieties of wind from the westward; being more or less mixed, more or less purely polar or tropical, as either one prevails in combination.

After a body of air has passed and gone to some distance southward or northward, it may be stopped by an advancing and more powerful mass of atmosphere, which is moving in a direction contrary to or diagonally across its line of force. If their appulse be gradual and gentle, only a check occurs, and the weaker body is pushed back until its special qualities, respecting temperature and moisture, are so masked by those of its opponent as to be almost obliterated; but if these currents meet with energy at very different temperatures and tensions, rapid changes are noticed as the wind shifts, and circuitous eddies, storms, or cyclones occur.

Otherwise, when their meeting is, as first mentioned, gradual, there is the return of a portion of either current (which previously prevailed), either direct or deflected—deflected even through more than one quadrant of a circle—by its advancing opponent, and retaining for some considerable time its own previous characteristics. Thus we have for short times cold dry winds from the south-west, instead of the usual warm and moist ones; or winds of the latter kind from the north, instead of cold ones.

The circuitous tendency of air in motion, and the numerous impediments to its horizontal progress, such as land, ranges of mountains, hills, or even cliffs, induce many a deviation from normal directions, extremely puzzling to the student of this subject; but so retentive is air of its tension and temperature for a time, that, like currents in the ocean, each may be traced by its characteristics as long as within our insular web of stations.

When the polar current is driven back by a tropical advancing from a southerly direction gradually, their action united becomes south-easterly (from the south-eastward); and as the one or other prevails, the wind blows more from one side of east or from the other. Time is required to produce motion in the air—horizon-

---

* Sir John Herschel's excellent term.

tally—and more time is indispensable for its gradual cessation from movement.

Statical effects are noticed at observatories, or by careful observers anywhere, some hours or days before notable dynamical consequences occur.

When a body of atmosphere is moving from or towards the pole, its impelling force (vis a tergo) may cease; while the mass itself has a certain impetus or momentum.

Diminishing tension then results at the place of checked energy, and the upper current (always present) descends. At the same time there is an alteration of tension at the farther extreme, which is meeting and mingling with, if not resisting, checked, and deflected by the advancing opponent.

Consequent on this an extent of air, reaching, perhaps, across some hundred miles, becomes, as it were, isolated. Detached from its original source and maintenance, whether polar or tropical, and then quite surrounded by air of a different character, it is impelled in new and varying directions, still retaining for a time more or less of its characteristics, until altered entirely, and totally incorporated with its conqueror.

Hence we sometimes have cold tropical wind, with electrical and other polar characteristics (for a limited time only), before the tropical predominates; or, on the other hand, a warm polar air-current, with tropical peculiarities.

Moreover, in addition to these causes of apparent inconsistency or irregularity are the results of circling currents—streams of air retaining their features, although changed, it may be even totally, in direction along the earth's surface; besides a variety of merely local alterations, such as are effected by high lands, or valleys, or coast-lines. All these, and many other minor considerations, ought to be familiar and present to a forecaster of weather, who would judge comprehensively according to observed facts and ascertained laws.

Lunarists and Astro-meteorologists support theories which, if in accordance with facts, would affect our whole atmosphere, or a hemisphere, or at least an entire zone, in a similar way, on account of the (supposed) influencing causes acting over all the rotating earth, and not only over Europe, or its adjacent islands.

---

At the Board of Trade from thirty to forty weather-telegrams are received daily (except Sundays), and the present forecasts, or premonitions of weather, are drawn up on the following arrangement. Districts are thus assumed :—

1. Scotland.
2. Ireland, around the coasts.
3. West Central (Severn to the Solway), coastwise.
4. South-West England (from the Severn to Southampton), by the coast.
5. South-East England (Wight to Thames).
6. East Coast (Thames to Tweed).

As newspaper space is very limited, and as some words are used in different senses by various persons, extreme care is taken in selecting those for such brief, general, and yet sufficiently definite sentences as will suit the purposes satisfactorily.

Such words as are commonly found on published scales of force, or nature of wind and weather, are generally understood, and therefore are used in preference to others, however apparently expressive.

In saying on any day what the *probable* character of the weather will be to-morrow, or the day after, at the foot of a table showing its observed nature that very morning, a limited degree of information is offered for about two days in advance, which is as far as may be trusted generally, on an average, though at times a longer premonition might be given with sufficient accuracy to be of occasional use.

Minute or special details, such as showers at particular places, or merely local squalls, are avoided ; but the general or average characteristics, those expected to be principally prevalent (with but few exceptions) the following day and the next after it, including the nights (not those of the weather actually present), are cautiously expressed, after careful consideration. Ordinary variations of cloudiness, or clear sky, cr rain, of a *local* or only temporary character, are not noticed usually.

That a broad *general average* or *prevalence* is kept in view, referring to a day or more in advance, and to a district, rather than only to one time or place, should be remembered by the reader.

The great practical difficulty is in separating the effect on the mind of present states of air, weather, and clouds, from abstract considerations of what may be expected on the morrow or next following day.

As meteorological instruments usually foretell important changes by at least a day, or much longer, we have to consider what wind and weather may be expected from the morning observations, compared with those of the days immediately previous, as indicative of the morrow's weather, and of the day after, at each place ; to take an *average* of those *expectations* for each district collectively, *in groups*; and then to estimate the dynamical effects which may be anticipated as the legitimate consequences of such relative tensions, temperatures, and dryness, occasioning more or less inequality in the atmospheric equilibrium, and thus causing greater or less horizontal motions of air-currents, or ordinary winds.

Comparisons of the moist and dry thermometers are very useful, if well observed, in telling the hygrometric condition of air; and thence, with other facts, showing how either current prevails, or has relative influence—a point of much importance in forecasting a change of wind either way, as well as the probability of rainy or dry weather. A good electrometer is not yet available at our out-stations, however desirable such an instrument would be, in expressing, not only relative electrical states of air, but what, till a better term is offered, may, perhaps, be called the *polarity* of our atmosphere (if not its polarisation).

Whether there is a condition, or relative position of the particles of air, in a tropical current, differing from either in a polar current—analogous to the polarisation of light—and whether there is a direct connexion between these main currents and electro-magnetic, especially those mysterious earth-currents, are questions easy to ask ; but excessively difficult to be answered, even by philosophical physicists of the highest eminence. To such authorities, however, the writer would appeal for some particular consideration of the following facts :—

With polar currents of air, electricity is above par, or plus ; the air is harsh, clouds in it have a hard, oily appearance, animal as well as vegetable life is peculiarly affected in various familiar ways, tension is above par ; and all these peculiarities are *constant* qualities independent of temperature of night or day, and of the time of year.

With the opposite or tropical current, different effects are well known to most people ; but the comparative absence of electrical tension (or plus electricity), the soft, watery aspect of clouds in such air, and the absence of hard edges or outlines, unless influenced in some degree by the polar element, have not been noticed generally, though they are properties expressive of tropical winds solely (west to south in this hemisphere) in their (unmixed) purity.

In all frequented parts of the world, these peculiar characteristics of the so-called easterly and westerly winds have been carefully noticed, and found to be irrespective of locality,—land or water, whether with an ocean to the east, or with a continent in that direction, or the converse. It may be remarked, in passing, that easterly winds everywhere (prevalent, not merely temporary currents), either mixed or deflected, are polar—derived more or less from the nearest pole; and that so-called westerly winds are tropical, from a tropical direction, or mixed tropical and polar currents. There is much to be remarked, in connexion with these distinctive features, respecting atmospheric colours, clouds, auroras, and meteors, but not admissible here.

---

Outline maps, with movable windmarkers, and cyclone glasses or horns, are useful in forecasting weather; and full consideration should be given to the probable position, direction, extent, and degree of progress of those centrical areas or *nodes* round which the principal currents usually circulate, or turn, as they meet and alter, combine with, or succeed one another.

Here dynamical considerations, with comprehensive comparisons of statical facts, are most important; and to treat them even approximately well, with such quick despatch as is requisite, demands aptitude and experience.

Those who are most concerned about approaching changes, who are going to sea, or on a journey, or on a mere excursion; those who have gardening, agricultural, or other out-door pursuits in view; may often derive useful *cautionary* notices from these published expectations of weather: although (from the nature of such subjects) they can be but scanty, and imperfect, under present circumstances.

Objection has been taken to such forecasts, because they cannot be always exactly correct, for all places, in one district. It is, however, considered by most persons that general, comprehensive expressions, in aid of local observers, who can form independent judgments from the tables and their own instruments, respecting their immediate vicinity, though not so well for distant places, may be very useful as well as interesting: while to an unprovided or otherwise uninformed person, an idea of the kind of weather thought probable cannot be otherwise than acceptable, provided that he is in no way bound to act in accordance with any such views, against his own judgment.

Like the storm-signals, such notices should be merely *cautionary*, to denote anticipated disturbance *somewhere* over these islands, without being in the least degree compulsory, or interfering arbitrarily with the movements of vessels or individuals.

o 2

Certain it is, that, although our conclusions may be incorrect, our judgment erroneous, the laws of nature and the signs afforded to man are invariably true. Accurate interpretation is the real deficiency.

Seamen know well the marked characteristics of the two great divisions of wind, in all parts of the world, and do not care to calculate the intermediate changes or combinations to two or three points. They want to know the *quarter* whence a gale may be expected—whether northerly or southerly—in general terms.

Every seaman will admit, that however useful, and therefore desirable, it would be to know exactly the hour of a storm's commencement—as our acquaintance with meteorology does not enable such times to be fixed—the next best thing is to have limits assigned for extra vigilance and due precaution, which limits are clearly stated, in all the printed popular instructions, to be from the time of hoisting the signal until *two* or *three days afterwards.*

But, say some, and justly—are ships to remain waiting to avoid a gale that after all may not happen? Are fishermen and coasters to wait idle, and miss their opportunities? By no means. All that the cautionary signals imply, is " Look out." " Be on your guard." " Notice your glasses, and the signs of the weather." " The atmosphere is much disturbed."

Perhaps sufficient thought has not always been given to the consideration of mere pecuniary loss by wear and tear, risk, accident, delay, and demurrage, caused by a gale at sea; balanced against the results of waiting for a tide or two, perhaps once in two months, when cautioned by a storm-signal.

Be this as it may with coasters, short traders, or even screw-colliers, the question is entirely different with ordinary over-sea or foreign-going ships; especially when starting from a southern or from a western port. To such vessels a gale in the Channel, or even during the first day or two after clearing the land, must always be very prejudicial. Officers and men are mutually strange; things are not in their places, often not secured; and the ship, perhaps, is untried at sea. Of course, however, these remarks are inapplicable to fine, first-class ships; and to powerful, well-managed steamers, independent of wind and weather, which start at fixed hours.

It is scarcely too much to say, even now, that if due attention be paid on the coasts to cautionary signals—and, at the Central Office, to the telegraphed reports—no very dangerous storm need be anticipated without more or less notice of its approach being generally communicated around the British Islands; or to those particular coasts which probably may be most affected by its greatest strength.

But this hardly applies to our extreme outposts, such as Jersey, Valencia, Nairn, and Heligoland, because their remoteness, invaluable as that condition is for warning other places nearer the centre, is an obvious reason why they cannot always be forewarned themselves.

In using the daily Weather Reports, it ought to be kept in mind that only one state of atmosphere in twenty-four hours is there recorded (excepting for rainfall); therefore it is only by comparisons and due reference to previous reports that probable consequences can be fairly inferred. It is advisable, in considering the forecasts, to look at the second as in some degree part of the first; time of weather continuing not being a certain or reliable notice.

In conclusion, it may be impressed on the reader, that this system is a tentative *experiment*. Each month, however, has hitherto added useful facts, and increased our acquaintance with the difficult, though not uncertain, dynamics of the subject. Nothing, however, could have been well effected in an attempt to apply meteorology to daily practice with confidence, had not a foundation of facts existed in the works of scientific authorities—whose statical records and invaluable deductions afforded a sufficiently extensive basis on which to rely while utilising modern powers of communication by telegraph, from any stations, simultaneously.

### Surveys of Spain.*

We learn from our correspondent, M. Coello, the accomplished geographer, who is now directing the topographical survey of Spain, that the following additions to our science have recently been made.

During the year 1861 persevering progress has been made in the great triangulation of the country.

All the chains of the triangles of the first order have already been studied, including those which relate to the whole circumference of the kingdom.

The chains of the meridian of Madrid, both to the north and to the south of that capital, have nearly all been measured, and will be completed before the end of the present year.

---

* Signor Coello, Corr. Member, R.G.S., Director of the Topographical Department in Spain. (Translated by Dr. Hodgkin, Hon. Foreign Secretary.)

The parallel of Madrid to the west has been finished as far as the frontier of Portugal ; and the measurement of the triangles of the parallel of Ciudad Real to Badajoz has been commenced.   The triangles required to complete the spaces to the west of the meridian of Madrid have been laid down as far as that of Salamanca.

The triangulation of the second order is finished for the whole province of Madrid, as well as that for a part of the adjacent country. We are now only waiting for the results of the last calculations for compensation, which have just been completed, in order to fix the length of the great base of Madridejos, and begin the long calculation of the work which has been done.

This year these different undertakings will be continued, and signals will be fixed for the measurement of the parallel to the east of Madrid, with the intention of making, concurrently with this work, simultaneous and reciprocal observations to determine the geodistic level, and settle with accuracy the elevation of Madrid above the Mediterranean, presumed at present upon the most received existing calculations to be 660 mètres, which is, perhaps, within ten inches of the truth.

The topographical labours thus undertaken in the province of Madrid will be continued during the year.   The corresponding land registration will at the same time be proceeded with, and the levels will be very carefully taken.

The maps are on the scale of $\frac{1}{10000}$, and of $\frac{1}{500}$ for cities and buildings.   The classifications, territorial valuations, and dispositions in the public archives, will commence as soon as a portion of the province is completed.   The topography is executed with very great accuracy.

During the past year a portion of the Tagus, and of its tributary the Gallo, has been mapped to form a portion of the hydrography of Spain.

The geological department has completed its work in the provinces of Burgos, Santander, and Madrid, and has commenced with those of Leon, Zamora, and Avita.

In the department of Woods and Forests various topographical details have been obtained in the provinces of Santander, Burgos, Valencia, Asturias, Oviedo, and Leon.

All these works have been executed under the direction of the Funta-General of Estadistica, who is appointed by the Government to take charge of scientific researches regarding the Spanish territory.

The Hydrographic Department has published various interesting works, more especially some on the Philippine Islands.

The War Department has completed the itinerary of Navarre, and published a beautiful atlas of the campaign in Africa, accompanied with very interesting topographical documents. The itineraries of different provinces are in progress, and some of them will be shortly published.

The results of the statistical returns made at the close of the year 1860 are now in the press, under the direction of the Statistical Board. This is also the case with a very complete Directory of all our provinces. Similar returns from the colonies have likewise been made, and will soon be published.

The same department has published Geological Memoirs regarding the provinces of Avita and Leon, and likewise the Topography of the province of Madrid, with a geological map. The whole of these are due to Don Coriano di Prado.

The plans for railways, canals, and roads, made for the most part by the Department of Public Works, have been prepared with zeal and activity, and some interesting results have been obtained in relation to topography and comparative levels of the country. A Memoir has likewise been published respecting the Public Works in Spain, and is accompanied with a map.

Other interesting works by private individuals have been finished, and in some instances published, amongst which are essays on the ancient Geography of Spain; and special mention must be made of a memoir on the site of the city of Munda, which obtained the prize of the Academy of History.

M. Coello has continued the publication of his Provincial Atlas, and has recently brought out the maps of four provinces. In the beginning of last year he published a general Map of Spain, corrected from the most recent data, a copy of which he has kindly presented to our Society.

## RUSSIA.*

Although important questions of social and political reform have been engaging the attention of all intellects in Russia, yet the advance of geographical science there, I am happy to say, has not been retarded.

The Imperial Geographical Society of St. Petersburg continues to display its wonted zeal and activity. Fresh materials are yearly

* John Michell, Esq., F.R.G.S.

contributed by it towards the elucidation and amplification of the geography both of Russia and of the regions by which that country is bounded.

The expedition sent to explore Eastern Siberia has made considerable progress in its labours. According to latest accounts from Port St. Olga, Mr. Schmidt, chief geologist of the expedition, had started to examine the coast from the estuary of the Amur to Possiet harbour. Mr. Glehn, his coadjutor, was employed in a geological exploration of the island of Sahalin, while Mr. Brylkin directed his attention to its ethnography. On the return of the expedition to St. Petersburg in the autumn of the present year, and on the termination of the labours connected with it, the Imperial Geographical Society will devote its time and means to further scientific enterprise. The Council have already under consideration the adoption of measures for organising three new expeditions. One will examine the causes that have led to the gradual shallowing of the Sea of Azof; the object of the second will be to explore that portion of the Russian frontier which adjoins the Chinese territory on the east; the character of the third will be statistico-ethnographical, and the field of its labours will be the interior governments of Russia.

The progressive shallowing of the Sea of Azof had attracted attention for many years. It was supposed to be caused by ballast being thrown overboard from merchant-vessels. On this supposition it was at one time proposed to prohibit the entrance into the Sea of Azof of all ships, either Russian or foreign, not ballasted with water. The Government, however, did not adopt this measure, as doubts were entertained of the correctness of the above supposition.

In 1860 the Academy of Sciences of St. Petersburg arrived at the conclusion that the shoaling of the Sea of Azof had been going on for centuries; that it was not general, but only limited to certain parts; that it was not produced by a discharge of ballast, but was attributable to different local conditions, such as the state of the sea-bottom, proximity of the steppe, violence of winds and currents, &c. It further expressed its opinion that a scientific expedition to examine these circumstances would be productive of useful results.

These conclusions met with the approval of the august President of the Imperial Geographical Society; and the Society was authorised to send a scientific commission to the Sea of Azof. An annual sum of 5000 silver rubles (810l.), for two years, was assigned from the imperial treasury to defray the expenses of the expedition, which is now being organised.

In October last the Russian Minister for Foreign Affairs informed the Imperial Geographical Society that a commission would proceed in the spring of this year to trace the boundary-line between Russia and China on the east, and invited the Society to take advantage of this opportunity for scientific exploration. The Council gratefully accepted the proposal, and have now under consideration the ways and means for acting on it.

According to the treaty concluded between Russia and China in 1860, the line of demarcation should extend from the sources of the Yenisei to the Tian-Shan range of mountains, south of Lake Issyk-kul. The starting-point to be taken is the landmark of Chabin-Dabaga, on the frontiers of the governments of Tomsk and Yeniseisk. This mark, erected in 1728, according to the treaty of Kiakhta, constituted then the most distant point of contact between the two empires. From Chabin-Dabaga the frontier runs in a south-westerly direction as far as Lake Dsai-San, extends along the ridge of the Djungarian Alataù, crosses the river Ili, and then follows the direction of the Tian-Shan to the confines of Kokan. This line of frontier, which has a length of about 2000 versts (1333¼ miles), has already been visited on many points by Russian scientific travellers. The country still presents a vast field for future exploration. The region extending to the west of the sources of the Yenisei has not as yet been visited by any traveller.

A commission has been appointed, on the recommendation of Mr. Bezobrazof, for organising an expedition into the interior of Russia, with the special object of collecting statistico-ethnographical data. The commission, presided over by Mr. Kalatchof, consists of MM. Artemief, Bezobrazof, Vernadski, Vtorof, Kalinofski, Kostomarof, Maksimof, Nebolsin, Neiharat, Stackelberg, and Schepkin.

Among the cartographical labours of the Imperial Geographical Society a map of Eastern Siberia, by M. Schwartz, deserves special notice. It consists of seven sheets, and embraces on a scale of $\frac{1}{1,680,000}$ the fluvial region of the Amur, the southern portions of the Lena and Yenisei, and of the island of Sahalin. Although many maps of Eastern Siberia have latterly appeared, that of M. Schwartz is the most reliably correct. As its indications are very detailed, and based on exact astronomical determinations, it will serve to complete and rectify the hitherto existing maps.

Mr. Helmersen has compiled a new geological map of Russia.

Several years have elapsed since the appearance of a similar map by Sir Roderick Murchison, M. Verneuil, and Count Keiserling, while the intervening period has been rich in geological discoveries in Russia. In many localities the limits of formation have been more distinctly defined; and this has induced Mr. Helmerson to construct a new map, with the assistance of the well-known Russian geologists, Pander, Hofmann, Abich, Auerbach, Barbot, Grewingk, Feophilatof, and Holmberg.

The 'Journal of the Imperial Geographical Society' for the past year contains, as formerly, articles of high geographical interest. The materials on Central Asia are, in particular, abundant. I may especially direct attention to the sketches of Djungaria, and to a description of the Chinese province of Nan-lu, or Little Bukhara, by Captain Valikhanof, the son of a Kaisak sultan. This traveller and Russian savant, as a native of Central Asia, intimately acquainted with the languages and customs of the countries he visited, enjoyed every facility for studying and describing these hitherto almost inaccessible regions. In the garb of a Kokand merchant, in 1859 he succeeded in reaching Kashgar, and now gives an interesting account of his journey. He minutely describes the atrocities committed by Valikhan, Hodja of Kashgar, who in 1857 ordered the execution of the deeply-lamented Adolphe Schlagintweit, and throws further light on the death of that traveller.

The Sketches of Djungaria, with a detailed description, historical and geographical, of Little Bukhara, will shortly appear in English before the public, and will doubtless prove a valuable addition to our knowledge of the geography of those countries.

### ASIA.*

The Russian traveller, N. de Khanikof, who has been engaged in making up the deficiencies in our imperfect knowledge of the Aderbeijan, in Persia, has made a new map of that region, which he has had engraved at Berlin. He has distributed several copies of it, and transmitted his observations regarding that interesting mountain district to the Academy of Sciences in Paris, and also to our secretary, Dr. Shaw, for the use of the Royal Geographical Society.

An uncommon degree of regularity characterises the mountain-ranges of this province of Persia, which is bounded both on the east and on the west by lofty longitudinal ridges. To the east the Talish

---

* N. Khanikoff (translated by Dr. Hodgkin, Hon. Foreign Secretary.)

mountains separate it from the basin of the Caspian; and to the west the chain of Kandilar forms a barrier between it and Mesopotamia. To the north and to the south of the Aderbeijan these two chains are joined by longitudinal elevations : the one, commencing at Mount Savalan (of 4752 mètres), joins the Kandilan chain in Kurdistan ; the other, coming off from the Talish mountains, and known as the Buzgush chain, joins Mount Sehend (of 3505 mètres). The space included between Mount Savalan and the Talish chain of mountains is occupied by the plain of Mughan, and the Salt Lake of Urmia is situated in the region lying between the Sehend and the Kandilan chain. The lowest point of this part of Persia, that is to say, the level of the Lake of Urmia, is 1250 mètres above the level of the sea ; and the highest point in the province of Aderbeijan is the summit of Ararat, 5169 mètres high. The line of perpetual snow varies in elevation from 3600 to 3800 mètres. This regular arrangement of the surface of the district, and the character of the climate, dependent on its high position, are very favourable for topographical work. The state of the atmosphere is generally so clear that one is never long without being able to see some one of the lofty summits which serve as landmarks for reference ; and it rarely happens that mirage or dry fog interrupts the distinct vision of objects for an entire day. Notwithstanding the precision with which the skilful topographers from amongst the officers of the Caucasus who acted under his orders, as well as himself, endeavoured to execute the work of laying down the itineraries of detached regions, it would be impossible to combine these independent labours without the basis of some well-determined astronomical or geometrical observations. These happily were not wanting, as he had latitudes and longitudes in Persia which had been settled by M. Lemm, and the results of the triangulation of the Caucasus under the direction of General Chosdzko. The former gave a series of fixed points in the neighbourhood of the Araxes ; and the latter supplied the like data, rigorously established, between Erivan and the basin of the Caspian. Hence the localities given in the north and middle of Khanikof's map have their exact bearings; and it is only in the south that he had no other data than such as were obtained by azimuths measured with the help of the magnetic needle. The errors to which such observations are necessarily liable will be corrected when the Anglo-Russian commission for defining the Turkish and Russian boundary shall have published its numerous astronomic data.

That part of the map which is strictly new is the southern portion, in which is situated the Lake Urmia, with its islands ; the itinerary from Marand to Khoi ; and the topographical details in the two provinces of Persian Kurdistan, Lahijan and Ushnu, in which he had the good fortune to complete the researches of his predecessors, Generals Monteith and Rawlinson.

## CHINA.*

Geography is already beginning to share ·in the advantages derivable from Lord Elgin's treaty, the conditions of which so greatly improve the position of the foreigner in China, whether traveller or official, merchant or missionary.    Until that treaty came into operation, our countrymen could only penetrate the interior of this vast country in the face of legal prohibitions, and with the liability of arrest at the hands of the native authorities. The new treaty gives British subjects the right of travelling with a passport through the whole land, and so readily has this permission been availed of, that, in the first year after this right was obtained, twelve out of the eighteen provinces of China have been visited by our countrymen, together with Manchoo Tartary, the cradle of the present dynasty.

First among these explorations comes the ascent of the Yang-tze-Kiang, so gallantly undertaken by Colonel Sarel, Captain Blakiston, Dr. Barton, and Mr. Scheresheffsky, the details of which are familiar to us all ; while the high sense entertained by this Society of the services these gentlemen have rendered to geography has been marked, as you have seen this day, by the presentation of the Patron's Medal to Captain Blakiston.    In tracing the great Yang-tze along 1800 miles of its course, those travellers crossed the six central provinces of Keangsoo, Nganhwuy, Keangse, Hoo-pih, Hoonan, and Sze-chuen ; and thus carried their explorations up-wards of a thousand miles beyond any point that had previously been openly visited by foreign travellers.    The first 700 miles of that river's course is now made familiar to Europeans by the opening of the port of Hankow to foreign commerce, and there is every prospect of the high expectations that have been formed of the capacity of that great central mart being fully realized.    Within eight months of the opening of that port it had been visited by nearly 200 foreign craft, consisting for the most part of small

* Sir Harry Parkes, K.C.B., H.B.M. Consul at Shanghae.

steamers; and the foreign trade thus conducted amounted during the first six months to two millions sterling.

Some particulars of no less than seven other journeys, undertaken by our countrymen in the north, centre, and south of China during the past year, have been made public. In the north, Mr. Morrison, our Consul at the new port of Chefoo, with Captain Harcourt as his companion, travelled overland to his post from Teentsin in the month of January, and profited by the opportunity thus afforded him to follow the Grand Canal along nearly 300 miles of its track, to visit the tomb of the great sage Confucius, which is to be seen at Kewfoo, in the charge of his own descendants, a family with a pedigree of 2500 years, dating from the time of the sage himself. Mr. Morrison also visited Tsenan, the capital, and other places in the hitherto unexplored province of Shantung, and the journey took these travellers over 700 miles of country, for the most part new to Europeans. Six months later, two other foreigners set out in an opposite direction, and travelled overland from Teentsin to Moukden, the capital of Manchoo Tartary. They were struck by the manner in which this once Tartar country has been virtually converted into a Chinese province by the superior energy of the Chinese emigrants, and report that the Manchoos, even in this their native land, have lost their ground entirely in all parts of the country where anything is to be made by agriculture and commerce; and that those who remain, by adopting Chinese manners, customs, and *language*, have become, to all intents and purposes, Chinese, and have been absorbed into the predominant race. Later in the year, in November and December, an expedition through the two northern provinces of China, Pe-chih-le and Shan-se, was undertaken by Messrs. Richards and Slossin. Starting from the same point—Teentsin—they appear to have ascended the high plateaus to the north of Peking, and to have skirted the Mongolian steppes until they reached Shan-se. They travelled in this province as far as its capital Tai-yuen, and then, turning westward, re-entered Pe-chih-le, and visited Paou-king, the capital of the latter province, on their way back to Teentsin. The journey occupied the travellers 46 days, during which time they appear to have crossed the Great Wall four times, finding it in a state of decay that may be feared is typical of the country of which it is the chief monument, and they estimate the total length of their journey at 1560 English miles. The flourishing and populous condition of most of the country through which they passed accounts for the success of the new northern port of Teentsin, the foreign trade of which, in the first year of its being opened, has reached the considerable sum of two millions sterling.

In the centre of China, four gentlemen—Messrs. Dickson, Thorburn, Beach, and Bonney—travelled, in the month of April, from Canton to Hankow, a distance of 756 miles, which they performed in 18 days; their journey differing from those above recited as being made entirely by water, with the exception of one day's land travel across the mountain-range that divides the province of Kwangtung from Hoo-nan. Following the course of the north river in the first-named province, and the Seang river in the latter, they thus traversed both those provinces from south to north, and were the first modern explorers of the great Tung-ting lake, by which they reached the Yang-tze and Hankow. In Chehkiang, Mr. Baker, having recently ascended the Tseentang river, and visited the celebrated green-tea districts of Nganhwuy, has again gone over ground previously travelled by Mr. Fortune, but to find in this instance that the previous prosperous condition of those important tea districts has disappeared before the rebel·scourge, and that scenes of industry have been replaced by desolation and destruction.

In the south of China, the Rev. Dr. Legge was the first foreigner to ascend, in April of last year, the east river in the Kwangtung province to a distance of about 300 miles; and the Rev. Mr. Irwin and companions have penetrated up the west river, in the same province, to a somewhat higher point than that reached by the expedition under Captain McCleverty in the spring of 1859, for a description of which we are indebted to our associate Lieutenant Brine. The opening of Formosa to foreign trade gives promise also of our shortly obtaining further information from that island, which is interesting not only from its commercial productions, but also from the presence of aboriginal tribes in its centre and eastern coast, of which little is as yet known.

It is satisfactory to hear from all these travellers that no serious obstacles were placed in their way either by the Chinese authorities or the people; and that, while inconvenienced at times by the not unnatural curiosity of the latter, when anxious to gaze on foreigners for the first time, they received from them, in most cases, friendly welcome and assistance. Our treaty-right to enter the country having thus obtained an effectual recognition, it will be seen that China is now thrown open to the researches of the traveller, subject, however, to the difficulties arising out of the deplorable disorders which are at present rife in so many of its provinces. Different parties of rebels or robbers, all acting independently of each other, were met by Colonel Sarel's party in Sze-chuen, by Mr. Morrison in Shantung, by Mr. Baker in Chehkeang, and by Mr. Irwin in Kwangtung; while Dr. Dickson's party, on the other hand, travelled from Canton to Hankow—or from the south to the centre of China —without falling in with any of these destructive hordes; and Messrs. Richards and Slossin traversed the provinces of Shan-se and Pe-chih-le under similar favourable circumstances.

## AUSTRALIA.*

Every new year brings with it, as we might well expect, recitals of fresh discoveries in this vast and important region of British colonization, of which, in a broad sense, it may be said that we have as yet only occupied the eastern, southern, and western coasts, and partially their adjacent interior lands. No sooner had we bestowed one of our Gold Medals on McDouall Stuart, for his adventurous exploration from South Australia to the northern watershed, than we heard of his having again started in the endeavour to reach the sea which bathes the northern shore of the continent. In the mean time, however, whilst he has again returned, after reaching the watershed of tropical Australia, that end has been attained on a more eastern meridian by the expedition under the command of Richard O'Hara Burke, assisted by the geographer William J. Wills. Notwithstanding the belief of a great number of old colonists and travellers, and which is still entertained, that horses and bullocks are to be preferred for these adventurous journeys, the ascertained fact is, that the scheme suggested many years ago by the Geographical Society, of employing camels as the beasts of burden, is that by which the continent has first been traversed from south to north by any of our countrymen.

Whilst two Australian colonies were thus eager rivals in these discoveries, and that the flourishing younger colonists of Queensland, on the north-east, have been extending the range of their feeding-grounds to zones almost intertropical, and approaching towards the Gulf of Carpentaria, the north-western limits of Western Australia have been vastly extended by the successful survey, by Mr. F. Gregory, of that large portion of the very exten-

---

* By Sir Roderick Impey Murchison, Vice-Pres. R.G.S.

sive lands which lie between the settled parts of that colony and the Cambridge Gulf.

Let us then devote, in the first place, a few words to the consideration of each of these last important discoveries.

The Victorian expedition, though perfectly successful in the main object of discovering a track to the north, through lands which are for the first time made known to us as being capable of occupation at no distant day, and in reaching the mouth of one of the tributaries of the Gulf of Carpentaria, had, alas! a tragical end. Its bold leader, Burke, as well as his companion, the accomplished geographer, Wills, have fallen, but not until their observations have assured us that they reached the northern shore, at the mouth of the Flinders River. And here we may well applaud the suggestion of Sir H. Barkly, that the great newly-discovered belt of good land between Cooper's Creek and the south end of the Gulf of Carpentaria should be called "Burke's Land;" so that the name of the gallant explorer will thus be perpetuated on the east, as that of Stuart has been properly associated with the chief highlands on the west. As the gallant Burke and his associates had long been absent, and reports arose of their failure and difficulties with which they were beset, it was highly to the credit of the coterminous colonies of South Australia and Queensland that they both made vigorous endeavours to aid in the rescue.

One of these efforts, as made by the direction of Sir Richard McDonnell and the Government of South Australia, proceeded over a considerable extent of new ground to the north-eastern part of that colony; and allusion to it will presently be made, as well as to other expeditions from Victoria and Queensland.

In considering the steps by which this great work of exploration of the interior has been brought to its present advanced state, we must not forget the feats of the laborious and able Surveyor-General of New South Wales, Sir Thomas Mitchell, who laid down sure bases of operation for those who were to follow him. It has also been well said by a recent traveller to the Darling,* and who has gone over much of the same ground, that, of all the expeditions subsequent to those of Mitchell, that under the command of our Medallist Sturt threw most light on the region to the north and north-west of Menendie. "The chivalrous Eyre," he writes, "had previously penetrated to the forbidden shores of Lake Torrens, and the indomitable Stuart has since very nearly crossed the continent;

---

* Mr. Haverfield.

but both of them I think would admit, that to Captain Sturt belongs the great honour of having opened the door to the vast central regions of Australia."

The Council of our Society has, indeed, judged well in assigning a Medal to the family of the lamented Burke, the leader of the Victorian expedition; and in offering a watch as a recompence to the sole survivor, the stout-hearted and faithful King, whose simple narrative of the deaths of his commanders, Burke and Wills, and of his own preservation of life among the kind natives, has touched the hearts of all who have read the tale.

The details of the labours of Burke and Wills in traversing and retraversing the continent have been so recently laid before the public, that it is unnecessary here to recapitulate them. We must not, however, pass over the Report of the Commissioners who were appointed by the Governor of Victoria to inquire into the circumstances connected with the sufferings and death of Burke and Wills. Endeavouring to ascertain the true causes of that lamentable result, they have thrown the chief blame on Mr. Wright, in not having left adequate supplies of provisions and clothing at Cooper's Creek. They also impute some discredit to the Exploration Committee, for not stimulating Mr. Wright to advance from the Darling, where he had been (as they say) in a state of "fatal inactivity and idling." And lastly, they reprove Mr. Brahe, for retiring from the relief depôt before he was rejoined by his commander, Burke; though, from the great responsibility and the want of sufficiently precise instructions, they excuse that gentleman for his unfortunate decision.

Whilst they regret " the absence of a systematic plan of operation on the part of the leader," they express " their admiration of his gallantry and daring, as well as of the fidelity of his brave coadjutor and their more fortunate and enduring associate King; and they conclude with recording " their feelings of deep sympathy with the deplorable sufferings and untimely deaths of Burke and his fellow comrades."

The friends of Burke must, indeed, derive great satisfaction from referring to the Despatches of Sir Henry Barkly, who generously vindicates the conduct of the gallant leader. In a letter to Sir R. Murchison he thus writes :—" It is true that he (Burke) was by nature impetuous, but we have in reality only heard one side of the case; and I do not feel quite sure that he did not leave definite instructions—possibly even in writing—with his second in command,

and at the Cooper Creek depôt, though none are forthcoming or acknowledged to have existed."   "At the worst," he says, "all that can be said of his conduct is, that he relied on others proving as brave and self-sacrificing as himself; that he was out of his reckoning on this point, and lost his own life in consequence." Finally, Sir Henry Barkly has well told Her Majesty's Secretary for the Colonies, that "a less daring leader might never have crossed the continent, or solved the problem so often vainly attempted."

But whilst from the expedition under Burke one man was saved, we have since been informed of the deaths of four white men, who were not long ago massacred in the interior, and of whose loss we should have been entirely ignorant, had not the Government of South Australia, under Sir Richard McDonnell, sent out, as before said, an exploring party from the south-west, to cut in upon the route of Burke.

After passing over lands, in some parts sterile and saliferous, in others watered and productive, the searching party of McKinlay and his assistant Hodgkinson (which was also well found in camels, as well as with horses and provisions) met with the relics of four white men, the skulls and skeletons of whom showed incontestable proofs of their having been murdered.   Having obtained possession of a native who had evidently been one of the murderers, since his body exhibited healed-up wounds, and the lodgment of a ball as well as of buck-shot under the skin, he gave to the explorers a recital of the massacre, and how the natives had eaten the flesh of their enemies.   As the hair of the victims was still adhering to their skulls, and seemed to the travellers to be of the same colours as those of Burke and his party ; and further, as what was taken for "camel" dung was found near the spot, they jumped to the natural conclusion that in this spot (lat. 27° 15' s., long. 139° 50' E., and consequently not far from the return route of Burke) they had really discovered the remains of Burke and his three companions. On their return to the settlements of the colony, however, this theory was entirely dispelled by the true account of the deaths of Burke and Wills, and of the safe return of the sole survivor, King. Who, then, were these unfortunate four explorers of the interior ? That they were British subjects, and not natives, is certain; not only from the skeletons and the colours of their hair, but also by the discovery of an English almanac of 1858.   We also know that they had made a vigorous resistance, which is established, not only by the testimony of the black man, but also by the gun-shot wounds inflicted on him.  Then, again, we have the proofs of the savage nature of this band of the aborigines, by learning that, after this one native left them, McKinlay's party were shortly assailed by a large well-armed body, who were only repelled by a hot fire from our countrymen.

What a mystery is this, then, and how are we to explain it? Surely we ought to be able to obtain, from the settlers on the outskirts of the colonies of Victoria and South Australia, some information to throw light on the journey into the interior of any persons who may be identified with these hapless men!  Again, is it not strange that, at so short a distance as exists between the site of this massacre and that of the deaths of Burke and Wills, the character of the aborigines should differ so essentially? for we are assured by the diary of the last days of Wills, that he and his associates were treated with great kindness by the natives.  We also know, from the testimony of the survivor King, that when these poor creatures (among whom he lived until the relief finally reached him) saw the bodies of Burke and Wills they wept over them, because they saw that they might have saved our countrymen from starvation.  We thus know that there are generous and tender-hearted aborigines in Australia, as well as those who appear to be irreclaimable and cruel savages; and this, too, in tribes not distant from each other.

Leaving this problem to be solved between our friends the ethnologists and philanthropists, we may in the mean time anticipate that with such energies as have been displayed by the explorers proceeding from our settled colonies in the last thirty years, including the older researches of Mitchell, Eyre, Sturt, Leichardt, and others, there can be no doubt that the colonists of Queensland will soon extend their pastures to the Gulf of Carpentaria; and that the northernmost settlers of South Australia, following up the track of Stuart, will ere long found establishments in the bosom of the noble recesses of Cambridge Gulf and the northern Victoria River, where fleets can anchor securely, and where the vegetation is luxuriant.

If the northern coast of this great continent is thus destined to be occupied by migrations from the east and south, it has recently been to a considerable extent successfully surveyed from the west by Mr. Frank Gregory; who, in extending the boundary of Western Australia, and in demonstrating the existence of large tracts of fine

P 2

land, reaching eastwards to beyond east long. 121°, in lat. 21°, has led us to hope that not many years will elapse before the warm desire of British geographers will be realised by actual occupation —at all events by the description of the headlands and inner portions which lie between Nickol Bay and Cambridge Gulf.

Having conveyed his party, with horses and provisions, by sea, from Perth to Nickol Bay, Mr. Gregory first explored the interior to the south-west, or towards the tracts lying on the north-western exterior of the settlements of West Australia, which he had surveyed in 1848. Following up a river, which he named the Fortescue, for 180 miles, and which flows through good lands, he reached elevations, which he termed the Hammels' Range, and through which he travelled by a pass 2000 feet above the sea, in lat. 22° 15', and east long. 118° 4'. Beyond this range he found extensive fertile plains running far westwards, or towards the colony, as far as the eye could reach. Travelling still further with a smaller party to the south-west, he fell in with a large river flowing from the E.S.E. This he named the Ashburton, from our noble President; and, judging from the fine pasture-lands on its banks, he believes that this tract (which he connected by triangulation with Mount Augustus and the Lynn River of his former survey) will become in a few years a valuable district of the province.

Having returned to the vessel, to recruit and replenish his stores after this his first journey of 780 miles, Mr. F. Gregory then pushed his survey south-east and eastwards, and passed in succession rivers which were called the Yule, the Shelley, and the Shaw, and then to the recipient of the two last rivers—a finer stream, to which the name of De Grey was given, in honour of our last President, under whose auspices the expedition was initiated. Again, much fine land was observed, the united journeys amounting to 2040 miles.

The clear and interesting sketch of this survey which has already been given by Mr. F. Gregory will be much enhanced when his maps are constructed in the accurate manner with which he works out all his data. In the mean time we already learn that this newly-discovered region, consisting of a succession of terraces that rise from the shore to lofty plateaux 2500 feet above the sea, has its culminating point in Mount Bruce, at an altitude of 4000 feet; whilst within the limits of the route followed not less than 2,000,000 acres are fitted for grazing purposes, and at least 200,000 acres are suitable for cultivation. The fruits and plants which are indigenous include, among the latter, tobacco, sandal-wood, and palms; and the author conceives that, notwithstanding its *quasi* intertropical position, the district is as well adapted to the growth of wool, as grounds in the same latitude in Queensland have proved to be; whilst he feels confident that there are also considerable tracts specially available for raising cotton.

The varied eruptive rocks of the country, whether of granitic or of volcanic origin, and the different sedimentary formations, from high plateaux of older sandstone to the youngest and more calcareous and sandy deposits, have been carefully observed. Again, meteorological and magnetical data have been carefully registered; and we are informed that the aborigines, who are of fine stature, some of them exceeding 6 feet in height, might be made useful in labour, and would by no means prove unmanageable or troublesome if properly treated; whilst a valuable pearl-fishery may also be established in Nickol Bay.

This survey, being the last of the very important services which have been performed by Mr. F. Gregory, is the more entitled to our approbation, as it was undertaken at our recommendation to Her Majesty's Colonial Secretary, the Duke of Newcastle; and we have to thank His Grace for countenancing this expedition in conjunction with the local Colonial Government.

The complete success of this exploration, without the loss of a man, is a decisive proof of the skilful and well-considered prearrangements and conduct of the leader, and will, we trust, induce Her Majesty's Government to continue to place reliance on any suggestions which may in future proceed from the Council of the Royal Geographical Society.

In concluding these observations on the recent progress of discovery in Australia, we may well advert to the strenuous efforts made by the colonists of Victoria and Queensland to succour Burke and his party. Naturally anxious as we have been respecting the issue of the searching expeditions sent from Victoria by sea, and overland from Queensland, the news just received is highly gratifying to all geographers and philanthropists. Sir Henry Barkly has written to Sir R. Murchison, stating that, notwithstanding the wreck of the *Firefly* tender, of which we had heard, on one of the reefs in Torres Straits, the good management of Captain Norman, the commander of the *Victoria* steamer, has been such that the *Firefly* was emptied of water and tugged round into the Gulf of Carpentaria, in spite of much stormy weather. Arriving at the mouth of the Albert River, men and horses, with abundance of stores, were landed from those ships, as well as from two colliers, which had also been sent round; so that Mr. Landsborough, who had been recommended for the search by Mr. Gregory, was at once enabled to explore for some distance into the interior.

In the mean time Mr. Walker, who was sent with a party of aboriginal troopers from Brisbane and Rockhampton, having gained the mouth of the Albert, passed in his route the river Flinders, near the sea, and there, to his delight, found the distinct tracks of Burke's party; thus realising the truth of the narrative of the sole survivor, King, that Burke and Wills really reached the salt water of the Gulf of Carpentaria.  This discovery further confirms the belief of the astronomers and geographers who inquired into the subject, that it was the mouth of the Flinders, and not of the Albert, which the gallant adventurers had reached.  Being supplied with provisions for four months, Mr. Walker then returned to the mouth of the Flinders, to follow up the trail of Burke; and, as he had been gone 80 days when Captain Norman left the mouth of the Albert, we may reasonably expect to hear soon of his arrival at Cooper's Creek and the colony of Victoria.

Whilst Walker is thus occupied, Mr. Landsborough is proceeding southwards, on the meridian of the Albert River, to Victoria; and thus by this double exploration the whole of the region to which Sir H. Barkly has worthily assigned the name of " Burke's Land " will be thoroughly made known to us.

That which to many cautious persons seemed to be a chimera a few years ago, but which the writer of these lines has always regarded as a most desirable result, will therefore ere long be accomplished, and the shores of Tropical Australia will, through its great indentations, the Gulf of Carpentaria and Cambridge Gulf, be fairly occupied by our colonists, who, communicating with the southern colonies, from whence they spring, by the lines opened out by Stuart and Burke, will carry on an advantageous intercourse with the Eastern Archipelago, and afford grand and useful bays of refuge to all imperilled vessels.  Truly we may now rejoice that our Council has wisely, as well as generously, judged in assigning a Medal to the family of Burke, and in not omitting to mark their sense of the faithful conduct and truthful narrative of the brave old soldier, King.

Whilst such has been the progress of discovery in hitherto unknown lands, our knowledge concerning the real mineral structure of the regions already colonised has been largely increased.

The admirable Geological Maps of Victoria, prepared by Mr. Selwyn, and the palæontological illustrations thereof, by Professor McCay, would do honour to the most advanced country in Europe; and though the other colonies cannot as yet boast of similar proficiency in maps and sections, every geologist knows how much his science is indebted to the Rev. W. B. Clarke, for his long-continued and successful endeavours in developing the true geological structure of New South Wales.

If from Australia we extend our observations to other regions of Australasia colonised by Britain, you perceive the rapid progress which is made in the development of wealth, commerce, and civilisation. Thus in Tasmania, thanks to the vigorous endeavours of my young and able friend Mr. Charles Gould, coal-fields of value in the north-eastern portion of that great island have been laid open, and the valuable substance, dysodile, has been extracted.

Again, in New Zealand the Local Governments are exerting themselves to procure the services of scientific men, who, possessing an acquaintance with geography and topography, are well versed in the sciences of geology and mineralogy, and can indicate upon maps the real value of the subsoil of each district. Thus, whilst the able geologist, Dr. Hochstetter, who was one of the men of science who sailed round the world in the Austrian frigate *Novara*, has made us well acquainted with the nature of the rocks and the usefulness of the fossils found around Auckland, my friend Dr. Hector (with whose merits this Society is so well acquainted, through his admirable labours as the senior scientific officer of Palliser's expedition in North America) is now the geologist, geographer, and naturalist of the thriving Scottish colony of Otago, in the southernmost of the New Zealand islands.

So earnest, indeed, are the colonists of New Zealand to obtain a scientific insight into the nature of their rocks, that applications have recently been made to Sir R. Murchison to secure the services of a competent person to conduct a geological survey of the newly-settled district of Wellington.

<br>

AFRICA.*

It is long since tidings have reached us from either of our two medallists, Livingstone and Speke, in whose explorations our Society takes especial interest, both from the brilliancy of their former

---

* Francis Galton, Esq., Hon. Secretary, R.G.S.

achievements and the importance of their present undertakings.
Just before the anniversary of 1861 we heard of Livingstone's departure from the Zambesi, in his small steamer, to examine the
Rovuma River and ascertain whether any basis existed for the often-expressed belief that that river would afford a convenient and a
neutral highway to the vast regions of the Niassa, independent of
the complications of Portuguese territorial claims.  The result of
his examination reached us shortly afterwards : it was far from
satisfactory.  His steamer of light draught was unable to ascend
the Rovuma for more than a few miles, before it became necessary
to return hastily, else she would have been left grounded by the
falling waters until the ensuing rainy season.  Livingstone then
revisited the Zambesi and established the members of the University
mission in the healthiest quarters he could find near the banks of
the Shiré.

We have heard nothing whatever of Speke since our last anniversary, except a fragment of news which is exceedingly satisfactory, though it left him at a stage and a date little removed from
where he last wrote to us.  It will be remembered that he had then
described himself in trouble.  The desert of Ugogo was peculiarly
parched in 1861 ; he and the natives had difficulty in .obtaining
food, and a large number of his porters had deserted and left him.
We have since learnt, through a native merchant who had interchanged a few passing words with him, that Speke was accompanied
by a fresh body of porters, that he had extricated himself from the
desert of Ugogo, and was travelling rapidly and in excellent force
on the way to Unianyembe.

Provisions will not fail him if he emerges this summer at Gondakoro on the White Nile, for by aid of the funds liberally subscribed
by many Fellows of this Society and by Mr. Consul Petherick's
furtherance, boats laden with grain were despatched by that gentleman, under a proper escort, from Khartum up the White Nile, early
in this year.

The present condition of the White Nile is such as to grieve
deeply those who believe commerce to be the most effectual agent
in civilizing Africa.  Fifteen years ago the natives along its shores
were mostly inoffensive and hospitable to travellers ; but the stream
of trade that has yearly passed along it, uncontrolled by any moral
supervision, and mostly in the hands of reckless adventurers and
lawless crews, has driven the numerous tribes along its banks into
so general and deep an hostility against strangers, that the White

Nile cannot now be ascended except by an armed force of considerable magnitude.

The hopes we entertained last year of an increased knowledge of the Upper White Nile, through the independent labours of M. Lejean and Dr. Peney, have failed us, owing to the illness and return of the former gentleman and the premature death of the latter. Dr. Peney did some good service to geography before he died : he travelled westwards from Gondakoro for 60 miles, and there apparently struck the penultimate stage of Petherick's former expedition. If this be the case—and the identity of the names of the places and tribes and geographical features leave hardly room for doubt—an enormous rectification becomes necessary in the estimated extent and direction of Petherick's itinerary. Peney also travelled above Gondakoro, through the cataracts, to nearly the furthest point of which we have even a rumour, and he places his goal at about one degree south of Gondakoro, and on absolutely the same meridian. ,

The determination of the altitude and snowy summit of Kilimanjaro, by the Baron von der Decken and his geological associate Mr. Thornton, has gladdened African geographers, who felt it was little creditable to their science that so interesting a subject should remain year after year open to question. It is a pleasure to find that the wanderings of missionaries, solely in the pursuit of their calling, should have led them here, as it has often done elsewhere, to be the first discoverers of new lands and pioneers to more accurate research.

An elaborate report on the dominions of Zanzibar, by Lieut.-Colonel Rigby, has been published in the Selections from the Records of the Bombay Goverment. It appears from subsequent accounts that the condition of that island has lately fallen into a very disturbed state.

On the coast of Africa opposite to Kilimanjaro, Captain Burton, our ever active medallist and now H. M. Consul at Fernando Po, has materially contributed to a survey of the large creeks and rivermouths which form a characteristic feature of those shores, and in the knowledge of which we are unduly deficient. We hear also of his ascent of the lofty Cameroon Mountain, and shall doubtless receive from him a detailed account of that extinct volcano, which in its origin, latitude, and proximity to the sea, as well as by its prominence, holds a position on the West Coast curiously corresponding to that of Kilimanjaro on the East of Africa.

The French have exerted themselves with energy in reconnoitring the tributaries of the great bay or estuary of the Gaboon, all of which take their rise in the flanks of the neighbouring mountain chain through which the Ogobai, familiar to us by the writings of Du Chaillu, bursts its way, in its course from a more distant interior.

Numerous explorations have been made in Senegambia and in the North-Western Sahara. The travels of Boo Moghdad are perhaps the most important. He left St. Louis on the Senegal, and passed to Mogador, on the coast of Marocco. Lambert's journey to Timbo is also of great interest. Duveyrier has returned to Algiers with large stores of information gathered in the Sahara, which he is preparing for publication, and which African geographers await with keen interest. We are sorry to hear that that energetic young traveller is suffering very severely from the effect of his many journeys.

Heuglin's expedition in search of information bearing on Vogel's fate, in Wadai, has made some advance in his necessarily circuitous route. He landed at Massowa and spent some months in Abyssinia, awaiting the favourable season for onward travel. His researches in that country have been original and minute, especially with regard to the geology and hypsometry of its northern borderland.

Our medallist Barth is engaged in the publication of a work of paramount importance to African ethnologists, namely, an elaborate collection of vocabularies of the tribes of Central Africa. It is mainly from a comparison of dialects that we may hope to unravel some portion of the mutual relations and early history of the various races which inhabit that large portion of the earth's surface, and we rejoice that the present work has been undertaken by so accomplished a philologist and geographer.

Finally, large maps of Africa are in progress of publication, the one by Dr. Petermann, in his comprehensive 'Mittheilungen,' and the other by Mr. Ravenstein, in England.*

---

* Since the Anniversary Meeting, intelligence has been received of Dr. Livingstone's navigation of the west coast of the Nyassa (in an open boat) up to lat. 11° 20'; during the whole of which distance (200 miles) its width appeared never to exceed 60 miles, no large river was seen to flow into it, and no certain account was obtainable of its northern termination. It lay between highlands; its waters were of great depth, and continually and dangerously stormy. The same mail informed us of the deaths, from fever, of Bishop Mackenzie and of another important member of the University mission.

## OUR OWN LABOURS.*

The relation of the Society to the wide range of science which it cultivates may be referred to with satisfaction. Through its influence, or by its Associates, it may be identified with most of the enterprises which enlarge the knowledge of the more remote regions or add to the details of those more intimately known. Although the progress of geography—a science which has been the growth of so many ages—can be but imperfectly estimated by the brief retrospect of the limited period to which this notice must be confined, still the past *two* years have been marked by some very important accessions to our knowledge.

It might perhaps be inferred that the industry of modern travellers, so well and so persistently carried on, would have left to these later times but few regions unexplored, or features to be noticed in primary discovery; but the late Transactions of our Society will lead to the inference that there lies hidden much more than has been revealed, and that our motto " Ob terrae reclusas," will still apply almost as justly to the countries close around us as to the still unknown mysteries of Africa or Australia. The last volumes of our Transactions publish the details of primary discovery and exploration more extensive and important, of countries absolutely unknown before, than those contained in the first, when the true course of the then mysterious Niger, or the earliest journeys into the interior of Australia, were described.

There is one evidence of the appreciation of the Society and its usefulness in the unbroken chain of travellers and labourers which are and have been connected with it; those of later times being often the friends, pupils, or associates of those who first enriched its volumes with the results of their enterprise, and whose works may be traced continuously from its origin to those which I shall briefly allude to presently. The Annual Addresses of former Presidents will show how large a share has been taken in the progress of Geography by the Royal Geographical Society since its foundation.

EUROPE.—In Europe the work of general research into the minute details of geography is far too great for individual labour, and the Addresses of your Presidents will show what great undertakings are carried on by various Governments; but that there is room for per-

* Alexander George Findlay, Esq., F.R.G.S.

sonal enterprise is shown by the communications of our well-known Associates Capt. Sherard Osborne, Capt. Spratt, and Major Stokes, on the course of the Lower Danube, descriptions of great national utility.

Our Corresponding Member, Professor Paul Chaix, has sent us an account of the surveys connected with the Great Federal Map of Switzerland, which have been in progress for half a century. Professor Holst, of Christiania, has also given an account, rendered for us by our Secretary, Dr. Norton Shaw, of the important and excellent surveys in Norway, which have been proceeding since the year 1779, a period at the dawn of geodetical science.

We have an interesting account of a portion of the Caucasus, the country of the Lesghi tribes of Hilly Daghestan, by the Baron de Bode, son of our deceased Associate. This communication, and a more widely extended dissertation on the Caucasus generally, by Captain D. Cameron, F.R.G.S., draws attention to an enchanting country and a most interesting people, or rather variety of races. As a region for tourists, the Caucasus would seem to present attractions and novelties far exceeding those met with on most beaten tracks.

Iceland was visited by the expedition which examined into the geographical positions for the proposed Atlantic telegraph by the northern route; and our excellent Associate and Medallist, Dr. Rae, has given us a graphic account of his crossing this interesting island.

ASIA has afforded a large field for the enterprise of those of our Associates who have penetrated into its less known regions recently laid open to us by political events.

The most important of these is the navigation and accurate survey of the upper portion of that great river which is the pride of China, the Yang-tze-Kiang. In a late volume of the Journal an account is given by our well-known Associate, Mr. Laurence Oliphant, the Secretary to the Embassy, of the ascent of the river to Hankow, 623 miles above its mouth. To this expedition was also attached our excellent Associate Capt. Sherard Osborne, who, in the Arctic regions, in the Black Sea, and elsewhere, has done such good service to geography. Another arctic officer, Mr. Court, who, under Sir R. M'Clure, performed the North-West Passage, also aided in this good work. Mr. Blackney's name must also be associated in this expedition, as having given us an excellent account of his observations. It will be fresh in the memory of all that these officers and their coadjutors ascended this mighty river in vessels of large draught of water to this great distance with our eminent Fellow Lord Elgin.

It must be a subject of gratification to the Society that the further exploration of this mighty and important river should have been executed through the personal zeal of our Associates, who have just received the highest mark of our appreciation, and who, like the officers of the preceding expedition, have won laurels in very different quarters of the globe. This topic is alluded to in another portion of this Address; but it is difficult to overrate the importance of these communications, either in a commercial sense or in relation to our future intercourse with that industrious and peculiar people.

In another part of China, the warfare led our Associate Lieut. Brine, with an expedition under Capt. M'Cleverty, R.N., up the Si-Kiang; and he has given us an account of the country through which the ships passed for 75 miles, and of the capabilities of the river for commercial purposes. This and the interesting communications of Capt. Sprye, and our Associate Dr. M'Cosh, on the countries on the west frontier of China, have been alluded to in a previous Address.

It is to be regretted that political circumstances prevented the expedition under Capt. Smyth, accompanied by Lieut. Jackson, Dr. Stewart, &c., from proceeding into Chinese Tartary last year. When our relations with China shall have attained a more firm basis, this important subject may be renewed, and will assuredly have again, as in the first case, all the support and countenance the Society can give.

Lieut. Oliver, R.A., has sent us some notes on the country west of Canton—another addition to our knowledge of this hitherto almost hidden country.

In an adjacent region we have had some interesting matter communicated by the late M. Mouhot, on Cambodia, where he had been resident for some years; and Mr. Edw. O'Riley has sent some notes on a tour through the Shan States. The communications of Mr. D. O. King of his journeys to the south-east of Bangkok, alluded to in a former Address, and the notes on the same country, collected by our Associate Mr. Jas. Campbell, demonstrate how busy is the spirit of inquiry respecting these countries, which have remained almost entirely closed to Europeans till recent times.

Foremost in the research stands our indefatigable Corresponding

Associate and Medallist Sir Robert H. Schomburgk, busy in the acquisition of information, and active in travelling through this hitherto little visited country and enervating climate. He has forwarded us several memoirs on the country of Siam, in which he represents the British Government: one on a boat-voyage to the town of Pecha-buri, and many particulars of a region which we only knew from vague conjecture or crude delineation. His Report on the trade and resources of this country are of high interest. Another of these communications was an account of a painful journey he had accomplished up the great river Menam, and thence on the backs of elephants to Moulmein, in our own possessions on the Bay of Bengal. It is thirty years since he gained his first reputation in the Transactions of the Royal Geographical Society, by his survey of Anegada in the West Indies, and twenty-three years since he claimed its Medal for his extensive and excellent researches in British Guiana and neighbouring countries. These are so well remembered that they need only be adverted to here to associate his earlier adventures with the later communications which we have welcomed.

In JAPAN the Society and our Associates have taken a deep and active interest, and have zealously endeavoured to advance our knowledge of this important country. It will be sufficient here to allude to the Papers sent by our Associate Mr. Rutherford Alcock, Her Majesty's envoy to that country. His accounts of his journeys into the interior, and of his ascent of their sacred mountain Fusiyama, form an epoch in geographical progress.

Another narrative is also most interesting, that of the journeys of Mr. Pemberton Hodgson into the interior of the untravelled and uncivilized island of Yeso. The discussions which ensued on these Papers, and the remarks of Mr. Laurence Oliphant, Sir Frederick Nicholson, Mr. Wylie, and others, must be of great interest to those who have watched the early stages of our intercourse with the Japanese. One fact of importance, often repeated by geographers, is manifest by the experience of Mr. Hodgson in these several journeys. Although unarmed, and accompanied by ladies, he travelled safely amid the demi-savage inhabitants, who had never before seen a European, without the slightest obstruction, and receiving perfect courtesy and hospitality. This fact, which may be also gathered from the experience of many in all parts of the world, teaches a lesson to those who first meet with untutored men, that they should be treated with that consideration the want of which has generally been the origin of that opprobrium too frequently bestowed upon what is retaliation.

Political events have placed another country prominently before the geographical world. The great river Amur has been found to be one of the most important rivers of Northern Asia, as by it the vast and isolated central steppes of Mongolia can be readily approached by water-conveyance; and it is even stated that, with a very small amount of road and canal, the traffic could easily be carried on from the Pacific to the Baltic. The Addresses of Sir Roderick Murchison will tell how much the Russian explorers and surveyors have done to elucidate the geography of this region, and the excellent map constructed by Mr. Arrowsmith will show its features at a glance.

In the last published volume of our Transactions we have a further accession to Asiatic geography—a translation of the narrative and account of a Journey to the Tian-Shan, or Celestial Mountains, in Russian Tartary, by P. P. Semenoff, which was undertaken under the auspices of the Imperial Russian Geographical Society. M. Semenoff was the first European who visited (in 1857) this gigantic range—one of the four which traverse Asia in a parallel direction, only two of which have been explored, the Himalayas from the south, and the Altai from the north. Another translated Memoir on the same country is also given, by M. A. Golubef, who has travelled on the Chinese frontier.

There are two Papers on the beautiful valley of Kashmir by our Associates, Mr. W. H. Purdon, c.e., and Capt. H. H. Austen. In addition to a description of the physical features of this interesting country, they give a farther account of that most remarkable and important work, the Trigonometrical Survey of India, as carried over it. In former Addresses and Memoirs this immense undertaking, carried on by the East India Company, first under Colonel Lambton, and then under the control of our respected Associates Sir George Everest till 1843, and Sir A. S. Waugh, has been dilated on. In these Papers the services rendered to science, and to geography in particular, by Capt. T. G. Montgomerie, are stated. The refined operations of a survey of this order, carried over a peaceful and accessible country, possess none of the interest or romance that these great Indian observations are invested with. In the triangulation and survey of Kashmir the officers met with great difficulties; much of the service was carried on during the great

Indian mutiny, surrounded by hostile people, and amid physical difficulties never before encountered in such a manner. The whole history of the vast survey of Northern India may be cited as a fine testimonial of the progress of primary exploration.

Of the large and almost unknown island of New Guinea we have had some account from our Associate Mr. A. Russell Wallace, for some time its sole European inhabitant. Mr. Wallace's zeal in the cause of science is well known, and his accessions to our knowledge of the natural history of this vast island have been shown in other places.

Mr. Spenser St. John, F.R.G.S., now in Haïti, has given us a most valuable account of the north-west coast of Borneo, where he was Consul-General—a further accession to our knowledge of the country first developed by our Associate Sir James Brooke.

The itineraries of Captain Claude Clerk, F.R.G.S., in Persia, in 1857–9, will be read with interest, affording valuable materials to the geographer. Captain Clerk describes his journeys between Tehran and Herat in the North, and Tehran and Bushire in Western Persia.

Proceeding to another part, we have a graphic and excellent account of the Andaman Islands, in the Bay of Bengal, by our Associate Dr. Mouat. This little group and its curious inhabitants seem to have been scarcely visited, though much in the way of commerce, till it was chosen as the place of exile for some of the Indian mutineers.

Sir Henry Rawlinson, who, twenty-three years since, claimed the Medal of the Royal Geographical Society as a comparative geographer of the highest order, and who, since his first recognition by this Society, has laboured so intensely, and with such admirable results, has advocated in our pages a most important proposal for connecting by electric telegraph our Indian possessions with this country. The route proposed is by way of Constantinople and the Euphrates, and thence through Persia, &c., to Kurrachi. The Ottoman Government has constructed the line as far as Bussorah, a route advocated in the early days of this Society by our respected Associate and Medallist General Chesney, as the readiest way to India for an overland transit. Although the progress of ocean steam-navigation has altered the relations which then existed, it is gratifying to know that the views endorsed by the Society have been so far recognised now as to form the basis for the modern system of telegraphic connexion. The discussion which ensued on Sir H. Rawlinson's proposition demonstrates that it was one of the highest geographical and national importance.

AFRICA has engrossed a large share of the attention of the Royal Geographical Society. From the time that the Society's first Medal was awarded to Richard Lander, thirty-one years since, for solving the great problem of the course of the Niger, to the present moment, when we are looking for the consummation of its endeavours to elucidate that other ancient enigma, the true sources of the Nile, the Society has been more or less occupied with obtaining information of the physical and moral condition of this great continent and its people.

At the first period above named, our maps of Africa exhibited its interior as nearly one universal blank, or with only the vague surmises of crude speculation. Now the geography of inner Africa presents a very different aspect. The pages of our Transactions are an index to the progress of discovery, which has been gradually displacing the imaginary arid desert by the well-watered and fertile country, or the supposed tenantless solitude with busy and populous tribes.

It is needless to advert to the early travels of Dr. Livingstone across the continent. The relation of the Geographical Society to that great traveller, and the wonderful successes due to his indomitable courage and untiring energy, must ever be a subject of congratulation.

The Society has for many years most zealously advanced those attempts to resolve the great geographical problem of the true sources of the White Nile; and all are now looking with great interest for tidings of the expedition under our Medallist Captain Speke and his companion Captain Grant, in the confident hope that the experience its leader gained when associated with Captain Burton in the Somali country, and in the journeys they had to the great African lakes, will enable him to complete successfully what was then commenced, and definitively set at rest that question of so many ages' standing. It is needless now to speculate as to any connexion there may or may not be between the head-waters of the Nile and the Victoria Nyanza, which he visited in July, 1858, as this will all be determined, it is believed, when we hear of the traveller's further progress. This topic is elsewhere adverted to, as is the expedition of Mr. Petherick, who also travels under the auspices of the Society to the aid of Captains Speke and Grant.

We look hopefully that before the next session we may welcome these gallant men on their successful return.

A brief account has been received from our Associate, Mr. Thornton, of an expedition to the great volcano Kilimanjaro, which has been thought to have some connexion with the physical geography of the Nile basin. Mr. Thornton was at first connected as geologist to Dr. Livingstone's expedition, but afterwards joined the Baron von der Decken, a Hanoverian gentleman, to the mountain. This journey is of great importance ; for while it fully confirms the accounts of the German missionaries given in our former Proceedings, it has the great additional claim of accurate survey and geological observation. Being an isolated volcanic cone, Kilimanjaro does not form part of that great eastern meridional axis which was so well argued upon by Sir Roderick Murchison in former years, and which has been reasoned on by some as the Mountains of the Moon of ancient geographers. The Baron von der Decken and his associate did not reach this great division between the Eastern and Western waters, and therefore the Nile question, probably, is not affected by the result of their journey.

Dr. Livingstone's proceedings are noticed in another part of this Address ; a brief allusion to them here will therefore suffice. His visit to the Victoria Falls of the great river Zambesi, and his farther observations on this important river, are of great interest. Connected also with his operations is the exploration of the river Shiré and the great Lake Shirwa. The more exact knowledge thus placed before us, instead of the imperfect accounts given by the Portuguese of former years, are of great importance in the future conduct of commercial or other relations with these regions. In the progress of this expedition an important part has been taken by our Associate Mr. Baines, well known as the artist of the North Australian expedition, and also in Kaffraria. Mr. Charles Livingstone, Dr. Kirk, the botanist of the expedition, and Mr. May, our Associate, have well seconded their leader in examining and reporting on the country. The examination of the Rovuma River, although not deciding whether it is the outlet of one of the chain of the East African lakes, is of much importance.

The geography of Eastern Africa has thus assumed an entirely new aspect within a very brief period. The exact knowledge we now possess contrasts in every way with the chaos of opinion and imperfect observation which before these expeditions were organised were our only guides. Although much may be required before we can have a perfect and accurate geographical picture of Eastern or Central Africa, yet the data thus laid down will be the foundation of that which will be subsequently acquired. The representations we now have demonstrate how imperatively necessary it is that astronomical observation should be connected with the necessarily vague estimates of a traveller over an unknown country.

On the shores of Western tropical Africa, our indefatigable Associate and medallist, Captain Burton, is active in the acquisition of information concerning the country where he represents Her Majesty's Government. The accounts of his visits to various places in the Bights of Benin and Benfia will be read with much interest, and there is no doubt but that his varied talent and extensive knowledge will accumulate much valuable information on these countries. He ascended and surveyed the Ogun or Abbeokuta River, in company with Captain Bedingfield, our Associate, who is well known to us in connexion with his examinations of the Congo, and as one of Dr. Livingstone's expedition.

Dr. Baikie, R.N., our Associate, who has been long on the Niger and Tchadda rivers, and has been endeavouring to establish a commanding position for England in Central Africa, has written hopefully of his prospects, should his expedition be retained. Intelligence has just arrived that the *Sunbeam* has ascended the river for 600 miles.

Another communication records the proceedings of Commander Dolben, F.R.G.S., during his ascent of the river Volta for 120 miles for the first time by white men.

With the increasing importance of the commerce of the Gold Coast and Western Africa generally, these narratives acquire great additional interest, and inspire the hope that a more intimate acquaintance with the physical condition of these countries will lead to a beneficial intercourse with the people who have so long been debased by the slave-traffic.

NORTH AMERICA.—For many years, as is well known, the Geographical Society took a most active part in the promotion of Arctic discovery, during the progress of which nearly the whole of the northern limits of America was accurately surveyed; and it is this service that developed the energies and skill of so many excellent officers, whose geographical labours have been so frequently mentioned in this and many previous Addresses, and are distributed throughout the pages of our Transactions.

During the period of these searching expeditions, one portion of the British dominions, now famous as British Columbia, was almost less known and visited than these icy and remote regions; and the explorations and surveys of our medallist Captain Palliser, with his coadjutors, Captain Blakiston, Dr. Hector, Lieutenant Palmer, C.E., and Mr. Sullivan, which have been treated of recently in former Addresses, have proved of immense service. The sudden interest with which the gold discovery has invested this country has given a high value to these explorations, which the Geographical Society so earnestly forwarded.

In the early days of the colonization of a country all exact information is of the utmost importance, and the reports of our Associate, Commander Mayne, R.N., of Lieutenant Palmer, C.E., of Mr. Justice Begbie, Mr. Downie, and others, as given in the Journal, must do great service. Captain R. W. Torrens has also given us an account of his ascent of the Nass River for 116 miles above Fort Simpson, near the borders of Russian America, and of the evidences of the existence of gold that were found in this novel journey. Our Associate, Captain Grant, has sent further notes on Vancouver Island and its capabilities.

On *Central America* we have had a paper on the republic of Nicaragua, by Mr. Vice-Consul G. R. Perry, and another from our well-known Associate Captain Bedford Pim, proposing a new transit-route across the American Isthmus through the lake of Nicaragua.

In *South America* our Associate Mr. Clement Markham, while engaged in the collection of the cinchona-plant among the mountains of Peru, which were to be transferred to the Himalayas for cultivation in our Indian possessions, has gathered much geographical information respecting the head-waters of the Purus, or Madre de Dios, one of the great affluents of the mighty Amazon, and also of the geography of the province of Caravaya, in Southern Peru.

From this same region we have a very curious narrative and illustration of a portion of the country to the south-east of Quito, sent us by Mr. R. Spruce, accompanied by his own remarks on the same region of the Quitonian Andes. Dr Jameson, of the university of Quito, has given us an account of an excursion from that city to the Mountain Cayambe, lying on the Equator.

AUSTRALIA.—The progress of Australia forms a very important chapter in the history of man. The rapidity with which exploration has been followed by colonization is remarkable. Almost all discovery made in this vast country may be said to have been made in connexion with the extension of its pastoral and commercial capabilities. The many explorations which the Society has encouraged and recorded since its establishment, have added a new world to the uses of civilised man. The first paper in its Transactions relates to the infant days of the Western colony, and its first volumes record the earliest discoveries of Sturt, Cunningham, and other travellers, who pushed over the boundaries of its limited Eastern settlements. How soon these important discoveries were utilized is familiar to us all; and in later days, since Mr. Eyre and Mr. Sturt, our worthy Medallists, first attempted to traverse the continent from south to north, the benefits which have accrued from their enterprise have well justified the awards of the Society. In the last volume of the Journal is an account of the ascent of the Murray and Darling Rivers, by Mr. Randell, in a steam-boat. This fact, and the account of the settlements on the courses of these rivers, is an example of the importance of these primary explorations.

But the Transactions of the last two years are not of inferior importance or interest to those adventures detailed in the earliest volumes of the Society, at a period when the whole continent of Australia was a field for vague conjecture. In another part of this Address the wondrous journeys of Burke and Wills, and of McDouall Stuart, are dilated on, and which, judging from the past, are destined to have as great an influence on the future of Australia as those of our early Medallists.

While thus recounting the travels in the Eastern portion of Australia, we cannot forget the claims of that family of Gregorys who have so advanced our knowledge of the Western part by their admirable exploring capabilities. Their merits have been fully explained in former Addresses, and the last journey of Mr. Frank Gregory will stand foremost in the ranks of discovery. These topics have been alluded to previously.

Besides those above, a long array of names may be cited as having added to our knowledge of Australia in the pages of our Transactions. Among these we have recently those of Wilson, Landor, Chimmo, Freeling, Hack, Flood, Babbage, Warburton, Sinclair, Governor MacDonnell, Selwyn, Dempster, Dalrymple, &c. &c. The actual social benefit which has been and will be derived from their observations must be very highly estimated.

We have had recently a very excellent account of the Fiji Islands, in the Pacific Ocean, by Mr. Bensusan, long a resident there, and by Dr. Berthold Seemann, whose long experience as a naturalist has added much to our knowledge of this beautiful group, as well as of the other numerous countries he has visited. Though there may be a difference of opinion as to the propriety of our colonising the Archipelago, there can be none as to the beauty and interest which belongs to the islands themselves.

The OCEAN has received some share of attention from our Associates. There are many features of marine physics which are still very obscure, notwithstanding the great accumulation of independent observation which has been collected. The depth, the movements, the constitution of the ocean, are each the subject of controversy, and in each branch of inquiry there is ample field for individual enterprise.

During the expedition undertaken for ascertaining the practicability of a northern route for an Atlantic telegraph-cable, the sounding-voyage in the *Bull Dog*, under our Medallist, Sir F. Leopold M'Clintock, of Arctic celebrity, has given us probably more exact data on the depth of the ocean than has been before obtained. We have now accounts of about 260 of these experiments in the North Atlantic, by which the depth has been stated at from one to four or seven miles. But many, nay most of these soundings, are open to very great doubt, and we have yet much to learn as to the depth of the ocean. In the voyage of the *Bull Dog*, besides the actual evidence of depth given by bringing up the bottom in most cases, there were some new facts elicited, which, while they overturn much previous speculation, create a desire for a great extension of the inquiry. The fact of a live star-fish and a worm brought up from enormous depths (1½ mile), would not have been thought possible prior to its being demonstrated. Another singular feature is that the specimens of mud brought up in these high northern latitudes, consisting almost exclusively of minute organisms, *alive*, principally foraminifera, globigerina, &c., are almost identical with those obtained by the United States officers, Lieut. Craven, U.S.N., &c., from great depths within the tropics, beneath the tepid waters of the Gulf-stream. This demonstrates that there must be a similar water-climate at each of these distant regions. Therefore the theory that there is neither light, heat, nor physical conditions necessary to support animal life at these enormous depths must be abandoned, and, while it overturns all this, it opens up a new and vast field for observation and speculation as to the actual constitution and influence which the ocean bears upon the great economy of nature.

Mr. Hopkins, a name well known to meteorologists, has given us a Paper on the conditions of the ocean and other topics relating to the North Pole.

Captain Irminger, of the Royal Danish Navy, has given us a very interesting dissertation on the ocean currents in the vicinity of Iceland, which brings forward several new features.

Another important ocean topic has been also added to by the observations of Lieut. Heathcote, I.N., on the difficult and complex system of currents in the Bay of Bengal. These are directly applicable to nautical purposes, and are of much value.

In this summary of the special application of geographical enterprise which it has been the sphere of the Royal Geographical Society to disseminate during the last two years, much is necessarily omitted for want of space. They are special as compared with the great extent of inquiry open to geographers. In the more extended sense of general geography, we may notice a paper by that eminent physical geographer, our Corresponding Member, Commander M. F. Maury, on the Southern Ocean and the Antarctic Pole. In mathematical geography Colonel Sir Henry James has described his new projection alluded to in a former Address, and Sir John Herschel has given us another communication on a similar subject. Our Honorary Secretary, Mr. Spottiswoode, has brought mathematical investigation to bear on the probable conditions of mountain ranges, and has given us another paper on a method of obtaining longitudes from the moon's greatest altitude.

Much more might be said as to the influence of the Society in the acquisition and future dissemination of geographical knowledge through the wide-spread influence of its numerous Associates, and of the cordiality existing among us, and of the many causes to which we may attribute the present prosperity of the Society.

---

Having now concluded the Report which the contributions of distinguished geographers have enabled me to lay before the Society, I may be allowed, perhaps, to say a few words on my own behalf.

This is the last time of my occupying this chair. Allow me, before I leave it, to thank you for the considerate kindness with which you have dealt with my frequent absences, my many shortcomings. I resign my office—for I have no doubt of his election—

to one whom you have long known, whose knowledge and skill
and conciliatory power you have long learned to appreciate. If the
Society has increased under me, it has been owing to his advice,
and that of the able Council with which you surrounded me.
It is to their zeal and efficiency that we are indebted for our
growing importance as a public body.

We have, in fact, become a public department, if that appellation
is to be assigned rather to the amount of service rendered than to
the cost incurred. We collect, revise, digest, and amplify all the
geographical information supplied to the various public offices, and
communicated to us. We keep it ready for their use, and for the
use of the merchant, manufacturer, and colonist. We organise and
direct missions of discovery, fitted out for public objects at the
public expense. We have no members of our body hanging on, in a
state of apathy and indifference, for the sake of salary or superan-
nuation. The Council is ever young in zeal and energy, if not in
years. Whatever is done, is done as a labour of love, with the
enthusiasm of votaries. Add to this that the subjects we treat of
are of universal interest, universal application. They appeal to all
our sympathies, whether of the present, the future, or the past.
Such a Society, so conducted, so supported, can never fail.

# PROCEEDINGS

OF

# THE ROYAL GEOGRAPHICAL SOCIETY OF LONDON.

## SESSION 1861-62.

*Fourteenth Meeting, Monday, June 16,* 1862.*

SIR RODERICK I. MURCHISON, PRESIDENT, in the Chair.

ELECTIONS.—*His Highness Said Pasha, the Vice-Roy of Egypt, as an Honorary Member, and Dr. H. Kiepert, Professor of Geography in the University of Berlin, as a Corresponding Member ; and Capt. the Hon. James R. Drummond, R.N., C.B.; Lieut.-Col. Elkington ; Vice-Admiral Sir Charles Howe Fremantle, K.C.B.; Capt. Edward Donald Malcolm ; Capt. John Puget ; Sir Henry Young, late Governor of Tasmania ; James Anderson ; Samuel Bruce ; Eugène Claude ; George Cockle ; Edward William Cox ; John Baily Darvall ; William Hardman ; Henry Schuback Hood ; Henry Lannoy Hunter ; Frederick Isaac ; Leonard Jaques ; David Lyon ; George Mitchell ; William Parry ; Mark Richardson, and William Whitmore, Esqrs., were elected Fellows.*

ACCESSIONS.—Among the Accessions to the Library and Map-rooms since the former Meeting were—St. John's 'Life in the Forests of the Far East;' part 3 of Philip's Imperial Library Atlas; 3 sheets of India, showing the districts bordering on the British Trans-Indus Frontier, by Major J. T. Walker, F.R.G.S.,; Routes of African travellers, by J. L. M'Leod, Esq., F.R.G.S.; Map of Aderbeijan, by N. Khanikof; L'Herzegovine, by H. Br. de Beaumont; Ellipso, donnant les inclinaisons, les déclinaisons, et les intensités magnétiques, &c., by Jules A. Lelaisant, Paris; République du Paraguay, by M. E. Mouchez, &c., &c.

EXHIBITIONS.—Charts and illustrations, resulting from Capt. H. M. Denham's Voyage in the Western Pacific, as well as weapons and instruments used by the Northern Australians and Pacific

---

* This Meeting, originally fixed for Monday, the 9th of June, was postponed to the 16th of June, in compliance with the request of the National Association for the Promotion of Social Science.

Islanders; Japanese Sketches, by R. Alcock, Esq., H.M. Minister in Japan : a suit of Japanese Armour, by Consul Pemberton Hodgson ; Sketches in the Holy Land, by Dr. Beke ; specimens of wood and iron from Lower Assam, by Sir M. Stephenson, F.R.G.S. ; map of the Holy Land, by E. Stanford, on 4 sheets, &c., were exhibited at the meeting.

THE PRESIDENT, in opening the business of the meeting, expressed his great satisfaction that the opinions of Mr. Arrowsmith and himself, and many other geographers, respecting the merits of M. Du Chaillu, as an explorer who had added materially to our acquaintance with the physical features of the Gaboon Region in Western Africa, had been recently confirmed by the well-known and clear-sighted German geographer M. Petermann.   In a letter to the President, M. Petermann referred particularly to a memoir of his own, published in the widely-spread and useful work the 'Mittheilungen,' which was accompanied by maps, showing by comparison how much more had been really accomplished by M. Du Chaillu than by any preceding explorer of Western Africa, of which country he might justly be called the geographical pioneer.   In lamenting that the map of M. Du Chaillu had been so inaccurately drawn, the President stated that no one had ever claimed for that explorer any pretensions to scientific skill ; the Geographical Society had recognized in him the character of a zealous naturalist, who, in capturing gorillas and in wandering among various native tribes, had incidentally been of great service in the cause of Geography.

THE PRESIDENT then read the following letter from His Excellency Sir H. Barkly, Governor of Victoria, dated Melbourne, 25th April, 1862 :—

" IN acknowledging your favour of the 25th February, I am glad to be able to send you (per Colonial Office bag) the printed Reports, with maps, &c., of the Explorative Expeditions to the Gulf of Carpentaria, as also a Map of Howitt's recent explorations near Cooper Creek.

" Walker's journey overland from the Fitzroy you will find most interesting, as, after penetrating the scrubs, which so baffled both Mitchell and Leichardt, he travelled through a fine basaltic country, finding the tracks of the latter explorer far beyond the point on the Alice to which they had been traced by Gregory.   Landsburgh was not so fortunate in the district he had to traverse in his attempt to reach Central Mount Stuart; but still he calls it ' fine sheep country,' and he saw it at its worst in the height of a tropical summer.

" We now await with great interest the news of the return of these two leaders and their parties to the South by Burke's route, which they proposed to follow down all the way to Cooper Creek ; and, to guard against accidents, Howitt has been directed to remain at the Depôt (Fort Wills) until they are both accounted for.

" As he has established his communication with the out-stations of South Australia at Mount Hopeless, and with those of the New South Wales squatters beyond Mount Murchison on the other side, and can draw ample supplies from either, there is no doubt of his being able to maintain himself here for any length of time that may be needed, especially as his relations with the Natives are most amicable.   He was about, when we last heard from him, to start in search of M'Kinlay, who, since the wonderful reports to which you allude, has not been heard of.

" You would, I fancy, conclude, from the evidence of King before the Burke and Wills Inquiry Commission, that the story of the discovery of remains, &c., made by M'Kinlay, referred to his finding the body of Gray, who died, you will remember, four days before the rest of the party got back to the Depôt. There was a certain amount of exaggeration in the accounts given, but no positive untruth.   Had not King survived to tell the tale, it would have been supposed that Gray, and probably Burke and the others, were killed by the Natives.

" Thanks for all you did at the Meeting of the Geographical Society, and for the trouble you have taken in communicating with Arrowsmith as to calling the new country Burke's Land. If, as I presume, the maps now sent find their way into the possession of that geographer, perhaps you will let him know that by next mail our Surveyor-general, Mr. Ligon, will have carried up his General Explorative Map of Australia to date, and that there will be some alteration of names, as I find, from there being so many exploring parties, that three or four rivers have been christened after myself, and some other people also; and I have told Mr. Ligon that I have selected that named after me by Walker—a new stream flowing to the south-west from the dividing watershed of the continent—and that he must find other names for the rest.

" Mr. Ligon's map will include the details of Mr. F. T. Gregory's recent tours on the west coast, which that gentleman, who leaves, I believe, in the present mail for England, has put at his disposal.

" Mr. Gregory's desire is to get the north-west corner of Australia proclaimed as a separate colony; and I hope he will succeed, as it would much facilitate its occupation for grazing purposes."

The Papers read were—

1.—*The Surveys of H.M.S. ' Herald' in the Pacific, under the Command of Captain H. Mangles Denham*, R.N., F.R.G.S., &c., &c.

[Captain Denham's original communication is printed at length in Additional Notices, p. 197.]

THE PRESIDENT called attention to this memoir, which gave a brief outline of the very remarkable labours of Captain Denham, R.N., who, in command of H.M.S. *Herald*, had most strikingly enriched maritime Geography in his numerous distinct surveys during nearly ten years, and had sent home to the Admiralty a multitude of data of the highest value in relation to terrestrial magnetism, tides, currents, deep-sea soundings, &c. Captain Denham was the first to ascertain the prodigious depth of the ocean (44,000 feet) between South America and South Africa, and to show that this depth far exceeded the altitude of the highest mountains above the sea. One of the most useful of the labours of Captain Denham was the establishment, after long and patient surveys, of the existence of a deep-sea passage, from South to North, of great width, and of upwards of 700 miles in length, to the east of Australia, wholly free from coral-reefs and sunken rocks; whilst his precise delineations of the outlines of the Fiji Islands, accompanied by numerous practical sketches, were precious contributions to our knowledge of that interesting group.

The second Paper read was—

2.—*Excursion to Harrān in Padan Aram, and thence over Mount Gilead and the Jordan to Shechem.* By CHARLES T. BEKE, Esq., PH. DR. F.S.A., F.R.G.S., &c.   (Gold Medallist R.G.S.)

THE author having expressed the opinion in his ' Origines Biblicæ,' published in 1834, that the Padan Aram of Abraham was the plain of Damascus, and not Mesopotamia beyond Euprates, was induced by Mr. Porter's subsequent discovery of a village called Harrān,

15 miles east of Damascus, to make a journey, in company with his wife, in order to visit it, and to track the route of the patriarch Jacob on his " seven days' journey " to Mount Gilead.   Harrān is a thriving village of 150 to 200 stone houses, plastered with mud, and contains numerous architectural fragments, especially three Ionic columns, from which it derives its local name of *Harrān-el-Awamid.* A fragment of an inscription was found, but it was too defaced to be deciphered.   There exists no local tradition bearing on the ancient history of the village.   Dr. Beke discovered a well on the western side of the town, which he conjectures to be the well " without the city " where Abraham's servant met Rebekah.

Leaving Harran on January 1st, the travellers first passed over " the river " Awaj, the Pharphar of Scripture, and then followed the great Haj road across the plains of Hauran till they came to Jebel Ajtun, or Mount Gilead, which they ascended.   On reaching the summit, near Mahnah,—the Mahanaim of Genesis,—they obtained an extensive view, embracing most of the remarkable places in Galilee.   Then descending Wady Ajlun by Kellat-er-Rubbud, crossing Wady Rajib, and passing by the tomb of Abu Obeida, they reached the Jordan, a little way to the north of Wady Zerka, the Jabbok of Scripture, near where Lieut. Molyneux's party were plundered by the Mashalka (" Messalliek ") Arabs, who, on the present occasion, escorted Dr. and Mrs. Beke across the river. After passing the Jordan, however, they had a skirmish with some Beduins; getting free from whom, they crossed the Makhrūd, and ascended Wady Fār'a to Nablūs, the ancient Shechem.

In Dr. Beke's elaborate paper the geographical correspondence of the chief places through which he travelled, with the events of the Bible narrative, are discussed with minuteness.   As regards the latter part of the journey, he considers that after the patriarch Jacob had left Succoth (which he places to the south of the Jabbok) and crossed the Jordan, he entered Wady Fār'a at its junction with the former river, passing between the Makhrud and Karn Sartebeh.

THE PRESIDENT begged the Society specially to return their thanks to Mrs. Beke, as well as to her husband, as that lady had shared in all the incidents of the journey which had been described.

---

3.—*Narrative of a Journey through the Interior of Japan from Nagasaki to Yeddo.*  By Sir RUTHERFORD ALCOCK, K.C.B., F.R.G.S., Ext. Min. Plen. and Consul-Gen. in Japan.

This journey, of which copious details are given in Additional Notices, p. 200, led through the inland sea of Japan to Hiogo and

Osaca, the great commercial emporium of the Empire, and thence overland to Yeddo. The usual obstructiveness on the part of Japanese officials and the feudal lords or Damios was displayed on this occasion, and overcome, not without danger of a collision, by the firmness of Mr. Alcock. It was essential that his journey should be made, for the time was fast approaching when these ports were to be opened to foreigners, and information on their capabilities had to be obtained. The result was that Osaca appeared beyond a doubt to be the most promising site in Japan for the principal seat of foreign commerce.

THE PRESIDENT commended the author in an earnest manner for his highly-interesting sketch of the social condition of Japan.

THE PRESIDENT then called the attention of the Fellows to the proposal of M. Jules Gérard to establish an African Society for explorations south-west from Algeria ; and, having complimented his associates on the increasing prosperity of the Royal Geographical Society, he adjourned the meetings till November next.

# ADDITIONAL NOTICES.

### (Printed by order of Council.)

1.—*The " Herald's " Voyage*, 1852-61.   By CAPTAIN DENHAM, R.N., F.R.S.
(See p. 195.)

IN 1851 strong representations were made to Her Majesty's Government respecting both the rapidly-increasing traffic between our Australian colonies and the western coast of America, and our inadequate knowledge of the intervening navigation among the insulated rocks and intricate clusters of islands which extend to the eastward of New Caledonia. It was urged also that distant commerce and maritime enterprise would derive great benefit from a thorough examination of that region, from having its dangers fully explored, and from having its harbours so charted and described that the seaman would know where he could either obtain supplies or repair for refit or refuge, or endeavour to fix his whaling or his coaling stations. An exploring and surveying voyage was accordingly undertaken in 1852, which, under Admiralty instructions, from time to time was conducted by Captain Henry Mangles Denham, of the Royal Navy, in Her Majesty's ship *Herald*, until 1861, when she was recalled in consideration of so long an absence from England.

The hydrographic results of this voyage being *transmitted annually*, the existing charts were forthwith corrected, and several new ones published, together with such hydrographic papers as would *at once* give the maritime world the benefit of those results ; and, in due course, the original matter, franked by the Duke of Somerset as First Lord of the Admiralty, and by Admiral Washington as the Admiralty Hydrographer, is now laid before this

Society ; comprising 163 determinations of latitudes and longitudes, 2601 magnetic results, 41 islands, 42 reefs and shoals, 22 barrier-reef prongs, 450 miles of Australian coast-line, with the estuaries Shark Gulf, Port Jackson, Moreton Bay, and the Derwent of Tasmania, 700 miles' contouring of the main bank, the edge of soundings off Capes Good Hope and Agulhas, thence along the Australian coast, and around the Lord Howe, Norfolk, and Kermadec islands ; 107,000 miles of ship-track notations of depths, winds, currents, ocean temperatures, meteorology, and natural history, with the researching evidence upon which twenty-three *vigias* (or fabulous reefs) were expunged. The detail of the above is set forth in the 144 charts and plans, together with 93 illustrative drawings, and 15 sheets of tabulations, also submitted to inspection.

The free use of the deep-sea lead throughout the passages out and home led to the delineation of certain ocean-banks of soundings in the South Atlantic ; one of which (the Victoria) in 20° 45′ S., 37° 47′ W., rises abruptly from no soundings to 19 fathoms, is of coralline structure, and spreads 80 miles by 12, attracting the fin-back whale, and affording haddock-fishing. The *Herald* was anchored for several days on these banks.

It was on the passage out that, in 37° S., and 37° W., about midway between Tristan d'Cunha and Buenos Ayres, soundings were obtained in 7706 fathoms, and other opportunities were taken of testing the depth at which the minimum temperature of the ocean is to be found (vide tabulation). The results shewed 41° as near the surface as 600 fathoms (although the surface-water was at the temperature of 80°), 40° at 900 fathoms, and not of lower temperature at 1500 fathoms.

The deep-sea lead frequently going, *always ready*, and the hand-leads *constantly going* when intersecting the assigned positions of vigias, precluded our mistaking earthquake tremor of the ship (as it will though out of soundings) for "grazing over a shoal." Tremors were experienced by the *Herald* (her leads *going*) when in the vicinity of the alleged *Equator shoals*, between the meridians of 21° and 22° W., affording reason for expunging such unnecessary terrors from our charts as the "Purdy shoals" of 1831 and 1842.

The region of the *Herald's* special exploration very soon became suggestive of a distinct oceanic designation, and that of "Western Pacific" was adopted, implying all that space embraced by the meridians 150° and 180° E. between the Equator and 45° S.

By determining the salient positions both of the islands and reefs belonging to the New Caledonia, Loyalty, New Hebrides, Fijian, and Tonga groups on the *north*, and also of Lord Howe, Norfolk, and the Kermadec islands, with the warning banks of soundings, which range about the parallel of 30° S., a clear passage is indicated of 300 miles wide for the first 1600 miles directly eastward of Australia. On this track the harbour of Matuku (the southernmost island of Fiji) is of easy access ; it is adapted for a coaling-station ; while the chiefs and a Christianized population present every facility.

Having mapped all that space embraced by New South Wales, New Zealand, Kermadec group, Tonga, Fiji, New Hebrides, and New Caledonia, so as to open up the first stage of communication between our Australian colonies and Western America, and having landed and established the Pitcairners at Norfolk Island, a detail survey of the Fiji group was taken in hand, which, however, had to be relinquished (when only its south-western section had been delineated upon a 3-inch scale), to meet the demand for a similar development of the Coral Sea as that which this expedition had wrought directly eastward of Australia ; in the course of which Captain Denham traced the fate of Mr. Benjamin Boyd, of the R.Y.S. yacht *Wanderer*, and punished his murderer at Guadalcana, of the Solomon group. The space to which Captain Denham's researches were then directed, is bounded to the westward by the great barrier-reef of Australia, and to the north-eastward by New Caledonia, Solomon Islands, and the Louisiade range—the trends of which converge to Torres

Strait. This coral sea, heretofore beset with vaguely-charted dangers, and rendered the more perplexing by many *reported* reefs, caused sad disasters, which, however, did not deter voyagers, who looked upon a *north-western* route to India as a great facility for ships of Tasmania, Melbourne, New Zealand, Sydney, and Queensland. In due course, however, this sea, with its isolated reefs (coming abruptly awash, though with no soundings around), became mapped; and now presents a clear 1200-mile route (free of current, and within the steady south-east trades), of 150 miles width; a route which may be availed of upon but three successive courses—viz. N. by w. ¾ w. 240 miles, N.W. ½ w. 700 miles, and w. ½ N. 220 miles—after crossing the parallel of 25° S., upon the meridian of 156° E., until sighting the (about to be lighted) Raine Island tower in Torres Strait. None of the six reefs (Cato, Wreck, Kenn, Lihou, Osprey, Willis) on the western hand, nor the Bellonas, Bampton, and Mellish reefs, on the eastern hand, need be neared; but, to give confidence, and to help a crippled ship to a sheltered anchorage,—which, happily, these reefs afford,—the Colonial Governments entertain Captain Denham's proposition of lighting Cato, Kenn, and Raine; in the same spirit his suggestions were adopted by the New South Wales Government regarding the coast-lights, beacons and buoys. The detailed examination of the reefs was such as to reveal their refuge capacities; and although 350 miles from land, light-house establishments can be formed and maintained (each having a cay free from surf, on sufficiently solid coralline substratum), and the landing of supplies would be easier accomplished than at our Eddystone or Smalls! each reef has upon its north-western and *leeward* aspect an eight-fathom shelf of fine coral grit. The plan-charts of these reefs, with a masthead look-out, will enable the cruiser or whaler to round-to under their lee, to all the succour of a Port-land or Plymouth Breakwater,—at once clear of a turbulent sea-way,—where she may caulk topsides, set up rigging, rate chronometers, obtain turtle, fish, and seafowl-eggs, and enjoy the priceless tropical comfort of open ports and scuttles. This "coral sea" development indicated such postal and commercial benefits as suggested the compliment of designating it the "Denham Route:" for, by it, and through Torres Strait, steamers of one-half the size now em-ployed to round Cape Leeuwin, can make the passage to Singapore in smooth water in one-fifth less time. Nor is it restricted to western monsoons for shipping to get to the *southward* through the Coral Sea, as the *Herald* worked the passage, against the south-eastern monsoon and trade, in twenty-six days.

To afford immediate, though temporary, means of "making-out" some of the more salient of these reefs, beacons were erected from the *débris* of wrecks and the *Herald's* stores so far as they would admit; while, with a view to permanent improvement, and for the sake of visitors or castaways, cocoa-nuts, shrubs, grasses, and every description of seed likely to grow and self-plant, were sown in the way most likely to clothe and promote the superstructure. These "cays," situated above high-water level, become the resort for seafowl to lay their eggs, and, as the birds die off, guano is produced and a vegetation is promoted that bids fair to render these ocean spots available refuges. Bottled-up papers were always left by the *Herald*, giving the latitude and longitude, and the course and distance to the nearest port, with such pro-visions, match-boxes, &c., and cooking-utensils, as could be spared, or had been collected from the wrecks fallen in with.

In 1858, the favourable season (January to June) for a sailing-passage along the southern aspect of Australia, and for a sojourn upon its western coast, was employed in determining the question as to Shark Bay being adapted for form-ing a settlement. Its position, and configuration of harbours on the maps extant had suggested it as a position for a penal settlement. The survey of this gulf was therefore prosecuted to the extent of its tidal interstices, which ramify over 400 miles of coast-line; its estuaries, however, were found to be inter-cepted by shallows only to be penetrated by the marine surveyors' step-by-step process; and eventually the region proved to be such a tissue of negatives as but ill-requited the time and toil expended upon its examination; for neither timber, water, nor stone, could be found near its shores; and but a few Natives were at last seen at the head of the innermost estuary, who meekly accepted biscuit and water (caring for nothing else of ours), they having but mud-bags to suck, and a thin parsnip-sort of root to eat.    The utterly desti- tute character of this region being determined by the beginning of June, when the dry moderate weather is quickly succeeded by storms — the furrowing effects of which, as traceable upon the semi-indurated sandhills, would indicate its being subject to hurricane visitations,—the *Herald* cleared this "gulf of negatives," with her last month's short allowance of water, on the 5th of June, 1858; the first 600 miles (being a *sailing* ship) was on the port-tack to the westward; but when in 32° s. and 104° e., she gradually got upon her 2600-mile track for Sydney (viâ Bass Strait), reaching it on July 12th for supplies.    She was soon again in the Coral Sea, clearing up its capacity as a route; and this being accomplished by October, 1860, she sailed homeward by Torres Strait, determining its middle passage, settling the position of its western dangers (Cook's Straits, Proudfoot, &c.), and then proving that the parallel of Booby Island, 10° 36' s., is a clear track down the "Arafura" sea, until abreast of Timor, when the soundings jump so abruptly from 100 to 12 fathoms, as to demand a "good look-out," and to indicate a bottom adverse to submarine telegraphic connexion of Australia by its north-western Cape.

Track-chart notations, as in the passage out, were continued viâ Java, Madagascar, Cape of Good Hope, St. Helena, Ascension, passing over certain reported shoals in 1000 fathoms, making the passage, with obvious advantage to a *sailing* ship (in the season of English Channel *easterly* winds), to the *eastward* of the Azores; and, on the 7th of May 1861, closing the opera- tions of this expedition in 777 fathoms, 52 miles outside the edge of soundings.

---

2.—*Extracts from Narrative of a Journey through the Interior of Japan from Nagasaki to Yeddo, in* 1861.   By RUTHERFORD ALCOCK, F.R.G.S., Min. Plen. and Consul-General in Japan.   (See p. 197.)

A PAPER was read in this Society last season, giving some account of my journey in the interior of Japan, which was undertaken for the ascent of the mountain of Fusiyama, and with the further purpose of visiting the sulphur- springs of Atami.   I had intended giving an equally detailed narrative of the incidents and principal objects of general and scientfic interest which came under my netice during a much more extended exploration of the interior of the country in a journey I undertook last year about this time, from Nagasaki to Yeddo, across the island of Kinsin, through the inland sea to Hiogo and Asaca, the great commercial emporium of the empire, and thence overland to Yeddo, the capital of the Tycoon.   I have unfortunately, however, arrived in England much too late in the season to give effect to this purpose now, and I owe, indeed, to the obliging courtesy of the President and Council the oppor- tunity of presenting to the Society even the very brief and imperfect sketch now before me, and for which I must beg the indulgence of all who are willing to listen to it.   Fortunately in my previous paper I gave such details of the general features of the country, the usual incidents of travel in Japan, and the social state and physical geography of the districts then traversed, that, to those who were present, or who may since have read it in the 'Transactions of the Society,' any repetition of such details would be superfluous, and they will be prepared without any further preface to take their place in the motley caravan which formed my cortège on the 1st of June last year, and start at once from the semi-Dutch colony of Decima in the bay of Nagasaki. It was such a morning as we have many in this pleasant climate of England, even in June. It began with a chilling drizzle, which soon deepened into a heavy drenching rain. The wet season of Japan had, in fact, commenced, beginning as it does with tolerable regularity about the end of May and extending into July. When it does not rain, in this season, the sun shines out with scorching power. I had thus a pleasant prospect before me of a thirty days' journey on horseback, either under a drenching rain or a tropical sun; for, although Japan has no pretensions geographically to a place in the tropics, during the summer months it asserts a claim to take rank with the best of the Spice Islands, both by its luxuriant vegetation and the power of the sun, and this so effectively and perseveringly that no traveller will feel disposed to contest the point. Were any evidence wanted, Japan would furnish another conclusive example that latitude only forms one element in the determining causes of heat and cold and of climate generally. In this little group of islands at this side of the globe, often compared to Great Britain and Ireland both from their size, distribution, and geographical position, the northern island of Yeso, in which our consular port of Hakodadi is situated, has a Siberian winter, where the inhabitants are snowed up several feet deep for many months; while at the capital of Yeddo, corresponding to London, in the larger island south, snow never lies beyond a day or two, and during October, November, and December, and often January, there is only an Italian winter in the most favoured portions of that favoured land. A bright sun, a clear atmosphere, and sky of the purest blue without a fleck or a cloud, sometimes for weeks together, are all to be counted upon. The trees put on their richest tints of every shade and hue, from the deep green of the camelia to the bright scarlet of the maple and the russet brown of the beech: these intermingled with a hundred varieties of evergreens, shrubs, and forest trees, of which the evergreen oak is one of the noblest as well as the most common. Nature has indeed lavished her wealth on the soil and vegetation, on all the physical features of Japan, and given an Italian sky and temperature with an eastern sun to enhance the beauty of all her other gifts. Unfortunately she seems to have exhausted her generosity when she made this terrestrial garden, and to have forgotten the children that were to live in it—some to till the ground and others to govern it—for one is often tempted to quote Byron's line descriptive of another Eastern land where all " save the spirit of man is divine." But in our impatience at a perpetual menace of violence, which all of Western race must live under, for many long years to come, I fear, we are apt to do injustice to the great virtues of the mass of the population. They not only are the most patient, untiring, and successful husbandmen and cultivators of the soil, but they are also a frugal, contented, and good-humoured race—docile and long-suffering, and to all appearance the easiest to govern and make happy of any it has been my fate to live among. They are, with all this, among the most ingenious and enterprising of Eastern races in all industrial pursuits; and I firmly believe, if they had fair play, could hold their own against either Birmingham or Manchester, Paris or Lyons, in many of the manufactures for which these centres of trade are noted.

As regards our relations and commercial interchange of products with the nation, however, all this is to a great degree neutralized and counterbalanced by one element in their institutions, and that is FEUDALISM. The iron hand of a proud, astute, and relentless class of feudal chiefs weighs heavily upon all the energies of the people. Proprietors of all the soil, exercising feudal sway with feudal privileges of life and death over all below them as their born thralls and subjects, they leave to the cultivators no more than is sufficient for a bare subsistence, and reduce the life of the mass to a mere animal existence. What Great Britain and France were in the times of the Crusades— what Venice was in the palmy days of its power, under a jealous and ruthless oligarchy, with its phantom sceptre in the hands of a powerless doge, ruled and coerced by a secret Council of Ten—Japan now is in all that concerns its privileged classes ; its feudal nobles and their armed retainers all ready to do battle, and to kill or be killed with equal promptitude at the beck and call of their chiefs.　These are the classes that consume all the surplus wealth and produce of the soil.　To maintain these idle and dangerous classes in their haughty privileges and unapproachable superiority, some thirty millions of the most industrious race on earth, perhaps, toil and spin, dig and delve in the fairest land of the East.　And for the last three hundred years, ever since the expulsion of the foreigners and the destruction of every trace of the foreign-imported Christianity under Taico Sama and his usurping and still more implacable successor Gongen Sama (the two most revered and glorified Tycoons of their history), this state of things seems to have been steadily maintained, and, what is perhaps still more remarkable, maintained without civil feuds between the Damios, insurrection against the sovereign executive vested in the Tycoons, or murmur among the oppressed masses, which, though politically dead, are yet like the busy inhabitants of a vast ant-hill, ever in movement, ever toiling, and seemingly within the limited range of a very material civilization, ever enjoying life without a thought for the past or a care for the future.　And yet with such a people, enterprising in all that lies within their field of exertion or vision, careless of life, proud of their nationality, with a warlike and belligerent class to head them, if once there were a cry to arms or revolt, who can say what a day or a year might bring forth, now that a new element is being infused into their national life ?

Japan, as I once wrote to Her Majesty's Secretary of State for Foreign Affairs, was not a country I could recommend just at present for a nervous man.　Fires every night destroying whole streets or quarters of a vast city ; earthquakes in every week, with an aggravating uncertainty as to the time or duration and extent of the shocks ; and a perpetual threat, every now and then enforced by an assassination or an attempt at a more general massacre of foreigners, and occasionally of their own ministers if supposed to be favourable to foreign relations, being the general conditions of life in Yeddo ; and I may be allowed to say they are not the pleasantest in the world, nor altogether satisfactory in any respect.　Such as they were, however, I had to make the best of it, not only for myself, but for others.　The time was approaching for the opening of new ports for commerce and the residence of foreigners, more especially Hiogo and Osaca on the inland sea of Surnada—ports the opening of which the Government of the Tycoon were evincing the most anxious desire to defer ; and it was very essential that I should, in the exercise of my treaty right, as the British Minister, to travel freely through the empire, have personal means of observation and satisfy myself, not only as to the real value of these ports, but of the state of feeling of the people there, and throughout the country generally, as well as of the actual relations existing between the mass of the population and the ruling classes.　I say it was essential, for these were data which constituted the very elements of any sound judgment as to the policy or expediency of the only two courses open to Western Powers—namely, either to insist on the full execution of the treaties in all their stipulations regardless of any consequences to the government of the country—or, in other words, disregarding and disbelieving all their predictions of disasters and revolution as the inevitable result ; or secondly, with or without certain conditions or equivalents, to accede to the proposal of the Tycoon and his Council of Ministers to defer the opening of the remaining two ports and two cities for a definite period of five years.　I had to give an opinion on this important question; and, before giving it, I was determined to seek the means of forming it on data collected in a larger and freer field than the capital afforded, and by my own personal observation, since I could place implicit trust in *nothing* that came from Japanese sources.　Once satisfied that this was the right course to follow, I made my arrangements in accord with my excellent colleague M. de Wit, the Dutch Consul-General, who also desired, following the track of his predecessors the Dutch Commissioners from ancient times, to make the journey from Nagasaki to Yeddo overland. And on the 1st of June, nothing heeding either the lachrymose and persistent remonstrances of the Governor of Nagasaki against the imprudence of our venturing on the highways beset by Lonins and enemies to the peace (as he had by especial desire ascertained), nor even the lachrymose state of the weather, which, however, was more sensibly felt, our cavalcade of some fifty or sixty persons began the journey—consisting of our own party of five Europeans, an escort of Japanese officials with their officers and servants, with baggage-horses, Norimons, and porters—the inevitable *impedimenta* and accompaniments of a long journey in Japan—and threaded our way through the stone-paved, but sloppy, streets of Nagasaki.

The route lies, in the first instance, across the north-western angle of the southern island of Kinsin to the fortified town of Kokura, at the entrance of the Sea of Sumada, stretching for 150 miles between the mainland of Niphon (the name the Japanese adopt when speaking of the empire) and the island of Sikopf. This part of the journey occupied nine days, travelling at the rate of 8 re a-day, or something less than 24 miles. During this part of the journey M. de Wit and myself had been persuaded to trust to the cattle we should find on the way as post-horses—a mistake no one will ever make twice. Whether it was the malice or idleness of our officials, or that only the most sorry beasts could be found for hire, may admit of some doubt. This was our one great misery, and I confess to have chafed under it, remembering that I had left a good horse behind me, under bad advice. As for the weather it rained most days, more or less ; and the mountain roads, especially down in the valleys, became at times all but impassable. But not even these untoward conditions, serious as they were, could rob the country of its picturesque features of continually alternating hill and dale, mountain and valley ; the former often terraced to the very summit, though the sterile sandstone might constantly be seen cropping up as if protesting against the continued miracle of patient husbandry which could draw verdure and food from such a soil. Indeed, so constant is this sandstone formation, that the fields below seemed little else than sand; and every river we crossed was choked up with sand washed down from the adjoining hills, and were chiefly remarkable for the absence or scarcity of water. In 300 miles, all the way to Yeddo, we only came upon two rivers navigable for boats, and one alone for junks—that on the banks of which Osaca is situated : yet by dint of patient toil and incessant irrigation, even Kinsin, which in most countries would be a desert, is made a fruitful soil. The wheat harvest was in progress ; but how, in the midst of so much rain, and in the wet season, indeed, the Japanese farmer manages to cut and house his corn is a problem we have never been able to solve. They do not pile it up in sheaves as we do on the ground, but hang the sheaves on horizontal pegs fixed to stakes scattered over the fields for that purpose. The rice harvest is in November, and fortunately under happier circumstances, as rice is the great staple of food, and a bad harvest of this cereal is a national calamity ; whereas wheat is grown in much smaller quantity, and is rather a luxury than a necessity. It is chiefly used for little cakes or as vermicelli, and mingled with beans in a sort of soft dough.

In June green plots of the brightest hue indicate where the seed-rice is sown, and the transplanting process was, in many places, going on ; while in others the peasant, with a light ploughshare, and sometimes with a harrow, and a bullock or a pony, was busily engaged breaking up the ground in preparation, and, with the water let in, was to all appearance reducing the soil to a state of liquid mud and manure.

The arum, a sort of lotus-plant with an edible root, the sweet potato and bearded wheat, and a bean from which they make the best soy in the East, furnished the chief crops. A few patches of tea, occasionally a cotton-field, or a home-plot of tobacco, and more rarely a few poppies, here and there appeared. The variety of timber and foliage is great. The vines and the vegetable-wax tree preponderate perhaps, but these are everywhere intermingled with the Cryptomeria japonica, the bamboo and the palm-tree, thus blending the vegetation of the temperate and tropical zones in a way I have never observed elsewhere. The hedgerows are mainly composed of evergreens; the yew, the camelia, and the gardenia growing wild with the cryptomeria, which is generally kept carefully clipped; and from the Japanese there is little doubt the Dutch borrowed and introduced into Europe the fashion of clipped trees and hedges, which go to this day by the name of Dutch gardens. I do not know whether Macadam went to Japan for the idea of his macadamised roads, or our American cousins for their knickerbockers, but I can confidently affirm all these things were old in Japan three hundred years ago.

On the third day, at Urisino in the morning and Takiwo in the evening, we found hot sulphur-springs in much request among the natives for bathing. The first which we reached at midday was open to the street, with a mat-roof only to keep off the sun. As we approached an elderly dame stepped out on to the margin, leaving half-a-dozen of the other sex behind to continue their bathing. The freedom of the matron from all self-consciousness or embarrassment was so perfect, that the charitable exclamation of John Huss, when he saw a pious old woman hastening to bring a faggot to his stake, seemed perfectly applicable,—*O sancta simplicitas!* O sainted simplicity and happy matron, with no fear of a censorious world, vexed by no arbitrary code of conventional proprieties, and feeling no shame in the absence of covering. She had washed and was clean; and with the consciousness alone that a duty had been fulfilled, she evidently saw no reason why all the world should not know, and see it too, if they chanced to come that way.

During this journey through Kinsin, the richness and fertility of the land, so far as agricultural produce was concerned, presented a strange contrast with the obvious poverty of those who tilled the ground and lived upon it. Even in the large towns, though better houses were to be seen than in the villages or hamlets, there was still no sign of commercial activity or prosperity. I was indeed struck by the fact throughout the whole journey, that only where trade existed was there any material evidence of activity or wealth. Of the exact conditions of the tenure of land, I have no reliable information, though it has been with me a constant subject of interest and inquiry. The rent exacted, according to different accounts, varies from two to four fifths. Whatever may be the proportion, I think I saw conclusive evidence that nothing beyond the barest subsistence is left to the cultivator. Absolute destitution in Japan seems rare, and the very beggars have rather a nonchalant and jovial air, as though begging were rather an amusement than a necessity; but accumulated wealth in the hands of the higher class would seem to be quite as rare.

On the third day of our journey, when near Takiwa, we came upon some coal-mines of the Prince of Vizens. The coals appeared of fair quality and bituminous, but exposed in heaps to the air, and liable to rapid deterioration. The mine itself was apparently worked in a very primitive fashion by horizontal adits.

Arrived at Kokura, the fortified capital of Bouzen, and one of the keys to the straits between the two islands of Kinsin and Niphon, we embarked for Leinonosaki, on the opposite shore, where .H.M.S. *Ringdove* was waiting to convey me to Hiogo, at the other end of the Surnada Sea. Leinonosaki is a long, straggling town, winding along the bay for a mile or more under the hills which rise at least a thousand feet above. It is only a depôt for native produce and foreign goods—the first to be sent into Nagasaki and other ports, the other for distribution inland.

I must not stop to dilate on the beauties of the inland sea. The scenery is really very fine, though I think it has been somewhat overrated by the few casual visitors. This Sea of Surnada is studded over with islands; its shores are evidently volcanic; many perfect cones may be seen in the ranges of hills, though none appear in a state of activity. The villages on the shores are but fishing-hamlets of the most miserable kind. The sea itself is, however, the highway of a great traffic. Admiral Hope, in the two days occupied in traversing its length, had the junks passing him counted, and they amounted to 1500.

On arriving at Hiogo we found Takiniobo, a Governor of Foreign Affairs, waiting to receive M. de Wit and myself. He had been sent express by the Government to arrest our further progress overland, and induce us to complete the journey by ship. The ground alleged was danger to us personally, but this failing in its effect, he was instructed to urge the importance to the Government, in a political point of view, of our abstaining from a visit to Miaco, the capital of the Mikado—a negotiation being nearly happily concluded for a marriage of conciliation between the Mikado's sister and the young Tycoon, in which foreigners would be great gainers. After two long interviews I and my colleague consented to waive our intention of visiting Miaco, but firmly refused to take ship, or otherwise change our course. The rest of the journey was accomplished much more satisfactorily to ourselves if not to our Japanese friends. Two of my own horses having been despatched to meet me at Hiogo, I found them waiting my arrival fresh and in excellent condition. Hiogo is a town of some considerable size on the edge of the bay, and may be considered to some extent the shipping port of the larger city and commercial capital of Japan, Osaca, which is situated in a valley some 30 miles distant. Through this valley a river runs, dividing into numerous branches, and further connected by a multiplicity of canals. We proceeded there on the following day. Its immense area and the signs of material wealth and commercial activity exceeded my expectations. Even a cursory glance sufficed to satisfy me that Osaca, not Yeddo, was the great centre of commerce in Japan; and that Ocasa and Hiogo together, in a commercial point of view, would be more valuable to us than all the other ports put together. We were nearly an hour in traversing the vast suburbs on horseback, before we seemed to gain the great thoroughfares, filled to overflowing with an immense but very orderly crowd. There was, indeed, much pushing and squeezing; and now and then a desperate raid on some luckless front rank was made by the police, and blows were furiously dealt on the shaven heads of the offenders; but the only weapon was a paper fan, and although in their hands it proved a most efficient instrument, it not only broke no bones, but had the additional advantage over our policeman's staff of not even ruffling the temper. We came at last to the main branch of the river, spanned by a substantial timber-bridge of 300 yards. Not a trace of hostile feeling was anywhere to be seen among the people. Here, as might be seen at a glance, was a vast population with whom trade is the chief occupation, and at every step I saw evidences of the greatest activity. Piled up near the bridge were glazed tiles and pipes for drains, and large earthen jars for coffins—the Japanese preferring to be buried as they sit—resting upon their heels. It seems to them, no doubt, more natural, and is decidedly more economical of space. Instead of the traditional six feet of earth, a Japanese can be buried in three; while, if he is poor, his body is reduced to ashes, and a homœopathic allowance of earth suffices for his grave. The Japanese have some strange superstition about either sleeping or being buried with their heads to the North, and my servant would on no account permit my bed to be laid down on the mats in a wrong direction; and, the better to avoid mistakes in all the houjens or hostelries, the points of the compass are distinctly marked on the ceiling of the principal apartment. I could not remain many days in Osaca, but long enough to perambulate it in all directions, and to pick up some interesting specimens of pottery very similar to Palissy and Majolica ware, and some good specimens of silk and tapestry for the Exhibition, but for which I had to pay a high price compared with the rates in Yeddo.  The sun was very powerful, and the second day we took boats, a sort of gondola, by the aid of which we traversed the whole city in various directions, and with the same facility as we might at Venice.  We visited the theatre, and I am only sorry time will not permit me to give any description of the dramatic performance as an illustration of Japanese life. Strangely enough I found, after my return to Yeddo, that I had actually witnessed here a rehearsal, as it were, of the scene of violence and bloodshed, in which I was destined to be a chief actor in the attack on the Legation by a band of armed ruffians the second night after my arrival : only the scene in the play was laid in a hostelry on the road instead of the Legation.

I was detained more than a month in Japan, when I had fixed a time for my departure, by an occurrence well illustrating the innate recklessness of the national character.  One morning as Ando Tsusimano Karni, the Minister of Foreign Affairs, was proceeding to the palace, not a hundred paces scarcely from his own residence, surrounded by his own retinue of officers and armed retainers, a shot was fired at him, wounding one of his servants, and a party of only eight men suddenly flung themselves sword in hand upon his Norimon. Before any defence could be made, he received a sword-thrust in the body, and other wounds.  The assailants were all slain on the spot, except two, one of whom, badly wounded, was taken prisoner; and the Minister informed me that some of the attacking party, according to this man's account, were survivors of the attack on the Legation, after our return from this journey. With men so ready for desperate enterprises, and so reckless of life, the policy to be pursued by Western Powers, in the interests of commerce and of civilisation, must needs be a grave and an embarrassing question.  Merchants, as is natural, are eager and impatient for the removal of all barriers and limitations —anxious for the immediate opening of more ports, but without very carefully counting the probable cost and the price to be paid.  What if this could only be carried out, or, indeed, attempted at the price of a social and political revolution in the country ; an outbreak of violence and slaughter on the part of the armed classes, and the overthrow of the existing Government, with a subsequent state of chaos and chronic war such as now exists in China ?  Is there any Western Power, with real interests at stake in the East, who would willingly accept the responsibility of measures of coercion to be followed by even a probability of such results?  And, if any could be found, who would be the gainers?  Not the merchants, assuredly, nor commerce ; for if it did not make all trade and residence in the empire impossible for half a century, it would at least put an end to both for the present, and it is not this country to whom such a policy could be acceptable.  Any further Eastern complication requiring squadrons and troops, and bringing all the horrors of war upon a well-disposed and unoffending population, could not fail to be unpopular to the last degree.  And the Western Powers collectively appear to have arrived at the conclusion that, bad as may be their prospects of rapidly overcoming the obstacles interposed by the ruling classes, there could be no advantage to commerce, or civilisation either, which would compensate, even if it could justify, the cost and the evils inseparable from a resort to force.  And, in the absence of this, merchants and statesman alike must, I believe, learn to be content to take patience, and trust something to time and persevering efforts of a more peaceable character.

3.—*On the most promising Fields for New Exploration in Eastern Africa.*

[THE following letter was written by a Sub-committee of the Council of the Royal Geographical Society, in reply to an application from the Geographical Society of Bombay.   It is now printed for general information.]

IN reference to the inquiries made by the Bombay Geographical Society, it should be observed that the extent of coast whence future explorations of importance may be directed into Eastern Africa, has become considerably limited by expeditions now in progress or recently completed.

Beginning at the south, we may look upon the Nyassa as entirely in the hands of Livingstone and other Zambesi travellers, such as Count Thurnheim. Livingstone, as we know, has established easy access to the southern end of the lake, and announced his intention of exploring the whole of it at the earliest opportunity.   It would be a waste of resources to direct new travellers to that same district.

Proceeding northward, the itineraries of native traders supply enough information for the present rude wants of African geography, of the country between Quiloa and Nyassa; and we have received slight but definite knowledge of the same through Röscher's ill-fated expedition, followed up as it was to some degree by the Baron von der Decken.

Taking yet another step, we arrive at the track of Burton and Speke, who have certainly left nothing of primary importance undescribed.

The fourth and last section of known country is to the eastward of Mombas, whence Baron von der Decken (accompanied by the English geologist, Mr. Thornton) has lately travelled to Kilimanjaro, and where he still proposes to travel.

Thus there is no urgent call for a new expedition that should leave the coast of Africa between the Zambesi and Mombas; but Eastern Africa is almost untouched between Mombas and the Red Sea.   The field that here awaits new explorations is too vast to be exhausted by any single expedition.   Three distinct undertakings may be specified.

The first is to ascend the Juba, the Ozi, and other rivers, as far as they are navigable.   They have all been visited by slavers, and opposition might be experienced on entering them, partly from that cause and partly owing to hostilities between the Somauli and the Massai; but no serious obstruction need be apprehended by a well-equipped party, large enough to command respect.

The second and the most difficult would be a land exploration through the Somauli.   Their language is an obstacle to a traveller from the side of Zanzibar, where interpreters cannot be engaged; while the religious and the political fanaticism of their northern tribes is an equal bar to travellers from Aden, where a suitable expeditionary party might, perhaps, be collected.   The most promising course would be to land at Mogadoxo, and to reside there for some months, learning the language and acquiring a hold on the goodwill of the people, before attempting further progress.

Additional interest is given to this exploration by the fact that Lieut.-Colonel Rigby, H.B.M.'s Consul at Zanzibar, is firmly persuaded that some Englishmen are now in captivity among the Somaulis; for a report to that effect has been confirmed by different witnesses.   He believes them to be a part of the crew or passengers of an East Indiaman, supposed to have been wrecked near the Mauritius in 1855, but whose cargo, or rather a number of miscellaneous effects resembling those known to have been carried by her, are come into the possession of the Somaulis.   An exploring party would find in this report an intelligible pretext for their presence in the land, and a stimulating object for their earlier movements.

The last course would be to adopt Mombas as the headquarters, and thence to pass into the interior by a route to the north of that travelled by the Baron von der Decken.   The country behind Mombas is a less unhealthy residence than other parts of the coast; and an expeditionary party might be organised there at leisure, with help from Zanzibar.   The Rev. Mr. Krapf resides in its neighbourhood; the natives are accustomed to Europeans; and the traders mostly speak Hindustani.   It would be impossible at the present time to plan an exploration in Africa that would afford hope of a more interesting discovery than one leading from Mombas round the northern flank of Kenia, and thence onwards towards Gondokoro.

*18th March*, 1862.

---

4.—*Calagouk, or Curlew Island, in the Bay of Bengal, as a Sea-coast Sanitarium.*   By Duncan Macpherson, m.d., Inspector-General of Hospitals, Madras Establishment.

The Moscos, contiguous to the mouth of Tavoy River; Tavoy Island, half-way between Tavoy and Mergui; and King's Island, opposite Mergui, have come respectively under our inquiries.   Of these various islands, the following is in every respect the most suitable for a sanitarium.

Curlew Island, the headquarters of the Alguada Reef lighthouse establishment, is situated in the Gulf of Martaban, 5 miles from the mainland of the Tenasserim coast, and 30 miles of Amherst Point, in lat. 15° 52′, and in long. 97° 42′.   It is 8 miles long, exclusive of Cavendish Island, which lies at its extreme south end, and which is half a mile in length.   The greatest breadth of the island is about $1\frac{1}{4}$ mile; and on its highest part, which is about 500 feet above the sea, are the " remarkable trees," a  point for navigators in making the coast.

The base of the island is primary rock, the superstratum being a rich mixture of open porous soil, composed of sand and vegetable mould.   Its formation is very peculiar, the northern and southern portions differing considerably. The northern half on the western side is composed of a long granite ridge, with an average perpendicular drop to the sea, varying from 250 to 300 feet.   To the east the ground descends to the sea in gentle or abrupt slopes.   The opposite side of the island is broken into alternate or isolated  hills, with level well-raised intervening spaces, forming three bays.   The first, Quarry-bay, where the stones are now being prepared for the Alguada lighthouse, is the deepest at high water; the beach is sandy, but at ebb tide an extensive mud-flat, covered in places with mangrove, is exposed : the somewhat narrowness of the channel between the island and the mainland on its side tending to the accumulation of mud.

The southern half of the island differs entirely from the northern, inasmuch as both sides are broken into bays.   To the west, Retreat Bay, Rocky Bay, Sea Bay, and Fish Bay are beautiful, hard, sandy beaches, well protected by high land on each side, and open to the ocean in front, with a fine rolling surf on the beach, and only divided from one another by projecting rocky points, and from the corresponding bays on the eastern side by well-raised necks of land, sloping east and west, free from all swampy ground, and ascending north and south to the hills which divide the bays.   The eastern bays look on the distant mainland, rising in bold outline on the horizon.   These very much resemble the western bay; in fact differ only by the mud uncovering at half-tides, the rise and fall at spring-tides being 22 feet.   All the bays on the eastern side are perfectly protected from the south-west monsoon; while during the north-east monsoon the bay on the western side, and the deep water close up to the ridge on the north, afford a free, open, and safe place for yachting

-and boating.   The bays on both sides are peculiarly well suited for bathing, the water on the western side especially being always pure and clear, except at spring-tides.

Ascending from Retreat Bay the ridge referred to above is reached.   This ridge, and indeed the entire island, is clothed with fine primeval forest, with trees of immense dimensions and height.   Under their overshadowing branches a well-shaded road might with ease be carried along the ridge, having the open ocean on one hand, with the view of the fine contour of the island itself and the bold coast of the Tenasserim provinces in the distance beyond on the other.   Here and there this ridge opens out into plateaus, forming beautiful sites for houses; and, with the exception of a slight rise about the centre, the road would nearly run on a uniform level for a distance of 5 miles. The same road might there be extended to the southward, encircling the bay and crossing the intervening points of land, and also to the northern part of the island, where there is a considerable space of garden and cultivable ground. The free percolation of air by means of these roads, judicious clearing for building sites, and the adoption of measures to facilitate the natural drainage, one year prior to the occupation of the island for sanitary purposes, are measures of the highest urgency and importance.

The island has now been occupied by a large party of workmen since April, 1860.   Usually the pioneers or first settlers in every locality suffer considerably, especially where no prior arrangements have been made to guard against disease.   In the present case a large body of natives of India, Burmah, and China, European officers and subordinates, entered on operations of a harassing nature, at the hottest season of the year.   Quarry Bay, where they settled, is, sanitarily considered, by no means the best locality to settle on.   But the presence of good stone, and the facilities for shipping it to the reef, induced the superintendent to fix his headquarters here.   I append a return of the strength of the establishment, the prevailing diseases, and the mortality, from the 3rd April, 1860, to the 30th April, 1861, from which it will be observed that, everything considered, the sick and death rate have been unusually small.   It must be borne in mind that the party for many months had little or no protection by night or by day, and that their huts occupied unwholesome sites in the midst of felled jungle, yet the report presents a gratifying immunity from the graver diseases.   The fevers were chiefly of an ephemeral nature, the sick-list being chiefly kept up by local injuries and their results,—diseases not contracted on the island and cutaneous affections, from the want of antiscorbutic articles of diet.

DAILY AVERAGE per Cent. of Prevailing Diseases, from 30th April, 1860, to 30th April, 1861.

|  | May. | June. | July. | August. | September. | October. | November. | December. | January. | February. | March. | April. | Averages. |
|---|---|---|---|---|---|---|---|---|---|---|---|---|---|
| Strength .   .   . | 212 | 209 | 295 | 367 | 400 | 433 | 495 | 502 | 480 | 480 | 705 | 710 | 440 |
| Dysentery .   . | ·09 | 2·07 | .. | .. | .. | .. | ·10 | ·36 | .. | ·14 | .. | .. | ·23 |
| Ulcers .   .   . | 0·7 | 5·1 | 3·1 | 4·1 | 5·5 | 3·8 | 2·6 | 3·5 | 4·1 | 2·1 | 2·08 | 3·64 | 3·38 |
| Fever .   .   . | 0·8 | 1·0 | 0·9 | 1·0 | 1·2 | 1·5 | 3·4 | 4·9 | 4·1 | 4·1 | 2·3 | 1·55 | 2·17 |
| Other diseases . | 5·05 | 8·61 | 6·13 | 6·14 | 7·05 | 8·01 | 4·25 | 8·99 | 8·30 | 16·74 | 11·99 | 22·22 | 6·13 |

There were nine deaths during the year from diseases contracted on the island, viz. :—Three from dysentery in January ; three from fever ; from ex-

posure, one in July, one in November, and one in January ; three from accidents and other diseases.   No deaths occurred amongst the Europeans.

During the ten days of my residence on the island, in the months of May
and June, the climate was exceedingly agreeable.   The nights were cool, and
no punkahs were necessary during the day.   In fact, a refreshing sea-breeze
was present at all times in every part of the island visited by me during the
day, and a blanket was always grateful at night.   The average of the thermometer at this period during the day is 75°, during the hot weather it is 88° ;
and Captain Fraser speaks in glowing terms of the climate at all seasons, as
compared with that in Calcutta.   Water of an excellent quality is procurable
at a depth of 15 feet ; and a perennial spring of sweet water flows through
the centre of the island.   The rainfall, Captain Fraser thinks, is under that
experienced on the mainland opposite.

The great advantage of this island is its proximity to Madras and Calcutta,
and to the principal stations in Burmah.

---

### 5.—*Topographical Notes on Tunis.*

["THIS paper appears to be a careful compilation of considerably more than
a century ago.   Some of the places described are correct, as far as the compiler
goes, but many changes have occurred in the interim.   His mention of mines
requires verification, for it is difficult to pronounce what is authentic and what
he gathered from itinerant Jews and others.   There are evidences of the manuscript having been ransacked, but I do not remember having met it in print."
—Vice-Admiral W. H. SMYTH, K.S.F., F.R.G.S., &c.]

*Biserta,* a large town about 50 miles north-west from Tunis, seated by the
sea-side ; about half a mile long, but narrow.   The lake, on the banks whereof
it is seated, discharges itself into the sea by the town walls, and forms the port.
Towards the east is the island where the Christians formerly lived.   The
inhabitants are pretty numerous, and are for the most part of the race of the
Andalusian Moors who were drove out of Spain.   They have about this town
very good arable land, which produces a great quantity of beans, chichorie,
and sundry other sorts of grain, which is exported for Italy and France, except
wheat and barley, that not being exported without a particular licence.   They
sow cotton and tobacco.   The lake reaches up 30 miles in the country ;
and there is an ebb and flow every six hours, and at the full of the moon then
it is more.   In the year 1755 there was found an old-built well of very fine
fresh spring-water ; it was stopt up ; it is in the market where they sell the
wheat.

*Ras El Gibel,* a town of about 300 houses, 8 miles west from St. Farina,
and about a mile from the sea.   There are seven churches with steeples.

*Porto Farina* is a an unwalled town of above 100 houses : a large lake is before
it, at the end whereof is a very handsome large bason for holding the men-of-
war and cruisers belonging to Tunis, it being the safest and best port belonging
to the kingdom of Tunis.   To the northward of the town is a salt-work.   In
1739, when I was first there, there were two men-of-war—one of 50 guns,
given by the Grand Signor in 1732, and the other of 50 guns, built by one
Mr. Markham, an English builder, which has never been at sea yet, nor, I
believe, never will.   Near this place, about 1750, was discovered, by a Milanese,
a quicksilver-mine, very good, but neglected by the Bey.

*El Alea,* a neat town seated on the top of a hill, whence its name (the high),
is inhabited chiefly by Andalusian Moors, about 10 miles south-west from Porto
Farina.   It is at this place only where the thistles grow which are used by the
capmakers at Tunis ; they will thrive nowhere else, as has been tried.

*Solyman,* a small unwalled town of about 200 houses, about 22 miles south-east of Tunis, is seated on a plain a mile from the sea, inhabited chiefly by Andaluses and Tripolines.   Saffron also grows hereabouts.

*Hammam Leef.*—This is a famous hot-bath seated at the foot of a very high, steep, rocky hill.   Here are two baths built, one for the men, and the other for the women : they go down three or four steps to them, and the water is up to their middle ; there is a bench of stone to sit on ; it is frequented chiefly for the cure of the French disease.   The water of this bath is entirely sulphurous ; it is about 12 miles south-east of Tunis.

*Galipia*, a small town situated at about 15 miles south-east from Cape Bona, and about 2 miles from the sea-side.   The castle stands on the top of a rocky hill close to the water-side, and is a very ancient building, and very difficult to go up.

*Zowwan*, a neat town of 450 houses, seated on a hill at the foot of a large hill, inhabited chiefly by Andaluses, who are dyers and gardeners, there being a very good spring of fresh water, which comes out of the hill above the town, which serves both for dyeing and for their gardens.   Where the head of the spring is, is the ruins of an old temple built over it ; it is round.

*Mesakin*, a small town of about 100 houses, inhabited chiefly by Sherifs, who won't allow neither Jew nor Christian to enter the town.

*El Jeridde*, a large tract of land lying on the borders of the Sahara or Desert and subject to Tunis.   It is a sandy soil, and the only produce of it is dates, with which they drive a great trade with the Moors round about them ; besides, they make great quantities of fine barracans and fine burnouses of wool they get from the Emamma, a tribe of Moors who are near them, in exchange of their dates.   The caravan that goes from South Barbary to Cairo every year calls at the Jeridde, both going and coming, and exchanges goods for dates.   The people are yellow and thin, and have bad sight by reason of the heat of the sand.   They reckon three days' journey from the Jeridde to Tuggurt.   The water of the Jeridde is purgative to strangers for a while, till they are used to it.   Madder is cultivated here ; and, upon a demand in Tunis, they carry it there from hence, it not turning to account, by reason of the land-carriage, unless very scarce and dear.

*Bahar Pharaon*, or the Sea of Pharaoh, is a kind of lake in the Jeridde ; some part water, but the most part sand, and in several places quicksands ; so that where the people passed over is marked with stumps of date-trees, otherwise there would be no finding the way.

*Tozer*, the chief town of the Jeridde.   Here is a palace built for the Bey, where he commonly resides when he cames to the Jeridde.   At this town the caravan that goes from South Barbary to Cairo and back again, calls here ; and the Codemsees pass here mostly.

*Nefta*, a town of the Jeridde, 15 miles south-west from Tozer.   They have plantations of date-trees and springs of warm water.

*Sfax*, or Sfacus, is a handsome town, four-square, and walled round.   The town is seated on a sandy plain about a stone's-throw from the sea.   It is about a mile in circuit, and very populous.   They make a great deal of linen cloth there.   This place drives a great trade to Alexandria for flax and rice ; and ships off from thence (when the Bey gives leave) oil, olives, and soap for Alexandria, and wool for Christendom, and henna for Tunis.

*Sminjah* is a plain so called, famous for the defeat of Hassein Ben Allie by the Algerines in 1735, and afterwards for the defeat of Sidie Jonas about two months afterwards by Hassein Ben Allie.   And in this plain are some quarries of black marble, pretty good.

*Mezezelbeb*, a neat town situated on a plain on the eastern bank of the river Mejerdah, inhabited chiefly by the Andalusians.   At this place is a fine bridge over the river, built by Mahomet Bey.   The river is very deep here, and as broad again as where the bridge is going to Porto Farina.

*Hammam Zreeba,* a hot-bath nine miles south from Zowwan. The water is impregnated with rock-alum and sulphur.

*Uselet,* a parcel of high mountains so called; they are about 18 miles square each way; and they reckon among these mountains about 6000 men inhabitants besides women and children. The mountains are craggy, and of very difficult access, being very narrow ways; but among the mountains they have valleys; and the caroub-tree is very plenty; and they keep a great many bees. They have several stone cisterns in the hollows of the mountains, which the rain fills and serves them for their drink. The people are very hardy, and very dextrous in handling small arms. I have been told by a Jew who used to travel in those parts selling trifles, that he had seen a great many stone statues in those mountains, dressed in a short dress, some with their heads off, others wanting their arms, defaced, I supposed, by the Arabs.

*Tabarca* is a small island near the borders of Algier, belonging formerly to Tunis, and afterwards to the family of Lomellini of Genoa, confirmed to them by a firman from the Grand Signor in 1740. There might be about 800 or 900 souls in the town, and 22 coral-boats thereto belonging. Facing the island is the ruins of the ancient Tagasta. The ruins of the town Tagasta are two miles in circuit; and there are three large magazines standing, and several sepulchres, which the Tabarkines broke down for the stones.

*Keph,* a strong town on the frontiers towards the Algier territories. The castle is a Roman structure. The climate here in winter time is very cold, and they have a good deal of snow-fall about the hills. Near this place is a very good copper-mine, and also an iron-mine, discovered in the old Bey's time. Near Chef are woods from whence they bring bark, which is used by the preparers of morocco-leather skins, and they also bring white galls from thence used by the said tanners.

*Gafsa,* a neat town a day's journey from the Jeridde. The houses are built of mud walls and palm-tree rafters. They make very fine burnooses and barracans here, and very fine worsted, of which the Turks, who are in garrison, make mahakas, which the women use to rub themselves with when they go to the bagnios; they put some of the inside of the date-tree under and sew the worsted over them. The wool they get from the Emama, a tribe of Moors not far from them. About a musket-shot from the town is a mountain called Gibel Gātōre, from whence they supply the kingdom of Tunis with flints for the muskets and pistols.

*Jerba,* an island belonging to Tunis lying just on the borders of Tripolie, near 60 miles in circumference. The soil is sandy and produces great quantities of water-melons. The people are very industrious, and are mostly merchants, but have the character of being very sharp and also close-fisted, which has caused a proverb in this country : " Como un Jerbino " (like a Jerbin)—that is, miserly ; and they are also reckoned one of the four of the greatest cheats, viz. a Jew, a Genoese, a Jerbin, and a Greek. They are mostly of a sect called Hamse.

*Gurbos,* a place about 12 miles to the northward of Soliman. Near the seashore at this place is a very hot bath : the water comes from the mountain above it, and is impregnated with alum; the water is so hot that it is hardly bearable. There are some ruins at this place.

*Susa,* a handsome walled town of about a mile in circuit, at about a stone's-throw from the sea-side, 15 miles south-east of Erkla. There are also several ruins about the town. The country round about is sandy, but produces great quantities of oil and olives. There is a great deal of linen cloth made here, being the best made in the kingdom. They have several wells of water : they are ancient, and built with large massy stones.

*Moraisah,* lying 6 miles north-east of Suliman, close by the sea-side. Here are very extensive ruins, and was formerly a city of some figure : they have brought away a great many stones from hence, which have served to build the castles at the Goletta and other buildings in Tunis. There is a great deal of ruins to be seen under water in calm weather, particularly a large gateway standing upright.

*Sahul,* a part of the country so called which comprehends all the land near the sea-coast from Ergla to Sfax: it abounds with olive-plantations. They cultivate and make indigo. The Moors of the Neageas, of Uled Saïde, and Dreid have their quarters in these parts.

*Arad,* a large tract of land, part plain and part mountainous; called also the Little Jeridde. It joins to the Sahul and the Jeridde, and goes as far as the borders of Tripolie. They have plenty of date-plantations, though not so good as those of the Jeridde; and they cultivate the henna.

*Carthage* is now only an heap of ruins: all the remains are the large cisterns, which are 17 in number, adjoining close to each other; there is one of them divided into two parts, with a cupola on each end. On the southernmost side are nine, and on the other side seven. They are all of equal dimensions, and are as follows :—

The length from within the walls is 90 feet, and in breadth 18 feet 10 inches.
The breadth of the wall that divides the two cisterns 4 feet 10 inches.
The breadth of the passages within the walls 6 feet 8 inches.
The depth from the top of the arch to the wall that divides the cisterns is 10 feet 3 inches.
The breadth of the cupolas 20 feet.
The thickness of the wall on the top is 2 feet 8 inches.
I measured the depth of one cistern that had some water in it, and found it to be 26 feet.

At the end of these cisterns, on the north side, is a wall built that one can go no further on the east side. The Moors have dug a hole in the wall to find treasure, and it is said they found some; but on the terrace of the cisterns, and adjoining to them on the west part, is a cupola which I measured the depth of, and found it 28 feet. The top of the cupola is broke down; and about 12 feet down is a square hole, for what use I don't know. In each cistern are eight small earthen pipes on the top—I suppose for the admission of the water—about 3 inches diameter. The cisterns on the south side are falling to ruin, several being fallen in.

Near the sea-side, at the distance of about 20 feet, and not far from the cisterns, are several fragments of ruins on a rising ground; and I went underground in an opening, and found it was an arched place supported on large pillars built of stone, and that there were four ways going always cross and cross. I could not go in far by reason of the rubbish. I was told by one that he had heard that some Turks had been in there, and came to a large hall supported by marble pillars, and that they could go under ground a great way; but it is now so filled up with rubbish that one can go only a little way in. I was told by one who lived at the castle, built near the cisterns, that in digging to make a garden they found several tombs, of two long stones for the sides, and one for the head, and another for the feet; they were narrow, and covered with a red-like slate: there were bones in them, and some bones of a child; their heads were laid north-west.

Near the cisterns, a little to the northward, is a spring of water, which comes out in a valley from a large mountain. The water in winter is good, but in summer it is something brackish: it comes into a kind of stone trough. Some Moors have been in, and say it is very spacious. About half a mile nearer Tunis are another set of cisterns; they seem to be shorter and broader than the others. The Moors have inhabited them.

There are several cisterns all about the hills of Carthage, and sundry other ruins, but nothing that deserves to be taken notice of.

*Beeban,* a place so called, about 40 miles east of Jerba, is the last place belonging to Tunis towards the eastward.

*Nabal,* a large open town, seated at about a mile's distance from the sea in a sandy plain. Near this place, on a mountain called Gibel Shib, or the alum mountain, there is an alum-mine. They don't know how to work it clean; they have formerly tried, but found the expense exceed the gains.

*Ras Sem,* in the kingdom of Tripolie. I have been told by a Corsican renegado, who had been Bey of Derna, that he had twice seen that place, and that he had seen there petrified palm-trees and also olive-trees, and like people's knee-bones, which were turned like flint-stones; and that people going there on purpose seldom found it because, lying in the sandy desert, the land being blown by the wind covered that place, and at some times the wind would drive it away, when what he told me of might be seen.

*Gamuda,* a place where are the ruins of a large town seated on the side of a hill. There are no inhabitants here. This is one of the stations of the winter camp. They find the abebile (?) here, and nowhere else in the kingdom; they are found in a plain on the surface of the ground.

*Cairoan,* a very large town, the next in bigness to Tunis. This town was supposed to have been built by the first Arabs who came down and conquered this country, there being several of the chiefs buried there. They have a handsome large church wherein is hung up the armour of the Arab chiefs, as helmet, breastplate, &c., as used in those times. The people pay no head-money, it being esteemed a holy place, next to Mecca; and the Moors say, that in case the Christians should take Mecca, then this town would be visited by pilgrims instead of that place. They reckon in this town 4024 houses. The people are very industrious, and much given to trade. They are reckoned very honest and just, but very sharp in their dealings, looking after the smallest matter, which they won't lose.

*Jibbel Iskill,* or Gebel Iskill, is a large high mountain about 16 miles from Biserta. At the end of the lake it is full of wild hogs, being full of woods. Here is a hot-bath, frequented by the Moors, and several ancient ruins. In the summer time, when the water is low, they send cattle to graze, there being fine pasture. In winter time they go there by water.

*El Hamma de Tozer,* a large village about 6 miles distant from Tozer. Here is a hot-bath : the water is not very hot, but after bathing it causes an abundant sweat, and is good in many diseases, and much frequented by the Moors. The water here is very good and sweet—the best in the Jeridde, and serves to water the date-plantations, being a copious spring.

*Cheps,* a large town through which a river runs that divides it in two parts, but it is joined by an ordinary stone bridge. The port is in the river, but it is very dangerous. The water of the river is sweet, but very heavy and unwholesome to strangers. The chief of their trade consists in the henna, of which they have many plantations. The water ebbs and flows very much, and at low water they can see the ruins of a large town. Some miles distant is the ruins of the old town of Cheps.

*Gem,* a large village built about half a mile from the famous Amphitheatre. In the Amphitheatre is a hole, and the Moors say that there is a passage under ground that leads to Medea. A Jew told me he had been a long way in it; and several Moors told him they had been a great way in it.

*Toburba,* a small town seated on the western side of the Mejerdah, inhabited chiefly by Andaluses. There is a handsome bridge built by Mahomed Bey out of the ruins of an amphitheatre. Here is a batan for milling caps.

*Weyd el Erg* a river about 6 miles east of La Calla. It is supposed that formerly there has been a port here, there being a great deal of ruins dispersed all about this track. There are otters in this lake : the Moors eat them.

*Biserta.*—The lake of Biserta is in two parts joined together by a narrow channel: that part towards Biserta is reckoned to be 25 Italian miles in circumference; the uppermost part is reckoned larger than the other; and within it, near the channel, is the fishery of Tingia.

*Truzza* is a very high mountain, and on the top of it is a large hole from whence ascend hot vapours, and it is used as a bagnio by laying wood over the hole, and a mat upon it, and the person lays down on it, being well wrapped up. Towards the foot of the mountain is a grotto; and some goats having gone in there, when they came out again their hair was turned yellow. Allie ordered people to go in, but they could find no end. At this place are woods of fir and pine.

*Gilma.*—Here are the ruins of a very large town built on the side of a hill. On the foot of it are several square towers, pretty high but narrow, covered on the top, and a door to go in; within each, on the floor, is a square stone about 4 feet high and as many square; and on the top is a round hole, about 6 inches diameter, which runs down into another larger; and within the tower, towards the top, are four figures cut out in gips, one on every side—one with a lance, another with bow and arrows, and such like arms.

Here is also a rivulet of fresh water.

In a large mountain, a day's journey on horseback from Tabarca, there is a lead-mine. They have ovens to melt and prepare it. They have several openings of the mine; but they don't take much care to melt it, being a good deal of dross mixed with it. It is a very large and plentiful mine, and is forbid to be worked but for the use of the Bey; but a great deal of it is sent in contraband to Bona in order to make their pots; and all the Arabs supply themselves here, also in contraband, with lead to make bullets; that for Bona is run to the sea-side, whence it is shipped on board the sandalls.

This is the road going to Tabarca, and is a very narrow and bad pass. The garrison of Tabarca have sometimes been set upon (in times of disturbance) here by the Moors.

A few miles from Bardo there is a copper-mine—very good ore; and not far from it is a silver-mine; and in the mountains above Tabarca is a silver-mine. Both these silver-mines were discovered in 1738 by a man who came here and gave himself out for a miner, and spoke several languages. I fancy he must have been a German renegade, though none knew what he was; and he tried the ore, and produced silver; but being accused of a design of running away, the Bey ordered him to be imprisoned, which he took so ill, that with a knife he had, he killed his servant, and then cut his throat.

The large copper-mine is beyond Chef, near the river Serat, on the Algier frontier. The mine is very rich.

At Spaitla is a copper-mine, and at Truzza is a silver-mine.

---

6.—*The Andaman Islands.* By Rev. Charles Parish, Chaplain, Bengal Service.

Communicated by Sir William Hooker, f.r.g.s.

Moulmein, Dec. 10, 1862.

My dear Sir William,—I have lately had an excursion to the Andamans, and, more interesting still, to Barren Island. Our new settlement at *Port Blair* in the southernmost of the three main islands, is at present not on the *mainland* (as we may well call the larger islands), but on three very small islets close to the mainland, in the bay or port. These are quite cleared, so hardly any botanising is to be done on them; and the mainland is not safe to visit without a guard of seamen, owing to the hostility of the natives. Moreover, when you visit it, you can yet do nothing more than skirt the shore, or, it may be, penetrate some 100 yards inland, as the country is one vast impenetrable jungle, swarming with leeches in the rainy, and with those still less delightful things *ticks* in the dry, season. Therefore, as I was there but four days—was poorly one day, and had duties to perform—you may suppose that I did not do much botanically. I strolled about, however, a little, and saw enough to show me that, generally speaking (although of course there must be some things new), the vegetation small and great is that of our Tenasserim coast. From the absence of palms of all kinds—at least about Port Blair (as far, that is, as my limited observation went)—and of large endogenous plants (at all events in sufficient numbers to catch the eye), you would hardly imagine, as you look down upon the scene from the top of one of the smaller islands, that it was a tropical one—although, indeed, as soon as you try to force your way through the vegetation, its rank growth speaks at once of heat and moisture such as temperate regions know nothing of. The land is not high; still there is no level land about Port Blair; the islands, as far as the eye can reach, form a series of gentle undulations densely clothed in green, the highest points being 700, 800, or even perhaps 1000 feet. The highest land in the whole archipelago does not, I believe, much exceed 2000 feet. I was at home among most of the herbaceous plants, ferns, and orchids, as they were my old friends of the coast. I found, however, a *Lindsiæ*, which I had not yet found here, and which I am not sure of, and a terrestrial orchid—*Platantheræ*, species new to me. But the fact that I have not yet met with these plants in our provinces, is no proof that they are not there also. It is very likely they are, but that I do not happen to have fallen in with them. One little interesting fact I discovered relative to the very limited *manufactures* of the poor Andamanese. It is, that they make their bowstrings of the fibre of *Dendrobia formosum* and *secundum*. Their bows are very powerful, and they are capital shots. The men and women go alike *in puris naturalibus*; and their life seems spent, poor creatures, in searching for food, chiefly shellfish, though they *shoot* other fish, and a pig occasionally. There are no other wild beasts known on the islands, as that expression is commonly understood, except one small carnivorous animal, which Mr. Blyth, of Calcutta, named to me; but I forget what he called it. Mr. Blyth requested me to search for frogs for him, as he said it was supposed by naturalists, that *Batrachians* were not found on islands at a great distance from continents. In this instance, however, they are; for I had no difficulty in catching him some frogs. But I must leave the Andamans now, hoping to make a better future acquaintance with them, and come to that place, which I have been long wishing to visit, Barren Island. I wish I were competent to describe this island and its formation geologically, for it is most interesting. Of its general structure and form, of course I need not speak, as every one knows that from Lyell, though he is mistaken wholly in one point; for he says that the sea flows round the base of the cone *inside* the outer wall of the island. It is difficult to understand where his information could have come from. Not only is it not so, but the valley, filled with rugged and broken blocks of lava, is much elevated above the sea—I should say, generally, 50 or 60 feet—and there are no appearances of any recent elevation of the island.

We landed (a party of five), early in the morning, at the only practicable landing-place—a breach in the summit of this submarine mountain, out of which the lava had flowed into the sea (the steamer meanwhile steaming gently to and fro, as there is no anchorage). It is only when opposite to this breach, as I call it, that you can get a sight of the inner cone, for the general elevation of the island is about the same as that of the cone, namely, about 800 feet. The cone is composed entirely of scoriæ and loose cinders, and is perfectly black; and, being excessively steep (about 45°), is, as you may imagine, very difficult to ascend. We ascended it, however. Near the summit the loose material of which the cone is composed is cemented into a tolerably hard surface or crust, by the deposits of sulphur and gypsum (I believe) which are precipitated from the vapours which are continually given out from it. There is a small crater on the top about 40 or 50 feet deep, and 100 feet in diameter. The bottom of it is quite smooth, and firm, and *cool* (*i. e.* was so at the time of our visit). It is along the *edge of this crater*, which is marked by long, narrow fissures, that the sulphureous vapours issue. Speaking generally, you may say that the cone is devoid of vegetation, as there is not enough upon it to be noticed at a distance, or to alter in any degree its prevailing black colour. Vegetation, however, does exist. Tufts of a species of *Juncus* are seen here and there, and a few miserably-stunted ferns—viz. *Nephrolepis hirsutula, Pteris longifolia* and *quadriaurita*, and that curious little plant *Psilotum*. These were the *only* plants growing on the cone. Round the base, and filling up the valley, flows (or has flowed at some distant time) a stream of black lava, which has evidently emptied itself into the sea at the breach in the side wall of the island, before mentioned. I say a *stream*, because I think it is impossible to view it from the top of the cone without coming to the conclusion that it was once a stream flowing round the base and rushing out into the sea; but the surface of the lava is neither smooth nor even, but consists of a mass of loose blocks, some solid and crystalline in their texture, and others (by far the greater number) porous and tufaceous, of every size and shape thrown and heaped together in the greatest disorder, as if (as I suppose must have been the case) thrown out from the crater on the top of the lava-current as it began to cool. No vegetation grows on this; but it is all as black as the cone, and is the most painful stuff to walk over that can be imagined, from the sharp points presented to the feet, the looseness of the blocks of tuff, and the horrible holes intervening. The inner sides of the island, facing the cone, are also generally of the same material as the cone itself, *i. e.* of loose cinders and scoriæ, black and steep, except here and there where the native rock projects and displays the stratification of the island. At the base of these slopes, and encroaching here and there on the lava, is tall rank grass; and a low jungle of three or four low shrubs, one of which is a species of *Mussœnda*. I wished to have gathered specimens of everything that grew in the interior of the island, and left a man on purpose to collect for me while I ascended the cone. Unfortunately, however, he injured his foot at the very commencement of his walking, and could do nothing; and I had enough to do to scramble up and down the cone, and look to my footing among the lava-blocks. I hope, however, to visit it again. If I do, I shall stay at the foot and botanise while my friends go up, as *once* is quite enough to have made the ascent. Looking to the interior of the island, it is well called "Barren Island," for it is truly a valley of desolation, dark and gloomy; but, as viewed from the sea, it is extremely fertile, all the slopes seaward being clothed with thick vegetation, though of what kind I had no opportunity of seeing.

The opportunities of landing there are of course very rare, as it involves a delay of the steamer, which is not always a thing to be managed, and there is no anchorage; and landing, except in very calm weather, is not possible, as there is but one spot where a landing can be effected, and the water must be very still to make it practicable even there. I forgot to mention that the sea becomes hot as you approach this landing-place, till, near the shore, it becomes scalding hot—a circumstance which occasioned a little meriment; for some of our men, not expecting anything of the kind, jumped out of the boat as usual into the water, and of course began dancing about very actively till they could either get in again or on shore.

But I think I have made my letter long enough, so shall conclude.

Believe me, my dear Sir William, very truly yours,

C. PARISH.

*7.—Journal of a Commercial Trip from Tientsin through the provinces of Shansi and Pechili.* By Messrs. RICHARDS and SLOSSIN.*

*24th Nov.* 1860.—Started this morning early before breakfast, as we had a long journey to perform. We still continued in the beautiful valley of Tientsin for some distance, till we came to a small walled town totally in ruins; here we commenced to ascend a mountain 2000 feet above Pekin, and proceeded along its top for some distance, till we came to a small town, where we watered our mules. The well here was 120 fathoms in depth.

From this we descended into a fine valley of some extent, and at 12 noon arrived at a small village named Ee-To-Chen, where we prepared a hasty breakfast. A short distance from here was a walled city, named Wha-Lee-Hien, where we were surprised to find the main street completely blocked up with people and, all along the street-sides, wares and goods of all descriptions displayed for sale; it was evidently a market-day.

We passed several small towns and villages, generally situated on rivers; and, after crossing a small river, continued on until sunset, when we arrived at a large town named Lu-Chu. In this district the roads were fine.

*25th.*—The weather this morning was intensely cold. The road still continued in this fine valley, which is very thickly inhabited; we passed small walled towns at short intervals, six of which were at one time counted within sight. We met a constant stream of carts and asses laden with coal, in which there must be an immense traffic.

At 12 P.M. stopped at a small town, where we had breakfast. We saw numerous joss-houses, all beautifully situated; every farm-house and village was neatly walled in, and had fine brick gates. The people of this valley, which is named Yu-chu, have every appearance of being in good circumstances; there are no poor nor beggars. The valley lies between ranges of mountains —the left range is very lofty, and covered with snow; that on the right is not so high, and gradually runs down into the valley. All over the country are numerous groves of trees, which generally enclose either a joss-house or a burial-place.

At 3 P.M. arrived at the city of Yu-chu, which is on the borders of the province of Shansi. Its walls can be seen at a great distance. The principal staples of trade of this city are coal and cotton: the cotton is grown in the valley; the coal-mines are about 5 li distant, of great extent, and of very superior quality.

Before entering Yu-chu we passed a handsome gate, and crossed a fine granite bridge, built over the moat which surrounds the city. There are four other large gates; the principal streets of the town are broad, and at short distances apart are handsome granite arches, which give to the street the appearance of an avenue of arches. Towers are built within the city, to about the same height as the walls, on which are erected fine buildings of three stories in height, and there are handsome steps to ascend them.

*26th.*—Received a visit from a young mandarin, the son of the chief magistrate, accompanied by his secretary and three more officials. They came to inquire whether we were going to stay long; and, if we were, the magistrate would give us rooms in his yamun, as he knew that our apartments were very small. Thanking them for their kindness, we informed them that we would start early in the afternoon.

---

* It has not been found possible to identify more than a few of the places mentioned in this Paper. The authors' own spelling has, therefore, been maintained in every instance.—ED.

The coal-mines here are very extensive, and the coal bears a famed name throughout the country ; it very much resembles the Cannel coal—not being dirty like the bituminous,—and when lighted it will burn for a long time, leaving nothing but fine white ashes, which are in great demand for manure. We were informed that, on account of there being no river communication, it would cost 5000 cash per picul to deliver it at Tientsin ; here the price is 150 cash per picul. It is in universal use, and is even transported as far as Mongolia, and is the main support of the city and valley of Yu-chu.

As our chart only gave the outlines of the province of Shansi, we inquired of the mandarin to give us some information we desired : and at 3 P.M. commenced retracing our steps to get upon the high road to Shansi, At 6 P.M. arrived at Koo-Yea-Thua, where we stopped for the night, and had miserable accommodation.

27th.—After a most uncomfortable night's rest we rose early, and went on. At 1 P.M. arrived at Tueo-Sheo, where we had breakfast, and after a long ride arrived at Ta-Too-Koo, situated on the high road to Shansi ; here we had a comfortable room in a joss-house, there being no suitable inn at the place. The people are very civil and quiet.

28th.—It is a cold, frosty morning, with a high wind. The country is not so rich in this valley, and the land is poor ; the roads are very rough, and fit only for a Chinese cart. Passed many walled towns, most of them in ruins ; and at 1 P.M. arrived at Pa-Ma-Fa, where we had breakfast, and again went on. It was bitterly cold, and the roads continued miserable, making it very uncomfortable. At 5 P.M. arrived at a large city named Si-Ning-Si, where we found a good inn, and stopped for the night. We were informed that we were the first foreigners that ever entered the city.

The streets of the city are very broad, and somewhat cleaner than we have lately seen ; they run at right angles, and have many ornamental arched gateways across them. This is the last city on the borders of the province of Pechili ; it is situated on the high road leading into Shansi, and we here begin to see some improvement in land and country.

The valley in which it lies is of great extent : on the right side the mountains almost wholly disappear, and on the left, at a great distance, we can see an extensive range of blue mountains running westward. Scattered over the face of the country are many patches of fine trees and extensive and handsome joss-houses ; besides, here and there, are Mahometan burial-places.

[29th.]—The day was a very pleasant one, but so hazy that the mountains on each side of us were scarcely visible. The roads are better than yesterday, and we went along nicely. About 12 noon we crossed a small river, which is the boundary-line between the province of Pechili and Shansi. A short distance from here we passed through a small walled city named the Heavenly City, and here there is a large country trade carried on. About 2 P.M. a strong west wind arose, which made it very dusty and cold, and the road was poor and shingly.

Our mules were very much exhausted when, at sunset, we arrived at a small walled city named Chu-Po, having had no water since we left in the morning ; and we were ourselves somewhat tired and faint, having had nothing to eat since 7 A.M.

30th.—Left this morning at daylight ; the weather clear but excessively cold, and the roads poor and indifferent. At 1 P.M. arrived at Pea-Tea-San, a small walled town of little importance. We here took breakfast ; and, after a disagreeable ride, at 4 P.M. arrived at the city of Tai-Tong-Fu, which is quite an important place.

The first part of the day's journey was continually on the ascent for about 40 li, until nearly on a level with the mountains on our right ; after which we descended into the valley in which this city is situated. We passed great numbers of carts all laden with coal, drawn by motley teams ; composed generally of a mule or steer, two donkeys and a horse : they carried from three to four tons of coal, all in large lumps.

When walking through the streets we were continally surrounded by numbers of people ; they never offered us any abuse, nor annoyed us by shouting, but were very civil. We were credibly informed that the walls of the city were 34 li in circumference, and that its population was very great, something over 800,000 souls. The principal streets are wide, and the shops and houses very fine, some of the latter being singularly handsome. The guard-houses over the gates of the city were three stories in height ; but they have been much neglected, and are now rapidly falling to pieces. The wall in some places is in good condition, but in many others shows symptoms of decay.

We received a number of visits from Chinese merchants, and also a letter written in Latin from a Chinese Catholic priest offering his services, for which we called upon him and returned thanks. Our business being finished about 1 P.M., we started ; and from the time of leaving our hotel to the gates of the city, a distance of more than two miles, the streets through which we passed were so jammed with people who had collected to have a look at us, that nothing was to be seen but a sea of heads.

The day was clear but excessively cold, and after a long ride we arrived at a small town named Su-nu-tsong, where we stopped for the night.

*2nd Dec.*—Before daylight resumed our journey, the weather fine, but still excessively cold. At 9 A.M. arrived at Way-zen-sec, where we had breakfast ; and after a long ride arrived at Wau-yah-lea, where we stopped for the night.

During the day we passed many villages, and saw many flocks of sheep and herds of cattle on the fields ; nearly every person we met was armed, and at short distances we passed guard-houses, there being many robbers on this road. There had been a convoy of three carts, carrying specie, with us for the last two days ; and they seemed desirous, although armed, of staying in our company, but we travelled too fast for them—they have just arrived at the hotel two hours after us.

*3rd.*—This morning before sunrise we started. After proceeding on some distance we passed through a large town named Tai-yau ; here there appeared to be quite a large trade carried on, some of the houses and shops being very fine. We passed a broad river completely frozen up ; its course was easterly.

Had breakfast at a wayside inn ; and just after sunset arrived at the village of Qun-woo, which is situated at the foot of the mountains, over which the Great Wall is built, and at the entrance of a pass. There are some very fine fortifications here, and the wall has well-built double bastions, but we saw symptoms of decay everywhere, and in many places the wall had nearly tumbled down.

There is an immense amount of traffic on this road ; during the day we passed thousands of donkeys and carts laden with coal and iron, besides numerous files of camels, in one of which we counted 527 ; we must have passed on the whole more than 1500. We also met many travellers in chairs, and the road was thronged with pedestrians ; the inns are numerous, and some of them very good. There is a great deal of competition on this road, and we often met runners at a distance of 5 li from the inns, soliciting custom.

The roads all through the valley are very inferior : sometimes they cover a space of over 200 yards in breadth, and are nearly impassable, being terribly cut up. In the summer time the farmers prevent the carts from encroaching on their grounds, by digging deep dykes along the roadside. Our course for the last three days has been about south-west.

*4th.*—Before sunrise proceeded on ; the day was clear but cold. A short distance from the hotel we passed the wall, which had been completely washed away for about 100 feet ; nothing remained to show where the gate had been but a part of an arch which could scarcely be distinguished. A fence was built across the gap, and we passed through a common gate.

The road led along the bed of a mountain-stream, which we crossed repeatedly during the day, and, as its water was frozen, the passage was difficult and slippery for our mules. The mountains on each side rose to a great height; on the summit of the highest of them were brick towers, varying from 100 to 200 feet in breadth.

For about two hours after leaving we were continually on the ascent, which in many cases was very steep, till we arrived at a small village on the top of a mountain, named Yea-Min-Quay. Here we passed through three gates, which are in a very ruinous condition. After passing the last gate the road descended so precipitously that our cartmen had to block the wheels or they could not have got down in safety; alongside the gate is a beautiful joss-house in good repair.

From here to the place where we had our breakfast, named Nan-Yen-Sawe, we were continually on the descent, and over a most wretched road, cut up and full of rocks. This place is situated at the end of the pass, which is 40 li in length. During our ride through, we met and passed carts and donkeys, generally laden with coal and iron, and nearly a continual stream of camels, more in numbers than we have seen on any preceding day.

We soon got out of the mountains into the valley, which is apparently of great extent; for, as far as the eye can reach towards the south-west, there is nothing to be seen but a level plain.

Directly south of us, about 80 li distant, is a large range of mountains; at a short distance from the foot of which is situated a walled city, named Tung-Chaw. Just before sunset we arrived at a stopping-place named Yun-Mun-Poo.

It had been our intention to stop here for the night; but, finding no decent accommodation, we proceeded on some distance and arrived at a hotel situated in the suburbs of a large city named Pein-Tien-Poo. The people here were curious but civil.

*5th.*—At 5 A.M. left our hotel, and fell in with a continuous stream of carts, donkeys, and camels, who travel all hours of the night; each cart having attached to it a lantern, which gives a beautiful effect when the train is seen winding along a road. The walls of the city are in good repair; and this is the first place in which we have seen them built with round towers; they are about 100 feet apart, are elevated 10 feet above the walls, and project about two-thirds of their thickness outside them. Usually the towers are square, here they are circular.

At daylight passed a walled city named Wang-Long-Poo. There is every indication of its being a very busy place. The streets are wide and clean, and ornamented with arches; the shops and houses are neat, some of them are large and extensive, and everything indicates great prosperity.

About 9 A.M. passed through another walled city, named Qua-shi-hien, beautifully situated on the summit of a hill, surrounded by a deep valley. This is crossed as you enter and leave the city by five granite bridges, which stand about 40 feet above the bottom of the valley.

At 10 A.M. arrived at a large village, named Nan-yu-see, where we had breakfast, and in the afternoon passed a large walled city, with extensive suburbs, named Yun-pin-sien. The shops and houses presented a neat appearance, being clean and handsomely painted. The streets were crowded with men, and filled with all kinds of produce; everywhere we turned we saw signs of prosperity.

About 4 P.M. passed a walled city, named Pin-dee-sien-e (Commercial City), which was built with bricks, and was evidently an opulent place, being the abode of many retired rich men.

At sunset arrived at Schien-kau, where we put up for the night, being much fatigued, having made four capital days' work.

All through the valley the soil is very rich, the villages numerous and well built with brick, and generally situated in beautiful groves of trees; and the inhabitants are generally well dressed. There was every indication of prosperity, and we seldom saw a beggar.

*6th.*—At daylight this morning passed a walled city, named Kin-san-poo, *i. e.,* Golden City, which does not deserve its name, as the houses and shops are poor and mean; there is no trade, and its inhabitants are merely supported by the travellers who make it a resting-place. Its walls are nearly totally destroyed.

At 9 A.M. passed another walled city, named Pan-Shi, somewhat in better condition than the latter one, but of little importance; it is likewise supported by the travelling community, nearly every house in the place being a hotel.

At 10 and 11 A.M. passed two small cities, named Urh-Shih-Li-Poo, *i. e.* Twenty-Li City, and Shih-Li-Poo, *i. e.,* Ten-Li City; both places of little importance. Shortly after leaving the latter place we sighted the extensive walls and high towers of a large city in the distance; and at 12 A.M. entered the city of Hin-chow, before which we passed four handsome gates. The main streets are paved with granite, and lined with handsome shops and houses, and crowded with all kinds of produce and merchandise. The city is situated partly on a hill; and in the suburbs are many fine residences, evidently the houses of men of wealth.

A short time afterwards, passed through a large place named Ma-Qua-Chun; soon after leaving it we entered a pass, the sides of which were about 90 feet in height. The road was much cut up, and full of large shingles, and its width rarely sufficient for one car to pass at a time; we were often detained a long time, to allow great trains of carts to pass. We passed villages, to each of which there were gates; and in all we passed eight gates. Many of the houses were built out of the ground, like those in Mongolia.

At 6 P.M. arrived at Sang-Wong-Tien, and took up our quarters just outside the gate, in a good hotel.

*7th.*—This morning before daybreak it was severely cold, but at noon it moderated and became quite pleasant. We passed during the day several walled towns, namely, Teh-Yu-Pe-Thin, Quaw-To-Soon, Chang-Tong-Chen, and several others, about six in number, of which we did not take the names. All these towns are doing a fair trade, owing to the great traffic on this road. This is especially the case with Chang-Tong-Chen, which is situated partly on a hill; and where are the residences of many retired men of wealth from the capital, Tai-yuen-Foo. The place is divided by walls, to each of which are gates; and during the day we passed more than four gates.

After leaving this place we entered into many ravines or passes; and spent the greater part of the day in going through them.

We did not see the city of Tai-yuen-Foo, the capital of Shansi, till we were nearly upon it, on account of its being situated in a valley; before we entered it, on our right hand, stood a fine pagoda, ten stories in height, neatly painted. The walls are of the usual height and in good repair, and the towers over the gates are of the same height as those at Pekin, having four stories. We were credibly informed that the city was 36 li in circumference, and that its population was immense—over one million of inhabitants. The suburbs are very extensive. We had just entered the city, and passed through the second gate, when we were stopped by the guard, who asked who we were, and requested our passports. We informed them that we would show them to the proper authorities when we arrived at our hotel. The streets of the city are quite broad, the shops numerous and fine; it is a great manufacturing place of iron and furniture-ware of all kinds and descriptions.   The streets were crowded with people, and along the side-walks were many beautiful joss-houses, one of which especially struck our attention, being beautifully ornamented with gilt and carved work.

After we had been some time in bed that night, we were awakened by a noise at the door, which, on opening, we found to proceed from the yard, full of the chief magistrate's retinue.   We asked what they wanted, and they said that the Quam-foo had come to see our passports.   We said that we were un-dressed, and requested him to come in, and he should see them.   The messenger soon returned, and said he would not come in ; when we told him that, as we did not wish to give our passport but to a man of authority, he should send in his secretary.   Then they sent in a man whom we saw from his appearance was not his secretary—but either a chair-bearer or coolie,—so of course we refused to give them up.

Finding that nobody else came, and hearing that the magistrate had gone into an adjoining room, we dressed ourselves and went in, and found him sitting in great state, evidently expecting us to kow-tow to him.   We bowed, gave him our passports, which he looked at hastily, took down our names and the date, and was folding them up to return, saying that was sufficient, when we told him that if he wished to take a copy of them he could do so at his leisure, but that they must be returned on the following day.   He took them and then bowed, showing that he would require us no more.

*8th.*—To-day stopped in the city to recruit ourselves and to gain informa-tion.   During the morning we were visited by many influential merchants, from whom we gained much valuable commercial information.

*9th.*—At daylight we left our hotel.

The country is very bare, and we passed a number of small towns.   All along the roadside, and over the country, are numberless wells used for the purposes of irrigation.

At noon arrived at a walled town, named Men-Ta-Hein, where we cooked our breakfast.

The face of the country presents a singular appearance, being cut up into numberless ravines, some of which are of great depth, 200 feet or more, and every spot of ground is under cultivation, being terraced off.   These commence at the bottom of the ravine, and rise one above the other to the top ; and pre-sent a very neat appearance, being neatly banked up with earth.

At 7 P.M. arrived at Tan-Ah-Yee, a distance of 120 li.   The houses of the town are well built of stones and bricks, with flat roofs—the roof of the lower house making a floor for the house built above.

Here is a considerable trade in the manufacture of agricultural implements.

A short distance from our hotel, on the righthand side of the valley, we noticed a pagoda four stories in height, situated on a hill ; alongside of which was a fine joss-house, nearly buried in evergreens.

We now commenced to ascend till we arrived at the summit of the moun-tain, on which we continued some distance ; even here every available spot of land was under cultivation and neatly terraced off.   After descending into a small valley, passing a large town in which there were many fine hotels, and crossing a river, we again ascended another range of mountains ; over which we continued some 40 li, till we descended into a very large and populous valley, in which there are many fine villages.   Shortly afterwards we sighted quite a large city, named Ching-Ping : its walls are about 60 feet high, and are far superior and in better condition than any we had yet passed. We entered at the west gate, which is a very handsome one, and evidently great care is taken of it.   The bastion is built in the shape of a half-moon. The city proper is not large, but the suburbs are very extensive, and the principal part of the business is carried on here.   The streets are broad, and filled with people and merchandize ; the inhabitants expressed no great curiosity, simply turning around to look at us.

Just before leaving the city we passed the yamun, which is really an ornament to the place, and the handsomest that we have yet seen.

It was our intention to take breakfast here ; but finding no suitable hotel we proceeded on until, at noon, we arrived at a walled town, named Too-che-lean.

From here the roads commenced to grow worse, being covered with rocks, and we were often detained by carts. After sunset we arrived at a town named Tsha-tsha, where we stopped for the night.

11*th*.—At daylight, when we left our hotel, the weather was delightful ; but the road, which still continued in the bed of a mountain-stream, was full of large shingles.

At 11 A.M. arrived at a large town, named E-chin, where we had breakfast. A short distance from here we commenced to ascend a range of mountains, over 2000 feet in height. The road had formerly been paved with large granite blocks; but now it is nearly destroyed by weather and heavy rains, and, being very steep, it was with great difficulty that our carts were enabled to surmount it. The pass is named Nan-lean-mun ; and on the summit of the mountain we passed through two handsome gates situated about 100 feet apart, over which are built extensive joss-houses.

This mountain is composed almost entirely of coal, and the Chinese are working pits ; they also gather it with ease from the surface.

From here we had a magnificent view of the surrounding country, as we were at a greater elevation than the neighbouring mountains.

We then descended into a valley in which there is situated a large walled city named Ping-sing-chow, through which we passed. The main street was crowded with men and produce, and was over three miles in length ; and at every 50 feet or so were erected handsome granite arches, which being neatly carved presented a beautiful appearance.

During the day we passed great numbers of camels, carts and mules, laden with raw cotton, Manchester goods packed in small bales, opium, sugar, &c. The camels travel generally all night through the passes, as the roads then are free from carts and other obstructions.

We passed through many villages, whose names we did not take down. The houses were built of cut granite ; and the people seemed to spare no pains in their buildings, which are unusually large and commodious.

12*th*.—At daylight left our khan and proceeded on. The road was a most fearful one, being nothing but a mere mass of rocks ; and at one place one of the carts was upset, and it was with great difficulty our mules could pull through.

Passed many fine villages neatly built of granite, and at noon arrived at Way-Seu-Chen, where we had a meal, 10 li from here. At 1 P.M. we came to the gates of the pass named Tong-Tiea-Mun. Here again we crossed the Great Wall for the last time, and from the province of Shansi entered that of Pechili, the wall at this place separating the provinces. We had travelled in Shansi to within one day's journey of the province of Ho-nan, and would have visited it but for want of time.

Shortly after passing the gates we ascended another range of mountains, on the summit of which we passed through two fine gates. The road was paved, but as usual in a most wretched condition, being mostly worn away. We then descended by a fearfully steep road, worse by far than any we had previously passed over, till we arrived at a small walled town, named Tsing-Kung, where we stopped for the night.

13*th*.—A short distance from our hotel this morning we passed a large town, named Na-Qua, and then descended into a valley and crossed the head of the river Hen-To-Ho ; passed through a large walled city, named King-Chung, on the righthand side of which stands a handsome pagoda seven stories in height. Formerly there had been a fine granite bridge spanning the river here ; but now two-thirds of it have been washed away, only six arches remaining. There are a few ferry-boats here ; but they are not in use, the river being very shallow and rapid. Saw here for the first time watermills used for grinding grain, &c. There are also numerous lime-kilns along the valley, some of which we visited, and on inquiry found the lime to be 100 cash per picul.

Passed through two large walled towns, the inn-yards of which were full of camels; and we met many strings of them, all laden with cotton, sugar, opium, &c.

At 12 A.M. arrived at E-Sen, where we had a meal. From here we crossed a high mountain, on whose summit were two fine joss-houses and gates ; then we made a precipitous descent into a valley, along which we continued till, after passing two remarkable-looking hills, we entered the extensive city of Wey-Lu-Hien : the walls are handsomely built of granite, save the battlements, which are brick and all in good condition.

We passed by the west gate, through an extensive grain-market, and entered the suburbs leading along the city wall. Here there is a great trade carried on, many fine shops and large warehouses filled with raw cotton, nankin, iron, sugar, opium, &c., and also many fine woollens. This city is a great central depot for all goods 'of foreign importation, before crossing the mountain and entering the province of Shansi.

We had intended to stop here for the night, as the sun was just setting ; but soon being surrounded by an immense crowd who became very annoying, we proceeded on, and at 9 P.M. arrived at Chaw-Chu-Poo, where we had most miserable accommodations. Shortly after leaving Wey-Lu-Hien we entered on to the vast plain of Pechili ; and here ended our mountain-travel, which commenced on the 9th of November, and had been most of the time at an elevation of over 2000 feet above Pekin.

14*th*.—Started this morning at daylight, and soon sighted the river which we had previously crossed ; it empties itself into a lake named Ta-Ten-Tse. Passed many fine villages, and saw that the yards of the principal inns were crowded with carts laden with goods of all descriptions bound over the mountains into Shansi. At a great distance over the plain we could just see the towers of some large city and a continuous stream of carts laden with cotton, &c., bound for Shansi.

At 6 A.M. arrived inside the walls of the city of Ching-ting-Foo, and were surprised at the dullness of the place, as contrasted with the great amount of traffic we had seen outside. We were informed that the walls of the city were 100 li in circumference ; but not more than one quarter of the space inclosed is inhabited, the rest being mere field, in which one can at any time find hares and pheasants : we bought one of the latter ; it was a splendid bird, and we were told it was shot in the city. Great quantities of cotton are grown in this neighbourhood.

Passed through a large town named Foo-Chin-Che, where we saw a beautiful black bear performing for the amusement of a crowd of Chinese.

At 7 P.M. arrived at a walled city named Shin-Loo-Hien, a place of little importance, being a mere travellers' resort.

Throughout the day the road was lined with carts, all laden with goods. Everybody goes armed in some way or other—whether with spears, swords, bows, or matchlock-guns ; we met many recruits going to Pau-ting-Foo, called thither, as they informed us, by the Viceroy of the province, who resides there. We passed a number of small villages and one walled town, named Men-Zen-Lien. At 11 A.M. arrived at the walled city of King-Chu, inside of which there is a very lofty and handsome pagoda of 12 stories in height, which we saw at a great distance. The walls of the city are of great circumference, but nearly in total ruins ; the trade here is a mere country one. Here we had a meal, and after a short rest went on, passing many small villages and a large walled city named Shin-Loo-Hien. At 5 P.M. arrived at Way-Lu, a large walled city, in the suburbs of which we took up our quarters for the night.

During the day we passed great quantities of marble in the shape of doorsteps, watertroughs, &c. It can be obtained a short distance from here.

16th.—The weather this morning was clear but piercingly cold when we left our hotel; we walked through the city, which is an unimportant one and doing a mere country trade.

At 9 A.M. passed through a walled town, named Fang-Luen-Chuw, where we had breakfast. Shortly afterwards passed King-Hien-Tien; here there is quite a trade: the main street through which we passed was thronged with people; it was evidently a market day, as there was a great quantity of cotton and other produce exposed for sale.

At 1 P.M. we sighted the walls of the capital of Pechili, Pau-ting-Foo, and proceeded to the north-west gate, where we stopped at a comfortable inn.

Before arriving here, we crossed two large stone bridges, the last of which spans a reservoir of water elevated some 8 feet above the moat which surrounds the city. About 100 feet from the city walls there is an embankment of earth, six feet high and pierced with loopholes for matchlocks or jingalls.

Shortly afterwards we entered the city. The streets are narrow, but the shops and houses are very fine, and some of them beautifully ornamented with gilt and carved work.

17th.—Left before daylight; the weather was bitter cold, and it was with great difficulty that we could keep ourselves warm in our carts. The road at first led along the city walls, and the scenery was very tame. We passed many villages all surrounded by trees, and at 11 A.M. entered a large place named Pang-Hean, where we had breakfast. There was a fair held here; and the streets were crowded with country people, who had different wares displayed for sale, besides cotton and grain.

At 1 P.M. passed a large walled city, named Ka-Yeng-Chen, a place of some importance.

At 6 P.M. arrived at quite a busy city, named Jen-Choey-Sun, where we stopped for the night.

18th.—Long before daylight we left our hotel. The road led through the city, which is a very extensive one and is situated in the high road from Pekin to Shansi, Ho-nan and the other provinces. The weather was intensely cold, everything being frozen up; the roads good, but the scenery tame and uninteresting.

At 10 A.M. stopped at a small town named Chang-chen-ho to get our breakfast; there was a fair held here also, and the principal staples exposed for sale were cotton and grain. At sunset arrived at a walled city, named Tai-hien, where we stopped for the night. The walls of the city have nearly disappeared; the houses are mean and poor, and the trade carried on is merely local.

19th.—Having 175 li to do before we could complete our journey, we determined to do it all in one day, and at 3 A.M. were on the road.

At 9 A.M. crossed the Grand Canal on the ice, and at 10 stopped at Tshianghai for breakfast. This city was once of some importance, but now is almost in ruins, caused by the Nankin rebels, in 1854, who nearly destroyed it; and traces of their work can still be seen, many of the houses being unbuilt.

A short time afterwards passed another walled city, also mostly destroyed.

About 3 P.M. we sighted, in the distance, the walls of Tien-tsin; and, after passing the walls built to protect the place from the rebels and English, at 4 P.M. arrived at our place of destination and home. We thus completed a journey of forty-six days; during which we crossed the Great Wall four times in four different places, visited above 100 cities, and traversed a distance of over 4700 li (Chinese miles), or 2566 English miles.

8.—*Excursion to the West of Canton.* By Lieut. OLIVER, R.A. Extract from a Letter, dated Canton, March 21st, 1861.

WE had eight days' leave, and everything was prepared. We procured an interpreter from the yamun, named Lee Asheen, passports from the consul, and letters of introduction to the magistrates of the districts, Sam-Shui and Shin-Hing, from the Governor-General of the two kwangs, Old Laou. The next thing was to get a boat. Nearly all the communication in China is by canals and rivers. We found a Chinese boatman who was willing to contract with us to take us in his vessel, the *Old Dragon*, as far as Shin-Hing and back in eight days. The *Old Dragon* was a fine boat, 70 feet long, covered all over like a Lord Mayor's state-barge, and propelled either by poling, tracking, or rowing. The crew consisted of the master, his mother, two brothers, a sister, cook, pilot, and 12 sailors. Our party consisted of Capt. Des Vœux, Lieut. Sandwith, Lieut. Malcolm, Lieut. Hunt, Ensign Hunter, and myself.

We had our beds, traps, &c., on board early on Monday morning, 11th of March, and breakfasted at the Custom-house. However, we did not leave the Shameen till 12 o'clock, when we were joined by Mr. Bonney, an American Wesleyan missionary. We were now towed up the Fatu Creek, leaving Howqua's Garden on our left. We kept in this creek till we reached Tung-kao, at 1.30, when we turned into a broader piece of water running west. At 2.15 we passed Pho-tien, and at 2.30 Een-Po. At 3 o'clock we arrived at Ng-Kai-How or Yun-Kin-Chung. Here was a fleet of braves, 20 boats full, each containing about 60 or 70 men. They all turned out to look at us, and blew their horns, and made a tumultuous noise with gongs and tom-toms. They were proceeding to quell an insurrection in the northern part of the province. At 4.30 we saw Upper Kuss-Kow on our left, and soon after Lower Kuss-Kow, and now Fatshan appeared directly in front of us. Fatshan is nearly as large as Canton, but is not walled. It took two hours to pass through Fatshan. The houses and quays were covered with human faces, and all their eyes centred on our boat. The Chinese ladies crowded their balconies and verandahs, but retired shrieking when we looked at them with our field-glasses. They have an idea that our binoculars have the power of representing them upside down, which hurts their vanity. However, they peeped at us through the chinks of the jalousies. It was 7 when we had left the town, and quite dark, so we anchored for the night.

We started at 3 A.M. on Tuesday, the 12th, and Malcolm and myself swam ashore at daylight, and had a run for a couple of miles, till we flushed a woodcock; then we swam on board again quickly, and aroused the others, who were sleeping soundly. We all dressed and went on shore at 6.15 A.M., at a place called Tsy-Tóng. Here was a fine towing-road, and high solid dykes to prevent inundations. The country here is very fine—large patches of sugar-cane, mulberry-trees by the mile together; sandy hills, like the Bournemouth cliffs, to the north. Here we shot divers, teal, doves, and kingfishers, but could not get any woodcocks, although two were reported hit. All this time our boat was going ahead with a favourable breeze from the east, and we had to run some miles to catch it up. 7.30 : Shay-ng-kow on the left, Kee-Shek on the right. At 8 o'clock we passed a long island covered with wheat-fields. At 9 o'clock the boat waited for us to come on board at Slong-Tung; the Si-cheou fine hills in the distance. We were now 20 miles from Fatshan. Here we breakfasted, and started again at 9.45, with the tide. At 10.45 we went ashore on the left bank. More brick-kilns and mulberry-fields. 11 A.M.: on the opposite coast was the Sy-Tsz-Tow, or Lion's Head Peak, with a new pagoda being built, near it. 11.15 : came to Ma-Sha, a village with about 1000 inhabitants, and surrounded by banyan-trees and fields of mustard and sugar-cane. Mr. Bonney and myself, with Captain Des Vœux, were behind, and the others shooting in front, when the young men of the village came out with shields and swords to kill us, shouting to one another to do so ; but none of them liked to begin, and the old men told them that they would get the worst of it. This is the only indication of hostility we ever saw or heard of, and is a remnant of the old Canton spite against us. Not long ago, the little urchins near Canton would sing whenever a foreigner appeared, "The White Devil comes !—sharpen the knife !—sharpen the knife !—off with his head !" Twelve sugar-mills are worked by oxen on the opposite side of the river Fawng-Teng. Returned to our boat at 12.30, and at 1.30 reached Sy-Nam. Large sandbanks. On the right we passed the finest temple in Sy-Nam, viz. Teen-How, and a three-storied pagoda on a small rocky island. Beyond were some strong batteries, with guns mounted, overlooking the town. The river here was covered with small ferry-boats, which took passengers across the river for two cash. At 3 o'clock reached Sam-Shui—Sam meaning *three*, and Shui *water*, as here three waters meet. The town of Sam-Shui is about 2 miles from the river ; it is a fine walled town, and has an elegant pagoda outside. We sent our interpreter ashore to the chief magistrate's yamun with our cards (in Chinese fashion on red paper, my name being O-LI-FA), and our letters of introduction, whilst we went for a short walk on shore, and up to the beautiful nine-storied pagoda. Unfortunately, we found the pagoda a mere shell ; the interior woodwork, staircase, &c., having been burnt out by the rebels in 1858. When we returned to the boat we found the chief mandarin's compradore with a noble present of ducks, geese, fowl-eggs, preserved fruits, oranges, annquots (a kind of citron), vegetables, cakes, &c.; also a message to say he was very sorry he had no milk or cream to give us, but if we were going to stay he would get some for our Excellencies. We left Sam-Shui at 5.15, and anchored off an island with a fortress on it. In the broad Si-Kiang River, which we had now reached, we were 56 miles due west of Canton. I was off duty this night, so slept soundly.

*Wednesday, 13th March.*—7 A.M. we passed Tsing-Kee, which contains one school and a pawnbroker's shop. Went ashore soon afterwards, and had a swim. Here are paddy-fields, dry now, and fine banyan-trees. At 7.25 passed Ni-Tawng, 150 inhabitants. We were now only 33 miles from Shia-Hing-Foo. At 7.40 came to Poo-e-Shai, a large academy here built in the first year of the present Emperor, Hien-Tung. Opposite were the Nam-Wan, or Southern Bay hills—we call them Mount MacCleverty—about 1500 feet high. Here also is a great salt depôt. At 9 A.M. returned to breakfast. On the left bank are large examination-halls, marked by a forest of mandarins' poles. Went on left shore at 12.20, under an avenue of tall banyan-trees, with the most beautiful beards. 12.40 passed Sha-Wan, a village of 60 people, with large fishponds and plenty of snipe, some of which were shot for dinner. There is a beautiful echo here from the hills. As we were walking along the bank I found in a pyramidal landmark a large and long lizard called Sha-ni, or a snake on legs. It is very venomous, and about 15 inches long. At 1 P.M. walked under 'the Sun-Tsüne pagoda, and through the To-Ki village, with 200 inhabitants. The mountains here converge to the river, and a magnificent gorge is formed by the river cutting its way between them—the mountains, rising on one side to 2800 feet high, called by us Mount Parkes, and on the other side Mount Straubenzee, 1800 feet. Beyond this, again, is Mount Malcolm, 400 feet high. At 1.45 we returned to our boat, and entered the pass. Water very deep—no bottom at 12½ fathoms. On the left a huge sugar-loafed peak, the sides covered with plantations. This pass is called the Shin-Hing-Huss. 2.40: still in the pass. The scenery so beautiful that we let our dinner get cold while admiring it. 3.45 reached the western entrance of the pass. See Shin-Hing-Foo in the distance, with a small pagoda and a hill on the right. We can now see seven pagodas. 5.15 passed the seven-storied pagodas. 5.45 passed a nine-storied pagoda. 6.20 anchored at the western suburb of Shin-Hing. 6.30 went ashore, but could not go far, as the city gates were shut, and it was dark by 7. Sent our cards and letters to the mandarin.

*Thursday, 14th March.*—We are now 93 miles west of Canton. After breakfast sent for palanquins, to pay our visit to the mandarin. Two braves on the bank extorted 33 cash from our chair-bearers. At 9.25 started in eight chairs to the yamun. Entered the city by the east gate; passed through several streets like those in Canton, noticed several bow-makers' and armourers' shops; also some handsome temples, with lions. Reached the yamun of Chaying-Kwank-Po. Received courteously by the mandarin, who asked us to be seated at a table, and regaled us with tea, cakes, almonds, pomelos, ginger, citron, &c. We reported the officials who squeezed our chair-coolies, and they were accordingly bastinadoed with split bamboos. He told us the people might throw stones at us at first, till they got used to seeing us, but he would send soldiers to guard us. We begged him not to take any trouble, as we were well able to take care of ourselves. As he, however, insisted, we were accompanied by a party of his braves, who made themselves very useful in carrying some biscuits and potted meat, our sketch-books, &c., up to the Marble Rocks. At 10·15 we went out by the north gate, over some stone bridges, and through paddy-fields, which were being harrowed—water-buffaloes drawing the harrows, which were guided by women, who, in this part of the world, much resemble the women at Saltash, near Plymouth. At 11 o'clock we reached the largest rock of the Seven Stars, Sam-Seen-Koon. We had seen the Marble Rocks from the city: they looked in the distance like the Needles of the Isle of Wight on a level plain, backed by a range of high mountains. There are seven rocks, about 200 feet high, of beautiful marble. These Seven Stars are very curious; and I do not know how to account for their presence, sticking up with their ragged-pointed tops and perpendicular sides in the middle of a large plain. We ascended to the top of the easternmost rock, the largest of the set. There are two temples to Buddha on this rock. In the lower temple there was an elaborate statue of Buddha, representing him with forty-eight arms. There are inscriptions of gigantic dimensions on all the rocks, of the reigns of Yong-Ching, Kang-Kee, and Keen-Long. We reached the summit of the eastern rock by 12 o'clock, and I found some ferns. We descended again and walked to the temple of Koon-Yum-Ngam, in the rock next to the eastern one, and the second in magnitude. Here was a wonderful cavern, or the "Cave of the Seven Stars." Part of it is cut to represent a joss-house, the idols being formed of choice specimens of marble. Two figures of warriors are in front of the altar, before the idol, and are not unlike similar effigies in old churches and cathedrals at home, also of white polished marble. The stalactites, in every imaginable form, reflecting the light from above with innumerable sparkling crystals, formed a beautiful canopy above. This hermitage, as it were, forms only the entrance to the large grotto, to which you descend by some forty steps, and then a splendid scene lies before you. The whole rock seems hollowed out, whilst large crystals hang down into the light; their source being in utter darkness up above, only revealed now and then when we let off rockets. When we discharged our rifles and revolvers the thunders and reverberations were grand, extending in hoarse murmurs into the very bowels of the mountain. It reminded me very much of the grotto at Hans, in Belgium. The effect was further heightened by the crystals being detached from the roof by the bullets of our pieces, and, tumbling headlong, scattering as they struck projections of the rocks with a myriad of scintillations. Our attention was next drawn by the Buddhist hermit to a hollow rock—a natural stone drum; when this was struck a sharp blow, it vibrated, and gave a not unmusical sound—in fact, a Chinese Memnon. We now lighted twisted bamboo torches, and penetrated a quarter of a mile through a narrow cavern; but, after all, saw nothing equal to the first grotto. However, the figures of the monk and our half-naked coolies, with the picturesque dress of the Chinese soldiers, looked very quaint and romantic by the light of the torches in these Tartarean regions. We spent nearly the whole day in the caves. I left some of the coloured pictures of the Christmas number of your ' Illustrated News ' with the old monk, who was greatly pleased. We returned to our boat in the afternoon, and in the evening dropped down again with the tide, commencing our homeward trip. I had filled my portfolio with sketches, and it will take me some time to finish them up. The captain of our vessel would not suffer us to go through the Pass of Shin-Hing-Huss at night, being frightened with the idea of the Lally-Lus and pirates, who infest those wild mountains; but we made him proceed, and consequently reached the eastern gap by midnight, when we anchored by a Chinese custom-house, at a place called How-Lik.

*Friday, 15th March.*—This morning we had intended to ascend Mount Malcolm, and take an aneroid to determine its height more accurately; but as we found it too cloudy and foggy to make it safe to attempt the ascent, we delayed it till the morrow. However, Messrs. Bonney, Malcolm, Des Vœux, and myself went up to the foot of the mountain to see a large Buddhist monastery we heard of; and the others crossed over to To-ki to shoot snipe for dinner. We started directly across some flat ground for nearly five miles, and then entered a valley leading to the monastery. A pretty stream tumbled over a rocky bed, like the Esk near Dalkeith; whilst in front rose a huge cliff with perpendicular sides, its top covered with woods, and Alps upon Alps rose beyond. The hills on each side were covered with bracken-fern, and the misty and cool day made it resemble Scotch scenery altogether, though presently it far surpassed it. The Chinese call this " The Mountain of the Golden Lake;" and the monastery and woods they call " The Groves of the Pleasant Mists." And rightly are they named. As soon as we turned the corner of the cliff, there was an exclamation of delight from everyone. It resembled some illustrations I have seen in Milton by the artist Martin. The vegetation and foliage was perfect—a blending of our tropical and your more northern flora in a sweet entanglement. Our guide led the way —his name, Teen-Tuk; and two Chinese boys, Ayon and Assam, carried our rifles and instruments. These Teng-Foo mountains are celebrated in Chinese literature, and deserve well all the admiration that their poets have heaped upon them. Here were tall cotton-trees; the tulip-tree with immense red blossoms; ferns twenty feet high; and pinus silvestris 'of enormous size; acacias, bamboos, teak-trees, parasites, and creepers; monkey-ladders and ropes of orchids festooning the vaulted roof of branches; beautiful little sandy squirrels, with grey stripes, leaped nimbly about, chasing one another, as tame as domestic cats. The cries of jungle-fowl and guinea-hens were answered by the shrieks of the pheasant and the song of the bulbul, interrupted by the sound of the beak of the toucan, one of which was killed, a magnificent specimen—green shot with gold, large yellow beak, thirteen inches long. Several squirrels fell victims to our death-dealing weapons, and Malcolm got a pretty black-and-white bird, with " an unprecedented length of tail." A little further on was a Chinese summer-house, with its usual accompaniment of Confucian precepts and Buddhist prayers. At a corner beyond, through an accidental break in the leafy covering overhead, we beheld trees growing out of the side of inaccessible rocks 1500 feet above our head, overhanging as though to crush us. We now ascended by zigzag narrow paths cut out of the rock for about 1000 feet, when we came to the Tek-chime Monastery at about 11.33 A.M. Here is a temple called Hing-Wun-Tz. The Principal or Abbot, named Chea-ne-Fan, received us courteously, and gave us a very good repast on rice and vegetables, principally mushrooms; for the Buddhist monks are not allowed to eat flesh. We saw the new temple, and the yet remaining charred relics of the old one, lately burnt by the rebels; also some splendid China tea-roses. We returned the same way to our boat, which we reached at 4 P.M.    After dinner, at 5.30, we took our dingy, and pulled over to the tea-plantations under the lofty Sugar-cone mountain, on the southern side of the Shin-Hing-Huss.    Near to these plantations we visited a quarry 800 feet deep, from which they dig the black stone which the Chinese use for inkstands, or rather what we should call palettes : the Chinese using solid Indian ink, rub it, when wanted, on these peculiar tablets.    The stone is valuable, but the quarry was not being worked, the mandarins having stopped the proprietors.    "But," said the inhabitants, "if you Taiwans (or Great Nation) will order the mandarins, they will be forced to allow us to work this mine"—showing that the people of China have a little notion of our power.    When we returned on board, we slipped our moorings, and went to Lo-un-Chun, a place nearer the Teng-Foo mountains, and situate at the bend of the river near Kwangli.

*Saturday, 16th March.*—Breakfasted at 7 A.M.    Started soon after to try to reach the top of the Teng-Foo Mountain.    Very misty.    Went up to the Monastery by 9.40 A.M.    Here we got some bamboo-poles, and continued the ascent.    By mid-day we reached a place beyond which our guide had never been.    No scenery but dense white clouds.    We, however, pushed up the steep rocks, and at length got to a peak of about 2000 feet elevation.    What was our disappointment to find that this was not the highest peak ; to reach which we should have to descend, and re-ascend on the other side of a tremendous chasm.    This was impossible, and with many regrets we returned to the Monastery, leaving the ascent of the real highest peak for travellers with more time.    As our leave would be up on the following Monday, we were obliged to make all sail back to Canton.    We returned to our boat, after seeing two beautiful falls, and a bell weighing 2000 catties.    At 7 in the evening we got back, and set sail for Poo-ne-Shui, but at 9 o'clock stopped at Wang-Sha on account of the rain.

*Sunday, 17th March.*—7.30 passed Tsing-kee ; 12 arrived at Synam ; 9 P.M. arrived at Fatshan, and anchored.

*Monday, 18th March.*—Seeing Fatshan all the morning.    Arrived in Canton at 6 P.M.

9.—*British Columbia, and a proposed Emigrant Route from Pembina to Yale.*  By WM. KELLY, Esq., F.R.G.S.

THE geographical position of British Columbia, with respect to the mother-country and other European fountains of emigration, places it at a serious disadvantage in competing for population with the great American and Australian regions, at least under the present arrangements for transport.    In fact, the only two recognised routes of approach to it are those by the Isthmus of Panama and round Cape Horn ; the former of which, whether direct from Southampton or by way of New York, is attended with so considerable an outlay, that it is utterly out of the reach of the class of emigrants alone fit for encountering the primary difficulties of pioneer colonization ; and although the latter may perhaps offer some trifling advantages on the score of economy, the extreme length, danger, and suffering inseparable from a voyage round Cape Horn to the westward, must operate as a complete bar to family emigration.

This state of things is the more to be deplored from the fact—which I can conscientiously aver from two years and six months' residence in British Columbia—that there is no other British possession more suitable or congenial to the Celtic or Anglo-Saxon race as regards climate, nor one which presents more genuine or substantial allurements to settlers in the extent and variety of its internal resources. To which may be added the probability of a steam communication between Australia and Fraser River—a consummation that hinges upon the formation of a highway from the Atlantic to the Pacific Ocean; Sydney being absolutely 900 miles nearer to New Westminster than to Panama, by which latter route it is at present contemplated to establish a mail route for the purpose of expedition.

The mean temperature of British Columbia approximates as nearly as may be to that of the British Isles. In the immediate valley of Fraser River, up to its junction with Thompson River, where it may be said to run through a grand mountain defile for over 120 miles, the winter season is perhaps somewhat colder and more protracted than ours save in the north of Scotland; but after emerging from the foothills of the Cascade Ranges into the vast open rolling territory lying between them and the Rocky Mountains, the seasons do not exceed the British average.

At Fort George, which approximates to the 54th parallel of latitude, all sorts of cereals and garden vegetables arrive at perfect maturity, and cattle, for the most part, can be safely wintered out; for even in seasons when the ground is covered with a tolerably deep coat of snow, there is a tall, coarse, succulent bunch-grass, which penetrates the surface, affording them abundant nourishment. Farther north, as we approach the Russian frontier, the natural variation of temperature, of course, is experienced; but to the southward, the newly-discovered valley of the Semilkameen, from the peculiar position and configuration of the country, enjoys a mild and genial atmosphere, altogether unusual in similar parallels of latitude. Throughout the colony, neither the heat of summer nor the cold of winter at all approaches the extremes of Canada or the more northern states of the Union. In ordinary seasons mining operations only suffer a brief interruption in the north—none at all in the valley of the Semilkameen. And if we are to measure the salubrity of the climate by the bills of mortality, it must rank wonderfully high indeed; for, with the exception of *scurvy*—inevitable at the outset from the dearth of vegetables and fresh provisions,—I was perfectly astonished at the general exemption from endemic disease, particularly considering the extreme hardships and predisposing causes attending a miner's life in a new country. In truth, a large proportion of the deaths that came under my cognisance were such as in an older country would challenge the inquiry of the coroner.

The salmon-fishery affords an immense scope for capital and enterprise. It is quite impossible to imagine the extent and density of the shoals of this fish in their full season. I have often stood on a rock and dipped out the fish with a large rude landing-net as quick as I could submerge it, and have seen Indians at the same time literally shovelling them ashore with canoe-paddles. Salt for curing them is obtainable in any quantity from the great saline springs in Vancouver Island; and as all the inhabitants of the Pacific islands, whether in the South Sea or Northern Archipelago, are excessively partial to cured fish, there could be no difficulty whatever in finding a ready and remunerative market for all that could be put up.

Next I would call attention to the endless supply of timber of the finest description and greatest variety—pine, fir, spruce, hemlock, cedar, oak, ash, maple, willow, alder, cotton-wood, &c. But the timber valuable as an article of export is the pine, which, from its prodigious size and uncommon straightness, is peculiarly suitable for masts and spars, a grand specimen of which may be seen in Kew Gardens. There is no doubt that vessels taking out merchandise could make splendid return-freights by loading with spar logs, which command an extraordinary price and ready sale in the home markets. These logs can be had of any dimensions. On the immediate banks of the Fraser, for at least 50 miles from its mouth, hundreds upon hundreds of most magnificent trees, cut down to clear the site of New Westminster, were burnt upon the ground.

Although there is scope enough of territory in British Columbia suitable for pastoral and agricultural purposes to satisfy the requirements of an independent state, I conceive that the colony is to be chiefly estimated for its unbounded mineral wealth. Its gold is well known.

Silver, too, has been discovered in many districts.

Cinnabar of the richest description was found in the Cariboo country by Captain Bowen, a gentleman with whom I am intimately acquainted.

Every one of the returning prospecters who came down last fall from the north and north-western districts, to make arrangements for the present season, brought specimens of one sort or another ; among which I can enumerate, from inspection, pure copper, platinum, agates, cornelians, coal, limestone, marbles of the purest and most beautiful kind. Lignite, or a species of bituminous wood of the earthy variety, is quite common in those districts, and is used by the miners for fuel. It is of a brownish-black colour, nearly as light as water, very friable. It burns freely when blown, sending forth a light blaze, which may be utilised for blacksmithing purposes.

Plumbago of the purest kind has been found in many localities by Major Downie in masses of magnitude sufficiently large to supply all the markets of the world. Mineral and hot springs, too, are features of this richly endowed colony.

As to the general character of the soil in the thousands of square miles fit for settlement, it is sufficient to say, that it is undeniably excellent in all its varieties for either agriculture or pasture. The cereals, fruits, and vegetables of Britain and France can be readily produced ; and stock, as I have already observed, can for the most part be wintered out without any supply of fodder. It is therefore abundantly manifest that British Columbia offers a field for emigration, now especially that the land-system has been liberalised.

Population is all that British Columbia requires to ensure its growth and unbounded prosperity ; but, in order to get that, we must have some practicable avenue of approach, which, as regards time, safety, and economy, shall be within the reach of the small farmer, tradesman, and navvie. Such a one, from the nature of the country, and from the estimates of highly qualified travellers, there is no doubt could be constructed for 250,000*l.*—made, too, after such a manner as to form a sound basis or foundation for future railway operations between Pembina, on the 49th parallel, and a central point in British Columbia—say Yale, the highest point of steamboat navigation on the Fraser River. The entire distance from point to point does not exceed 1100 miles, 250 of which can be accomplished by river-steamers in the South Saskatchewan.

In the Royal Speech, Her Majesty indulged in the hope "that my new colony on the Pacific, British Columbia, may be but one step in the career of steady progress by which my dominions in North America may be ultimately peopled in an unbroken chain from the Atlantic to the Pacific by a loyal and industrious population"—a hope certain to be ultimately consummated, as well from the grand prospects growing out of eastern policy, as from the fact that the splendid country lying between the Red River settlement and the Vermilion Pass is in the wheat-growing parallel ; that vast and varied mineral discoveries have recently been made in British Columbia ; and that the embouchure of the Fraser furnishes one of the finest harbours in the world. At present the most direct route is *viâ* Portland, U.S., whence Chicago can be reached in ten days by the Grand Trunk Railway. From Chicago to St. Paul's, a distance of 350 miles, can be accomplished in one day by rail ; and thence to Pembina, about 450, in one day, when the railway is finished (at present it takes eight days). From this point it is that recent explorers suggest the formation of an emigrant trail, diverging north-westerly, to Elbow on the South Saskatchewan in an oblique direction, instead of diverging at right angles to Assiniboine. Several small parties of Canadians and Americans travelled this trail in 1859 and 1860; one of which was under the conduct of a Mr. McQueen, a gentleman of intelligence and discrimination, whose acquaintance I had the good fortune to make. He describes the route as one easily made into a good waggon-road—much superior to the overland Oregon one. It is sparsely wooded at intervals, and abounds in feed and water all the way, affording many most eligible localities for settlement. He estimates the distance from Pembina to Elbow at 420 miles. From Elbow his party proceeded along the Saskatchewan about 150 miles, and found it perfectly navigable the entire way for good-sized steamers. They then diverged in a direct westerly course (finding the river took a great southerly sweep), and, after travelling 100 miles over grassy prairies, they struck the river again, and followed it up to Fort Bow, about 80 miles; and even here Mr. McQueen pronounces it navigable for stern-wheel steamers. From Fort Bow, as Dr. Hector says, "The ascent to the water-parting on the Vermilion Pass is scarcely perceptible, being only as 1 in 135"—an opinion fully confirmed by Mr. McQueen, who, with his party, weary and footsore, under heavy packs, reached the forks of Thompson and Fraser rivers (the heart of British Columbia) in twelve days, stopping very frequently each day to prospect for gold, and make inquiries from the various digging-parties they came across. To recapitulate, then: throwing in one day of grace for contingencies, Pembina can be reached from Portland in five days; and, admitting that the remaining 1100 can be accomplished at the same average rate that the American overland-mail contractors do their work, the entire distance from Portland, on the Atlantic, to New Westminster, on the Pacific, could be performed readily in twenty-five days. With such a line once started, Her Majesty's expression would soon become developed, and a thoroughfare within reach of all classes of emigrants fairly established.

If Government will make moderate concessions of the public domain along the route, capitalists can readily be found who will undertake to construct a good, well-graded waggon-road, suitable for the basis of a future railway, under conditions to allow Government to re-enter possession of the grant whenever it should be required for public purposes. In a short lapse of time we would then have pony-expresses, soon followed by stage-coaches for the heavier mails. Although I am aware that at the present juncture it is not prudent to cite American precedents on any subject, I nevertheless feel confident that ascertained results, fortified by well and long-proved experience, cannot be hastily ignored. The United States Government has invariably found the granting subsidies to overland-mails was putting out the public money to fructify at the best advantage, by at one and the same time enhancing the value of the public domain in opening it up for settlement, and by improving the revenue and trade in encouraging the spread and increase of population. This, to my positive knowledge, has been remarkably demonstrated in subsidising the daily overland mail from Sacramento city, in California, to Portland, in Oregon, a distance above 700 miles over what was theretofore a perfect wilderness; and although the service has been little over one year at work, nearly all the fertile tracts along the route have been taken up, while the stages for horse-changing and refreshments have become the nucleus of townships, where land now sells by the foot. There is no doubt whatsoever that similar results would follow if a like system were adopted on the line I propose. Or if the Government undertook the scheme as a public work, I believe the necessary funds would be forthcoming, ere its completion, from the sale of public lands for farms and townships.

The Government of British Columbia, in excusable anticipation of a Pacific Railway, is constructing its highways into the interior at such easy grades that on a future day they may be available for laying down rails upon. And that such a railway will be made there seems every plausible assurance, as well from the exigencies of our newborn eastern commerce, as because the whole range of the Rocky Mountains south of the 49th parallel does not furnish one single practicable pass, while that called the Vermilion Pass, in the direct line, is in British territory, and does not exceed 4944 feet in altitude.   Dr. Hector describes it as "not presenting any difficulty whatever to the construction of a railway, connecting the fertile prairies of the Saskatchewan with the auriferous valleys of British Columbia."

I think I shall abundantly prove, by the following extracts from a letter written by a distinguished member of this Society (Captain Richards, of the surveying-ship *Hecate*, in reply to an address from the corporation of New Westminster), the excellence of that port as a point of departure :—

> "Her Majesty's Surveying Ship, 'Hecate,' off New Westminster,
> October, 30th, 1860.

" . . . However highly you may estimate our services, it is yet to natural causes alone that the Fraser River owes its immunity from dangers and difficulties, almost always incident to Bar harbours.   Effectually sheltered and protected as it is, in common with the coast of British Columbia, by the natural breakwater which the sister colony affords, your noble river is accessible at *all times of tide* to vessels of from 18 to 20 feet draught and 1000 tons.

"It is free from risk of life and property in a higher degree than any river I am acquainted with on the western side of this continent ; and when a lightship is stationed at the Sand Heads, or the entrance marked by permanent buoys, the seaman may guide his vessel through at *all times* with ease and safety."

---

10—*Ascent of Um Shaumur, the Highest Peak of the Sinaitic Peninsula,* 1862.   By the Rev. T. J. PROUT, M.A., F.G.S., Student and late Censor, Christ Church, Oxford.*

THE mountain Um Shaumur, the loftiest and grandest in the peninsula of Sinai, is situated about 12 miles south-south-west of Gebel Katherin, but from the rugged nature of the intervening country, a somewhat circuitous journey of 10 or 12 hours' duration is required to reach it.   The mountain rises precipitously in three peaks or base-tops, of which the western is considerably the highest (say 300 feet above the central, and 100 feet above the eastern peak).   The height of the western peak above the sea has been given at 9200 feet ; but I cannot vouch for the correctness of the statement ; and indeed all figures in this account must be understood as approximative, as we had no means with us of taking accurate measurements.   The camel-road to the mountain, from the Convent of St. Catherine, lies first of all in a south-easterly direction up the Wady Shu'eib, and along the track leading to Shurm, for about two hours ; and then, turning more to the southward, winds through rather a dull valley as far as regards scenery, but possessing some interest geologically from the extensive deposits of recent sandstone and conglomerate which have been formed along its bed by the wearing away of the mountains above.   About two hours more, at the ordinary rate of camel-travelling, bring us to some high ground at the upper end of this valley, from whence we obtain a fine view full in front of the cone-shaped "Jebel-el-

---

* A narrative of a previous ascent of one of the minor peaks of Um Shaumur, accompanied by a sketch of the mountain, has been forwarded to the Society by the Rev. Frederick Howlett.—ED.

Odha." Descending from the height on the further side, we enter the Wady Rahabeh—a wady of the same general character as the last—and in other two hours arrive at an Arab resting-place, under shelter of some fallen rocks on the western side of the wady. Not far from this spot, but more in the centre of the valley, are several Arab storehouses or magazines—desolate-looking buildings of stone rudely and loosely put together, and furnished respectively with a single entrance of about a yard square in size. Whenever the Arabs to whom these magazines belong, deposit property within, they merely fill up the entrance with brushwood arranged in a peculiar manner, and leave it without any other protection whatever. Moreover we were informed, that although the removal of the brushwood would be an easy matter, yet that no case was known of the sanctity of a storehouse so sealed having been violated. Travellers intending to ascend Um Shaumur will probably be disposed, if they have no tents with them, to pass the night under the shelter, such as it is, of this resting-place; but if they have brought tents with them, they will do better to push on about an hour and a half further, and encamp in a small lateral valley, the "Wady Zeitûneh," so called from an ancient olive-tree (probably the only one for many miles round) which stands not far from its entrance. The particular advantage of the place for encampment is, that close to the tree there is a well of tolerable water. And here it may be added, that along the whole route, from the Convent of St. Catherine to this spot, no other water is passed, with the exception of a very indifferent spring some distance to the north of the resting-place in the Wady Rahabeh.

Supposing, however, for the present that we start in the morning from the resting-place in the Wady Rahabeh, a walk of an hour and a half over a low ridge, and along the bed of a narrow winding valley floored with deep sand and gravel, brings us to the top of the corrie at its upper end, from whence, on the further side, we obtain a view of the more eastern portion of Um Shaumur. The way to the mountain, however, does not yet lie straight before us. The ravine in front is so deep and difficult to traverse that it is advisable, if not absolutely necessary, to make rather a long circuit by some still higher and much steeper ridges to the westward. A stiff climb of an hour and a quarter up to and along these ridges brings us to a point from which the whole of the northern face of Um Shaumur is visible from top to bottom. The view of Um Shaumur from this point is very striking, the whole mountain being nearly sheer precipice with the exception of a gully below the central peak filled with scattered fragments of every size, from masses weighing many tons to small stones. The said gully is an important feature in the mountain; for by it alone, as far as we could see, are the higher parts to be approached. Before commencing the ascent of Um Shaumur proper, it is necessary to descend some thousand feet to a narrow neck or isthmus of rock connecting the hill on which we stand with the main body of the mountain. Both on the east and west sides of the neck are very deep and narrow ravines; and but little reflection is here required to convince one that Um Shaumur could not well have been the "Mount of the Law," as some have conjectured it to be. For, independently of its lying so much out of the probable track of the Israelites, there is not room in the crevasse-like ravines which surround its base for any large number of people to encamp. In the gorge on the western side of the neck are the ruins of the old chapel or convent of St. Antony, and near it there flows a stream of excellent water having its source high up in the gully above.

Having at length reached the base of Um Shaumur itself, we now commence a scramble over or round or under the various fragments of rock which choke the gully by which, as already stated, our ascent must be made; and after about an hour's steady climbing, but without any real difficulty, we reach the central peak. To this point several travellers have ascended before us; and it is a little higher up that *the* difficulty of the mountain occurs. The huge masses of syenite which support the western summit are so precipitous as to be, at first sight at least, quite insurmountable without the aid of a ladder.   But on further inspection the perpendicular face of one of the largest of these buttresses is found to be rent from top to bottom by a fissure of some width indeed at the aperture, but gradually contracting until there is barely room for a man to turn or even to stand in it.   On the floor of this part of the fissure there is an accumulation of detritus which raises us just within reach of a small ledge or shelf formed by a few stones which have fallen from above and stuck fast between the lateral faces of rock.   To this ledge it is necessary to worm oneself up as one best can.   There is no room for a spring or other display of gymnastic activity, and the smooth sides of rock afford no hold for booted feet.   In our case, however, the lean and wiry Arab who acted as our guide, having divested himself of his sandals and other impedimenta, saved much time and trouble by first screwing himself up to the ledge, and then giving my friend and myself a hand, which slight aid was all that was required.   I may, however, here remark, that on mountains like Um Shaumur the possession of a rope, if not always necessary, is at least desirable by way of precaution.   The ledge once gained, a few minutes more scramble placed us on the summit of Um Shaumur; the first Europeans, we believe, who have scaled this the highest point of the Sinaitic peninsula.   As probably Um Shaumur is surmountable only by the way I have described, it is possible that former travellers have been baffled by not finding the fissure in the Hagar-el-Bint; or perhaps the ledge itself by which we ascended is the result of a fall of stones which has taken place since the mountain was last attempted. The view from the summit of Um Shaumur is extremely grand.   We have first, from north-west to north-east, a sea of jagged peaks and bare rugged hills of dark-red granite and syenite, shut in in the distance by Serbâl, Katherin, Mûsa ; and other mountains of the Sinai range ; while more towards the east the eye ranges across the Gulf of Akaba to the lofty mountains of Arabia. On the south again, or rather the south-east, the ridge on which we stand is continued with more or less interruption of its deeply-serrated outline until it ceases at the Cape "Râs Mohammed."   Turning westward, at some little distance, not immediately at our feet, we discern the plain of Ka'a', extending to the shore of the Gulf of Suez ; and further off, beyond an expanse of deepest blue, the high and sometimes sharp-topped mountains of Africa stretching away in the distant horizon.

The mountains of the southern part of the peninsula of Sinai consist of coarse-grained granite and syenite, both occasionally porphyritic, and weathering for the most part into a dark-red colour.   These coarse rocks are, however, sometimes traversed by veins of red felspathic syenite of much finer grain, and also by veins of greyish-white quartz ; but dykes and outpourings of trap are much more frequent than either.   In the detritus along the hillsides and valleys I observed great quantities of yellow mica, together with specimens of tourmaline, augite, prehnite, &c.   But our visit was of too cursory a nature to admit of a minute examination of the geology, geography, or otherwise of the Peninsula.   I may, however, state in conclusion, that in the red sandstone region abutting the granite district on the north, and lying generally between it and the limestone range of Et-Tîh is abundance of iron and copper ; and not only so, but there are in several localities traces of extensive works having been carried on for the extraction of both these metals.   More especially is this the case in the neighbourhood of the hill called "Surabit-el-Kadim."   A thorough exploration of the wadies there would probably not only show that the history of the peninsula is not to be confined to the few years of its occupation by the Israelites, but would at the same time do much to clear up the mystery which still hangs over the question of Sinaitic inscriptions.   I might say a good deal more on this subject ; but, as it is difficult to separate the results of my own observations from information which I received, I feel that it is not fair towards the gentleman who gave me that information, and whose hospitality in the desert I gratefully acknowledge, to anticipate in any way the publication of discoveries which rightfully belong to him, and which, I trust, he will himself ere long communicate to the world.

11.—*Account of the Ascent of the Camaroons Mountain, in Western Africa.* By Captain RICHARD BURTON, H.B.M. Consul at Fernando Po, Gold Medallist. (Communicated by the FOREIGN OFFICE.)

*Consul Burton to Earl Russell.*

Fernando Po, February 22, 1862.

MY LORD,—I have the honour to report that I have made two ascents of the hitherto unexplored Camaroons Mountain, and have discovered a magnificent site for a sanitarium, a convict station, or a negro colony. I have enclosed a report, to be forwarded, if your Lordship thinks proper, to the Secretary of the Royal Geographical Society.

I have, &c.,      (Signed) RICHD. F. BURTON.

(Enclosure.)

*A Reconnaissance of "Theon Ochema," Camaroons Mountain.*

"Τέτταρας δ' ἡμέρας φερόμενοι, νυκτὸς τὴν γῆν ἀφεωρῶμεν φλογὸς μεστήν. Ἐν μέσῳ δ' ἦν ἠλιβατόντι πῦρ τῶν ἄλλων μεῖζον ἁπτόμενον, ὡς ἐδόκει, τῶν ἄστρων. Τοῦτο δ' ἡμέρας ὄρος ἐφαίνετο μέγιστον Θεῶν ὄχημα καλούμενον.

"Post cursum dierum quatuor, noctu terram conspiciebamus flammis refertam. In medio autem erat excelsus quidam et ceteris major ignis, ipsa, uti videbatur, tangens astra. *Is interdiu apparuit esse mons altissimus, qui Theon Ochema vocatur.*"

[This remarkable passage in Hanno's 'Periplus,' chap. 16, is to be explained only by the firing of the grass and the burning solfaterra on the Camaroons Mountain.]

THE Royal Geographical Society may, at first sight, not be disposed to think much of an exploration which appears only to have reached a mountain district 14 miles of direct, and 21 of indirect distance from the sea. But a little knowledge of the subject gives another view of it. Water is often wanting; provisions are never to be found on these tropical heights. The wild people are a notoriously bad, though cowardly race, and everywhere, as the late expedition to Kilimanjaro proves, if such proof be required, savages are unwilling to see their mountains ascended for the first time. Add to this, that the only escort in these lands must be krooboys—sturdy fellows, but the most arrant poltroons. They hate land-work; they malinger by inducing sore feet; they run away; and at the best of times they are fond, as Murphy is, of depending on Pat to ask Corny to think about coming some day and help to carry a small bundle of straw to repair the roof.

For nearly four centuries this magnificent pile of mountains, the "Theon Ochema" of Hanno and Pliny has been looming before the eyes of the passing European mariner, yet the summit has been ever virgin. Two attempts have lately been made. In 1847 a Mr. Merrick, of the Baptist Mission on the Camaroons River, succeeded in emerging from the forest into the open grassy levels. But pure water failed him; his people suffered from cold and thirst, and he was compelled to return. Two years afterwards he died. In 1860, M. Gustav Mann, a young Hanoverian botanist, travelling and collecting in West Africa under the patronage of Sir William Hooker, ascended a few hundred feet, when press of time persuaded him to stop. Here, then, remained for me a mountain whose "glorious pinnacle never yet felt the foot of man."

Geographically speaking, the Camaroons Mountain is a parallelogram laying between 3° 57' and 4° 25' north latitude, and 9° 25' and 9° 1' east longitude. It is bounded on the east by the Bimbia River, a stream probably discharged by the mountains. The western limit is a branch of the Rio del Rey, or Rumbi River. The Atlantic washes the southern face, and the area towards the north still wants exploration. The distance from the southern foot to the summit, as laid down in the charts, is 14 miles; allowing the same for Country Cape, 28 miles will be its length; and its breadth from the Bimbia to the Rio del Rey is not less than 24 miles, forming an area of 600 square miles. Captain Owen, R.N., estimates the diameter at nearly 20 miles, which would give an area of about 314 miles; but he does not include the high lands to the north-east, extending to the Rumbi range.

This huge volcanic mass is one of a long line of basalt islands, beginning at the unexplored Rumbi range, and stretching from 33° north-east to 33° south-west through Camaroons, Fernando Po, Prince's Island, St. Thomas', and Ascension. It occupies the bottom of the Bight of Biafra, in the very centre of the Gulf of Guinea, where the coast of Western Africa—after that long sweep eastwards which made the later classical geographers shear off the vast triangle south of the equator—bends almost at a right angle towards the Antarctic pole. The lands behind it being still unexplored, it is difficult to say whether this basaltic buttress to the Atlantic waters does, or does not, communicate through the Rumbi Mountains with those West African ghauts, the Sierra del Crystal. On the other hand, it may be connected by the Kwa Hills to the north-westward, and by the Bassa Mountains upon the Niger, with that mass of high ground east of Sierra Leone, and known upon our maps as the Kong Mountains.

My first visit to Victoria—the little missionary station whence the ascent was to be made—was on the 10th December, 1861, in H.M.S. *Bloodhound*, Commander Dolben. There I found Mr. Mann eager to begin the journey, but still "palavering" with the petty chiefs on the road. An official visit to the Camaroons—an odious "trust river"—procured another volunteer, the Rev. A. Saker, for eighteen years a resident in these parts, a linguist and ethnologist highly respected by the people. Returning to Fernando Po to complete the outfit, for which four days sufficed, I had yet another volunteer for the expedition, which gave it an international character. Señor Atilano Calvo Iturburu, Assessor or Assistant Judge and Secretary to Government, Fernando Po, was as weary as myself of "palaver," and at least as anxious for a mouthful of fresh air. You must not confound him with certain awful personages in pepper-and-salt wigs and ample gowns, but rather think of him as a fast young pig-sticking Anglo-Indian magistrate.

The dawn of the 18th December found Judge Calvo and myself lying in H.M.S. *Bloodhound*, off the lovely Bay of Victoria, where Mr. Saker was awaiting us. Mr. Mann had set out in advance to await us at the highest village, and we were to follow on the next morning. Precisely at 6 A.M., as agreed upon, we arose, despite the ravages of mosquitoes and sand-flies, and fifty minutes afterwards found ourselves *en route* with a hurrah! The party consisted of Mr. Saker and his two kroomen, who carried his bed, his bunker, and his carefully-locked box of creature comforts—the veteran traveller never lost sight of his fellows. He was accompanied by the interpreter, Mr. Johnson, who having begun life as a factotum to Governor Beecroft, had settled down in his old age as a teacher in the Camaroons Mission. Judge Calvo's escort was composed of four kroomen—all of them hopeless convicts from the cuartel of Fernando Po—and King Eyo, a youth whose idleness and uselessness were admirable and exemplary even in Africa. My party consisted of six krooboys under their head man, Black Will. They were placed in charge of my steward Selim Agha, an invaluable man, a native of Tegulet, and a protégé of the late venerable Mr. Robert Thurburn, of Alexandria. He had spent a dozen years of his life at a school in Scotland, where he learned to cook, doctor, spin, carpenter, shoot, collect specimens, and stuff birds—briefly every-thing.

Our route lay through a bush—such is the magnificent Anglo-African term for a forest of trees often 100 feet high—composed of palms and acacias, a variety of figs and cardamoms, the kola-tree (*Sterculia acuminata*), and three kinds valuable for timber, namely, the African oak (*Oldfieldia Africana*), the scrubby oak of Sierra Leone (*Sophira alata*), and the brimstone-tree or yellow wood (*Mormida lucida*). This also is the region of huge grasses which extend to 4000 feet above sea-level, where dwarfened growths take their places. The whole of this country is admirably adapted for cacao (*Theobroma cacao*), coffee, and sugar; it is a pity to see it wasted on plantains and koko (*Colocuia escu-lenta*). We twice forded the bright little mountain-stream which supplies Victoria with the purest water, and ascended some tough heights, passing west of Mount Henry—a site which I at once fixed upon as a provisional sanitarium, to be prepared before the grand institution near the summit of the mountain. After four hours—2h. 20m. of actual walking—we entered the settlement of the Chief Miyombi, passed some outlying huts, and halted for breakfast at Bosumbo, the head-quarter village, lying 23,420 feet from Victoria. These and other distances were measured by my factotum Selim, with a line sup-plied to me by Lieutenant Dolben. At Bosumbo Mr. Saker's French aneroid showed 29.6, and Mr. Mann's B.P. apparatus gave 210.5°; temperature, 67.5°.

We now stood upwards of 1000 feet above sea-level, and at noon merrily resumed our way. The path, a mere rut, led through dense bush and grass, with a general northerly direction bending westwards. After passing through a somewhat populous district, we entered upon a vile series of rocky ridges, separated by ravines, and impassable during the rains.

At 4.30 P.M. we made Mapanya, the district of the Chief Botani, and the highest village on this part of the mountain. It lies 17,300 feet from Bosumbo; the aneroid showed 28.23, the B.P. 207.5°; temperature, 72.5°.

The first person we saw was Mr. Mann, who at once informed us that he had just returned from reaching the summit. Faces fell at the announcement: it had been understood that he would wait our arrival. Presently we were reassured. The time of his walking rendered it impossible that he could have been near the mysterious spot. Eventually it became clear that he had never seen his bourne.

The next trouble was the ceremonious welcome with which we were received. The Chief Botani, a yellow man with a bright blue pair of tattooed regulation-whiskers, appeared before us in his royal garb, tall black tile, old scarlet and gamboge coatee of Royal Marines, and a pocket-handkerchief. Thus habited he performed a lively dance, apparently borrowed from the movements of excited poultry. I did not enjoy it. In Africa, when the King dances you have to pay for the honour.

Mapanya is the usual Bakwiri village, a single street separating four huts on the northern from two on the southern side. The site is a little clearing, well grown with plantains, and backed by a glorious screen of wooded heights. The huts are oblong, with pent roofs. The walls are of wattle, supported by posts of the strong and fibrous tree-fern, and provided with sheets of bark to keep out the wind. The roofs are thatched with palm-leaves. The inner space is divided into three "pieces;" at one end of the long walls is a closet, partitioned off by posts and party-walls; the centre, where the only door is, represents the hall; whilst the other third is devoted to the fire-place, with a platform above it for storing and drying wood. The ceiling is black, as if painted with coal-tar, and the floor, which ignores a broom, is at once the chair, the bed, and the resting-place of man, woman, and child, goat and sheep, pig and poultry, to say no more.

The tribe to whom this part of the mountain belongs is called in our charts

Bakwileh.	The proper word is Bakwíri, from "kwiri," a jungle, and meaning literally Boyesman or Bushman. They are allied in language to Ilubu, or people of Bimbia, and their dialect is a branch of the great South African family, whose type is the Kafir tongue. The Bakwíri are a light-coloured race like the Bubis of Fernando Po, and have well-made legs, like mountaineers generally. They bear a bad reputation; they are harmless only because each village of five huts has a "palaver" with its neighbours, and because the poison-ordeals sadly thin their numbers. They can hardly be persuaded to part with their flocks, or even their poultry, except by the inducements of rum, a tall hat, or an English shirt. Mr. Mann's scarlet blankets excited, however, the utmost admiration. The people offered successively in exchange for one, a pig and a goat, a small boy, and a large girl.

We halted at Mapanya on the 20th December, having sent the krooboys to Victoria for a reinforcement of provisions. A lively scene met our eyes at 2 P.M. The dancing Chief Botani had been "dashed" by Mr. Mann, and had received a similar present from me. Not content with that he demanded more, which was refused. Then he and his followers, drunk with "bilám," or trade rum, attempted to seize Mr. Mann's interpreter, a child known as "Poor Fellow." They drew their long knives, and had laid forcible hands upon the little wretch, when Mr. Mann energetically rescued him. Upon which the war-drum was beaten, the women began to leave the village, and the men to flock in. Mr. Saker being unarmed, there were only three of us, and the fun soon became fast and furious. We stood to our weapons, and occupied the doorways of the huts so as not to be taken in rear. Presently the fumes of the rum ceased to affect their brains, and all excitement disappeared—Botani, the Chief, wearing a very hang-dog look.

The next day, however, matters were worse. Our kroomen returned from Victoria, accompanied by the Chief Miyombi, of Bosumbo, much the worse for liquor. On being refused more rum he persuaded Botani to demand 500 "big tings," i.e., 500l., for his gracious permission to ascend a place upon whose top cloth would be found growing. The demand was lowered to 300l., when we laughed in his face. He then ordered us down the mountain. We showed our guns, and told him that we should start up the mountain that day. Botani then declared that he would allow no carriers to accompany us. We had loads for twenty-five men, at least, and there were only fourteen: so he retired to another village, and quietly waited there to hear of our failure.

A little after noon, Messrs. Saker and Calvo set out with fourteen kroomen, and reached a place in the forest which was afterwards called "Ridge Camp." The bearers were then sent back, and only nine came, causing us a trouble which brought back to my mind bygone days in East Africa. Shortly after 5 P.M. we effected a start. The distance is 6000 feet, and there are five very bad ascents. The road is a copy of that leading to Mapanya—high pitches, ladders of rock and root, tall grasses, ridges, hollows, scrambling-places, nettles, and legions of biting ants. The palm had disappeared near Mapanya, and now we saw the last of the plantain, and the first of the graceful tree-fern. As darkness was imminent, we heard shouts above us, and those who had rested came down to assist the wearied. I arrived at 6.30 P.M., and Mr. Mann shortly afterwards brought up the rear of his luggage. At Ridge Camp the aneroid showed 27.2. We passed a comfortless night in the forest. The inhospitable Bakwíri had refused us water, the ground was uneven, and the total loss of rest was a bad preparation for the hard day's work that awaited us.

Before dawn on the 22nd of December we left Ridge Camp, made a cache for our extra loads, and determined to reach water before the night. The real march began at 8 A.M. The characteristic of the scenery now was the fern—fern, fern, everywhere. Some were like palm-trees, 10 to 20 feet high, surpassingly fair to look at; others were dwarfed epiphytes, springing moss-like from the arms of their parent trees. There were beds of ferns upon the ground, and others running creeper-like up the trunks. Never had I seen a more beautiful fernery, set off as it is by the huge tropical growth around it. The path, however, was vile.

After 2510 feet, which consumed a good hour of our valuable time, we passed under a natural arch of fallen trees, which we called "Fern Gate." The B.P. here showed 120.4°, the temperature 66°. Beyond it lay a new land. Bush and forest suddenly ceased as if felled with the axe; and, O, joy! we had emerged from the regions of the tall grasses. Nothing met the eye but a broad green slope of small moss and larger fern, all of it the *F. nephrolapis*, based upon a rugged bed of old and degraded lava. We called this first stream Lava Bed No. 1, and specimens of it, and of the other fire-rivers long since quenched, have been forwarded for the inspection of a certain ex-President of the Royal Geographical Society, whom it were needless to name here. The direction of the bed is from 291° to due north, that is to say, it has flowed from north to south with a little easting. I afterwards found this a rule which safely guided us to the topmost peak. The craters may open irregularly and in all directions, but the lava-flow follows the direction of the wind. More expert volcanists will determine if there be any connection between the two facts. The breadth of the bed may be half a mile; the lower part finding little slope thins out, and ends in a dense forest. The banks are girt on both sides by giant trees; and looking down from the half-way heights, the idea of a huge fir* is suggested.

Having breakfasted and eaten blackberries (*R. apetalus*), we began the ascent at 9.50 A.M. The hunters' path led up the western edge of the lava-river, and gradually curved to the eastern. It was severe work: six particularly steep pitches presented themselves, and the way often wound up prisms of lava from 15 to 25 feet high. In the lower part, where the blocks cannot be seen, there was imminent risk of spraining an ancle. Higher up, the ascent became more rocky and bare. Salvia scented the air, and the surface was spangled with bright blossoms unknown even to our expert "botaniker." There was also heath, but, ah! how different from what you understand by such word—an *Ericanella* 15 feet high, thin and rugged as an old tamarisk. The bees now began to settle upon us, but no one was stung. As we ascended, the heat of the sun became terrible. The kroomen tailed off; Selim Agha remained behind in charge of them, and verily I believe saved several lives by squeezing water out of the thick mosses that hung from the banks.

The last third of the road is the most rugged of all. The bed now nears the place whence it issued, and the unequal cooling of the masses has made it uncommonly rough walking, or rather climbing. You look up and see a high, abrupt, and broken transverse wall; you reach this in half an hour, more than half-exhausted, and you see nothing but another. I found it impossible to keep my eyes open; something fiery and feverish had got into my veins. So requesting my companions, who were far fresher, to keep going, I lay down upon a lava block, slept soundly for an hour till 4 P.M., and was thus able to finish the ascent.

Lava Bed No. 1 issues from a dwarf cone which, from its exceptional darkness, we called "Black Crater." It is a punch-bowl, opening towards the south, long extinct; the western lip rises 200 feet from the level platform below, or 356 feet measured along the slope. The crater is about 100 yards in diameter, and the circumference of its middle height may be 600 yards. The outer surface is fine cinder, mostly bare, very sparsely overgrown with now dry grass and with stunted shrubs, and there is a little green vegetation

---

* Manuscript illegible.

inside the crater. It is distant 8350 feet from Fern Gate. The B.P. showed 200.2°, the temperature being 63.25°.

Mr. Mann kindly volunteered to set out with a krooman, and to bring back a beaker of water. His offer was accepted by a most grateful public, and we afterwards named the fountain which an old Mokwiri had shown to him " Mann's Spring." Without such discovery, indeed, our work would have been trebled. By degrees our kroomen appeared with bed and baggage; five of them, however, remained behind. Another bad camping-place had been selected. The high north-east wind roared over us all night, and a change from 78° to 40° Fahrenheit in a few hours is a severe trial of strength. Even at 6 A.M. the mercury stood at 48°.

A lovely morning, when the large red sun had

　　　" Retinged the dark and livid air with bloom,"

made amends for past troubles. Before us, beyond a grassy hollow, about one mile broad, rose, separated apparently by a great gulf, the awful form of Mount Trestrail, stern, solitary, and rising one-third higher than Vesuvius, without neighbour or rival. The charts give it 5820 feet. Captain William Allen calls it " Mongo Mt. Etindet," which would mean the " separate mountain," but Mr. Saker had never heard the word.

As Selim Agha and his squad did not appear at 2 P.M., we sent them a beaker of water, and set out for Mann's Spring, distant 9594 feet. Our direction was northerly, with a little westing. The walk is charming by contrast, winding round the grassy shoulders and folds of various hills. On the right we passed a crater, whose double effusion of lava united at the base, inclosing a clump of vivid verdure, probably the *Hypericum angustifolium*, a European growth which had now become common. The path, a mere rut, struck, after forty-five minutes, into a thickly-wooded ravine, nearly the highest limit of large vegetation. After the fiery sun there was pleasure in its cool shade, and its air scented with a garden of blue labiates and white clematis hanging from lofty trees. The forest, except where herbaceous plants clothed the ground, rather resembled an English wood than an African jungle, and the birds twittered from morning to night upon the moss-bearded branches.

We at once paid a visit to Mann's Spring. It is a little runnel of pure cold water, issuing from peaty earth, at the foot of a small rock-bank, and sinking into the dark brown mould beyond. It is embowered in blue flowers, and surrounded by nettles, which supplied us with a Scottish spinach. A few yards from it the kroomen had cleared a slope for our camp: we expected even then to remain here for some time. Shortly after our arrival all the stragglers came up, happily without an accident, except some chafed feet, which they afterwards improved into laming sores. At Mann's Spring Camp the B.P. ranged between 199·5° and 200°, temperature 65°, which would give it in round numbers 7000 feet of altitude. It is in the Tierra Templada of this mountain, where the wooded lands of the Caliente climate below touch the Pays Brûlé, the Tierra Fria, above. During a residence there, lasting from the 23rd December, 1861, to the 31st January, 1862, I made up my mind that it would be an admirable spot for a Sanitarium or a Colony. Materials for a road and for house-building lie all around. Of the 60,000 runaway negroes in Canada give me but 300, and I will make a path practicable for mules at the end of a dry season. Pestilent Lagos will require a " sick bay," and where can a Lebanon be found equal to the beautiful, the majestic Camaroons?

Christmas-eve and Christmas-day were spent in taking bearings, and rambling about the hills, and in naming the places. According to Captain Allen the Bimbia people call the topmost heights " Mongo Ma Lobu," or the Mount of Heaven. We loyally christened them " Victoria " and " Albert," being then ignorant of the awful event which had destroyed Christmas merriment in Old England. As the natives have no distinguishing terms for the several heights, we thought it not ungeographical to seize the opportunity.

The ascents of "Earthwork Crater," so called from its extreme regularity of outline, and "Mount Helen," in honour of Mrs. Saker, who had supplied the Christmas plum-pudding, showed us a wonderful prospect. The mind was thrown back upon the wild scenes that Nature must have worked here. A wondrous confusion reigned around. A vast circle of thick white cloud, irridescent by the sun, and careering round and round us whilst we were standing in limpid air, forms a setting for the tumbled mass of craters—we counted twenty-eight—gashes, deep crevasses, thick lava-beds, and ribs of scoriaceous rock, marshalled in the region before us. But after a brief *coup d'œil*, every eye was turned from the lesser to the greater giants northwards, where, clear and distinct in the thin air of morning, rose the grand presence of the Peak. It was manifestly divided into a pair of distinct heads, which at once suggested the two most fitting names. The deep metallic blue that invested the monarch of West African mountains, compared with the brown, dotted with points of blackish verdure, on the nearer rocky parallel, suggested that a chasm would separate fore from back ground. The idea proved, happily for us, erroneous.

On Christmas-day, 1861, Mr. Saker left us for a season, his presence being required at Victoria. Mr. Mann had been confined to his hammock for some time: the Judge and I therefore determined upon a reconnaissance of the Great Mountain; and at 5·30 A.M. on Friday, December 27, 1861, we set out, accompanied by three kroomen, upon our eventful walk.

Emerging from the forest that clothes the base of Earthwork Crater, we found ourselves on the grassy tract, and presently saw Mount Helen bearing 75° 25'. After about 2000 feet we came upon a bed of lava, which we called No. 2. Following it up we arrived at the base of Mount Helen, distant 7814 feet: here the B.P. showed 198°, temperature 66°, whilst on the summit it was B.P. 195.4°, temperature 57.5°.

Having enjoyed a pipe under one of the few wind-rung trees that dot its south-western side, we struck over a long grassy and rocky reach of mountain slope, separating us from a magnificent mountain, which, as a dutiful husband, I had named Mount Isabel. Its distance from Mount Helen is 8648 feet, and the B.P. was 193.75°, temperature 60°. We then ascended a steep cone, after which a kind of *terre pleine* led us to a sheltered spot, which we judged well fitted for a depôt of water and for breakfast.

Before us northwards, however, was a spectacle that robbed me of appetite; there, straight in front of us, they rose in ineffable majesty—those towering peaks,—tangible, as it were, in the morning æther. There was no chasm. Beyond the base of Mount Isabel the ground swelled gradually upwards, forming a labyrinth of green-black lava-streams, and a congeries of grass-grown craters extending up to the main cone. A faint verdure seemed to streak the eastern slopes, which were far less abrupt than the western; a long and highly-inclined sweep of blue—the effect of fine black cinder—separated Victoria from Albert Mountain; and whilst the latter showed a distinct but small crater, the former was beautified with descending stripes of red and yellow, falling, as it were, from a cliff or niche a few feet below its apex.

I seized the Judge's arm, and urged an instant advance. He meekly shook his head, and referred me to my breakfast, which stuck in my throat. Our krooboys had required driving the whole morning, and with increased fatigue I expected a rare afternoon.

At 10.30 A.M. we arose once more, with an uncommon elation of spirit; "excelsior" being now the word. The direction—path there was none—lay along the steep side of a hill, where we walked upon the edges of our feet. After a quarter of an hour we had reached, at a running pace, Lava Bed No. 3. It issues from a crater below, and south-westward of, the main peak. Appa-

rently the oldest formation, the material is overgrown with dry green moss, and crumbles like pumice under the tread. Turning the head of the stream which is suddenly arrested by a rise, we followed a smooth groove along the eastern flank of a small cone on the proper right, and then struck across the bed towards another on the left of the lava-river. The passage occupied half-an-hour. The mossy part was 800 feet broad, and the last 400 feet stretched over a stream of ruddy-black clinkers, detached stones, hard and rough, which caused torture to our feet. I afterwards observed the same formations to extend under the friable outer coat of lava. Meanwhile the contrast of the small dark vein with the large, soft, green artery is curious in the extreme.

At 11.30 A.M. we reached the cone on the proper left of the stream, much encouraged by seeing that we were sensibly nearing our destination. After a ten minutes' walk along its clean-cut edge, encumbered only by tussocks of wiry yellow grass, we found ourselves again compelled to cross the same lava-river higher up the bed, where, though narrower, it is far more ridgy and broken, being near its source.

This second passage led us to what appeared to be two grassy cones, which lie at the foot of the grand crater. Not knowing that they were outliers disconnected with our destination, we thought proper to ascend them. It was the last straw that broke the Judge's back. The incline was unusually steep, the surface stiff grass, and patches of hot black scoriæ; and the sun was oppressive. After a painful clamber we reached the summit, and found that the two cones were one, with a central depression. We stood on the rim of a beautifully defined crater, narrow and edge-like at the top, about 100 yards in circumference, sloping inwards like a punch-bowl, and grass-clad to the very floor, which was a jetty pavement of fragmentary lava.

There, after that waste of labour—the cone could easily have been rounded —we allowed ourselves to rest for fifteen minutes by the watch; we abandoned ourselves to the charm of the situation, and made eternal silence vocal with a cheer. We were the first Europeans certainly—probably the first men—who had ever stood within gunshot of the giant sugar-loaf whose now-extinguished fires caught the old Carthaginian's gaze.

We then debated upon the mode of ascent. The Judge preferred the long eastern shoulder, which was green with lichens, as being the easier. I preferred to breast Victoria Peak by the nearest path, towards the red and yellow fire-tinged scoriæ, and to leave on the left the smooth steep black slide of dust-like lava that, separating the two eminences from afar, wore a blue tinge. At 1 P.M. we began by walking round the crater of the grassy cone; here, however, the Judge stopped. Looking at the wall before him—I afterwards found by measurement that it measured 3300 feet along the slope—he judged it beyond his powers, and advised me to reserve it for another day. Subsequent events almost make me regret that I had been less obstinate. But on second thoughts —no! to be the first is everything; to be second is nothing.

Descending the tufted cone I began the last ascent, accompanied by a single krooboy and by a flask of anisado and water, which the Judge had kindly lent to me. At first the walking was easy, and the slope gentle, but the loose cinders caused fatigue by slipping from under foot. Arriving after a long elbow to the left at blocks of basalt, which we afterwards called " Half-way Rocks," I turned to the right, and, steadily keeping the red and yellow cliff in sight, ascended along the ragged edge of a little ridge, which afforded mossy lava to support the tread. In places there were thin scatters of a quartz conglomerate, which I never saw except upon that cone. The sun was fiery, and the high north-easter left its marks upon me for a fortnight afterwards.

At 1.30 the easier slope was surmounted, and walking became so troublesome that I preferred an occasional " all-fours." As we neared the summit my krooman sank down with thirst-glazed lips, and he was allowed to remain behind. A few moments more saw me upon Theon Ochema, where a new and unexpected set of objects met my sight.

Victoria Peak I now discovered was but the outer walls of a double crater, black, and, to judge by the eye, 250 feet deep, opening southwards, where it has discharged a prodigious lava-stream, and divided into two by a thin partition-wall. Unable to boil at that visit, I afterwards found the mercury rise to 193·5°, temperature 60°, at the base; and at the summit of Victoria Peak 189·75°, temperature 59°. Mr. Saker on one occasion made B.P. 188°, temperature 59°; but I am disposed to doubt this observation. To the north-west of Victoria Crater lies Albert Crater, a far smaller formation, but remarkable for its high back wall, where the B.P. was 189·5°, temperature 59·6°. The two craters are parted by a curious V-shaped dyke of compact greystone, in large blocks, like a ruined Cyclopean wall, and 25 feet high. To the west-north-west of Albert Crater, and divided from it by a jagged wall of basalt, lies Prince's Crater, by far the smallest of the three.

But these were subsequent discoveries. Time forced me to be content with a cursory look at Victoria Crater. By way of recording my claim, I made a little cairn of stones. The krooboy had rejoined me with the B.P. apparatus, but the others had lagged behind with my poncho. The furious north-easter charging round the black summit threatened to make a Phaeton of me—to sweep us like flies off the peak; and after sundry attempts I desisted, promising myself better luck next time.

In such doings 2.30 P.M. had sped: there was a reverse to our bright medal, a night in the wild and open. The descent of the cone occupied half an hour. I tried the Vesuvian style of gravitation, and found the cinders so loose and the slope so great that a wreck upon the boulders studding the base was imminent. This descent occupied thirty minutes, and when I threw myself down to rest at the foot it was already 3 P.M. I had taken upwards of seven hours to finish off the five miles of ascent, and still hoped to effect a return in three hours.

I hurry over the homeward march. Arrived at Mount Isabel we refreshed exhausted nature, and hastened on after a ten minutes' halt. A wind was already blowing, which sent the mercury to 40°. Shortly after 6.30 P.M., as we passed our guide and beacon Mount Helen, a cloud-bank was all we could see in the west. The pace now became frantic: twilight, though longer upon the mountains than in the plains, is short. Before 7 P.M. we were surrounded by a darkness that could be felt. We were compelled to halt. The kroo cry, however, at last brought a response, and presently we saw fire-sticks—the excellent Selim being as usual to the fore—making their way towards us. The cold night-wind whispering pleurisy kept us moving till assistance came, and we reached camp at 8.30 P.M., instead of 6 P.M.; twelve hours having been employed in finishing ten miles. After the supper of hungry men we retired to rest, but not to sleep; the sun and wind had sorely burned our hands and faces, our legs ached, and that African plague, spasmodic cramps of the lower limbs, awoke me every half hour.

In the morning the reconnoitrers were distinguished from their fellows by hobbling about like cheap screws after a long field-day. Another African plague supervened. In an evil hour I made that march in a pair of loose waterproof boots, which began by softening the feet, and ended by half flaying them. Wounds in these lands are hard to heal; I have heard of a man losing his leg in consequence of a mosquito-bite. Briefly, a hurt which in England would have passed away in a week, wasted thirty days of my precious time.

A variety of expeditions followed this first exploration. Messrs. Calvo and Mann ascended, on the 3rd of January, 1862, Albert Peak; left a maximum and a minimum thermometer there, discovered the V-shaped dyke above alluded to, and returned on the next day prematurely. The cause was the recurrence of Mr. Mann's complaint; a week reduced him so low that he listened to our advice and accompanied to Victoria the Judge, now homewards bound.

On the 5th of January the Rev. Mr. Saker again joined our party. He had brought up with him Mr. R. Smith, a coadjutor, who eventually became too unwell to venture higher.

On the 13th January, Mr. Saker made the third ascent, and the first boiling of thermometer upon Victoria Peak. He returned on the next day at 6 P.M. sadly tired, and on the 15th January he descended the mountain.

Mr. Mann was as unlucky as I was: fifteen days out of the four months which in these latitudes compose the botanist's year, are a terrible loss. He reappeared in camp on the 25th January, having accomplished the severe ascent from Ridge Camp to Mann's Spring in seven hours. My foot had permitted me to crawl about since the 22nd January, at present one of my lucky days. We made all preparations for a final visit to the summit without delay. The tornado season was setting in: the thunder was now above, not below us; and globular lightning shooting like Roman candles across the path is not pleasant.

At 7 P.M. on the 27th January we set out for the fourth expedition, resolved to pass two nights near the summit. The first day was spent in sketching, taking bearings, and collecting plants; we passed the hours of darkness on Mount Isabel. The next day took us to "Saker's Camp," a cone at the foot of the great mountain: beyond exploring the interior of Victoria Crater, and vainly attempting to measure the circumference of the huge cone, we did nothing. At night the cold caused itself to be felt, the mercury sank to 33·5° Fahrenheit, our waterproofs were white with hoar, and the peak was powdered with frozen dew. And yet there are those who doubt that snow has been seen on the Camaroons Mountain! The minimum thermometer upon the back wall of Albert Crater showed 27° Fahrenheit.

The next day enabled me to make a happy discovery. Mr. Mann and I started by different roads: they had told me it was impossible to ascend the blue slide between Victoria and Albert. The word is naturally somewhat irritating; I resolved, therefore, to try, and agreed to meet my fellow-traveller on the summit. At 2 P.M. we took formal possession of the place; flew the union jack; drank the health of the Sovereign Lady with our last bottle of champagne; and left our names upon a leaden plate, with two sixpences—rather a bright idea, but not emanating from my cranium.

After this ceremony, Mr. Mann returned to camp. I was not satisfied, and wanted something more, especially a view of the country to the north-east and the north-west. Accompanied by my factotum and a krooboy, I climbed up the dyke separating the two great chasms, and walked down a smooth cinder-valley trending north-east between Victoria Crater and the northern wall of Albert Crater. Fortune favoured me with a sight of the utterly unknown land; the wind-driven clouds melted away, and I saw that the land to the north exactly reflects the land to the south. Still disappointed, I turned to the north-west, behind Albert Crater, and observed some suspicious cracks and gashes, long, narrow, and deep, which raised my hopes sky-high; they proved, however, thoroughly extinct, nor could I detect in them the least smell of sulphur. Disappointed, I ascended the highest wall of Albert Crater, where the krooboy was sitting, B.P. thermometer in hand.

Hardly had the candle been lighted when Selim, who had struck over certain dwarf and broken hillocks, stained with red and yellow, and lying due north of where I stood, re-appeared, highly excited. When he told me the cause, his feelings were shared; we started on grand gallop, and presently met our reward.

My factotum had discovered a complete solfaterra. It lies north-north-east of Albert Crater, somewhat below the highest point, and where the downwards slope begins. Smoke arose in puffy volumes from the long lines of white marl and sulphur which, divided by small ridges of moss, ran in a northern and southern direction. During rainy weather the phenomenon must be seen from the low lands, and perhaps may still be visible from Fernando Po.

This discovery accounts for many detached reports. If, as the guides say, Mont Blanc smokes his pipe, then Ochema's pipe is not yet put out. The fiery mountain noticed by the old Punic navigator; the flames which the people of Bimbia described to Captain Allen as proceeding from the earth; the flashes seen by the cloth merchants at Camaroons River and by the people of Fernando Po, are now satisfactorily explained. I am pleased to announce to the Royal Geographical Society of Great Britain the addition of another volcano, not wholly extinct, to the list of those already known.

Nothing now remained but to descend and dine. On the next day we again separated. Mr. Mann ascended Albert Peak to remove his thermometer, whilst I returned to camp and finished the measurements. The event of the day was a hailstorm, the stones being of a size approaching to the inconvenient. I reached camp at 4 P.M., and my fellow-traveller arrived about an hour afterwards.

All of geographical interest being now ready, on the 31st of January, 1862, I left, not without regret, "Mann's Spring Camp," where so many peaceful happy days, without sand-flies or prickly heat, had sped. The Chief Botani received me with a civility bordering on servility. After leaving his village, however, a fellow in the lower districts presented a musket at my men, hoping to make them run away and cast their loads; they had learned, however, that the danger of being shot was problematical, but that the punishment of desertion was certain. Finally, on the 2nd of February, 1862, I once more saw the scattered bungalows of Victoria, where the kindly Mrs. Saker, who would not leave the place till our safe return, received me with all hospitality.

In concluding this hurried sketch of a highly-interesting region, I must express my regret that my instruments were wholly inadequate to the task. An aneroid is the poorest substitute for the mountain-barometer; I had no hygrometer; and even a clinometer was not at hand.

These few lines will, it is hoped, show the adaptability of the Camaroons Mountain for a sanitarium, a colony, or a convict station. A locale which shows every morning hoar-frost during the hot season in a region removed but 4° from the equator is not to be despised in the days when it is proposed to remove Calcutta to Simla. The Anglo-Scandinavian race cannot, it is true, thrive in all climates: but there are few, and those are valueless, in which choice of site would not make him a cosmopolite.

---

12.—*Geological Notes on Campana, in the Province of Esmeraldas, Ecuador.* By JAMES WILSON.

[IN communicating the following short letter from Mr. James Wilson, Sir Roderick Murchison makes this comment:—"Athough Mr. Wilson (known to geologists and geographers by his explorations in California and Tropical Australia) has not been able to make any extensive surveys in Ecuador, where he has been labouring hard as the surveyor of a land company in the province of Esmeralda, yet the discoveries which he has made of the existence of the works of man in a stratum of mould beneath the sea-level, and covered by several feet of clay—the phenomenon being persistent for 60 miles—is of the highest interest to physical geographers and geologists. These facts seem to demonstrate that, within the human period, the lands on the coast of Central America were depressed and submerged, and that after the accumulation of marine clays above the terrestrial relics the whole coast was elevated to its present position."]

"25th April, 1862.

" DEAR SIR RODERICK,—I fear I am now nearly lost to your memory, in that, although sojourning in an interesting country, I have not sent a single line to keep me remembered at the Meetings of the Geographical Society, as I had hoped to do when I first set out for Ecuador in the service of the Ecuador Land Company. My work has been most arduous in surveying these dense forests of the equator, though my recompense, I am sorry to say, is by no means commensurate. With the exception of a journey through the forest of Quito, I have seen little of the country ; being confined to the locality of the Pailon, which presents only one kind of rock, a sort of volcanic conglomerate, consisting principally of a vast bed of volcanic sand or ashes, in which are irregularly embedded stones of various shapes and sizes, up to massive boulders of tons in weight, the whole bearing a striking resemblance to the northern drift. There is, however, one remarkable feature in the formation of the coast of this locality ; and, so far as I have been, along the coast of this province : it is a stratum of mould, in which fragments of pottery and articles of gold, and other remains of human work, are found. Over this lies a bed of clay, varying from 5 to 10 feet in thickness. The bed of clay rises above the tide, more or less ; but the stratum of mould containing these relics is below that level. I have found it at various points, for a distance of 60 miles ; and I believe it might be traced to a much greater distance. In the course of a few months my engagement with the Company terminates ; when I shall be able to travel more freely, and to greater distances, and be able again to afford the Geographical Society a paper. Captain Melville White (to whom I entrust this, and who has visited us in this retired locality), has travelled very extensively in these countries, and will most probably afford much geographical information.

" Wishing you good health, I remain, Sir Roderick, your very obedient servant,

" JAMES S. WILSON."

---

### 13.—*Planispheres.*   By the Chevalier IGNAZIO VILLA.

THE Chevalier Ignazio Villa submitted seven planispheres to the Society, accompanied by a printed description, from which the following is extracted :—

No. 1. *Grand Terrestrial Planisphere.*—The northern hemisphere is laid out with radial meridians, the antarctic pole being in the centre. All the earth is thus represented within a single circle ; the highest mountains and the active volcanoes are marked on the plan, and elevated at the circumference of the outer circle on the French metrical scale. This planisphere, being made to rotate, exhibits the hour in all countries, and their longitudinal differences in time. Clockwork movement can also be applied, so that one may see the phenomena relative to local times that in the course of twenty-four hours follow each other upon the earth.

No. 2. *Celestial Planisphere.*—This planisphere represents the entire heavens on a single circular plane, indicating all the constellations visible to the naked eye in their angular positions. Round this planisphere there is a girdle, on which is portrayed an epitome of all the countries of the earth ; so that they may be found at once in their longitudinal positions. In this system the earth is immoveable, and the celestial planisphere rotates in sidereal time. It shows at a glance the constellation which passes at any moment under any meridian, and places in direct relation all terrestrial and celestial points, as well as the right ascensions and declinations of the latter, and verifies the distances of the moon and stars from the sun. This celestial planisphere will be useful in marine schools and in the study of astronomy ; and, when a clock is attached, it can be framed, and mounted on a pivot, so as to be used on board ship. It is also applicable to watches.

No. 3. *Grand Cosmographic Table.*—At the centre is the terrestrial system in its orbit, with its partial and total eclipses, the phases of the moon, its tides, the refractions of the sun, the day and night of the polar circles, the position of the sun in regard to the poles, the constellations of the months, and the signs of the Zodiac. In the four corners are portrayed four globes in perspective: two for the solstices, and two for the equinoxes, with their inclinations to the terrestrial axis; the shadows representing the precise curves as they are projected each day upon the earth. By means of these curves, the rising and setting of the sun can be easily found for any latitude. Beneath are placed two synoptic scales, one indicating the length of the day and night in all countries or parallels of the earth; the other is an equatorial band, divided at the tropics with a solar scale, by which may be seen immediately the right ascension of the sun for all days of the year.

No. 4, *Grand Map of a Quarter of the Earth*, exhibits part of Asia, Europe, the northern parts of Africa and the American continent down to the Equator, thus including all the most interesting parts of the commercial world, projected according to Mercator. It enables any one to find, without calculation, the differences which result from the rotation of the earth between any country and the longitudinal zero.

Nos. 5 and 6 are Planispheres on a smaller scale, illustrating the theory of the winds, terrestrial magnetism, and other subjects of physical geography.

No. 7, *an Universal Meridian*, indicates the equation of time of each day in minutes, seconds, and hundredths.

The terrestrial planisphere (No 1), after having been examined by a Special Commission appointed by the Austrian Government, obtained the reward of a gold medal and has been adopted for the use of the Imperial schools throughout the empire. The series of seven plans have been adopted in all the Lycea of Tuscany; and were subsequently purchased by the Italian Minister of Public Instruction, for the schools of that kingdom.

Index.

# INDEX

### TO

## VOLUME THE SIXTH.

END OF VOL. VI.

LONDON . PRINTED BY WILLIAM CLOWES AND SONS, STAMFORD STREET, AND CHARING CROSS.

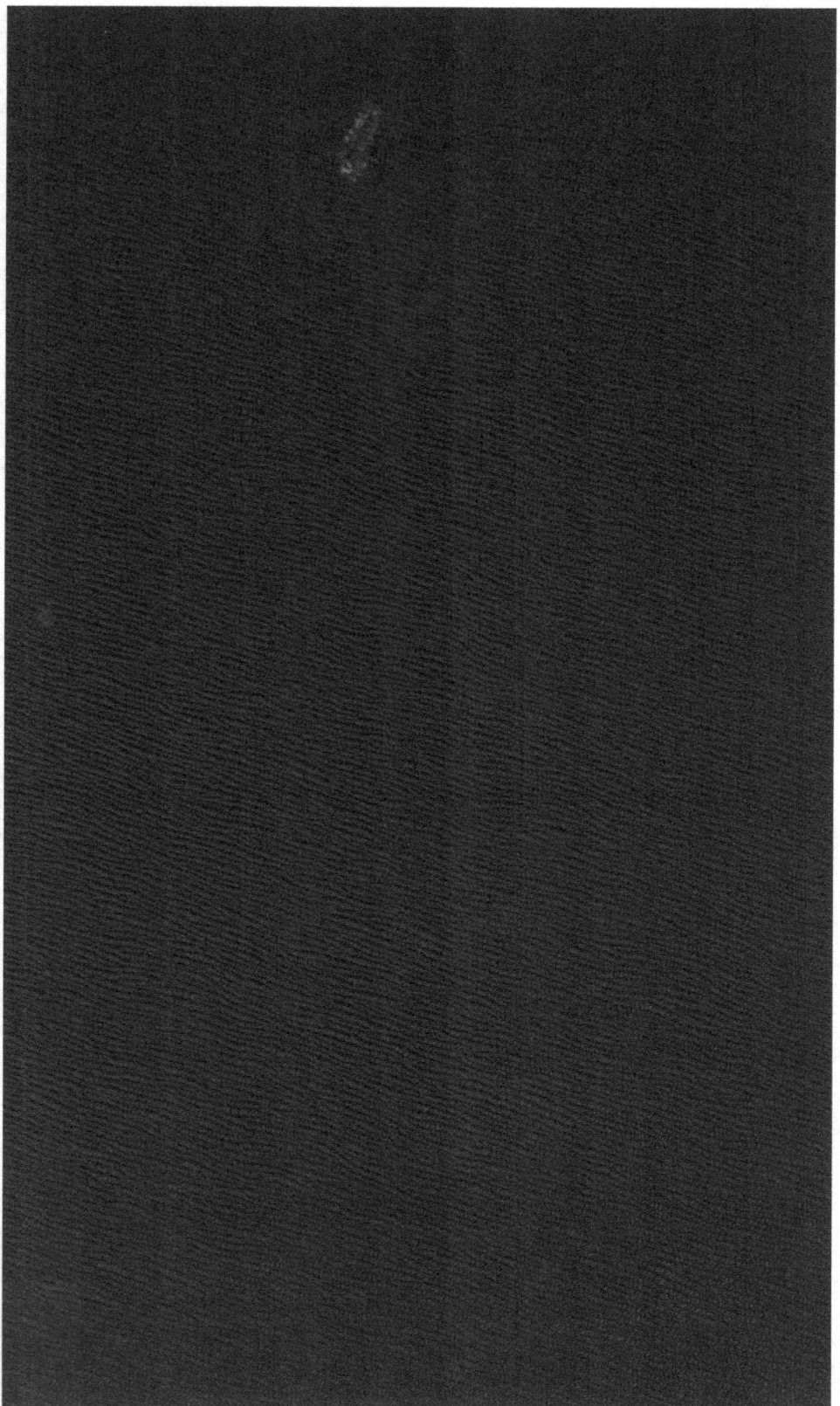

Check Out More Titles From HardPress Classics Series In this collection we are offering thousands of classic and hard to find books. This series spans a vast array of subjects – so you are bound to find something of interest to enjoy reading and learning about.

Subjects:
Architecture
Art
Biography & Autobiography
Body, Mind &Spirit
Children & Young Adult
Dramas
Education
Fiction
History
Language Arts & Disciplines
Law
Literary Collections
Music
Poetry
Psychology
Science
…and many more.

Visit us at www.hardpress.net

CPSIA information can be obtained
at www.ICGtesting.com
Printed in the USA
BVHW081818120819
555665BV00016B/1898/P